Introduction to Applied Ethics

Introduction to Applied Ethics

Robert L. Holmes

For more resources:
www.bloomsbury.com/holmes-introduction-to-applied-ethics

Bloomsbury Academic
An imprint of Bloomsbury Publishing Plc

B L O O M S B U R Y
LONDON · OXFORD · NEW YORK · NEW DELHI · SYDNEY

BLOOMSBURY ACADEMIC
An Imprint of Bloomsbury Publishing Plc

50 Bedford Square	1385 Broadway
London	New York
WC1B 3DP	NY 10018
UK	USA

www.bloomsbury.com

BLOOMSBURY and the Diana logo are trademarks of Bloomsbury Publishing Plc

First published 2018

British Library Cataloguing-in-Publication Data
A catalogue record for this book is available from the British Library.

ISBN: HB: 978-1-3500-2980-4
PB: 978-1-3500-2981-1
ePDF: 978-1-3500-2979-8
ePub: 978-1-3500-2982-8

Library of Congress Cataloging-in-Publication Data
Names: Holmes, Robert L., author.
Title: Introduction to applied ethics / by Robert L. Holmes.
Description: New York : Bloomsbury, 2018. | Includes index.
Identifiers: LCCN 2017049049 (print) | LCCN 2017052267 (ebook) |
ISBN 9781350029798 (PDF eBook) | ISBN 9781350029828 (EPUB eBook) |
ISBN 9781350029804 (hardback) | ISBN 9781350029811 (pbk.)
Subjects: LCSH: Applied ethics–Textbooks.
Classification: LCC BJ1012 (ebook) | LCC BJ1012 .H6575 2018 (print) |
DDC 170–dc23
LC record available at https://lccn.loc.gov/2017049049

Typeset by Newgen KnowledgeWorks Pvt. Ltd., Chennai, India.
Printed and bound in Great Britain

For
Savannah, ShuLan, Matthew and Noah

Contents

10 Moral Consideration for Animals 317

Part IV Autonomy and the Individual

11 Privacy 357

Part V The Nonconsensual Taking of Human Life

14 The Death Penalty 451

15 Terrorism and War 471

Acknowledgments

Appreciation to the following authors and publishers for permission to use material they control:

Chapter 2: NPR interview with Barbara King: "Is It Sexism to Say That Women Are Superior?" April 16, 2015, containing an email exchange between King and anthropologist Melvin Konner. Used with permission of Barbara King. Use of extract on "gender," from *The National Geographic Magazine*, January 2017, p. 86. Used with permission of National Geographic Magazine. A passage from Christina Hoff Sommers, *The War against Boys: How Misguided Feminism Is Harming Our Young Men* (New York: Simon and Schuster, 2000), pp. 23–6. Used with permission of the author. Chapter 6: Passages from Thomas Donaldson, *Corporations and Morality* (Prentice-Hall, 1982), pp. 2–6. Used with permission of the author. Chapter 7: An extract from Peter Singer, "Famine, Affluence and Morality," *Philosophy & Public Affairs*, Vol. 1, No. 3, Spring 1972, 229–44. Used with permission of Blackwell Publishing, Ltd. Chapter 8: Quote in Definition Box 8D and subsequent quotations from Milton Friedman, *Capitalism and Freedom* (Chicago: University of Chicago Press, 1962) used with permission of the University of Chicago Press. Passages from Ayn Rand, *For the New Intellectual* (New York: Signet Books, 1963) (originally appearing in Ayn Rand, *Atlas Shrugged).* Used with permission of Richard E. Ralston, Publishing Manager, Ayn Rand Institute. Chapter 10: Tom Regen, extracts from "The Radical Egalitarian Case for Animal Rights," from *In Defense of Animals*, ed. Peter Singer, pp. 13–15. © 1985 Basil Blackwell Publishers. Used with permission of the publisher. Carl Cohen, "The Case for the Use of Animals in Biomedical Research," *The New England Journal of Medicine*, Vol. 315 (October 2, 1986), 865–8. Used with permission of The Massachusetts Medical Society. Jonathan Foer, *Eating Animals*, Back Bay Books, Little, Brown and Company (Hachette Book Group), pp. 41–4. Extracts used with permission of Hachette Book Group. Chapter 11: Passages from Jonathan Shaw, "The Watchers: Assaults on Privacy in America," *Harvard Magazine*, January–February 2017, 56–61, 82–3. Used with permission of Harvard Magazine. Chapter 12: Passages from Judith Jarvis Thompson, "A Defense of

Abortion," *Philosophy & Public Affairs*, Vol. 1, No. 1, Fall 1971, 48f., and R. M. Hare, "Abortion and the Golden Rule," *Philosophy & Public Affairs*, Vol. 4, No. 3, Spring 1975, 207f. Used with permission of Blackwell Publishing, Ltd.

I would also like to express thanks for permission to the following publishers to use portions of my previous publications: Chapter 5: Oxford University Press, for use of material from "Sexual Harassment and the University," *The Monist*, Vol. 79, No. 4, October 1996. Chapter 13: "Is There a Slippery Slope from Suicide to Assisted Suicide to Consensual Euthanasia?" from Loretta Kopelman and Kenneth DeVille (eds.), *Physician-Assisted Suicide: What Are the Issues?* (Boston: Kluver Academic, 2001). Used with permission of Springer. Chapter 14: passages from "The FOR and the Death Penalty," *Fellowship Magazine*, Vol. 66, Nos. 5–6, May–June 2000, used with permission of the Fellowship of Reconciliation.

Special thanks to Frankie Mace, assistant philosophy editor at Bloomsbury, for supporting the project at an early stage and for guidance throughout the book's preparation and production. Without her the book would not be in print. Thanks also to Predrag Cicovacki for unwavering support from the outset. Thanks as well to S. Rebecca Holmes-Farley for valuable research assistance, as well as for use of a portion of her unpublished manuscript "The Legal, Moral and Social Implications of Physician-Assisted Suicide" in Chapter 13. Finally, thanks to my wife, Veronica Slivinski Holmes, for her wise suggestions and help in editing the entire manuscript; and most of all for her understanding, patience and encouragement throughout.

Introduction

Most books on applied ethics consist primarily of readings, often preceded by a section on ethical theory. Many such readings were written for professional philosophers. While some are accessible, few are in their entirety, and most that have philosophical depth are difficult for the average undergraduate. Those not written for professional philosophers, on the other hand, often lack philosophical substance and are used mainly to represent "a position" on the issue.

This book is written especially for students approaching applied ethics for the first time, with their interests, needs, and limitations in mind. It proceeds the way I believe we first begin thinking ethically, which is by encountering practical moral problems and then taking up more theoretical issues as they become relevant. In what follows, theory is introduced only where it is immediately relevant (in "theory boxes" and definitions of key terms in "definition boxes") and only to the extent required for understanding the issues at hand. Few people make moral judgments by learning theory first and then "applying" it to practical moral problems. If students don't know which of a bewildering array of theories served up at the outset is correct, they don't know what they're supposed to "apply." If they're expected to decide which is the correct theory (which philosophers don't agree on) *and* at the same time decide what moral judgments it yields in particular cases, they're likely to pick the theory that supports what they're predisposed to believe; either that, or come away thinking that different theories are correct for different issues—a relativism to which many of them are inclined anyway. Worst of all, they may come away not knowing what to think at all.

The "theory boxes" are more frequent in the early chapters and are cross-referenced in later chapters for easy review. The philosophical analysis of the text becomes increasingly difficult in some later chapters, with Chapter 13, on physician-assisted suicide, perhaps being the most difficult.

Although there are no readings per se, the book quotes liberally where appropriate (e.g., with regard to Supreme Court decisions and social commentary), and discusses many of the now standard arguments with regard to specific problems (e.g., Thomson on abortion, Singer on animal rights). Rather than present a disconnected series of problems, I try to emphasize the interconnections among issues. On some issues (e.g., racism and sexism), I present and defend a position; I don't consider it a seriously open question whether those practices are wrong. On others (e.g., abortion and capitalism versus socialism), I analyze the issues but don't take a stand. In any event, students are encouraged not to accept uncritically what I or anyone else says about the issues. The aim is to foster informed, independent, critical thinking on their part. Each topic is contextualized, to give students a perspective on social commentary on that topic as well as the views of philosophers. Instructors, for their part, may want to criticize, reject, or elaborate on any of my analyses, which are intended to invite further thought and discussion of that sort.

The book is intended as a core text for courses in contemporary moral problems. It contains more than enough material for a full semester. The intent of each chapter is to give students a comprehensive grasp of the issues. This will enable instructors to proceed almost immediately to discussion at class time rather than having to do extensive lecturing themselves unless they choose to do so.

For more resources:
www.bloomsbury.com/holmes-introduction-to-applied-ethics

Part I

Race, Gender, and Ethnicity

Racism

Racists have to claim that certain of the crucial moral properties of human beings are genetically determined: that some races are less intelligent, less capable of high moral consciousness, and the like ... But all claims about innate cultural differences are unsustainable in the light of human history.
—Charles Taylor[1]

Introduction

Although racism is a prominent topic in discussions of contemporary moral problems, there is surprisingly little understanding of precisely what it is and why it's wrong. We shall in this chapter provide a definition of racism and explore the moral issues involved in its practice. In so doing, we will distinguish primary and secondary racism, examine a racist philosophy, consider whether the concept of *race* is even meaningful, and examine the burden of proof racists would have to meet to justify their position.

1.1 Three basic questions about racism

Racism has been a dominant force in shaping the modern Western world. Settlers from England established slavery in North America, while the Portuguese and Spanish were the major slaveholders in Latin America. During the slave-era, more than ten million slaves were forcibly brought to the Western world by Europeans. By the outset of the Civil War, there were four million slaves in America alone. Although they were freed by Lincoln's Emancipation Proclamation in 1863, systematic discrimination plagued them until civil rights legislation in the 1960s began to counteract some of the worst effects of racist practices in employment and education.

Three questions provide the focus of our examination of racism:

1. What is racism?
2. Why is it wrong?
3. What may we justifiably do about it?

By "wrong" in question (2) we mean morally wrong. And in (3) we are asking about moral justifiability. Racism isn't illegal (though many racist practices are, such as school segregation). And although some responses to racism are legal (e.g., affirmative action in some of its forms), their moral justifiability is contested. Our primary concern is with the moral issues. Where relevant, we'll take up legal issues as well.

Let's begin by considering some of the basic moral issues. These were expressed in 1908 by the philosopher Josiah Royce (1855–1916):

Race: The Moral Issues

[W]hen … we turn back to our own country, and think how many different race-problems confront us—we then see that the earliest social problem of humanity is also the most recent problem. This is the problem of dealing with the men who seem to us somehow very widely different from ourselves, in physical constitution, in temperament, in all their deeper nature, so that we are tempted to think of them as natural strangers to our souls, while nevertheless we find that they are stubbornly there in our world, and that they are men as much determined to live as we are, and are men who, in turn, find us as incomprehensible as we find them. Of these diverse races, what ones are the superior and what ones are the inferior races? What race or races ought to rule? What ones ought to yield to their natural masters? To which one of these races has God, or nature, or destiny, ordained the rightful and final sovereignty of the earth? Which of these types of men is really the human type? Are they by their presence and their rivalry essentially perilous to one another's interests? And if so, what one amongst them is there whose spread, or whose increase in power or in number, is most perilous to the true cause of civilization? Is it a "yellow peril," or a "black peril," or perhaps, after all, is it not rather some form of "white peril," which most threatens the future of humanity in this day of great struggles and of complex issues?[2]

Question (3) (What may we justifiably do about racism?) may seem puzzling. If something is wrong, we should stop doing it. But how we should respond to wrongdoing by others is itself a moral issue. Our *response* to any act of wrongdoing is itself an act and as such needs justification. Not just any response is justified. It's wrong, for example, to steal candy from a baby but also wrong to burn someone at the stake for doing it. Even people who agree that racism is wrong often disagree over what should be done about it. In particular, they disagree over whether affirmative action is justified (a topic we'll take up in Chapter 4). So, even where there's a consensus over the wrongness of an act, we must be prepared to justify any particular response to it.

But is there a consensus that racism is wrong? There is not. Most people, say, in Britain or America, condemn racism. But some—white supremacists, for example—defend it. And even some who condemn racism are often accused of perpetuating it, knowingly or unknowingly. These facts establish the relevance of questions (1) and (2).

Even if there were a consensus that racism is wrong, it would still be important to understand why it's wrong. Otherwise we might with the best of intentions unwittingly perpetuate it in subtle ways. In the absence of such a consensus, it's doubly important to show why it's wrong. But to do this requires understanding in the first place precisely what racism is. For although most people think they understand racism—and they no doubt do well enough for most practical purposes—a full understanding is more difficult to come by than one might suppose.

1.2 What is racism?

Let us begin with a brief historical and moral perspective on the nature of racism in the United States. It was written in 1957 by Martin Luther King, Jr. (1929–68):

Racism in the United States

The first Negroes landed on the shores of this nation in 1619, one year ahead of the Pilgrim Fathers. They were brought here from Africa and, unlike the Pilgrims, they were brought against their will, as slaves. Throughout the era of slavery the Negro was treated in inhuman fashion. He was considered a thing to be used, not a person to be respected. He was merely a depersonalized cog in a vast plantation machine. The famous Dred Scott decision of 1857 well illustrates his status during slavery. In this decision the Supreme Court of the United States said, in substance, that the Negro is not a citizen of the United States; he is merely property subject to the dictates of his owner.

After his emancipation in 1863, the negro still confronted oppression and inequality. It is true that for a time, while the army of occupation remained in the South and Reconstruction ruled, he had a brief period of eminence and political power. But he was quickly overwhelmed by the white majority. Then in 1896, through the *Plessy v. Ferguson* decision, a new kind of slavery came into being. In this decision the Supreme Court of the nation established the doctrine of "separate but equal" as the law of the land. Very soon it was discovered that the concrete result of this doctrine was strict enforcement of the "separate," without the slightest intention to abide by the "equal." So the Plessy doctrine ended up plunging the Negro into the abyss of exploitation where he experienced the bleakness of nagging injustice.

A Peace That Was No Peace

Living under these conditions, many Negroes lost faith in themselves. They came to feel that perhaps they were less than human. So long as the Negro maintained this subservient attitude and accepted the "place" assigned him, a sort of racial peace existed. But it was an uneasy peace in which the Negro was forced patiently to submit to insult, injustice and exploitation. It was a negative peace. True peace is not merely the absence of some negative force—tension, confusion or war; it is the presence of some positive force—justice, good will and brotherhood.

Then circumstances made it necessary for the Negro to travel more. From the rural plantation he migrated to the urban industrial community. His economic life began gradually to rise, his crippling illiteracy gradually to decline. A myriad of factors came together to cause the Negro to reevaluate himself. And so he came to feel that he was somebody. His religion revealed to him that God loves all his children and that the important thing about a man is "not his specificity but his fundamentum," not the texture of his hair or the color of his skin but the quality of his soul.

This new self-respect and sense of dignity on the part of the Negro undermined the South's negative peace, since the white man refused to accept the change. The tension we are witnessing in race relations today can be explained in part by this revolutionary change in the Negro's evaluation of himself and his determination to struggle and sacrifice until the walls of segregation have been fully crushed by the battering rams of justice.

Quest for Freedom Everywhere

The determination of Negro Americans to win freedom from every form of oppression springs from the same profound longing for freedom that motivates oppressed peoples all over the world. The dynamic beat of deep discontent in Africa and Asia is at bottom a quest for freedom and human dignity on the part of people who have long been victims of colonialism. The struggle for freedom on the part of oppressed people in general and of the American negro in particular has developed slowly and is not going to end suddenly. Privileged groups rarely give up their privileges without strong resistance. But when oppressed people rise up against oppression there is no stopping point short of full freedom. Realism compels us to admit that the struggle will continue until freedom is a reality for all the oppressed peoples of the world.[3]

Against this background, let us distinguish two kinds of racism, primary and secondary. The importance of distinguishing them will become clear as we proceed. We may begin by defining "primary racism."

Definition Box 1A

Primary Racism: The beliefs, attitudes, and practices of racists.

This relates racism not only to actions, but also to beliefs and attitudes. Although racist actions are of foremost moral and legal concern, actions grow out of beliefs and attitudes. Without an understanding of racist beliefs and attitudes our understanding of racism is incomplete. This definition, of course, shifts the burden to the term "racists," so we need to understand what a racist is in order to understand racism. It's individual persons, after all—their beliefs, attitudes, and practices—that are at the heart of racism. (Notice, of course, that it's the beliefs, attitudes, and practices of racists *as racists* that concern us; not their beliefs, say, about higher mathematics or attitudes toward campaign finance reform.)

When racists predominate in a society—particularly in positions of power—primary racism will be pervasive. It can be expected to take the form of open and systematic discrimination. Slavery is but the extreme case. But even where those discriminated against are "free"—in the minimal sense of not being slaves—they still may be disadvantaged in virtually every area of human undertaking. They may be expressly prohibited from social, political, or economic advancement and deprived of all but the most rudimentary of human goods, such as health care, education, proper nutrition and equal employment opportunities.

A society that perpetuates such inequalities is still characterized by racism. But it's a racism that has a more complex explanation than primary racism. For that reason it's useful to recognize:

Definition Box 1B

Secondary Racism: The perpetuation of racial inequality, sometimes unwittingly, through conduct motivated primarily by non-racial (e.g., economic) considerations.

We shall deal with secondary racism at greater length in Chapter 4. For the present, we need to understand primary racism. To do this requires understanding what a racist is, as that's a key concept in our definition of "primary racism."

1.3 What is a racist?

Here the issue becomes more complex. The term "racist" is used in many ways, some of which are useful to understanding racism, some of which aren't. But all are illuminating in various ways. To understand them better, let's call upon ethical theory to distinguish two different senses of meaning:

Theory Box 1A

Descriptive and Emotive Meaning

Descriptive Meaning: The beliefs a word or sentence tends to express (on the part of the speaker) or to produce in others.

Emotive Meaning: The feelings or attitudes a word or sentence tends to express (on the part of the speaker) or evoke in others.

Consider the following sentences:

1. She's computer literate.
2. He's a philosophy major.
3. They're both cool.

(1) and (2) have almost exclusively descriptive meaning. Each formulates a belief the speaker could normally be assumed to hold about the person in question, and which a hearer who believed the speaker would then come to hold. Each describes something about the person. (3), on the other hand, has predominantly emotive meaning. To call people cool isn't so much to describe them (they aren't literally cool as opposed to warm) as it is to express approval or admiration. Characteristically, this is done with a view to getting others to feel the same way.

Some words have both descriptive and emotive meanings. The word "bastard," for example, has a descriptive meaning: "an illegitimate child." But this descriptive meaning has now largely receded. Many people don't even know the word's descriptive meaning and few use it any longer to convey that meaning. It's now used almost exclusively with its emotive meaning, which is to insult or demean someone.

The word "racist," like the word "bastard," has both descriptive and emotive meaning. The emotive meaning is negative; people usually call others racists to express disapproval of them and their conduct. Most people, in turn, are offended at being called "racist." In short, "racist" is an emotion-laden word. Its descriptive meaning, however, is less clear. So we need to ask what that meaning is (or if there isn't a clear descriptive meaning, we need to ask what meaning it can plausibly be given to help in discussing the problems of racism).

Our concern with the descriptive meaning of the word "racist" doesn't preclude that the descriptive meanings we shall discuss also have associated emotive meanings. Nor does it mean that the descriptive meanings are necessarily more important than the emotive meanings. Both are part of our common discourse about race. It means only that for purposes of understanding the moral and philosophical issues, the descriptive meaning is central.

Let us consider three possible definitions of the descriptive meaning of "racist," with varying degrees of complexity.

Definition Box 1C

Racist$_1$: One who practices racial discrimination.

But what exactly is discrimination? Note that there are perfectly innocuous senses of the verb "to discriminate." For example:

To discriminate:

1. To distinguish or make distinctions (e.g., counting or enumerating).

To discriminate in this sense by itself has nothing to do with racism. You discriminate in this sense if you distinguish apples from oranges or categorize things by quality. The wine connoisseur has discriminating taste in wine; the gourmet, in food. The same may be true even where ostensibly racial classifications are involved. You aren't engaged in racial discrimination if you're asked to count the number of Hispanics, African Americans, Caucasians, and Asians in a room.

2. To *treat* differentially.

To discriminate in the first sense may be nothing more than an intellectual activity, but to discriminate in this sense involves treating people differently. But even doing this may have no connection with racial discrimination. Students on probation are treated differently from those in good standing; convicted criminals are treated differently from innocent persons. In these cases there are good reasons for differences in treatment. Such treatment isn't discrimination in the sense relevant to the moral issues of racial discrimination. Even where ostensibly racial criteria are employed, differential treatment needn't constitute racial discrimination.

If you were making a movie and wanted someone to play Frederick Douglass, you doubtless would exclude white males from consideration. And you certainly would exclude white females. However, if you were casting for someone to play the part of Queen Elizabeth, you would do the reverse. You'd exclude black females and certainly black males. Meryl Streep wouldn't be convincing as Frederick Douglass, or Denzel Washington as Queen Elizabeth. No one considers this racial discrimination[4] (though one might well consider it discrimination that there are disproportionately fewer starring roles for blacks than for whites). And in certain areas of personal preference, differential treatment likewise doesn't constitute racial discrimination. It's not discrimination if you have more African American friends than white or more Hispanic American friends than either African American or white. Nor is it discrimination if you prefer a marriage partner from one or the other of these groups, any more than it is discrimination if a gay or lesbian person prefers a same-sex marriage partner. In these domains, autonomy and personal privacy hold sway.

3. To treat prejudicially.

It's when you treat others prejudicially or preferentially on the basis of their membership in a racial group that you're practicing racial discrimination. Let us say then:

Definition Box 1D

Racial Discrimination: The prejudicial treatment of persons on the basis of supposedly racial characteristics.

There are two sides to discrimination. If you treat members of one race prejudicially you will by comparison be treating members of other races preferentially. Discrimination always implies the *comparative* treatment of persons. If everyone is treated badly, that may be wrong, but it's not discrimination. A racist in this first sense, *racist₁*, is anyone who practices racial discrimination. We may take this to include those who approve of racial discrimination and would practice it if they could but are unable to because of lack of opportunity or incapacity of some sort. The fact that racial discrimination involves the prejudicial treatment of one group of persons by comparison with the treatment of other groups means that discrimination by its nature raises questions of *justice*. The basic idea of justice can be explained as follows:

Theory Box 1B

Racial Justice
Justice concerns fairness in the treatment of two or more persons or groups. All other things being equal, if persons defined by supposedly

> racial characteristics (such as skin color) are treated prejudicially (or preferentially) by comparison with the way in which others are treated, that's a case of racial injustice.

This helps us understand what racial discrimination is, but it's only a first step toward understanding racism. This is because the definition of racist$_1$ refers only to conduct. It says nothing about beliefs, attitudes, or motives. It doesn't even require that one *knowingly, deliberately, or intentionally* practice discrimination. Why is this a shortcoming?

People practice racial discrimination for various reasons, some of which have nothing directly to do with race. Suppose you own a restaurant in a community prejudiced against a particular race at a time when such discrimination was legal. (Racial discrimination in restaurants was legal in the United States before prohibited by Civil Rights legislation.) If you serve members of that race, others will boycott your restaurant and you'll go out of business. If, to preserve your business, you refuse to serve members of that race, you're practicing racial discrimination. But—assuming that you wouldn't do it otherwise—you'd be doing it for economic reasons. That doesn't make it less wrong. But you wouldn't be discriminating for racial reasons. Your conduct wouldn't be governed by beliefs or attitudes about race (beyond, of course, those reflected in the economic judgment). Your motivation would be economic self-interest.

Racial discrimination, in other words, can have different *explanations* depending on why it's practiced. Consider the following news article:

Racial Disparities in NYC Restaurant Jobs

While more than 26 percent of New York City's population is Black, only 10.5 percent of its 48,176 waiters and waitresses are Black, according to 1996 census data. Since many of those are working in low-end neighborhood restaurants, the racial disparity among waiters in mid-to-high-priced places is greater ...

"People are so used to the exclusion of African-Americans, you don't even notice," said David A. Paterson, a black state senator whose district includes Harlem and part of Washington Heights.

The reasons for the disparity are as complicated as diners' orders. Interviews with dozens of restaurant owners and waiters, and with state, city and labor leaders reveal an industry that acknowledges a dearth of black waiters, but offers several reasons for their absence.

At many Chinese, Japanese, Italian and other ethnic restaurants, for instance, owners say that they employ no blacks as waiters because they need to hire employees sharing their own backgrounds. They say that customers demand the authenticity implied by the presence of ethnic waiters in ethnic restaurants.

Other restaurateurs say few blacks apply for the jobs even though new restaurants are plentiful and waiters are scarce. And both black waiters and leaders acknowledge that black Americans may be rejecting what they perceive as a servile profession.

But many blacks working in high-end restaurants in New York City say that the real reason their numbers are so small is racism ...

"Restaurant jobs are stepping-stones into careers and opportunities for many," said Lloyd A. Williams, president of the Greater Harlem Chamber of Commerce. "There is absolutely no question that blacks are being discriminated against as waiters and waitresses."[5]

The article suggests three possible reasons for the underrepresentation of blacks as servers in the better New York restaurants:

(1) that ethnic restaurants want members of their own ethnic group as servers (Chinese want Chinese, Japanese want Japanese, etc.), because it gives an appearance of authenticity, which is good for business;

(2) that some blacks think of such jobs as servile and for that reason don't apply for them; and

(3) that blacks are discriminated against in restaurant hiring, presumably *because they are black*.

Here we have a fact to be explained: the disproportionately low number of black servers in New York restaurants. If explanation (3) is correct, this fact represents a clear case of racial discrimination. If explanation (2) is correct, it isn't a clear case of discrimination because it has been brought about by the choices of blacks themselves (even if past discrimination may be one of the reasons some blacks feel this way and make that choice). What if explanation (1) is correct? Here the matter is more complicated. If treating people prejudicially on the basis of supposedly racial characteristics is discrimination, and if bypassing them in the hiring process for servers is prejudicial to them, then this is a case of racial discrimination.

By the definition of racist$_1$, these restaurant owners are racists. But most of them probably don't think of themselves as racists and would probably be offended to be so called. They'd probably argue that they're just trying to run a successful business, and that economic interest dictates that they take race or ethnicity into account in hiring. That is, they might not *knowingly or deliberately* be practicing racial discrimination. And their motivation might be purely self-interest and have nothing to do with race. This isn't to say that self-interest is an honorable motivation; only that it's different from a racist motivation.

If, however, the owners refused to serve blacks in their restaurants— even if for reasons of economic self-interest—then they would be running segregated restaurants. Their practice would then be clearly discriminatory and prohibited by law. Purely from the standpoint of the conduct involved, it's difficult to see why if the one is racial discrimination (refusing to serve blacks in restaurants) the other isn't as well (refusing to hire blacks in restaurants). The question remains, however, how to judge the restaurant owners as persons. Even if they are practicing discrimination, are they, as persons, racists? By the definition of racist$_1$ they are. To those who use the term "racist" in this way, conduct alone suffices to make one a racist, without regard to beliefs and underlying motivation. By this, even if you were to engage in practices which unbeknownst to you were prejudicial to one race, you would still be a racist. For others, however, the notion of a racist implies something more.

Whatever the truth of the various explanations in this particular case of New York City servers, those examples reinforce the view that to identify racists simply with those who practice racial discrimination gives us, at best, a minimalist conception of a racist. It limits racists to those who engage in certain conduct, pure and simple, without regard for context, beliefs, attitudes, or motivation. Our definition of "primary racism" requires that we say something about racial beliefs and attitudes as well. If we want an understanding of what a racist is that illuminates racism more fully, we need to look further.

Let us therefore consider another sense of the term "racist."

Definition Box 1E

Racist$_2$: A racial bigot.

What is a bigot?

Key Quote 1A

A bigot is "one obstinately and irrationally, often intolerantly, devoted to his own church, party, belief, or opinion." (*Webster's Third International Dictionary*)

In view of this, we may say that a racial bigot is anyone devoted to his or her own race, racial beliefs or attitudes or practices in an obstinate, irrational, or intolerant way.

Bigotry is typically associated with attitudes (including feelings and emotions). And the attitudes common to racial bigotry include: hostility, hatred, resentment, fear, suspicion, and mistrust. We've seen that the term "racist" has a negative emotive meaning; it tends to express disapproval. Those who don't think of themselves as racists are characteristically insulted by being called racists. As philosopher Judith Lichtenberg puts it:

Key Quote 1B

"Racism" is inescapably a morally loaded term. To call a *person* a racist is to impugn his character by suggesting deliberate, malign discrimination, and it is therefore natural that those who think their hearts . . . are pure should take offense at the accusation.[6]

But some people admit to being racists. They aren't insulted by being called racists. The emotive meaning of "racist" might express the disapproval of the speaker but in their case it wouldn't have the intended effect upon the hearer. On the other hand, virtually anyone would be insulted by being called a bigot.

So while racist$_2$ defines yet another use of the term "racist," it applies to only some of the persons we would normally think of as racists. Many American slaveholders were thoughtful, educated people. Thomas Jefferson was an example. They weren't clearly irrational. And they weren't obviously obstinate and intolerant in the ways associated with bigotry. But they were certainly racists in some sense. And we need a conception of racism that includes them. Racist$_1$ refers only to racial conduct without regard to racial attitudes and beliefs. Racist$_2$ refers to attitudes and not explicitly (though by implication) to conduct and beliefs. It does refer to some unspecified beliefs. We need a conception that makes reference specifically to racial beliefs.

Consider the following belief: some races are innately superior to others. And consider the following passages. The first is from a speech given by Abraham Lincoln in 1858:

White Superiority but Moral Equality?

I have no purpose to introduce political and social equality between the white and the black races. There is a physical difference between the two, which in my judgment will probably forever forbid their living together upon the footing of perfect equality, and inasmuch as it becomes a necessity that there must be a difference, I ... am in favor of the race to which I belong having the superior position. I have never said anything to the contrary, but I hold that notwithstanding all this, there is no reason in the world why the negro is not entitled to all the natural rights enumerated in the Declaration of Independence, the right to life, liberty and the pursuit of happiness ... I hold that he is as much entitled to these as the white man. I agree with Justice Douglas he is not my equal in many respects—certainly not in color, perhaps not in moral or intellectual endowment. But in the right to eat the bread, without leave of anybody else, which his own hand earns, *he is my equal and the equal of Judge Douglas, and the equal of every living man.*

[Justice Douglas] avows that the Union was made *by* white men and *for* white men and their descendants. As a matter of fact, the first branch of the proposition is historically true; the government was made by white men, and they were and are the superior race. This I admit.[7]

Lincoln, of course, liberated the slaves with the Emancipation Proclamation of 1863. He's the last person most people would think of as a racist. But he clearly believed in the superiority of the so-called white race. It's just that he combined this belief with a belief in equal rights. So what do we say of him? Was he a racist? Some would say so. But if was, he wasn't your typical racist. Perhaps a better term is one that isn't used often today but was common during the nineteenth century. Let us say that Lincoln was a *racialist*. And let us define "racialist" as follows:

> ## Definition Box 1F
>
> **Racialist: One who believes that some races are innately superior to others.**

Most racialists in this sense are no doubt racists$_1$. And many of them are racists$_2$ as well. But some, like Lincoln, are not. Racialists in this sense needn't share the attitudes or engage in the conduct typical of racists. They may in fact oppose racial discrimination and even support equal rights. As rare as such persons might be—persons who can believe in the superiority of one race but oppose racial injustice—it's important to distinguish them from racists in the first two senses.

Recalling that Royce (Section 1.1) speaks of superiority and inferiority and domination and submission in connection with racism, let us now define a third sense of "racist" that combines central beliefs and conduct pertaining to race.

> ## Definition Box 1G
>
> **Racist$_3$: One who knowingly practices or approves of racial discrimination in the belief (a) that some races are innately superior to others, and (b) that innately superior races ought to dominate inferior races.**

Notice that the reference in (a) is to *innate* superiority. This typically means biological or genetic superiority. For full-fledged racists, the alleged superiority of some races over others isn't simply due to cultural, political, or environmental conditions. It's due to the very nature of the races, whatever the conditions under which they exist. The racist$_3$ believes that this is what justifies the domination of one race over another.

In slavery, the masters own and dominate the slaves. They control virtually every aspect of their lives. There are societies, however, in which there isn't such overt domination but things are nonetheless designed socially, politically, and economically so that one race is systematically treated preferentially over others. That is, there can be profoundly racist societies that fall short of being slave societies. We shall take (b) to include the belief that superior races ought to enjoy such preferential status.

Primary racism can be overt or covert. It's covert to the extent that racists try to conceal their racial beliefs and attitudes, which they may do consciously or unconsciously. Some people fear that others may disapprove of their racist beliefs and attitudes, so they try to conceal them. Others conceal their racist beliefs and attitudes even from themselves, rationalizing their actions in such a way that they don't think of them as racist. Their racism is unconscious. In both cases, the racism is covert. When there's no attempt to conceal racist beliefs, attitudes, and conduct, the racism is overt. With this understanding, we may fill out our earlier characterization of primary racism as follows:

Primary Racism: The beliefs, attitudes, and practices of racists.
Overt: Racist beliefs and attitudes are openly held.
Covert: Racist beliefs and attitudes are consciously or unconsciously concealed.

It's important to see that racists$_3$ can be thoughtful, intelligent, educated people; otherwise one underestimates the difficulty of eradicating racism. Some slaveholders were otherwise decent human beings. Some, like Thomas Jefferson, as we've said, were exceptional. It's easy to see what's wrong with racism if one identifies it exclusively with the beliefs, attitudes, and conduct of nasty, ignorant, irrational people. The challenge is to show what's wrong with the racism of thoughtful, intelligent people. Only if you can do that have you refuted racism in a meaningful way. It accomplishes little to show what's wrong with ill-considered, irrational, or incoherent versions of a moral or philosophical position. You need to be able to show what's wrong with the strongest version of it.

With that in mind, let's look at a classic racist statement. Then we can proceed to examine the moral issues in the evaluation of racism. The following racist philosophy is by the nineteenth-century French writer Arthur de Gobineau (1816–82), sometimes called "The Father of Racism." Seeking to understand the course of history and the causes of social problems, he thought he found the answer in the study of race.

1.4 A racist philosophy

Gobineau on Race
Then, passing from one induction to another, I was gradually penetrated by the conviction that the racial question overshadows all

other problems of history, that it holds the key to them all, and that the inequality of the races from whose fusion a people is formed is enough to explain the whole course of its destiny.

I find these races naturally divided into three, and three only—the white, the black and the yellow. If I use a basis of division suggested by the colour of the skin, it is not that I consider it either correct or happy, for the three categories of which I speak are not distinguished exactly by colour, which is a very complex and variable thing; I have already said that certain facts in the conformation of the skeleton are far more important ... So I may say, once and for all, that I understand by *white* men the members of those races which are also called Caucasian, Semitic or Japhetic. By *black* men I mean the Hamites; by *yellow* the Altaic, Mongol, Finnish and Tartar branches. These are the three primitive elements of mankind ...

The negroid variety is the lowest, and stands at the foot of the ladder. The animal character, that appears in the shape of the pelvis, is stamped on the Negro from birth, and foreshadows his destiny. His intellect will always move within a very narrow circle. He is not however a mere brute, for behind his low receding brow, in the middle of his skull, we can see signs of a powerful energy, however crude its objects ... Many of his senses, especially taste and smell, are developed to an extent unknown to the other two races.

The very strength of his sensations is the most striking proof of his inferiority. All food is good in his eyes, nothing disgusts or repels him. What he desires is to eat, to eat furiously, and to excess; no carrion is too revolting to be swallowed by him ... to these qualities may be added an instability and capriciousness of feeling, that cannot be tied down to any single object, and which, so far as he is concerned, do away with all distinctions of good and evil ...

The yellow race is the exact opposite of this type. The skull points forward, not backward. The forehead is wide and bony, often high and projecting. The shape of the face is triangular, the nose and chin showing none of the coarse protuberances that mark the Negro ... The yellow man has little physical energy, and is inclined to apathy; he commits none of the strange excesses so common among Negroes. His desires are feeble, his will-power rather obstinate than violent; his longing for material pleasures, though constant, is kept within bounds ... He tends to mediocrity in everything; he understands easily enough anything not too deep or sublime ... The yellow races are thus clearly superior to the black. Every founder of a civilization would wish the backbone of his society, his middle class, to consist of such men. But no civilized society could be created by them; they could not supply its nerve force, or set in motion the springs of beauty and action.

We come now to the white peoples. These are gifted with reflective energy, or rather with an energetic intelligence. They have a feeling for utility, but in a sense far wider and higher, more courageous and ideal, than the yellow races; a perseverance that takes account of obstacles and ultimately finds a means of overcoming them; a greater physical power, an extraordinary instinct for order, not merely as a guarantee of peace and tranquility, but as an indispensable means of self-preservation. At the same time, they have a remarkable, and even extreme, love of liberty, and are openly hostile to the formalism under which the Chinese are glad to vegetate, as well as to the strict despotism which is the only way of governing the Negro.

The white races are, further, distinguished by an extraordinary attachment to life. They know better how to use it, and so, as it would seem, set a greater price on it; both in their own persons and those of others, they are more sparing of life … At the same time, they have discovered reasons why they should surrender this busy life of theirs, that is so precious to them. The principal motive is honour, which under various names has played an enormous part in the ideas of the race from the beginning. I need hardly add that the word honour, together with all the civilizing influences connoted by it, is unknown to both the yellow and the black man.

On the other hand, the immense superiority of the white peoples in the whole field of the intellect is balanced by an inferiority in the intensity of their sensations. In the world of the senses, the white man is far less gifted than the others and so is less tempted and less absorbed by considerations of the body, although in physical structure his is far the most vigorous.

Such are the three constituent elements of the human race. If the three great types had remained strictly separate, the supremacy would no doubt have always been in the hands of the finest of the white races, and the yellow and black varieties would have crawled forever at the feet of the lowest of the whites. Such a state is so far ideal, since it has never been beheld in history; and we can imagine it only by recognizing the undisputed superiority of those groups of the white races which have remained the purest.[8]

For Gobineau, not only is the white race superior to the yellow and black races, but within the white race so-called Aryans are superior to Semites (said to be a combination of white and black races) and to Slavs (said to be a combination of white and yellow races). Hitler, in this same vein, took Aryans to be the superior race. The Nazi extermination of Jews (a Semitic people) and contempt for Poles and Russians (Slavic peoples) shows how racism can turn whites against whites as well as whites against nonwhites. It can in principle also turn nonwhites against whites and nonwhites against nonwhites.

Notice that Gobineau doesn't take skin color per se to be a defining racial characteristic. Rather, he takes skin color to correlate with other properties, such as skull shape, facial features, and pelvic structure. He then correlates both skin color and these properties that make up "conformation of the skeleton," as he calls it, with still other properties: intelligence, sense of honor, capriciousness, heightened capacity of the senses, apathy, courage, inventiveness, and valuing of life. Finally, he arrives at his fundamental racial classification:

GOBINEAU'S RACIAL CLASSIFICATIONS

Black: Carefree, capricious, musical and artistic ability, low reasoning power.
Yellow: Practical, stubborn, apathetic, uninventive.
White: Rational, energetic, resourceful and creative.
Semitic: (combination of white and black)
Slavic: (combination of white and yellow)
Aryan: White.

In this way, Gobineau produces a tidy scheme. He thinks that by recognizing these races and their characteristics, one can trace how the interaction and mixing of races has determined the course of history.

1.5 The racist's burden of proof

Gobineau leaves unquestioned the assumption that there is such a thing as race. That there are races is presupposed by the two principal beliefs of primary racism, namely, that some races are innately superior to others, and that superior races ought to dominate inferior ones. So let us now add it explicitly to the other two:

RACIST BELIEFS:
1. There are races.
2. Some races are innately superior to others.
3. Innately superior races ought to dominate inferior races.

There are many attitudes associated with racism. The following, though not the only ones, are conspicuous among them:

RACIST ATTITUDES: Condescension, patronization, disrespect, contempt, suspicion, resentment, envy, hostility, fear, and hatred.

With regard to conduct, we've so far focused upon racial discrimination. In a sense, all mistreatment of persons on the basis of race is discrimination of some sort. But we might distinguish verbal conduct, on the one hand, and outright violence, on the other, from the commoner forms of discrimination:

RACIST CONDUCT:
1. Verbal abuse: slurs, insults, innuendoes.
2. Racial discrimination: the prejudicial treatment of persons on the basis of supposedly racial characteristics.
3. Racial violence: the causing of harm or death to persons on the basis of perceived racial characteristics.

Beliefs and attitudes may not be under people's control. But conduct is.[9] This includes verbal conduct. Hate speech can be as damaging in its own way as physical violence, as the following passage emphasizes[10]:

Key Quote 1C

The racial insult remains one of the most pervasive channels through which discriminatory attitudes are imparted. Such language injures the dignity and self-regard of the person to whom it is addressed, communicating the message that distinctions of race are distinctions of merit, dignity, status, and personhood. Not only does the listener learn and internalize the messages contained in racial insults, these messages color our society's institutions and are transmitted to succeeding generations.[11]

Beliefs may be true or false, correct or incorrect, justifiable or unjustifiable. And both they and attitudes may be good or bad. But conduct—including verbal conduct—may be either right or wrong. By this, I mean *morally* right or wrong.

Verbal abuse, discrimination, and violence are all presumptively wrong. That has nothing to do with racism per se. If you verbally abuse, disadvantage, harm, or kill *anyone* for whatever reason, the burden is upon you to justify such conduct. Treating people this way on the basis of race similarly needs to be justified. Otherwise it's wrong.

So the burden is upon racists to defeat the presumption of the wrongness of treating people as racists do. Racists$_1$, as we've seen, may try to do so on grounds that have nothing to do with race. They may reason, as in the earlier example of the restaurant owner who discriminates out of self-interest (Section 1.3), that economic considerations warrant it. Racists$_2$—the racial bigots—are unlikely even to be willing to try to justify their conduct, at least in a reasoned, systematic way.

Only the racist$_3$ has a fully-fledged and coherent set of views about race. So let us suppose that we're confronting a racist of that sort. Suppose the racist$_3$ genuinely believes the views he expresses and is willing to engage in a rational defense of them. Such a racist must, as we have noted above, defend at least the following three propositions:

1. There are races.
2. Some races are innately superior to others.
3. Innately superior races ought to dominate inferior "races."

How might a racist go about trying to defend these views?

1.6 Is there such a thing as "race"?

Key Quote 1D

Race may be America's single most confounding problem, but the con-founding problem of race is that few people seem to know what race is.[12]

The first step, of course, would be to provide good reason to believe that there even is such a thing as race.

People speak and act as though they know what race is. But there is no consensus that there is even a scientifically useful conception of race. There are physical differences among individuals, of course. Some are short, some tall, some fat, some thin; some have black hair, some blond; some have blue eyes, some brown; some are light-skinned, some dark-skinned, and so on. No one disputes this. The question is whether the observable properties of people (like skin color) correlate with *other* properties, such as intelligence, strength, creativity, talent, industriousness, laziness, aggressiveness, passivity, kindliness, and so on, which aren't as readily observable. If they do, then one could infer these other properties from the presence of the observable properties.

But even if there were such a correlation, that would be of limited interest. We'd need to know what *explains* the correlation. If it were simply the result of social or cultural circumstances, that wouldn't provide any basis for founding racial distinctions on those differences (in the way that racists do).

Consider the following two groups of people, with identifiable common properties, and alleged correlates of those properties:

Group A	Group B
Common property: being rich	Common property: being poor
Correlative properties:	Correlative properties:
a. being well-nourished	a. being malnourished
b. being well-clothed	b. being poorly clothed
c. being well-educated	c. being poorly educated

Suppose someone said that Group A is innately superior to Group B by virtue of being better educated, better clothed, and better nourished. Would that be a convincing argument? It wouldn't, of course. Let us see why.

Theory Box 1C

Essential and Accidental Properties

There's an old but useful distinction between **essential** and **accidental properties** that's helpful here. Being a human being is an essential property of yours; it's part of what makes you what you are. No matter what you do, you'll be a human being for as long as you live. Being a New Yorker or a Londoner, on the other hand, is an accidental property; you lose it by moving to San Francisco or Manchester, even though you remain the same person.

Both essential and accidental properties correlate with other properties in either **necessary** or **contingent** ways. The property of being human, for example, correlates *necessarily* with the property of being an animal. Biologically, anything that is human is an animal (as opposed to, say, a plant or mineral). But it correlates only *contingently* with the property of being a meat eater. Some humans eat meat, but others don't.

And you can be a meat eater at one time in your life and a vegetarian at another. You remain a human being, and the same human being, all the while.

Racists allege essential differences among groups that warrant categorizing them as races. The differentiating properties are thought to be part of the very nature of races. As we saw earlier (Section 1.3), racists don't simply say that racial superiority and inferiority are a result of social or environmental conditions. They believe that they depend upon the essential and not merely the accidental properties of races. That Race A was oppressed by Race B for 300 years would be an accidental property of Race A. But that Race A is inferior to Race B would be a supposedly innate and essential property of A. This means that we can speak both of essential and accidental properties, and of necessary and contingent correlations among properties in discussing the moral issues involved in racism.

Now, with regard to Group A and Group B, the properties *being rich* and *being poor* are accidental properties. If the rich lose their money, they become poor; if the poor come into money, they become rich. A person remains the same person whether he's rich or poor, since the properties of being rich or being poor aren't essential to his being the person he is. And these properties correlate with all sorts of other properties. Being well-nourished, well-clothed, and well-educated correlate with *being rich* more than they do with *being poor*. And being malnourished and of limited education and poor health correlate with poverty more than they do with wealth. But the reasons for these correlations are obvious. They depend upon social and economic conditions.[13] Rich people can buy whatever they want in the way of food, clothing, and education. Poor people can't. There's no need to look beyond social, economic, and political conditions to explain these facts.

Consider another two groups:

Group C	Group D
Common property: having skin color C1	Common property: having skin color C2.
Correlative properties:	Correlative properties:

Group C	Group D
1. Being healthy	1. Being unhealthy
2. Being wealthy	2. Being poor.
3. Being wise	3. Being foolish

Unlike being rich or being poor, having a particular skin color is an invariable property. You can't change your skin color (other than through extraordinary measures of the sort Michael Jackson undertook), though you can decorate your skin with tattoos. It's arguably an innate property as well. Some might even think it's an essential property of the person you are, though that's more problematic. At the least we can say that what skin color has in common with essential properties is that it's invariable. Suppose it were argued that Group C is innately superior to Group D because members of Group C tend to be healthy, wealthy, and wise, whereas members of Group D tend to be unhealthy, poor, and foolish. Would that be a good argument?

Once again, it wouldn't. But the reason it wouldn't is different from the case of Groups A and B. There the problem was that the common properties were purely accidental. A person could be rich at one time and not at another. Here the properties aren't accidental. If you have a particular skin color, you have it for good. The problem here is that the properties of having C1 and having C2 correlate only contingently with the other properties. There is no known causal or necessary connection between skin color and being healthy, wealthy, and wise. If there's sometimes a correlation between C1 and those properties, it will almost certainly be due to social, cultural, economic, or other variable conditions. (Perhaps Group C has dominated Group D for centuries, enabling it to cultivate health, wealth, and wisdom.) There would be nothing about having C1 per se that destined you for health, wealth, and wisdom, and nothing about having C2 that destined you to poverty, ill health, and foolishness.

By the same token, if people with skin color C1 were healthy, wealthy, and wise, and those with skin color C2 were poor, foolish, and unhealthy, we'd still need to know whether those correlations were necessary or merely contingent. If they were contingent (as they would be if they were due to social and economic conditions), then the obvious response (morally speaking) would be to remedy the conditions that produced them.

While skin color arguably is an essentially unchangeable property of individual persons, it is not an invariable property of groups. Even racists acknowledge there can be wide variations in skin color among groups. So, properties like C1 and C2, whatever they are, couldn't be essential properties of races. And even if they could, the correlations with the other properties mentioned would still be contingent. So the idea of race typically differentiates groups of people according to two sorts of properties:

A. Physical properties: for example, skin color, body structure, hair texture, brain size, facial features, strength, genetic material.
B. Mental properties: for example, intelligence, creativity, energy, moral instincts, ambition.

Mental properties define what can broadly be called *character*. According to racists, we're supposed to be able to infer certain mental properties from physical properties. Elevated to the level of a so-called science, this practice is called "physiognomy." Thus "those animals with the longest snouts are always considered the most stupid and gluttonous," it was once maintained; and those races with traits most noticeably similar to the traits found among animals were believed to have the traits of those animals.[14] A variant of this approach, "phrenology," sought to infer mental properties from the shape and protuberances of the skull. Thus people with large eyes were once judged to have good memories, those with protuberances of the forehead to be benevolent. It's not just that the mental properties happen *by chance* (through cultural, environmental, or social conditions) to be correlated with the physical properties. They are *necessarily* correlated with them. According to racists, the groups ("races") having those properties therefore possess certain characters.

But even where there are no readily apparent physical properties identifiable as "racial," racists often think that ancestry, as indicative of certain genetic material, suffices to define race. But there is a problem with doing this. Mark Twain made it central to his novel *Pudd'nhead Wilson*. In it, his central character is a young African American slave woman named Roxy, whom Twain describes as follows:

Racial Identity in *Pudd'nhead Wilson*
From Roxy's manner of speech, a stranger would have expected her to be black, but she was not. Only one-sixteenth of her was black,

> and that sixteenth did not show ... Her complexion was very fair, with the rosy glow of vigorous health in the cheeks ... Her face was shapely, intelligent, and comely—even beautiful. She had an easy, independent carriage ... but of course she was meek and humble enough where white people were. To all intents and purposes Roxy was as white as anybody, but the one-sixteenth of her which was black outvoted the other fifteen parts and made her a negro. She was a slave, and salable as such. Her child was thirty-one parts white, and he, too, was a slave, and by a fiction of law and custom a negro.[15]

Twain focuses upon skin color in the above passage. But there are properties of a third sort that racists appeal to. We may call these "cultural" properties:

C. Cultural properties: higher religion, political advancement, scientific, artistic, and musical achievement.

Thus, innate physical and mental properties are taken to define "races." Different races, then, are thought to manifest different cultural properties in various social settings throughout history.

But have racists established that there are such things as "races" in this sense? They have not. There's no convincing racist argument to establish that claim. There is, in fact, no consensus among anthropologists that the whole concept of race is even meaningful or useful.[16] As anthropologist Ashley Montagu writes:

One Anthropologist's View of Race

[T]he indictment against the anthropological conception of race is (1) that it is artificial; (2) that it does not agree with the facts; (3) that it leads to confusion and the perpetuation of error, and finally, that for all these reasons it is meaningless, or rather more accurately such meaning as it possesses is false. Being so weighed down with false meaning it were better that the term were dropped altogether than that any attempt should be made to give it a new meaning.[17]

Even assuming there are races, there's no reason why being one-sixteenth of one race would make one a member of that race when being fifteen-sixteenths another race wouldn't make one a member of *that* race. One's ancestry is a matter of fact. How one is categorized on the basis of that ancestry is a matter of judgment. Thus it's said that former Haitian ruler "Papa Doc" Duvalier claimed that 96 percent of Haiti's population was white, because "in Haiti they used the same procedure for counting whites that Americans used for counting blacks."[18] Along similar lines, it's been observed, much in the spirit of Mark Twain, that "[r]acial categories, especially in the United States, are often more poetry than science. American blacks almost invariably have some white ancestry, so their classification has more to do with politics and culture than with genes."[19] President Barack Obama, the first American black president, reportedly was half black and half white. Although he self-identified as black, he was by ancestry as much white as black. "Who is white and who is not," one anthropologist observes, "is a matter of politics, not biology, and it is important that our children understand this."[20]

If this should be true, what are its implications? Royce, again, draws this same conclusion and suggests the beginnings of an answer.

Race Problems Not Grounded in Natural Differences

In brief, then, there is hardly any one thing that our actual knowledge of the human mind enables us to assert, with any scientific exactness, regarding the permanent, the hereditary, the unchangeable mental characteristics which distinguish even the most widely sundered physical varieties of mankind ... What, then, in the light of these considerations, is there which can be called fundamentally significant about our numerous modern race-problems? I answer, scientifically viewed, these problems of ours turn out to be not so much problems caused by anything which is essential to the existence or to the nature of the races of men themselves. Our so-called race-problems are merely the problems caused by our antipathies.[21]

Even if racists haven't established that there is such a thing as "race," there are, as Royce notes, still "so-called" race problems. However confusedly, people still think and speak as though there are races. The term "race," in other words, has a vague, commonsense meaning. And it figures prominently in personal, social, political, and legal discourse. As philosopher Paul C. Taylor writes, "People still use the language of race, and they thereby impose on us the burden of understanding how they use it and what they use it to do."[22] The following passage by an African American columnist Leonard Pitts confirms this:

Genetic Equality Doesn't Erase Racism

In the same week that scientists announced they had unlocked the secrets of the human genetic code, I tried—and failed—to hail a cab in New York City. All in all, it seemed an ironic confluence of events.

We could render disease a thing of the past, the scientists said. We could eliminate birth defects, manipulate intelligence, stop the aging process. And then there was this: The genome researchers mapped the genetic codes of five people, self-identified as Caucasian, African-American, Asian and Hispanic. When it was done, they couldn't tell one from the other. As one scientist put it, "The concept of race has no scientific basis."

About the same time he was saying this, I was opening the back door of this taxi on 44th Street, only to have the driver tell me he was off duty. When I pointed out that he didn't have his off-duty light on, he promptly remedied the situation.

Now, let's be fair. It's entirely possible the guy had simply forgotten to turn the light on until I mentioned it. But as a black man who has frequently found it impossible to snag a cab in New York without appealing to some hotel doorman for help, well, let's just say I have my suspicions . . .

Right about now, of course, someone is getting ready to reel off the usual bogus statistics purporting that cabbies are justified in by passing guys like . . . me because nine out of 10 black men are serial killers. I could respond in kind—I've pretty much had to memorize the FBI's Uniform Crime Reports as a means of self-defense.

But that misses the point. I ain't no statistic. I'm me—a man who, science just reconfirmed, is not fundamentally different from other men.

Unfortunately, the sameness of men has always been hard for men to grasp. We tend to be drawn to the differences instead, to define ourselves against the alien ways of this tribe or that. That's not an American trait but, sadly, a human one. Which is why we live on a planet of perpetual war and constant refugees, of ethnic cleansing and ancient grudges. We define by difference.[23]

Whether or not there's a meaningful concept of race, so-called racial problems are real. So we want to try to understand those problems. In so doing, let's assume for purposes of discussion that there is such a thing as race, bearing in mind that there's no consensus on this issue and that, in any event, racists haven't established this fact. As a reminder that the concept is a contested one, I shall henceforth put the term in quotation marks in section headings.

1.7 Are some "races" superior to others?

Let us remember the three central claims the racist$_3$ must establish. They are:

1. There are races.
2. Some races are innately superior to others.
3. Innately superior races ought to dominate inferior races.

We've discussed (1) and concluded that racists haven't established its truth. Nonetheless, let's assume, for purposes of argument, that (1) can be established. The question then is whether (2) and (3) can be shown to be true.

Before proceeding, we should take account of the differences among (1), (2), and (3) and the implications of those differences.

Theory Box 1D

Facts, Values, and Is/Ought
Proposition (1) is a **factual** or **descriptive statement**. Racists believe that to speak of races is to speak of certain virtually unalterable facts about the world. That there are races is the way things are.

Proposition (2), on the other hand, is a **value judgment**. To call one thing superior to another is to assign it a higher value; it's to say that it is better than the other. Notice, however, that even if (1) were true, we couldn't simply conclude from the fact that there are races that some are superior to others. That is, we can't (without further support) infer a value from a fact. So we need to recognize a distinction between **facts** and **values**.

Proposition (3), however, differs from both (1) and (2). Like (2), it differs from (1) in that it doesn't describe the world or seem to report a fact. On the other hand, it differs from (2) in that it doesn't assign value (goodness) to anything. It differs from value judgments. It *prescribes* a certain way of acting; it refers to conduct. It is, we may say, an **ought judgment**. Although there are both moral and nonmoral ought judgments, we shall take them to be moral judgments.

So, there are two further distinctions to be recognized: first, between value judgments and ought judgments; second, between factual statements and ought judgments. Where "is" stands for factual or descriptive statements and "ought" for prescriptive or ought judgments, this distinction is commonly referred to as a distinction between **is** and **ought**.

Thus, linguistically, we have a distinction among three kinds of sentences:

1. Factual statements
2. Value judgments
3. Ought judgments

And we also have two important distinctions: **facts/values** and **is/ought**. Although some philosophers contest this, we cannot (without further support) infer values from facts or ought from is. Put linguistically, we cannot infer value judgments or ought judgments directly from factual statements. To try to do so is to be in error. It's to commit what has been called the **naturalistic fallacy**.
EXAMPLES:
From the fact:

1. People desire drugs (factual statement)

it doesn't follow that

2. Drugs are good (value judgment)

Similarly, from:

3. Cannibalism is practiced in some societies (factual statement)

it doesn't follow that

4. Cannibalism ought to be practiced (ought judgment)

Let's apply these considerations to the problem of racism. Given that we can't simply infer that because there are races (which now we're assuming) some races are superior to others, what must a racist do in order to establish that some races are superior to others?

First, the racist must identify the essential, differentiating properties of various races (such as skin color, body structure, or brain size). Second, he must show which of those properties (e.g., brain size) make some races superior to others. Third, he must show *why* the possession of those properties makes some races superior to others. (If, e.g., it could be shown that brain size correlates with intelligence, he would have to show why being more intelligent makes one superior.)

But there are serious difficulties in trying to do this. Let's see why. For purposes of illustration, let's talk about (nonhuman) animals. We may say that each of the land animals below is superior in the indicated respect to the others:

Elephants: size
Giraffes: height
Cheetahs: speed
Kangaroos: jumping ability
Peacocks: plumage
Cows: giving milk
Chickens: laying eggs
Roaches: tolerance of radiation

While probably every animal is superior in some respect to most or all other animals, each is also inferior in some respects to most or all other animals. Birds are inferior to elephants in size, but they fly better. Fish aren't as fast as cheetahs, but they swim better. Tortoises live longer than kangaroos but can't jump as far. Chickens are inferior to cows at giving milk but better at laying eggs. Roaches are superior to all of them at surviving radiation, but they're not as pretty as peacocks.

But what type of animal is superior overall? There's no obvious answer. If you're interested in certain abilities—such as size, capacity to withstand heat or cold, longevity, and so on—some animals are superior to others with regard to those abilities. But these don't make them superior overall to others. There is, in fact, no accepted set of criteria by which some animals are superior overall to others.

You might say, here, that we're talking about different species. In the case of humans, we're talking about members of the same species. This is true, though at least some races were once thought by racists to represent different species (which was considered blasphemous by Christians, because the Bible represents all people as being descendants of Adam and Eve). It enabled racists to say that some inferior races were subhuman, standing somewhere between humans and animals.

Even if we consider different types of animals within the same species, we encounter similar difficulties. Which is better overall among dogs, beagles, or poodles? While poodles make better house pets, beagles are better for hunting rabbits. Bloodhounds have a keener sense of smell, but greyhounds are faster. Setters are better at pointing, but German shepherds are better at guarding junkyards.

One possibility with regard to humans is contained in the following passage from British philosopher G. E. Moore (1873–1958):

Key Quote 1E

Let us suppose it to be held ... that what is meant by saying that one type of human being A is "better" than another type B, is merely that the course of evolution tends to increase the number of Type A and to decrease those of type B. Such a view has ... been often suggested ... it amounts merely to the familiar suggestion that "better" means "better fitted to survive."[24]

Were this to be the criterion of superiority of races, it would provide a quantitative standard by which to determine racial superiority. We would simply have to count. The race with the largest number of members would be the supreme race, those with the second highest would be next best, and so on.

The problem is, first, that every living person represents a lineage that has survived through the course of evolution. Every existing race (still assuming there is such a thing) has survived equally with every other race. Although at one time racists thought that certain races were dying out in evolutional terms, there is no reason to believe that's true.

Second, even racists acknowledge that there are no pure races any longer. If not, the question would be how we determine to what race a person belongs. Is a person who is one-sixteenth black, as Roxy is in the Mark Twain novel (see Section 1.6), black? If so, then most people of African ancestry in America are black, which would swell the number of blacks in the count. Or is a person who is one-sixteenth white, white? If so, then most African Americans are white, which would diminish significantly the number of blacks in America and inflate the number of whites. And why settle on one-sixteenth as the defining fraction, rather than, say, one-eighth or one-thirty-second? The supposed neutral, quantitative standard is almost invariably going to degenerate into value judgments.

Third, and finally, even if it could be established that one race predominates quantitatively over others, why would that be a reason to say it was innately superior to others? To draw that conclusion without further argument would be, as we've seen, to infer a value from a fact, hence to commit the naturalistic fallacy (which, interestingly, G. E. Moore called attention to in another connection). That is, the reasoning:

1. Race A tends to increase through the course of evolution
2. Therefore, Race A is innately superior to all other races

is fallacious. The racist needs to justify taking the property of tending to increase through the course of evolution to be one that confers inherent value on what possesses that property. Even if it could be established that there are races, and even if criteria of superiority could be agreed upon by which to evaluate the various characteristics of races, it would likely turn out that some races are superior to others in some respects, inferior in other respects. Absent convincing reason to weigh some criteria more heavily than others, there would be no way to establish that some races are superior overall to certain others or that one is superior to all of the others.

Summary: To establish that some races are innately superior to others, racists would have to:

1. Establish that there are races
2. Show that their differences are inherent
3. Justify the selection of criteria of superiority from among those differences
4. Justify weighting those criteria in such a way as to warrant concluding that some races are innately superior overall to others

Racists haven't done this in any morally, philosophically, or scientifically convincing fashion. There is, therefore, no good reason to conclude that, even if there are races, some are innately superior to others.

Let's suppose, however, that racists could establish convincingly that some races are innately superior to others. Would that then provide a good reason for asserting proposition (3). That superior races ought to dominate inferior races? Let us now turn to that question.

1.8 Ought supposedly superior "races" to dominate supposedly inferior "races"?

Recall we saw earlier (Theory Box 1D) the importance of three distinctions: **fact/value, value/obligation**, and **is/ought**. Just as we can't conclude that simply because there are races, some are superior to others, so we can't conclude that simply because (as we're assuming for the moment for the sake of argument) some races are superior to others, they ought to dominate others. To establish that something is good doesn't in and of itself tell us what we ought to do. For that we need some further reason. In this case, we need to see a connection established between superiority (meaning "of higher value than") and obligation.

Suppose the racist proposes the following argument regarding races A and B:

1. Race A is innately superior to Race B.
2. Innately superior races ought to dominate inferior races.
3. Therefore, Race A ought to dominate Race B.

This argument asserts a connection between superiority and obligation in premise (2). If that premise could be established, and if (1) is true (as we're assuming for the moment), then (3) would have been established.

We should then have to ask what reason there is to believe that (2) is true. There are many directions a racist might go in attempting to show this. The following three possibilities are among those most commonly found:

A. Natural Law Ethics
  1. Innately superior races dominate inferior races by nature.
  2. One ought to act in accordance with nature (the principle of natural law ethics).
  3. Therefore, innately superior races ought to dominate inferior races.
B. Divine Will Theory
  1. God wills that innately superior races dominate inferior races.
  2. One ought to do as God wills (the principle of divine will theory).
  3. Therefore, innately superior races ought to dominate inferior races.

C. Utilitarianism
1. The domination of inferior races by superior races promotes the greatest general happiness.
2. One ought to promote the greatest general happiness (the principle of utility).
3. Therefore superior races ought to dominate inferior races.

Let us consider what is meant by Natural Law Ethics, Divine Will Theory, and Utilitarianism.

Theory Box 1E

Natural Law Ethics, Divine Will Theory, and Utilitarianism
Natural Law Ethics, Divine Will Theory, and Utilitarianism are types of ethical theory. Each has many forms. In simplest terms, they assert the following:

Natural Law Ethics: rightness and obligation are grounded in nature (cosmic nature or human nature).
Divine Will Theory: rightness and obligation are determined by God's will. (When expressed in terms of God's commands, this is called the Divine Command Theory.)
Utilitarianism: rightness and obligation are determined by what maximizes value. (A classic formulation by John Stuart Mill [1806–73] holds: One ought to promote the greatest general happiness, where happiness is held to be the highest good.)

Racists might attempt to justify claiming that Race A ought to dominate Race B by appeal to any one of these (or other) theories. We cannot undertake here to determine which (if any) of these theories is correct. Suffice it to note that a thorough defense of racism would require that one provide good reason to accept any theory alleged to support racism. But serious problems confront the racist even assuming the correctness of the theory to which he appeals.

With regard to *Natural Law Ethics*, for example, one might question whether A1 is true; that is, whether superior races dominate inferior races by nature. To support that claim, the racist would need to identify the supposedly superior races, then show that those races in fact dominate inferior races. Racists can't define "superior" as those races that dominate, because then to say that superior races dominate inferior races would be circular. Notice three obstacles to doing this. *First*, if, as most racists maintain, there are no longer any "pure" races, how would one know whether superior races naturally dominate inferior races? We can verify historically that certain peoples conquered other peoples, and that, in modern terms, certain nations defeated others in war. But in virtually all of those cases (certainly in modern times), both the victors and the vanquished are a mixture of races. It would be difficult if not impossible to show which strains in the mixture are responsible for the dominance of one over the other. *Second*, if, as racists maintain, superior races have been lowered in quality by intermixture with inferior races, then one might take that as showing that it's inferior races that dominate by nature, not the superior. For if superior races are supposedly lowered in value by mixing with inferior races, it would seem plausible to suppose that inferior races are elevated in quality by mixing with superior races (a claim which some racists actually make); in which case it would look as though inferior races are gradually prevailing over superior races. *Third*, even if there were pure races, it would be hard to show that they dominate inferior races in light of the fact that, historically, no kingdom, empire, or civilization lasts forever. They come and go with the shifting tides of history. It's unclear what evidence the racist can appeal to here.

If the racist says, well, yes, superior races haven't dominated but argues that that's because their racial purity has been defiled (a common claim racists make), then they can explain the fact that the superior races don't in fact dominate. But in so doing they are thrust back to the first problem, of not being able to produce convincing evidence for the claim. If there were clearly identifiable races of at least a high degree of purity, then we could at least in principle review the historical record and look at the world today and begin to see what evidence there is of their dominance. Once one accepts that there aren't clearly identifiable races, or that there are, but they have become impure over time, then one undercuts the evidence for the factual claim that they dominate by nature.

With regard to the *Divine Will Theory*, the central problem, of course, is to substantiate whether there is a God, and if there is, what God's will is. Christians, Jews, and Muslims agree there is a God, but they aren't in complete agreement about what God's will is. To answer this, Jews appeal to the Old Testament or Hebrew Bible; Christians appeal to the Old and New Testaments; Muslims build upon the Bible but appeal ultimately to the Koran. Hindus, on the other hand, believe in a plethora of gods with variable wills, and Buddhists deny that there's a God at all. Biblically, it was God's will that the Israelites conquer the Canaanites. Does the Israelites being a "chosen people" biblically mean that they were innately superior to the Canaanites? The Puritans likewise thought of themselves as a chosen people. Does that mean that they and the white settlers who followed them were innately superior to native Americans? And in either case, should they dominate other peoples because of their convictions (unshared by those other peoples) that they are divinely favored? Muslims believe that God has ordained that Islam (the Muslim faith) be spread throughout the world. When that conviction comes up against the convictions of Jews and Christians about their role in the world, which is correct? Once the racist steps into the realm of faith to back his views, he has removed himself from the realm of rational discourse. That doesn't mean that one of these faiths isn't correct. But they can't all be correct. They could all be incorrect, however, or correct only in part. If these issues are matters of faith and faith alone, their correctness or incorrectness can't be established either by rational argument or scientific investigation.

Finally, if the racist appeals to *Utilitarianism*, the burden is to show that domination of inferior races by superior races promotes the greatest general happiness. To argue this, of course, one would have to contend with many of the same problems as with Natural Law Ethics and the Divine Will Theory. One would have to be able to identify the superior races, and show that at the present, or in times past, they have dominated inferior races. And one would have to show that their dominance has maximized happiness. From what we know of the dominance of some peoples by others (whether thought of as races or not), the evidence seems overwhelming that such dominance has caused more suffering and misery than happiness. Slavery, the Holocaust and genocide against Native Americans are but three historically recent confirmations of this.

But let's suppose the racist could make a plausible case that it would promote the greatest general happiness to have superior races dominate inferior races. Would that suffice to establish that Race A ought to dominate Race B? Let's consider two reasons why it would not.

1.9 "Race," rights, and utility

The first reason why promoting general happiness wouldn't justify superior races dominating inferior races has to do with rights. A large part of Western tradition believes that there are *human rights*, rights that every human being possesses simply by virtue of being human. These rights don't depend upon historical, cultural, or sociopolitical circumstances. Unlike political rights, they aren't possessed only by people who live in democracies. They may or may not be honored by dictatorships and totalitarian regimes. But people living under those regimes possess them nonetheless. And they cannot be taken away. They can only be respected or not respected. The UN Declaration of Human Rights states what they are commonly thought to be:

UN Declaration on Human Rights
Whereas recognition of the inherent dignity and of the equal and inalienable rights of all members of the human family is the foundation of freedom, justice and peace in the world …
   Now, Therefore,

THE GENERAL ASSEMBLY
Proclaims

Article 1. All human beings are born free and equal in dignity and rights. They are endowed with reason and conscience and should act towards one another in a spirit of brotherhood.

Article 2. Everyone is entitled to all the rights and freedoms set forth in this Declaration, without distinction of any kind, such as race, colour, sex, language, religion, political or other opinion, national or social origin, property, birth or other status …

Article 3. Everyone has the right to life, liberty and security of person.

Article 4. No one shall be held in slavery or servitude; slavery and the slave trade shall be prohibited in all their forms.

Article 5. No one shall be subjected to torture or to cruel, inhuman or degrading treatment or punishment.

Article 6. Everyone has the right to recognition everywhere as a person before the law.

Article 7. All are equal before the law and are entitled without any discrimination to equal protection of the law …

Article 8. Everyone has the right to an effective remedy by the competent national tribunals for acts violating the fundamental rights granted him by the constitution or by law.

Article 9. No one shall be subjected to arbitrary arrest, detention or exile.

Article 10. Everyone is entitled in full equality to a fair and public hearing by an independent and impartial tribunal, in the determination of his rights and obligations and of any criminal charge against him.

Article 11. (1) Everyone charged with a penal offence has the right to be presumed innocent until proved guilty according to law in a public trial at which he has had all the guarantees necessary for his defence. (2) No one shall be held guilty of any penal offence on account of any act or omission which did not constitute a penal offence, under national or international law, at the time when it was committed ...

Article 12. No one shall be subjected to arbitrary interference with his privacy, family, home or correspondence, nor to attacks upon his honour and reputation. ...

Article 13. (1) Everyone has the right to freedom of movement and residence within the borders of each state. (2) Everyone has the right to leave any country, including his own, and to return to his country.

Article 14. (1) Everyone has the right to seek and to enjoy in other countries asylum from persecution. (2) This right may not be invoked in the case of prosecutions genuinely arising from non-political crimes or from acts contrary to the purposes and principles of the United Nations.

Article 15. (1) Everyone has the right to a nationality. (2) No one shall be arbitrarily deprived of his nationality nor denied the right to change his nationality.

Article 16. (1) Men and women of full age, without any limitation due to race, nationality or religion, have the right to marry and to found a family. They are entitled to equal rights as to marriage, during marriage and at its dissolution. (2) Marriage shall be entered into only with the free and full consent of the intending spouses. (3) The family is the natural and fundamental group unit of society and is entitled to protection by society and the State.

Article 17. (1) Everyone has the right to own property alone as well as in association with others ...

Article 18. Everyone has the right to freedom of thought, conscience and religion; this right includes freedom to change his religion or belief, and freedom, either alone or in community with others and in public or private, to manifest his religion or belief in teaching, practice, worship and observance.

Article 19. Everyone has the right to freedom of opinion and expression; this right includes freedom to hold opinions without interference and to seek, receive and impart information and ideas through any media and regardless of frontiers.

Article 20. (1) Everyone has the right to freedom of peaceful assembly and association. (2) No one may be compelled to belong to an association.

Article 21. (1) Everyone has the right to take part in the government of his country, directly or through freely chosen representatives ...

Article 22. Everyone ... has the right to social security and is entitled to realization ... of the economic, social and cultural rights indispensable for his dignity and the free development of his personality.

Article 23. (1) Everyone has the right to work, to free choice of employment, to just and favourable conditions of work and to protection against unemployment. (2) Everyone, without any discrimination, has the right to equal pay for equal work ...

Article 24. Everyone has the right to rest and leisure, including reasonable limitation of working hours and periodic holidays with pay.

Article 25. (1) Everyone has the right to a standard of living adequate for the health and well-being of himself and of his family, including food, clothing, housing and medical care and necessary social services, and the right to security in the event of unemployment, sickness, disability, widowhood, old age or other lack of livelihood in circumstances beyond his control. (2) Motherhood and childhood are entitled to special care and assistance. All children, whether born in or out of wedlock, shall enjoy the same social protection.

Article 26. (1) Everyone has the right to education ... (2) Education shall be directed to the full development of the human personality and to the strengthening of respect for human rights and fundamental freedoms ...

Article 27. (1) Everyone has the right freely to participate in the cultural life of the community, to enjoy the arts and to share in scientific advancement and its benefits ...

Article 28. Everyone is entitled to a social and international order in which the rights and freedoms set forth in this Declaration can be fully realized.

Article 29. (1) Everyone has duties to the community in which alone the free and full development of his personality is possible. (2) In the exercise of his rights and freedoms, everyone shall be subject only to such limitations as are determined by law solely for the purpose of security during recognition and respect for the rights and freedoms of others and of meeting the just requirements of morality, public order and the general welfare in a democratic society …

Article 30. Nothing in this declaration may be interpreted as implying for any State, group or person any right to engage in any activity or to perform any act aimed at the destruction of any of the rights and freedoms set forth herein.

If there are human rights, then even if there were inferior races, those rights would be possessed by the members of those races equally with the members of superior races. And they would be possessed even where they are disregarded. And they would be possessed even if disregarding them would promote a greater good. That is, there may in principle be a conflict between *rights* and *utility*.

Some American slaveholders were convinced that slavery promoted the greatest good. Some of them even thought it was good for the slaves (because, e.g., it served to Christianize them). Even if they had been right in this judgment (note: we're *not* saying that they were right), slavery still violated the human rights of the slaves. It was cruel and unfair and it institutionalized a gross injustice. People have a right to be treated fairly and justly even if they are thought inferior to others.

We widely recognize this with regard to individuals. Certain individuals are arguably superior to others in certain ways. Einstein was a better physicist than most, and Emily Dickinson a better poet than most. *Elitism* would maintain that some individuals are even superior overall to others. Even if that could be established (which is questionable), we wouldn't say that such individuals should dominate others (though some like Nietzsche and Hitler said they should; and others, like Plato and Aristotle, thought they should be elevated to leadership roles). If there are human rights, then all people are equal in rights. Individuals, even if superior in certain respects—and even if superior overall, if that could be shown—are constrained by the rights of others like anyone else. They shouldn't be treated preferentially. Conversely, people who are blind, disabled, ill, or elderly shouldn't be treated detrimentally. Although perhaps not equal in strength, speed, eyesight, or hearing, they're equal in rights.

Similarly, even if it could be shown that some races, like some individuals, are superior to others, and even if it could be shown that their domination of others would maximize value, that wouldn't suffice to show that they ought to dominate others. One would still have to take account of human rights.

1.10 Racism and universalizability

The racist's judgments concern *groups* of persons (as "races" are), whereas our conduct always has consequences for *individuals*. And it's arguably a condition of our treatment of individuals that we be consistent in such treatment. This notion is embodied in what is sometimes called a principle of *universalizability*.

Theory Box 1F

Universalizability
Universalizability by itself doesn't tell us what we ought to do, but it requires that, as rational beings, we be consistent in our judgments and conduct. This principle, closely associated with the ethical theory of Immanuel Kant (1724–1804), has many formulations.

For our purposes we shall take it to assert:

U: Persons ought to be treated similarly unless there are morally relevant dissimilarities among them.

According to U, it's a necessary (though not a sufficient) condition of your acting rightly that you treat people similarly unless you can point to morally relevant differences among them (or the circumstances) that warrant different treatment.

Let us now consider how *U* might come into play when we shift from groups to individuals. Suppose someone thought that being tall is a mark of superiority, and that tall people deserve preferential treatment over the vertically challenged. Let's call this *Heightism*. Height is a measurable quality. We can verify, for example, that Americans are taller than Japanese. But this means only that *on average* Americans are taller than Japanese, not that every

American is taller than every Japanese. Some Japanese are taller than some Americans. Some Japanese, in fact, are taller than most Americans. It might even be that the tallest Japanese is taller than the tallest American.

Now if you reasoned that Americans are superior to Japanese because they're taller, and that they should dominate Japanese because they're superior, what would you commit yourself to in treating individual Japanese and Americans? Given two individuals, an American and a Japanese who are identical in height, you would treat them differently. You'd treat the American preferentially, the Japanese prejudicially. Yet there would be no morally relevant difference between them *as individuals*. This would violate *U*. By treating them differently when there were no morally relevant dissimilarities between them, you'd be acting inconsistently. Because a necessary condition of your acting rightly would not be met, such conduct would be wrong.

Returning now to racism, to be even remotely plausible, any claim that Race A is innately superior to Race B will have to mean only that members of Race A are *on average* superior to members of Race B. And that, as with height, is perfectly consistent with some members of Race B being superior to some members of Race A. If then you treat those individuals differently from members of Race A to whom they are superior (i.e., if you treat the superior individual prejudicially, the inferior individual preferentially), then you're in violation of *U*. In that case, your conduct can be shown to be wrong *even if* it's conceded that Race A is superior to Race B. The racist won't have shown that it's right for Race A to dominate Race B.

1.11 Conclusion

We argued earlier (Section 1.5) that racist treatment of persons is presumptively wrong, and that in order to defeat that presumption the racist must be prepared to defend the central claims:

1. There are races.
2. Some races are innately superior to others.
3. Innately superior races ought to dominate inferior races.

Racists, we've concluded, haven't successfully defended even claim (1), because it hasn't been convincingly shown that races even exist. But even if we assume that there are races, it hasn't been shown that some races are innately superior to others. And even if that were shown, it wouldn't follow that superior races ought to dominate inferior races, any more than that superior individuals (if there are any who can plausibly be said to be superior overall) ought to dominate inferior individuals. Racists, we may say, haven't defeated the presumption that racist conduct is wrong; hence racism is wrong.

Study questions

1. What are the differences between *primary racism* and *secondary racism* (Section 1.2)?
2. What constitutes *racial discrimination*? Why is it a complex issue whether the low proportion of black servers in NYC restaurants represents racial discrimination (Section 1.3)?
3. How does the text define *racism*? What are the definitions of *racist₁*, *racist₂*, and *racist₃* in Section 1.3? How does a racist in any of these senses differ from a *racialist* (Definition Box 1F)?
4. Who was *Gobineau* (Section 1.4)? What were the main points of his racist philosophy?
5. Cite three problems a racist has to confront in trying to establish that there are races and that some are innately superior to others (Section 1.6)? What role does the distinction between *essential* and *accidental properties* play in helping to understand these problems (Theory Box 1C)?
7. What do you take to be *Mark Twain's main point* in the passage from his novel *Pudd'nhead Wilson* (Section 1.6)? What implications does it have for the problems of race today?
8. If there were races and some were superior to others, why would it not follow from those facts alone that superior races ought to dominate inferior races (Section 1.8)?
9. What are *Natural Law Ethics*, *Divine Will Theory*, and *Utilitarianism* (Theory Box 1E)?
10. What is the *principle of universalizability* (U)? What role does it have in evaluating a possible conflict between *utility* and *rights* on the question of racial justice (Section 1.10)?
11. Do you understand racism better from having read this chapter? If so, in what ways?

Notes

1 Charles Taylor, *Sources of the Self: The Making of Modern Identity* (Cambridge, MA: Harvard University Press, 1989), p. 7.
2 "Race Questions and Prejudices," *The Basic Writings of Josiah Royce*, Vol. 2, ed. John J. McDermott (Chicago: University of Chicago Press, 1969), p. 1090.
3 From Martin Luther King, Jr., "Nonviolence and Racial Justice," in James M. Washington (ed.), *A Testament of Hope: The Essential Writings of Martin Luther King, Jr.* (San Francisco: Harper & Row, Publishers, 1986), pp. 5–7. Originally published in *Christian Century* 74 (February 6, 1957): 165–7.
4 One might well consider it discrimination, however, that there are disproportionately fewer starring roles for blacks, male and female, than for whites; and fewer opportunities overall at various levels of a lucrative industry.
5 *The New York Times*, May 10, 2000.
6 Judith Lichtenberg, "Racism in the Head, Racism in the World," *Report from the Institute for Philosophy & Public Policy*, University of Maryland, Vol. 12, No. 1, Spring/Summer 1992, 5. I have relied heavily, particularly in the discussion of secondary racism, upon Lichtenberg's excellent analysis.
7 Abraham Lincoln, first debate with Douglas, August 21, 1858; the second quotation is from another speech against the Kansas-Nebraska Act.
8 Arthur de Gobineau, *Inequality of Human Races*, trans. by Adrian Collins, Introduction by Dr Oscar Levy (London: William Heinemann, 1915), pp. xiv, 146, 205–208; emphases in the original.
9 Conduct may not fully be under people's control, of course, if it's governed by compulsions, addictions, cognitive impairment, or unconscious motives.
10 Richard Delgado, "Words That Wound: A Tort Action for Racial Insults, Epithets, and Name-Calling," in Richard Delgado (ed.), *Critical Race Theory* (Philadelphia: Temple University Press, 1995), p. 159. Originally published in HARV. C.R.-C.L. L. REV. 133 (1982).
11 Ibid.
12 Ian F. Haney Lopez, "The Social Construction of Race," in Richard Delgado (ed.), *Critical Race Theory* (Philadelphia: Temple University Press, 1995), p. 193. Published originally in HARV. C.R.-C.L. L. Rev. 1 (1994).
13 These reasons weren't always obvious. In the nineteenth century it was widely believed that poverty was due to heredity. The idea that poor people are inherently lazy, indisciplined, and unambitious—hence deserving of their poverty—persists even today. In a more complex view, Hinduism traditionally embodies a caste system, according to which different people, by nature, are suited for certain roles, such as leadership or servitude.

14 Quotation taken from Thomas F. Gossett, *Race: The History of an Idea in America* (New York: Schocken Books, 1965), p. 70. I am relying heavily on Gossett's analysis here.
15 Mark Twain, *Puddn'head Wilson* (New York: P.F. Collier & Son company, 1922), pp. 11f.
16 Steven A. Holmes reports that "[i]n a 1985 survey of physical and cultural anthropologists, 50 percent agreed that there is such a thing as race, biologically speaking, and 41 percent disagreed." *New York Times*, October 23, 1994.
17 Ashley Montagu, "The Concept of Race in the Human Species in the Light of Genetics," in Ashley Montagu (ed.), *The Concept of Race* (London: Collier-Macmillan, 1964), p. 9.
18 "Seeing Race," *Michigan Today*, June 1996, Vol. 28, No. 2, 2. Quoted from Lawrence Hirschfeld, *Race in the Making: Cognition, Culture and the Child's Construction of Human Kinds* (Cambridge: MIT Press, 1996).
19 Holmes.
20 "Seeing Race," *Michigan Today*.
21 Royce, p. 1107.
22 Paul C. Taylor, *Race: A Philosophical Introduction* (Cambridge: Polity, 2004), p. 84.
23 Leonard Pitts, Jr., columnist for the *Miami Herald*. From *Rochester Democrat and Chronicle*, July 12, 2000.
24 G. E. Moore, *Philosophical Studies* (Patterson, NJ: Littlefield, Adams, 1959), pp. 255f.

For more resources:

www.bloomsbury.com/holmes-introduction-to-applied-ethics

2

Sexism

[R]eason and experience convince me that the only method of leading women to fulfil their peculiar duties is to free them from all restraint by allowing them to participate in the inherent rights of mankind.

—Mary Wollstonecraft[1]

Society, as organized to-day under the man power is one grand rape of womanhood, on the highways, in our jails, prisons, asylums, in our homes, alike in the world of fashion and of work.

—Elizabeth Cady Stanton[2]

Introduction

Like racism, sexism is often discussed with little understanding of precisely what it is. In this chapter, we'll define "sexism" and explore the reasons why it's morally wrong. In so doing, we shall consider the question of whether sexism is analogous to racism. And we'll also consider the contentious question of whether men are superior to women or vice versa, and whether superiority is even relevant to whether either sex should dominate the other.

2.1 Three basic questions about sexism

Women make up half the world's population. Every person has been born of a woman, and most have been nurtured by women. Women are the major influence in the early childhood of the overwhelming majority of people. Yet women and girls have been, and still are in much of the world, severely oppressed. Even where the worst of their oppression has ended, they are often systematically disadvantaged. Gloria Steinem, the founder of *Ms.* magazine illustrates this in her comments on attitudes toward women's accomplishments in literature:

Women Have "Chick Flicks." What about Men?

Think about it: If "Anna Karenina" had been by Leah Tolstoy, or "The Scarlet Letter" by Nancy Hawthorne or "A Doll's House" by Henrietta Ibsen—if "The Invisible Man" had been "The Invisible Woman"—would they have been hailed as classics? Suppose Shakespeare had really been the Dark Lady who some people still think he/she was. I bet most of her plays and all of her sonnets would have been dismissed as ye olde Elizabethan chick lit and buried until they were resurrected by stubborn feminist scholars of today.

Indeed, as long as men are taken seriously when they write about the female half of the world—and women are not taken seriously when writing about ourselves, much less about men and public affairs—the list of Great Authors will be more about power than talent, more about opinion than experience.[3]

Taken as a group, women represent by far the largest body of persons who have been discriminated against throughout history, far more than any so-called race or ethnic group. Sexism is the label for this phenomenon.

There are, however, radically different perceptions of what sexism is and how serious a problem it is. As you think about this topic, consider the following report of a poll tabulating different perceptions of the extent of sexism in the United States:

Sexes Differ on Persistence of Sexism

To be a woman in the United States is to feel unequal, despite great strides in gender equality, according to a poll about gender in post-election America ... It's catcalls on the street, disrespect at work and unbalanced responsibilities at home. For girls, it's being taught, more than boys, to aspire to marriage, and for women, it's watching positions of power go to men.

But men don't necessarily see it that way.

Those are some of the findings from the poll, by PerryUndem, a nonpartisan research and polling firm whose biggest clients are foundations ...

Eighty-two percent of women said sexism was a problem in society today; 41 percent said they had felt unequal because of their gender. Men underestimated the sexism felt by the women in their lives, the survey found. And while most respondents agreed it's a better time to be a man than a woman in our society, only Republican men thought it was a better time to be a woman than a man ...

Over all, only 37 percent of respondents thought it was a good time to be a woman in the United States. Fewer thought it was a good time to be a minority woman; 24 percent said it was a good time to be a Latina, and 11 percent a Muslim woman ...

Despite the widespread support for gender equality and certain feminist policies, only 19 percent of respondents said they considered themselves feminists. There was no clear consensus on who best represented feminism today. The largest shares of people named two black women: Michelle Obama and Oprah Winfrey.[4]

The differences in perception of sexism documented by the above report almost certainly represent differences in understanding of what sexism is. So, let us begin by trying to clarify precisely what sexism is. As with racism, we'll frame our discussion of sexism around three questions. How far the parallels between racism and sexism extend is a controversial issue, which we'll discuss later (Section 2.4).

1. What is sexism?
2. Why is it wrong?
3. What may justifiably be done about it?

We shall defer question (3) until our discussion of affirmative action in Chapter 4, much of which will deal with measures to counteract discrimination on the basis of both race and gender.

2.2 What is sexism?

Although males as well as females may experience sexism, women have been by far its primary victims. This is clear from the classic nineteenth-century Declaration of Sentiments, patterned after the Declaration of Independence and authored principally by Elizabeth Cady Stanton. It was adopted in 1848 at the first women's rights convention in upstate New York:

Declaration of Sentiments
Seneca Falls, New York, July 19–20,1848

...

We hold these truths to be self-evident; that all men and women are created equal; that they are endowed by their Creator with certain inalienable rights; that among these are life, liberty, and the pursuit of happiness; that to secure these rights governments are instituted, deriving their just powers from the consent of the governed. Whenever any form of Government becomes destructive of these ends, it is the right of those who suffer from it to refuse allegiance to it, and to insist upon the institution of a new government, laying its foundation on such principles, and organizing its powers in such form as to them shall seem most likely to affect their safety and happiness. Prudence, indeed, will dictate that governments long established should not be changed for light and transient causes; and accordingly, all experience hath shown that mankind are more disposed to suffer, while evils are sufferable, than to right themselves by abolishing the forms to which they are accustomed. But when a long train of abuses and usurpations, pursuing invariably the same object, evinces a design to reduce them under absolute despotism, it is their duty to throw off such government, and to provide new guards for their future security. Such has been the patient sufferance of the women under this government, and such is now the necessity which constrains them to demand the equal station to which they are entitled.

The history of mankind is a history of repeated injuries and usurpations on the part of man toward woman, having in direct object the establishment of an absolute tyranny over her. To prove this, let facts be submitted to a candid world.

He has never permitted her to exercise her inalienable right to the elective franchise.

He has compelled her to submit to laws, in the formation of which she had no voice.

He has withheld from her rights which are given to the most ignorant and degraded men—both natives and foreigners.

Having deprived her of this right of a citizen, the elective franchise, thereby leaving her without representation in the halls of legislation, he has oppressed her on all sides.

He has made her, if married, in the eye of the law, civilly dead.

He has taken from her all right in property, even to the wages she earns.

He has made her, morally, an irresponsible being, as she can commit many crimes with impunity, provided they be done in the presence of her husband. In the covenant of marriage, she is compelled to promise obedience to her husband, he becoming, to all intents and purposes, her master—the law giving him power to deprive her of her liberty, and to administer chastisement.

He has so framed the laws of divorce, as to what shall be the proper causes of divorce: in case of separation, to whom the guardianship of the children shall be given, as to be wholly regardless of the happiness of women—the law, in all cases, going upon the false supposition of the supremacy of man, and giving all power into his hands.

After depriving her of all rights as a married woman, if single and the owner of property, he has taxed her to support a government which recognizes her only when her property can be made profitable to it.

He has monopolized nearly all the profitable employments, and from those she is permitted to follow, she receives but a scanty remuneration.

He closes against her all the avenues to wealth and distinction, which he considers most honorable to himself. As a teacher of theology, medicine, or law, she is not known.

He has denied her the facilities for obtaining a thorough education—all colleges being closed against her.

He allows her in Church as well as State, but a subordinate position, claiming Apostolic authority for her exclusion from the ministry, and, with some exception, from any public participation in the affairs of the Church.

He has created a false public sentiment, by giving to the world a different code of morals for men and women, by which moral delinquencies which exclude women from society, are not only tolerated but deemed of little account in man.

He has usurped the prerogative of Jehovah himself, claiming it as her right to assign for her a sphere of action, when that belongs to her conscience and her God.

He has endeavored, in every way that he could to destroy her confidence in her own powers, to lessen her self-respect, and to make her willing to lead a dependent and abject life.

Now, in view of this entire disfranchisement of one-half the people of this country, their social and religious degradation,—in view of the unjust laws above mentioned, and because women do feel themselves aggrieved, oppressed, and fraudulently deprived of their most sacred rights, we insist that they have immediate admission to all the rights and privileges which belong to them as citizens of these United States.

In entering upon the great work before us, we anticipate no small amount of misconception, misrepresentation, and ridicule; but we shall use every instrumentality within our power to effect our object. We shall employ agents, circulate tracts, petition the state and national Legislatures, and endeavor to enlist the pulpit and the press on our behalf. We hope this Convention will be followed by a series of Conventions, embracing every part of the country.

Firmly relying upon the final triumph of the right and the True, we do this day affix our signatures to this declaration. (Signed by 68 women and 32 men)

Although the declaration focuses on American women, it claims that women generally have suffered discrimination throughout history, a "long train of abuses and usurpations, pursuing invariably the same object." That object "evinces a design to reduce them [women] under absolute despotism." It is a pervasive and systematic sexism that is being charged. This is the notion we want to examine.

Let us distinguish between primary and secondary sexism, as we did with regard to racism. We'll define both now but discuss some of the issues central to secondary sexism in Chapter 3.

Definition Box 2A

Primary Sexism: The beliefs, attitudes, and practices of sexists.

This shifts attention to what is distinctive of the beliefs, attitudes, and practices of sexists qua sexists, and invites the question: what is a sexist?

Much of the problem with sexism and racism is that the inequities they cause extend well beyond the deliberate subordination of a race or sex implied by primary racism and sexism. Those who benefit from those inequities (in our society, whites and white males) may not themselves be racists or sexists (or, at least, may not think of themselves as such); and for that reason they may be reluctant to acknowledge these inequities or to feel any responsibility for trying to remedy them. At the same time, those who are disadvantaged by the inequities (in our society, principally African Americans, Native Americans, Hispanics, and women) are likely to be unwilling to settle for progress that proceeds at a glacial pace. It's important for these reasons to recognize secondary sexism as well as secondary racism:

Definition Box 2B

Secondary Sexism: The perpetuation of sex-inequality by conduct that is motivated primarily by nonsexist (e.g., economic) considerations.

If women have been prevented from voting and owning property; if they've been confined to the household to rear children and be obedient wives; and if, moreover, they've been subjected to violence and abuse at the whim of men; if, that is, they've suffered discrimination for centuries; then even if that discrimination ceased overnight and the legal barriers to their advancement were lifted, women would still find themselves socially, politically, and economically disadvantaged. Men would still control the government, the military, and the judiciary, and own most of the wealth. Even if they weren't personally responsible for past discrimination, they would benefit from it, and by resisting change would help to perpetuate the inequities that are its legacy.

In other words, even if you abolished primary sexism at a stroke, secondary sexism would remain. We shall take up one of the principal means thought best to deal with it—affirmative action—in Chapter 4.

Let us continue with our examination of primary sexism. As noted, to understand primary sexism requires understanding what a sexist is.

2.3 What is a sexist?

The term "sexist," like the term "racist," has various uses. Sometimes it's used with a predominantly, or even exclusively, *emotive meaning* (as explained in Chapter 1, Theory Box 1A, Section 1.3), and other times with a predominantly *descriptive meaning*. It most often has both emotive and descriptive meaning. To call someone a "sexist pig," for example, is to use the term emotively, typically to express disapproval of someone. (The word "pig" has a literal descriptive meaning referring to a certain type of animal, but it's not that meaning one has in mind when calling someone a "sexist pig.") We shall, again as with racism, be concerned with the descriptive meaning.

Definition Box 2C

Sexist$_1$: One who practices sex discrimination.

People can treat others prejudicially or preferentially on the basis of sex as well as on the basis of supposedly racial characteristics. In that case, it's not so much the properties of persons as individuals that are singled out as it is properties they share with the larger group to which they belong—in this case, defined by sex. All members of that group are singled out for prejudicial treatment. Prejudicial treatment can consist of verbal abuse, discrimination, and both physical and psychological violence. While all three are wrong, only discrimination and violence on the basis of sex are illegal; much (though not all) of verbal abuse isn't.

While people are often called sexist simply because they practice sex discrimination, that gives us only a minimalist conception of a sexist. It doesn't even require that one knowingly or intentionally discriminate. So we need to consider other uses of the term. We can also distinguish:

Definition Box 2D

Sexist$_2$: A chauvinist with regard to sex.

To understand what it is to be a sexist$_2$ we need to understand what a chauvinist is. The term can be most broadly defined as follows:

Definition Box 2E

A chauvinist is "a person whose patriotism is unreasoning and fanatical; 2. A person unreasonably devoted to his own race, sex, etc. and contemptuous of other races, the opposite sex, etc." (*Webster's New World Dictionary*)

A chauvinist about sex is anyone unreasonably devoted to his own sex and contemptuous of the opposite sex. A *male chauvinist* (the typical use of this term with regard to sex) favors men and is contemptuous of women. Male chauvinism carried to the extreme is *misogyny*, the hatred of women. A *female chauvinist* favors women and is contemptuous of men. Hatred of men is *misandry*.

The male chauvinist is to sex as the racial bigot is to race. Just as the bigot is unlikely to offer much in the way of justification for his outlook, the same is true of the male chauvinist. But typically the male chauvinist believes in the superiority of men. We need to take account of this belief in trying to understand what a sexist is.

When discussing racism, we had a convenient term for someone who believes in the superiority of some races over others (see Section 1.3). We called such a person a "racialist." But we don't have a ready label for someone who believes in the superiority of one sex over another but doesn't necessarily support discrimination on that basis. For that reason, I shall coin the term "sextist" for that purpose.

Definition Box 2F

Sextist: One who believes in the innate superiority of one sex over the other.

While a $sexist_1$ no doubt often is a sextist in this sense, he needn't be. One might practice sex discrimination for reasons (again, including economic) that have nothing directly to do with beliefs about the superiority of one sex over the other. The $sexist_2$, however—often a male chauvinist or misogynist—is probably almost always a sextist. The male chauvinist typically believes that males are superior to females. The misogynist may believe this as well, but he may not. Unlike the chauvinist, the misogynist might actually believe that females are superior to males and resent them for that reason. Perceived female superiority might explain his hatred of females.

We can now define the full-fledged sexist with the same reference to beliefs and conduct as in the case of the racist.

Definition Box 2G

$Sexist_3$: One who knowingly practices or approves of sex discrimination in the belief (a) that one sex is innately superior to the other, and (b) that the innately superior sex ought to dominate the inferior sex.

Primary sexism, then, can be taken to refer to the beliefs, attitudes, and practices of sexists in these various senses. We won't go over them again, but you should be aware that the same distinctions between overt and covert, and conscious and unconscious, that we made with regard to racism (Section 1.3) apply in the case of sexism. People can *be* sexist even though they try to conceal their sexist beliefs and attitudes and even if they're not themselves conscious of them.

2.4 The sexist's burden of proof

Since the sexist (by which we shall henceforth mean the sexist$_3$) practices, or at least approves of, sex discrimination, and discrimination is the prejudicial treatment of persons, the burden is upon the sexist to justify such treatment. We've seen (Section 2.2) in the 1848 Declaration of Sentiments a catalogue of the discriminatory treatment of women. Lest it be thought that sex discrimination is a thing of the past, consider the following summary by an African American feminist of the evolution of women's issues in the latter part of the twentieth century. It will help to show why there is a burden of proof upon the sexist:

The "Second Wave" of Feminism
Almost exactly forty years ago, the "second wave of feminism" emerged in the wake of the gains made by the black civil rights movement. In 1961, President John F. Kennedy issued Executive Order 10980 establishing the President's Commission on the Status of Women and appointed Eleanor Roosevelt as its chair. Two years later, the second-class status of the female gender was documented in the Commission's final report, *American Women*, edited by noted anthropologist Margaret Mead. The comprehensive document identified widespread discrimination against women in employment, educational access, social security, divorce laws, service on juries, insurance rates, access to credit, and many other public policies. Special studies authorized by the Commission also addressed the double impact of race and gender on black women's lives.

In short, *American Women* provided important data to support the inclusion of gender in the spate of civil rights laws passed at the national and state levels during the 1960s and 1970s. It also spurred the formation of local and state women's commissions throughout the nation, brought new militancy to existing women's organizations, generated dozens of new "feminist" groups, and turned the spotlight on the systems of gender bias that, for centuries, had affected opportunities for women and girls.

As a result, in the ten-year period between 1965 and 1975, dramatic changes were made: a woman's right to reproductive choice was affirmed by the Supreme Court; gender restrictions on virtually all jobs were removed; girls' access to school sports and previously male-dominated educational fields was expanded; violence against women and girls was exposed to public view; credit discrimination was banned; the number of women entering the political arena significantly increased; gender equity was added to affirmative action programs; and a long-dormant "equal rights amendment" was resurrected in a serious, though not successful, effort to assure constitutional protection for women.

This second wave of feminism is complex, with many facets and many "leaders." Its focus has varied from the personal to the universal—addressing the root causes of social, economic, and political inequity. Because women are everywhere (one cannot move to a suburb to escape them), the rumblings of change are also everywhere. The movement has broadened its message, attracted new supporters, and lost some old ones who were more comfortable with a narrower vision of feminism. What was once categorized as a white, middle-class phenomenon now includes all races, ethnicities, classes, and sexual orientations. Asian Pacific Islanders, Latinas, black women, indigenous women, lesbian, bisexual, and transgender women, women with disabilities, young women, older women have all formed groups to address their unique concerns. Coalitions and collaborations on issues of general concern—and there are many—have replaced the pressure to define any one organization as "the movement." ...

It has taken more than 200 years, but ... [t]he "tribe" of women, in all its diversity, has indeed grown discontented and is combining its voices with those of enlightened and liberated men to define the new millennium. We have come a long way, but there is still a long, long way to go![5]

While our main concern will be with sexism in the United States, some of the worst forms of discrimination against women are found in other countries. In some less developed countries, girls receive less nutrition, education, and medical care than boys. Infanticide against newborn girls is often practiced, as well as sex-selection abortions to prevent the birth of girls in the first place. Female genital mutilation is practiced in some African societies. There is sex trafficking of young women from some Eastern European nations into Europe under conditions tantamount to slavery. Some work as domestics under similar conditions. Not least of all, domestic violence against women is widespread and often condoned. A form of violence against women in Bangladesh is reported in the following account:

> The village elders met under a litchi tree, applying their collective wisdom to put a value on Peyara Begum's grotesquely ruined face.
>
> The crime was hideous, they somberly agreed. A young man had become obsessed with her, but she was married and he was turned away. He took his revenge with sulfuric acid, to erase the beauty that had once enchanted him and to empty her life of happiness.
>
> Her cheeks melted. Her right eye was blinded and hollowed like a crater . . .
>
> No one is sure why this crime occurs here at such a high pace, for this nation is not so different from many others in its poverty or its treatment of women. Inexplicably, some aberrant ripple is moving through the countryside. Nariphokko, a woman's rights group, has kept statistics: 80 attacks in 1996, 117 in 1997, 130 in 1998 . . .
>
> Some victims die, but that seems unintended. The purpose of the attackers is to manufacture a living hell, and in that there is most often fulfillment.
>
> Survivors are left not only with their deformities but also with the peculiarities of village reckoning. One young woman was forced by her parents to marry her attacker, solving the urgent matter of who would support a woman unwanted as a bride. Another was forbidden to come home until she allowed her husband to take a second wife.[6]

The above simply recounts a particularly grisly practice. There is a preference for boys in much of Asia, which sometimes leads to the killing of unwanted girls. With the development of ultrasound technology enabling people to determine the sex of a fetus, incidences of the aborting of female fetuses has soared. This led India, for example, to ban prenatal sex-determination testing. According to a *Time* magazine report, the effects of the ban have been minimal:

Key Quote 2A

The results of India's 2011 Census reveal that far fewer girls than boys are born in the country each year, indicating a rapidly declining gender ratio that reflects pervasive sex-selection practices ... In the past twenty years, India has seen 10 million female lives lost to abortion and sex selection ... The numbers illustrate a long-standing problem in countries like India and China whose cultures view male children as more valuable.[7]

These practices are part of the vast pattern of systematic abuse of females. Even in countries like the United States, where practices like the above are considered barbaric, these forms of discrimination are felt. Consider the following report:

She arrived in New York less than four years ago, a bride from India hoping for a good life with a man who bragged of being a millionaire. The reality broke her heart and nearly cost her life.

Pervinder Kaur, the hopeful bride, knew very little English and less about America. Alone and vulnerable, she saw herself turned into a prisoner in her in-laws' home, forbidden to make friends outside the family. Her husband tried to force her to turn over money, then beat her, she said.

But two phone calls set her free. Finally, she called the police, who got an ambulance and sent her to the hospital. Later, she called Sakhi ...

Sakhi—the name means "female friend" in Hindi—is a still struggling, 10-year-old support group based in Manhattan and run by South Asian women to help other women from India, Bangladesh, Pakistan, Nepal and Indian communities in the Caribbean. It is part of a growing movement led by young South Asian-Americans who want to confront social issues that have often been taboo subjects in their homes and neighborhoods.

Sakhi teaches women about their rights and how to exercise them in the United States. Among its services, the group helps women find places to live. It also offers language assistance and legal advice in court cases and dealing with city services. Sakhi volunteers may accompany women to meetings with the police, the courts, and other agencies.

> Similar organizations have formed in recent years in Connecticut, Pennsylvania, Illinois, Texas, California and Washington State. They all offer not just help, but the comfort of a familiar culture in an alien world …
>
> The organization's volunteers have seen women in New York who have been psychologically wounded, physically battered, beaten and burned. In India, by its government's own figures, at least 6,000 brides are burned to death every year because the dowry they bring into a marriage is deemed too small—or because a husband decides he doesn't really like the woman selected for him by his parents …
>
> The majority of women in South Asia are illiterate, and as more are brought here as brides or domestic labor, the pool of vulnerable women grows. To them, the outside world is strange and terrifying. Even taking a subway train can be intimidating. That was Pervinder Kaur's story.[8]

Race discrimination and sex discrimination are similar in many respects, but there are important differences. Unlike with racism, some of the attitudes contributing to women being disadvantaged have consisted in their being valued rather than devalued. The following writer makes this claim:

> ### Racism and Sexism: A Disanalogy?
> Male prejudice against women is often combined with respect for women. In this way male prejudice is very different from racism. The denial of women's rights to work and live as they individually choose is often associated with contempt for women's intelligence and capacity, but at the same time with a desire to protect those who have the main responsibility for perpetuating human life. The slogan, 'Women and children first,' invoked in shipwreck or other disaster, is not an expression of contempt or hostility but of a belief in the special *importance* of women and children in the crucial moments when the choice of who among many are to deserve survival is a real one. The racist would not be crying 'Jews and blacks first'; on the contrary, racially despised groups would be the expendable ones.[9]

The sinking of the *Titanic* illustrates Dummett's point. Women and children were given priority in the lifeboats, and they constituted the majority of survivors. So what's wrong with that, you might ask? Shouldn't women be grateful for being given preferential treatment? The problem is that many of the other modes of treatment associated with this outlook have had the effect of depriving women of equal opportunities for education, and political and economic advancement. Worst of all, in the view of some, it has had the effect of infantilizing women, turning them into permanent children who are dependent, not upon parents, but upon men, primarily their husbands. The existentialist philosopher Simone de Beauvoir (1908–86), captures that thought in the following passage:

Women as a Passive "Second Sex"

Woman herself recognizes that the world is masculine on the whole; those who fashioned it, ruled it, and still dominate it today are men. As for her, she does not consider herself responsible for it; it is understood that she is inferior and dependent; she has not learned the lessons of violence, she has never stood forth as subject before the other members of the group. Shut up in her flesh, her home, she sees herself as passive before these gods with human faces who set goals and establish values. In this sense there is truth in the saying that makes her the "eternal child." Workers, black slaves, colonial natives, have also been called grown-up children—as long as they were not feared; that meant that they were to accept without argument the verities and the laws laid down for them by other men. The lot of woman is a respectful obedience.[10]

Whereas the typical forms of racial discrimination in primary racism involve an open devaluing of those discriminated against, at least some of the forms of sex discrimination result from *valuing* women—and valuing them over men. This can have the unintended effect of disadvantaging women, hence becoming a part of pervasive discrimination against them.

In this connection, it's important to take note of a controversial issue. No one would maintain, say, that African Americans do better than Caucasians in contemporary American society. The long-term effects of slavery and racism are easily documented. But some argue that in contemporary American society it's actually girls who are doing better than boys. Philosopher Christina Hoff Sommers contends:

A War against Boys?

Inevitably, boys are resented, being seen both as the unfairly privileged gender and as obstacles on the path to gender justice for girls.

There is an understandable dialectic: the more girls are portrayed as diminished, the more boys are regarded as needing to be taken down a notch and reduced in importance. This perspective on boys and girls is promoted in schools of education, and many a teacher now feels that girls need and deserve special indemnifying consideration. "It is really clear that boys are no. 1 in this society and in most of the world," says Dr. Patricia O'Reilly ...

It may be "clear," but it isn't true. If we disregard the girl advocates and look objectively at the relative condition of boys and girls in *this* country, we find that it is boys, not girls, who are languishing academically. Data from the US Department of Education and from several recent university studies show that far from being shy and demoralized, today's girls outshine boys. Girls get better grades. They have higher education aspirations. They follow a more rigorous academic program and participate more in the prestigious Advanced Placement (AP) program. This demanding program gives top students the opportunity of taking college-level courses in high school. In 1984, an equal proportion of males and females participated. But according to the United States Department of Education, "Between 1984 and 1996, the number of females who took the examination rose at a faster rate ... In 1996, 144 females compared to 117 males per 1000 12th graders took AP examinations." ...

According to the National Center for Education Statistics, slightly more female than male students enroll in high-level math and science courses ...

The representation of American girls as apprehensive and academically diminished is not true to the facts. Girls, allegedly so timorous and lacking in confidence, now outnumber boys in student government, in honor societies, on school newspapers, and even in debating clubs. Only in sports are the boys still ahead ...

Girls read more books. They outperform males on tests of artistic and musical ability. More girls than boys study abroad. More join the Peace Corps. Conversely, more boys than girls are suspended from school. More are held back and more drop out. Boys are three times as likely as girls to be enrolled in special education programs and four times as likely to be diagnosed with attention deficit/hyperactivity disorder. More boys than girls are involved in crime, alcohol, and drugs. Girls attempt suicide more than boys, but it is boys who actually kill themselves more often.[11]

Assuming the statistics on which these conclusions are based are accurate, we'd need to ask what explains them. If, as Sommers believes, it's the attitudes of "misguided feminism" that are harming boys, then arguably in addition to discrimination against girls there is a reverse discrimination against boys. As we saw earlier (Section 1.3), discrimination involves the comparative treatment of groups. If either boys or girls as a group are treated prejudicially by comparison with the ways in which the other group is treated, that's discriminatory. The question is whether males suffer from a reverse sexism, or as one writer puts it, a "second sexism." Consider the following:

"The Second Sexism"

In those societies in which sex discrimination has been recognized to be wrong, the assault on this form of discrimination has targeted those attitudes and practices that (primarily) disadvantage women and girls. At the most, there has been only scant attention to those manifestations of sex discrimination whose primary victims are men and boys. What little recognition there has been of discrimination against males has very rarely resulted in amelioration. For these reasons, we might refer to discrimination against males as the "second sexism," to adapt Simone de Beauvoir's famous phrase. The second sexism is the neglected sexism, the sexism that is not take seriously even by most of those who oppose (or at least claim that they oppose) sex discrimination . . .

Male disadvantages include the absence of immunity, typically enjoyed by females, from conscription into military service. Men, unlike women, are not only conscripted but also sent into combat, where they risk injury, both physical and psychological, and death. Men are also disproportionately the victims of violence in most (but not all) non-combat contexts. For example, most victims of violent crime are male, and men are often (but again not always) specially targeted for mass killing. Males are more likely than females to be subject to corporal punishment. Indeed, sometimes such punishment of females is prohibited, while it is permitted, if not encouraged, for males. Although males are less often victims of sexual assault than are females, the sexual assault of males is typically taken less seriously and is thus even more significantly under-reported. Fathers are less likely than mothers to win custody of their children in the event of divorce . . .

Perhaps the most obvious example of male disadvantage is the long history of social and legal pressures on men, but not on women, to enter the military and to fight in war, thereby risking their lives and bodily and psychological health. Where the pressure to join the military has taken the form of conscription, the costs of avoidance have been either self-imposed exile, imprisonment, or, in the most extreme circumstances, execution … In those times and places, where the pressures have been social rather than legal, the costs of not enlisting have been either shame or ostracism … It may be hard for people in contemporary western societies to understand how powerful those forces have been in other contexts. However, young men, and even boys, have felt, and been made to feel, that their manhood is impugned if they fail to enlist. In other words, they would be cowards if they failed to respond to the call to arms. Women, oblivious to their own privilege in being exempt from such pressures and expectations, have sometimes taken a lead in shaming men who they thought should already have volunteered.[12]

However one evaluates these claims, if sexists condone sex discrimination of any sort, whether against women or men, the burden of proof rests with them to justify such discrimination.

We've pointed out one apparent dissimilarity between racism and sexism. There is a second one to note. The idea of race is a contested one. There's no consensus on whether there is such a thing as race. There is a consensus that biologically there are sexes. But the matter isn't that simple. As many as one in a thousand babies is born with some sort of sex ambiguity. Of practical importance is the difficulty in finding reliable criteria to certify that an athlete is actually a female and not a man, since in competitions requiring strength and speed men in general have an advantage over women. Even science has long found the problem complicated, as indicated in the following report:

Determining Sex

Who is a man and who is a woman? For all its dazzling discoveries about the genes that guide a human embryo along its path to maleness or femaleness, science, it appears, cannot provide a simple answer.

Scientists say that dozens of birth defects can blur gender and impossibly complicate the search for a simple genetic test to certify someone as female. A person can be born with "male" sex chromosomes, but because of a mutation in a gene on another chromosome be unable to respond to those hormones. She will look like a woman and see herself as one. Other women will have normal female sex chromosomes, but due to defects in hormone production, have a man's muscles and masculinized genitals, usually an enlarged clitoris. Still others will have the two X chromosomes that most women have, but also a Y chromosome, like most men.[13]

Of even greater practical importance than certifying the gender of athletes is empowering young people to identify with gender in a way that enables them to lead rich and fulfilling lives. At one time, sex was thought to be a purely biological category and gender a socially defined category. But now the concept of gender has been expanded, as the following passage makes clear:

Key Quote 2B

Gender is an amalgamation of several elements: chromosomes (those X's and Y's), anatomy (internal sex organs and external genitals), hormones (relative levels of testosterone and estrogen), psychology (self-identity), and culture (socially defined gender behaviors). And sometimes people who are born with the chromosomes and genitals of one sex realize that they are transgender, meaning they have an internal gender identity that aligns with the opposite sex—or even, occasionally, with neither gender or with no gender at all ... But people today—especially young people—are questioning not just the gender they were assigned at birth but also the gender binary (boy/girl, male/female) itself.[14]

Recall the example of Roxy from Mark Twain's novel *Pudd'nhead Wilson* in Chapter 1, Section 1.6. She was one-sixteenth black but fifteen-sixteenths white, yet considered black by society. Today, society tends to expect gender conformity from people, that is, conformity to society's norms for behavior of the sexes. But transgender people combine masculine and feminine characteristics often in complex ways, even more so than in Roxy's case with regard to black and white ancestry. Although a third of countries now allow gender change, there is extensive discrimination against lesbians, gays, bisexuals, and transgenders

(LGBT). We cannot here examine discrimination against LGBTs, but it needs to be recognized along with the discrimination of racism and sexism.

Despite the growing complexities in understanding sex and gender, we may say that the concept of sex, biologically considered, isn't a contested concept in the way in which race is. Thus, although the sexist holds (relatively uncontroversially) that

1. There are sexes,

the important questions concern the other two of the sexist's principal beliefs:

2. One sex is innately superior to the other.
3. The innately superior sex ought to dominate the inferior sex.

Unless the sexist can justify both of these propositions, he hasn't defeated the presumption that sexism is wrong. Let's examine these in turn.

2.5 Is one sex innately superior to the other?

There are examples throughout history of the disparagement of women and the representation of them as inferior to men, either in certain respects or overall. Let us consider a few passages from the history of philosophy.

Aristotle

(384–322 BCE)
Again, the male is by nature superior, and the female inferior; and the one rules, and the other is ruled; this principle, of necessity, extends to all mankind. (*Politics*)

In human beings, the female fetus is not perfected equally with the male … For females are weaker and colder in nature, and we must look upon the female character as being a sort of natural deficiency. Accordingly while it is within the mother it develops slowly because of its coldness … but after birth it quickly arrives at maturity and old age on account of its weakness, for all inferior things come sooner to their perfection or end, and as this is true of works of art so it is of what is formed by nature. (*On the Generation of Animals*)

Again, one quality or action is nobler than another if it is that of a naturally finer being: thus a man's will be nobler than a woman's. (*Rhetoric*)

Kant

(1724–1804)
Nothing of duty, nothing of compulsion, nothing of obligation ... I hardly believe that the fair sex is capable of principles. But in the place of it Providence has put in their breast kind and benevolent sensations, a fine feeling for propriety, and a complaisant soul. (*Observations on the Feeling of the Beautiful and the Sublime*)

Schopenhauer

(1788–1860)
The Nobler and more perfect a thing is, the later and slower it is in arriving at maturity. A man reaches the maturity of his reasoning powers and mental faculties hardly before the age of twenty-eight; a woman, at eighteen. And then, too, in the case of woman, it is only reason of a sort ... That is why women remain children their whole life long, never seeing anything but what is quite close to them, cleaving to the present moment, taking appearance for reality, and preferring trifles to matters of the first importance. ("On Women")

Nietzsche

(1844–1900)
Woman wants to become self-reliant—and for that reason she is beginning to enlighten men about "woman as such": *this* is one of the worst developments of the general *uglification* of Europe. For what must these clumsy attempts of women at scientific self-exposure bring to light! Woman has much reason for shame; so much pedantry, superficiality, schoolmarmishness, petty presumption, petty licentiousness and immodesty lies concealed in woman ... From the beginning, nothing has been more alien, repugnant, and hostile to woman than truth—her great art is the lie, her highest concern is mere appearance and beauty. (*Beyond Good and Evil*; emphases in the original)

Notice that Schopenhauer makes a similar observation to that of Simone de Beauvoir (Section 2.4) about women remaining children all their lives. But whereas de Beauvoir attributes this to the enforced dependence and passivity of women in male-dominated society, Schopenhauer attributes it to the inferiority of women. Men, he says, are "nobler" and "more perfect." Kant, in this passage, doesn't say that women are inferior, but he may be taken to imply it. His moral theory emphasizes the preeminence of duty and principles, and he regards women as incapable of acting on such notions.

Although what we're calling *sextism* (the view that one sex is superior to the other; see Section 2.3) typically holds that men are superior to women, some women (and some men) hold the reverse. They contend that women are superior to men. Consider the following column by writer Anna Quindlen:

Women Are Superior

My favorite news story so far this year was the one saying that in England scientists are working on a way to allow men to have babies. I'd buy tickets to that. I'd be happy to stand next to any man I know in one of those labor rooms the size of a Volkswagen trunk and whisper "No, dear, you don't really need the Demerol; just relax and do your second-stage breathing." It puts me in mind of an old angry feminist slogan: "If men got pregnant, abortion would be a sacrament." I think this is specious. If men got pregnant, there would be safe, reliable methods of birth control. They'd be inexpensive, too.

I can almost hear some of you out there thinking that I do not like men. This isn't true. I have been married for some years to a man and I hope that someday our two sons will grow up to be men. All three of my brothers are men, as is my father. Some of my best friends are men. It is simply that I think women are superior to men. There, I've said it.

The other day a very wise friend of mine asked: "Have you ever noticed that what passes as a terrific man would only be an adequate woman?" A Roman candle went off in my head; she was absolutely right ...

The inherent superiority of women came to mind just the other day when I was reading about sanitation workers. New York City has finally hired women to pick up the garbage ... There was something about all the maneuvering that had to take place before they could be hired, and then there were the obligatory quotes from male sanitation workers about how women were incapable of doing the job. They were similar to quotes I have read over the years suggesting that women are not fit to be rabbis, combat soldiers, astronauts, firefighters, judges, ironworkers and President of the United States ...

I keep hearing that there's a new breed of men out there who don't talk about helping a woman as though they're doing you a favor and who do seriously consider leaving the office if a child comes down with a fever at school, rather than assuming that you will leave yours. But from what I've seen there aren't enough of these men to qualify as a breed, only as a subgroup.[15]

Males and females generally differ in verifiable ways physically (body structure, reproductive organs, average size, etc.). One could question whether those differences alone make one sex superior to the other. The more interesting question is whether these physical properties correlate with what we earlier (Section 1.6) called mental properties. To justify the claim that one sex is innately superior to the other, sexists must identify these mental properties and show that there is a necessary (and not merely a contingent) connection between them and the physical properties. They must show that it's not just due to social and cultural circumstances that the mental properties are associated with the physical properties. They must then show why the possession of certain mental properties confers innate superiority upon one sex.

An attempt by anthropologist Melvin Konner to identify some such physical properties, and to suggest that they may make for the superiority of women, is challenged by another anthropologist, Barbara J. King. The following is an email exchange between them on the issue as reported in a National Public Radio interview with King:

Is It Sexist to Say That Women Are Superior to Men?

"Women are not equal to men; they are superior in many ways, and in most ways that will count in the future. It is not just a matter of culture or upbringing. It is a matter of chromosomes, genes, hormones, and nerve circuits. It is not mainly because of how experience shapes women, but because of intrinsic differences in the body and the brain."

It's not every day my jaw drops when reading the Chronicle Review, a section of *The Chronicle of Higher Education*. But drop it did when I read the opening paragraph, above, of "The End of Male Supremacy" by Emory University anthropologist Melvin Konner, published on April 3 [2015].

Konner's article, which is adapted from his new book, *Women After All: Sex, Evolution, and the End of Male Supremacy*, sits in conflict with three central conclusions that I impart to my anthropology students: Women and men are more alike in their behavior than they are different; sex differences that do exist arise in large part from variation in how children are raised and other experiences of living and working, attesting to the magnificent plasticity of the human bring; and no group of people, regardless of gender identification (I'm no fan of an oversimplified male vs. female binary) is biologically superior to any other. Those conclusions emerge from books, such as neuroscientist Elise Eliot's *Pink Brain, Blue Brain*, that insist the tiny sex differences present at birth are magnified through socialization. Konner, even while affirming that not all men are violent and not all women are nurturing, fearlessly advances his women's superiority thesis. Maleness is "a birth defect," he declares.

Curious to engage directly with Konner, last week I sent him questions by email and he kindly replied. Here is our exchange:

Could you outline what you consider to be the most significant evidence that women are superior to men because of "intrinsic differences in the body and brain?"

Recent brain imaging studies show that a part of the brain that helps produce violence, called the amygdala, is larger in men than in women.

Also, the frontal cortex (frontal lobes), which help to regulate impulses coming from the amygdala, is (are) more active in women. Mounting evidence supports the claim that male and female brains are different in many species, including us, partly because of androgenizing masculinizing) influences of testosterone on the (anterior) hypothalamus, amygdala, and other parts of the brain involved in sex and violence.

Genetic evidence also suggests that selection for aggressive and hypersexual traits has been strong in at least parts of our species in the human past. Roughly one in twelve men in Central Asia has a Y chromosome consistent with descent from a single man who lived in the time of Genghis Khan. Something similar is true of Ireland, harking back to the era (the Middle Ages) when that island was thoroughly dominated by warring tribes.

How do you respond to the view, or, maybe more honestly put, the complaint, that in attempting to support women, you are essentially erasing women's agency by reducing them (or I should say "us") to bodies and brains?

If reducing behavior to the brain is erasing agency, then none of us has agency. Every knowledgeable person since Hippocrates has located our thoughts, emotions, and feelings in the brain. Agency is something subjective that every person has. I think that using brain science (or evolution for that matter) to argue against agency is foolish.

As a woman and a feminist, I winced when reading your equating "maleness" with "a birth defect," "a disorder" and "androgen poisoning." Doesn't this language do more harm than good, in that it describes negatively an entire group of people in an unnuanced, stereotyped way?

You are not the first person to wince at that, but many others, mainly but not only women, have smiled. Would you object if I said "whites are bad because they oppress blacks," or "Anglos are bad because they oppress Latinos," or "rich people are bad because they oppress the poor"? How come after 12 millennia of oppression of women by men, I can't say men are bad for doing that?

In my view, we are living in a time when a corrective is sorely needed. Although in the article and the book I am careful to say "not all men" are bad, it is still true that "yes all women" have to fear the many, many bad ones. And unlike the racial, ethnic, or class categories, the difference between men and women is substantial and biological.

I'm sorry if some people don't like that, but it's true.

You state with confidence and optimism that "millennial male dominance is about to end." You take care to extend that prediction cross-culturally: "Even in the poorest lands, the increasing availability of women's suffrage, health services, microloans, and saving programs is giving them control over their destinies." How do we square this with what we know is happening to women in numerous places, including but not limited to places that fit your "poorest lands" descriptor: gender-based violence; rape; and other physical and emotional traumas?

Paradoxically, the small minority of men in ISIS, Boko Haram, and the like actually tell us more than all the books in the world about what men are like and what they have done to women (and by the way, to each other) through most of history. They are throwbacks, but instructive ones. They are part of a terrified lashing out by men against the inevitability of women's rights. They are representatives of the dominant men of the past who could not stand the idea of women being equal. The major trends in the developing world are against them, and they know it. Some men can't adjust. Look at Afghanistan, where almost no girls went to school 15 years ago under the Taliban, another throwback. Today the vast majority of Afghan girls are in school. The youngest person ever to win the Nobel Prize was Malala Yousafzai, the Pakistani girl who promoted girls' education. Men like that tried to kill her, but they only strengthened her and her cause.

* * *

[King summarizing]: We are left, then, with dueling perspectives from scientists on sex differences. Konner is certainly not alone in insisting that they are real. Eliot is not alone in insisting, instead, that they are largely explicable by culture and socialization.

This debate around the scientific evidence and how to interpret it is not going to vanish because Konner writes "I'm sorry, but it's true" about biological sex differences. The language Konner uses to make his case strikes me as problematic: It wrongly makes women out to be primarily about some set of (supposedly) biological characteristics called femaleness, and men primarily about some set of (supposedly) biological characteristics called maleness.

And by the way, I would object if Konner had said: "Whites are bad because they oppress blacks." I endorse an alternative statement: "Whites who oppress blacks are bad." The distinction is significant and applies equally to men's treatment of women.

I'm going to take a stab at the question posed in the heading to this post. Is it sexist to say that women are superior to men? Yes, in a way that hurts men and women. (http://www.npr.org/sections/13.7/2015/04/06/4000757/Is-it-sexist-to-say-that-women-are-superior-to-men. Used with permission from Barbara J. King)

Despite King's characterization of his claim, there's no indication here that Konner is a sexist, though he may well be a sextist. What's clear, however, is that there's no consensus among scientists as to whether there are properties that make one sex significantly different from the other. Even less is there a consensus as to whether, if there are such properties, they make one sex superior to the other. Some people believe there are significant differences in the character or mental makeup of males and females. Others think there aren't, and that what differences we find are largely socially determined.

There are, however, stereotypes of men and women. They are prominent in contemporary culture. Some of them figure prominently in discussions of this issue. Whatever the facts, it's what people believe that determines how they act and how they treat others. This makes it important to understand conventional thinking. These stereotypes are as follows:

Typical male/female stereotypes

Male	Female
Dominant	Submissive
Rational	Emotional
Aggressive	Passive
Rough	Gentle
Analytical	Intuitive

The burden is upon the sexist to show, first, that these (and/or other) "mental" properties characterize males and females respectively, and that they derive from permanent physical differences between the two. Having done that, the burden is to show, second, that certain of these properties are "good-making" in the sense that to possess them, or to possess them in a higher degree than another, makes one better than the other. This is a formidable task. This point is made in the following passage from psychologist Anthony Storr:

Innate Differences without Superiority?
And it is highly probable that the undoubted superiority of the male sex in intellectual and creative achievement is related to their greater endowment of aggression. It is true that women have often been

badly treated by men, deprived of opportunities of education, denigrated, or forced to be unnecessarily subservient. But, even when women have been given the opportunity to cultivate the arts and sciences, remarkably few have produced original work of outstanding quality, and there have been no women of genius comparable to Michelangelo, Beethoven or Goethe. The hypothesis that women, if only given the opportunity and encouragement, would equal or surpass the creative achievements of men is hardly defensible: and it is only those who exalt intellectual creativity above all else who are concerned to demonstrate that women can compete with men in this respect.

It is a sad reflection upon our civilization that we should even be concerned with such problem, for its existence demonstrates our alienation from our own instinctive roots. No doubt it is important that men should reach the stars, or paint the Sistine Chapel or compose nine symphonies. But it is equally vital that we should be cherished and fed, and that we should reproduce ourselves. Women have no need to compete with men; for what they alone can do is the more essential. Love, the bearing of children and the making of a home are creative activities without which we should perish; and only a civilization in which basic values have become distorted would make these sterile comparisons.[16]

Storr appeals to one of the stereotypes in our list (aggression) and uses that as an *explanation* of why men and women have some of the other stereotypical characteristics often ascribed to them: men being intellectual and creative, women being loving and nurturing. Many would question whether men are superior to women and women to men in the above ways. But the important questions are whether there are some such differences, and whether, if there are, their possession makes men (or women) superior.

As we noted in connection with the *fact/value* distinction (Chapter 1, Theory Box 1D, Section 1.7), you cannot go from a statement of fact (e.g., that there are certain innate differences between the sexes, whatever they are alleged to be) to the conclusion that one sex is better than the other without supporting argument. The burden is to show that if it should turn out that one sex is better than the other in certain respects, and vice versa, these values are weighted in such a way as nonetheless to make one sex superior overall to the other. This hasn't convincingly been done by sexists. As we've seen, there isn't even agreement that there are any innate mental differences between males and females, much less that there are differences that confer overall superiority upon one or the other.

2.6 Ought one sex to dominate the other?

Let us suppose, however, as we did with racism, that the sexist can establish that one sex is innately superior to the other. Would that show that the superior sex ought to dominate the inferior sex? It would not. We've already seen that just as one cannot go from *fact* to *value* or from *is* to *ought* without supporting argument, one can't go from *value* to *obligation* without supporting argument. Just because a particular individual is superior to others in some respect (such as ability to play the violin or shoot baskets) doesn't mean the person is superior overall to others. And even if we agreed that such a person is superior overall to others, it wouldn't follow that the person ought to dominate others. One would have to produce reasons for such a conclusion.

Among the likelier candidates for ways of trying to argue that one sex ought to dominate the other are appeals to nature, God, and utility. Since most of the reasoning of this sort has supported male domination of females, we'll use for illustration possible arguments to show that men should dominate women. As we did in connection with racism (see Chapter 1, Theory Box 1E, Section 1.8), we shall use Natural Law Ethics, Divine Will Theory and Utilitarianism for illustration:

A. Natural Law Ethics
   1. By nature males dominate females.
   2. One ought to act in accordance with nature (the principle of natural law ethics).
   3. Therefore, men ought to dominate women.
B. Divine Will Theory
   1. God ordains that men dominate women.
   2. One ought to do as God wills (the principle of divine will theory).
   3. Therefore, men ought to dominate women.
C. Utilitarianism
   1. The domination of women by men promotes the greatest general happiness.

2. One ought to promote the greatest general happiness (the principle of utility).
3. Therefore, men ought to dominate women.

Regarding argument A: The factual claim in A1 is false. It's not true that in all of nature, males dominate females. Wolves and hyenas have dominant females. And among the bonobos, a type of ape that is very similar to human beings, females are dominant.[17] Even if one narrows the claim to assert only that among humans, males dominate females, the claim is far from obviously true. To evaluate it fully, we would have to examine what is meant by dominance, then look at the anthropological evidence. If, for example, we were to take leadership roles in government and prowess in war-making as criteria of dominance, then it would generally be true that men have dominated women. But if we were to take influence in the rearing and education of children as a sign of dominance, then the picture wouldn't be so clear. Certainly in the early years of child-rearing women are the predominant influence. There would be definite areas in which women dominate that would have to be taken into account. Some allege that women's domination of men is potentially pervasive and in the course of evolution will become a fact. Consider the following passage from Valerie Solanas:

Female Supremacy

Eventually the natural course of events, of social evolution, will lead to total female control of the world ...

If all women simply left men, refused to have anything to do with any of them—ever, all men, the government, and the national economy would collapse completely. Even without leaving men, women who are aware of the extent of their superiority and power over men, could acquire complete control over everything within a few weeks, could effect a total submission of males to females. In a sane society the male would trot obediently after the female. The male is docile and easily led, easily subjected to the domination of any female who cares to dominate him. The male, in fact, wants desperately to be led by females, wants Mama in charge, wants to abandon himself to her care.[18]

Even if it could be shown that males or females are innately superior, it wouldn't follow from that value judgment alone that the superior sex ought to dominate the inferior sex—even if (contrary to the evidence) it could be shown that one sex has in fact dominated the other historically.

Regarding argument B: There are numerous examples of alleged religious bases for male dominance of females, of which the following are two from Christianity and Islam:

Key Quote 2C

The Bible
Let the woman learn in silence with all subjection. But I suffer not a woman to teach, nor to usurp authority over the man, but to be in silence. For Adam was first formed, then Eve. And Adam was not deceived, but the woman being deceived was in the transgression. (*New Testament*, 1 Tim. 2:11–15)

The Koran
Men have authority over women because God has made the one superior to the other, and because they spend their wealth to maintain them. Good women are obedient. (4:34)

If God endowed males with certain attributes which make them superior to women, then it should be possible to identify those attributes (say, among physical and mental properties, as discussed above) and show why they make men superior. But even if it were assumed that men are innately superior to women, it still wouldn't follow from that fact alone that men ought to dominate women. As we saw in the previous chapter (Section 1.7), from the value judgment that one being is better than another, whether innately or not, it doesn't follow without further argument that the superior ought to dominate the inferior. The passage from the Koran seems to presume that it does. If, on the other hand, God made men superior to women in the way in which you make someone captain of a ship or of team, then God confers authority upon men. In that case, the issue becomes a matter of religious faith, and is moved out of the realm of rational scrutiny and evaluation.

Regarding argument C: Some might maintain that a greater good is promoted if one sex dominates the other; things simply operate more smoothly, both socially and within the family. Such reasoning might proceed along the following lines. Consider ballroom dancing. If two people are waltzing, it's important that one of them lead and the other follow. Things break down immediately if both try to lead. The same, it might be said, is true within a family. A greater harmony is achieved if, say, the husband is dominant, the final authority. Most families would be chaotic if husband, wife, and children were equal in authority, children having an equal say in all decisions, from bedtime and meals to the city they live in. Typically, husband and wife presume to have control and guidance—to be dominant, if you like—over the children, at least at the young ages. But that leaves the question of the relations between husband and wife. If they're constantly at odds, bickering, arguing, each trying to have his or her way, then the situation may be less chaotic than if the children are involved, but it will be unharmonious. How much better if one person is the final authority, so that his or her judgments ultimately resolve issues, and other family members accept this? This wouldn't necessarily require that every family member agree with every decision of the father or husband. That would be unrealistic to expect. But they might accept that authority and act accordingly in the interests of family and marital harmony.

There is support for such a way of thinking, both psychological and theological. Plato, in his dialogue in the *Republic*, gave a psychological analysis of the makeup of the soul. It consists, he said, of reason, a spirited element (accounting for anger, sense of honor, ambition, and the like), and appetites (desires for food, drink, sex). He argued that harmony (hence the virtue of justice) was achievable within the individual soul only when reason was in charge and the other elements of the soul were performing their proper functions under reason's superintendence. Otherwise, it would be as though each of us had a person (reason), a lion (the spirited element), and a many-headed beast (the appetites) within us, with the person dominated by the lion or the beast.

St Augustine, in somewhat similar vein, reasoned that just as God is the supreme authority over all of his creation, so among humans it's part of the natural order God has conceived that there be a ruler over each society (or state or country)—typically a king. The king might not always be the wisest or the most just, but having authority centralized in him helps maintain order and minimize the bad effects of human sinfulness. The same is true within the family, in this view, with the husband or father in control.

So, it might be presumed (according to this argument), if one sex dominates the other overall—whether or not that sex is deemed to be innately superior—a greater harmony will be achievable within marriage, within the family, and within society at large. That is, there will be a utilitarian justification for one of the tenets of sexism.

Suppose a greater good was achievable by having males dominate females (or vice versa, as Valerie Solanas maintains). Would that be the end of the matter from a moral standpoint? It wouldn't, of course. Just as we saw in connection with racism (Section 1.9), there would be the question of rights. If there are such things as human rights—that is, rights that every person has simply by virtue of being human, and which aren't dependent upon standing in society or cultural or social circumstances—then women have those rights equally with men. Male domination of females (or female domination of males) would violate human rights *even if* it were true that it promoted a greater good. (Notice that the Seneca Falls Declaration of Sentiments [Section 2.2] emphasizes rights—*inalienable* rights—and the convention at which it was adopted was a *women's rights* convention.) *Rights* and *utility* may, it seems, come into conflict. When and if they do, we can't simply assume that utility holds sway.

But what if rights aren't universal? What if they're culturally relative? This would provide an opening for sexists to concede that women have equal rights, but still maintain that those rights can be overridden by other considerations. The last decade of the twentieth century saw attention focused upon this issue at the UN World Conference on Human Rights, as brought out in this news report:

United Nations World Conference on Human Rights

From United States delegates to the Dalai Lama, most everyone in Vienna for the United Nations World Conference on Human Rights is condemning suggestions by several Asian, Middle Eastern, and Northern African governments that human rights are culturally relative ...

Democracies in the developing world, the argument goes, must give more weight to the rights of the collective society than to individuals who may threaten its stability. "Human rights are vital and important," says Indonesian Foreign Minister Ali Alatas, "but so are efforts at accelerated national development." When the two conflict, he says, development must take priority.

Anticipating such challenges, UN Secretary-General Boutros Boutros-Ghali opened the two-week conference on June 14 by urging the nations to reaffirm what he called "the imperative of universality" of human rights ...

Sudan's Lt. Gen. Omar Hassan al-Bashir opposes universality with an argument based on religion. Since he took power in a coup four years ago, General Bashir has accrued a dismal human rights record, chiefly by waging a bitter war against non-Muslims in the south. Although Sudan had ratified many human rights agreements, including key provisions of the Universal Declaration of Human Rights, Bashir maintains that they are inconsistent with Islamic law ...

Countries such as China and Indonesia have objected to foreign intervention for decades, but by adopting the language of economic development [some allege] ... they hope to make their position more defensible. Nevertheless, a recent change in US policy may help to buttress the view that all human beings are born free and equal in rights and dignity.[19]

President Bill Clinton sounded a similar theme in a talk to students and faculty at Beijing University in China 5 years later:

Human Rights as Universal

We do not seek to impose our vision on others. But we are convinced that certain rights are universal, that, as one of the heroes of our independence, Thomas Jefferson, wrote in his last letter 172 years ago: "All eyes are opened, or opening, to the rights of man."

I believe that everywhere, people aspire to be treated with dignity, to give voice to their opinions, to choose their own leaders, to associate with whom they wish, to worship how, when and where they want. These are not American rights or European rights or developed world rights. They are the birthrights of people everywhere.[20]

Women have insisted that women's rights be recognized as human rights. But if rights are relative, then rights in one social and cultural setting might not be rights in another. But what exactly is ethical relativism?

Theory Box 2A

Ethical Relativism

To understand ethical relativism (or "relativism" for short), it will be helpful to distinguish three theses:

   A. Moral beliefs and practices vary from culture to culture.

B. Morality depends on (1) *human nature* (e.g., human reason, motivation, capacity for pleasure and pain); or (2) the *human condition* (the way human life is constrained by the natural order—such as that all humans are mortal); or (3) specific *social and cultural circumstances* (e.g., local traditions and customs); or all three of these.

C. What is morally right or wrong (as opposed to what is merely thought to be right or wrong) may vary fundamentally from person to person or culture to culture.

Thesis A simply affirms cultural diversity. It doesn't mean that every moral belief and practice varies from culture to culture, only that some do.

Thesis B asserts that morality is determined by, or conditional on, the nature of human beings and/or the world they live in.

Thesis C represents ethical relativism. It implies both Thesis A and Thesis B but goes beyond them. It's a thesis about what is *actually* right and wrong, not merely about what is *thought* to be right and wrong.

Only **skeptics** seriously question whether some acts are right and others wrong. And only **nihilists** deny such distinctions outright. Most people differ only about which acts are right and wrong.

Ethical relativists are neither skeptics nor nihilists. They believe in moral right and wrong. It's just that they contend that what is basically right for one person or culture may be wrong for another.

The qualification "basically" is important here. There are some differences in right and wrong that can be accepted by anyone, relativist or not. No one says, for example, that everyone of whatever size should eat exactly the same food and in the same amounts; or that everyone should wear the same clothing regardless of climate. That is, no one denies that some acts are right under some conditions, wrong under others. The question is (1) whether *all* actions depend exclusively on variable personal, social, cultural, or environmental conditions; and (2) whether that results in variations in what is basically right and wrong for different peoples and cultures. Relativism answers yes to both questions.

If sexists argue that all rights are relative, in the sense that people (in certain cultures) may have them and others (in different cultures) not, then they're denying the existence of *human* rights. For these, as we've seen, are rights one has simply by virtue of being human. They aren't conferred by anyone and aren't dependent on social or cultural circumstances. It isn't coherent to say both that there are human rights and that they're relative.

If, however, sexists concede that there are human rights but they can be superseded by other kinds of moral considerations, there's no incoherence in their position. But then they're not ethical relativists. They're simply maintaining that rights and utility may conflict, and that when they do, sometimes utility overrides rights. This in fact seems to be the position in the article above (regarding the UN World Conference on Human Rights) when it's said that human rights may conflict with economic development. What's implied is that economic development is a greater good and sometimes human rights have to take a backseat to the greater good. Applied to sexism, a similar argument might be that male dominance promotes a greater good, and that the human rights of women have to take a backseat. Theoretically, this is an intelligible position, but it requires that one provide some grounds for choosing utility over rights. That would seem to be prohibited by Article 30 of the UN Declaration on Human Rights (see Chapter 1, Section 1.9), which denies to any state, group, or person "any right to engage in any activity or to perform any act aimed at the destruction of any of the rights and freedoms set forth herein."

Even if it should be conceded that violating rights sometimes promotes a greater good, that wouldn't by itself justify such violations. We would still need to take account of the principle of *universalizability* discussed in the previous chapter (Theory Box 1F, Section 1.10). That principle, once again, asserts:

> U: Persons should be treated similarly unless there are morally relevant dissimilarities between them.

Applying this to the case of sexism (still using as an example sexism against women), even if the prejudicial treatment of women should promote a greater good (whether in terms of happiness or economic development or whatever), it violates U. For it's in the nature of sexism to treat people defined by sex differently *whether or not* there are morally relevant differences among them. If there are human rights, then all men and women possess them and possess them equally. If you respect the rights of some and violate the rights of others, you're treating people differently in the absence of morally relevant dissimilarities among them.

2.7 Conclusion

The principal beliefs associated with primary sexism are (1) that one sex is innately superior to the other, and (2) the innately superior sex ought to dominate the inferior sex. The first is a value judgment, the second an ought judgment that purports to be moral. We've seen that sexists don't support either judgment convincingly, hence that the views of the full-fledged sexist (what we defined as sexist$_3$) haven't been justified. In the absence of such justification, the presumption against sexism stands, and sexism should be considered wrong.

Study questions

1. What does the text propose as the *three central questions* to be asked with regard to sexism?
2. What are *primary sexism* and *secondary sexism* (Section 2.2)?
3. What are the definitions of *sexist$_1$*, *sexist$_2$* and *sexist$_3$* (Section 2.3)? How do they differ from the proposed definition of a *sextist*?
4. What disanalogies are there between *racism* and *sexism* (Section 2.4)?
5. How do *sex* and *gender* differ (Key Quotes 2A and 2B)?
6. The main focus of sexism is upon *discrimination against girls/women*. What grounds do some recent writers cite for saying that there is also *discrimination against boys/men* (Section 2.4)?
7. What are the *stereotypical differences* between males and females (Section 2.5)?
8. Part of the *burden of proof* of the *sexist$_3$* is to show that one sex is innately superior to the other (Section 2.5)? What difficulties does the text cite in trying to do that?
9. What are *human rights*? How do they differ from *legal rights*? What role do human rights play in the understanding of sexism?
10. What is *ethical relativism* (Section 2.6)? Can there be human rights if ethical relativism is true?

Notes

1 Mary Wollstonecraft, *A Vindication of the Rights of Woman* (New York: The Modern Library, 2001), p. 181.

2 Ellen Carol DuBois (ed.), *The Elizabeth Cady Stanton-Susan B. Anthony Reader* (Boston: Northeastern University Press, 1992), p. 123.

3 Gloria Steinem, Op Ed, *The New York Times*, March 2, 2017.

4 Claire Cain Miller, "Sexes Differ on Persistence of Sexism," *The New York Times*, January 19, 2017.

5 "Riding the Second Wave," by Aileen C. Hernandez, *Research Report*, Vol. 22, No. 2, Spring/Summer 2001, 16–17. Published by the Wellesley Centers for Women, Wellesley, MA.

6 From Barry Bearak, "Women Are Defaced by Acid and Bengali Society Is Torn," *The New York Times*, June 24, 2000.

7 Jenny Wilson, *Time*, April 16, 2011.

8 From Barbara Crossette, "Amid the Pain and Isolation, Finally, a Friend," *The New York Times*, October 16, 2000.

9 Ann Dummett, "Racism and Sexism: A False Analogy," in James Rachels (ed.), *Moral Problems*, 3rd edition (New York: Harper & Row, 1979), p. 45.

10 Simone de Beauvoir, *The Second Sex* (New York: Vintage Books, 1989), p. 598.

11 Christina Hoff Sommers, *The War against Boys: How Misguided Feminism Is Harming Our Young Men* (New York: Simon & Schuster, 2000), pp. 23–6.

12 David Benatar, *The Second Sexism: Discrimination against Men and Boys* (Oxford: Wiley-Blackwell, 2012), pp. 1, 2, 27.

13 Gina Kolata, "Testing for Athletes: Who Is Female? Science Can't Say," *The New York Times*, February 16, 1992.

14 Robin Marantz Henig, "Rethinking Gender," *National Geographic*, January 2017.

15 Anna Quindlen, *The New York Times*, September 10, 1986.

16 Anthony Storr, *Human Aggression* (London: Allen Lane, The Penguin Press, 1968), pp. 68–9.

17 Natalie Angier, "Bonobo Society: Amicable, Amorous and Run by Females," *The New York Times*, April 22, 1997.

18 Valerie Solanas, "SCUM (Society for Cutting Up Men) Manifesto," in Barbara A. Crow (ed.), *Radical Feminism: A Documentary Reader* (New York: New York University Press, 2000), p. 217.

19 *Christian Science Monitor*, June 18, 1993.

20 *The New York Times*, June 20, 1998.

For more resources:

www.bloomsbury.com/holmes-introduction-to-applied-ethics

3

Hispanic/Latino Immigration and Rights

[I]t is in the best interest of Hispanics to retain our ethnic/ cultural identifications and insist on some form of political representation based on group classifications.

—Ofelia Schutte[1]

Introduction

We shall in this chapter consider the history of Hispanics in the United States, examine the question of whether they constitute a race or an ethnic group, and in so doing look at the importance of "naming"—the choice of labels for groups. We'll then examine anti-Hispanic discrimination as it relates to social justice.

3.1 Hispanics in America

Hispanics are the largest minority in America. Numbering 37 million, they now surpass blacks, at 36.2 million. The reasons for the increase are many, but they include increased immigration due to deteriorating economic conditions in areas of Latin America and high birth rates. In any event, important questions are being asked:

Key Quote 3A

Will the current tide of poor, low-skilled Hispanic labor migrants (legal or not) gradually blend into the American mainstream like their

European predecessors? Or will they remain a growing but segregated population, marginalized by race, class, language, and culture? Has this country's capacity to absorb the most vulnerable foreigners diminished during the past 50 years, or are we simply witnessing the pains of transition to a new stage of American diversity?[2]

Blacks were forcibly brought to America. Most Hispanics chose to come. But some found themselves in the country as a result of historical events. Texas and California (along with other southwestern states) were once part of Mexico. When Mexico won independence from Spain in 1821, it initially encouraged Americans to settle in its sparsely populated province of Texas. But when the settlers demanded independence and the right to hold slaves, Mexico tried to stem further immigration. Conflict broke out. Texans eventually prevailed, establishing the Lone Star Republic which the United States annexed in 1845. War between Mexico and the United States broke out in 1846, at the conclusion of which Mexico ceded California and other territory (much of what is now Arizona, New Mexico, Nevada, and Utah) as well to the United States.

Those Mexicans who weren't driven out of Texas, California, and other territories during the violence found themselves incorporated into the United States. Much the same was true of Puerto Ricans following the 1898 war with Spain when the United States acquired Puerto Rico. Many other Hispanics fled to the United States from Cuba following the overthrow of the Batista regime by Fidel Castro in 1959.

Thus, although most Hispanics came to the United States voluntarily, often for economic reasons, many found themselves in this country as a result of shifting national boundaries brought about by war and violence. Still others sought refuge here from what they saw as tyranny.

Whether they came for economic, political, or other reasons, Hispanics brought with them a culture different from the one they encountered here. Some think this destines them for a distinctive role in American society; others think it makes them a threat to American culture. Immigration—mainly from Latin America—was a major issue in the 2016 presidential campaign, and President Donald Trump in 2017 ordered the deportation of undocumented immigrants and the building of a wall between the United States and Mexico. In any event, many Hispanics find themselves disadvantaged in American society, which brings the issue of their rights to the fore.

Let us begin by considering an Hispanic perspective on this legacy and its importance:

The Making of a New People

The year 1492 marked not just the so-called discovery of the New World, but also the culmination of the expulsion of the Muslims from the Iberian peninsula [Portugal and Spain], as well as the ultimatum to the Jews to either leave the peninsula or convert. The discovery and conquest of the New World was deeply influenced by the drive to establish both religious homogeneity and territorial unity in the Iberian peninsula. The worldview of the Spaniards was constituted by a confrontation with the infidel, or Muslim, and the traitor, or Jew ... When the Spaniards discovered the new World, they faced a choice: to see these new people as either infidels or betrayers. But the radical otherness of the Amerindians, the original impressions that they were primitive, even innocent, creatures, made it difficult to assimilate them to the established schemas ... Amerindians were not ... enslaved, corralled into auction blocks, or vilified because they were seen as threatening and contaminating.

So much for the discovery and the first encounters. But what about the conquest and the period of colonization? ... Cortes and Pizarro never would have accomplished their feats of conquest had it not been for the aid of dissenting tribes of Amerindians who in fact were carrying out a civil war by aiding the Spaniards ... Furthermore, once the Spaniards imposed themselves as rulers, they did so by essentially taking over the Aztec and Inca hierarchies. A modus vivendi was established between the old hierarchies and the new rulers. In Peru, Pizarro and his brothers were essentially allowed to rule because it was thought they would be temporary dictators. The Spaniards, in short, were so successful in their conquest because they knew how to work with the already existing structures of social and political control. In fact, Spanish and Aztec as well as Inca cultures lived side by side ... Today Mexico and central South America remain areas with large indigenous populations, and this betrays the fiction that the Amerindians were everywhere exterminated ...

For Latin Americans, race has been more a question of skin pigmentation, nose shape, and height than of human dignity and thus exclusion from socio-economic and political power. Indeed, the central category in Latin America is class, not race ... While there is racism, this has more to do with access to extremely scarce social resources than with question of the purity and hybridization of peoples who have been in a continuous process of *mestizaje* ...

Anglo-Saxons, on the other hand, who arrived in the New World in the seventeenth century, almost 150 years later than the Iberians, came with very different goals and a very different worldview. Germán Arciniegas has described the differences between Hispanic America and Anglo America in terms of four stages of encounter with the New World: discovery, conquest, colony, independence. Whereas Hispanic America began with discovery, proceeded with the conquest and then the colony, and finally gained independence in the eighteenth and nineteenth centuries, Anglo America began with independence, proceeded to establish its colonies, then conquered the continent, and began only in the nineteenth and twentieth centuries to discover it ...

The fact is that most of the Anglo-Saxons who established the first colonies on the northern part of the North American continent came after a rupture had already taken place with their world. They came to establish a new Jerusalem, but one that was certainly different from that of the Old World. To this extent, their relationship to Amerindians was determined by belligerence and conflict, animosity and resentment. The fact that the Anglo-Saxons did not encounter great Amerindian civilizations, as Cortes and Pizarro did, also determined the ways in which the Anglo-Saxon colonizer would look upon the Amerindian. Another fundamental difference between Anglo American and Hispanic America is that by the seventeenth century a highly elaborate and detailed European discourse on face had already developed to legitimize the enslavement of Africans, the ghettoization of Jews, and the creation of imaginary nations based on racial purity and homogeneity ... As the colonies grew, the economy expanded, and the Anglo-Saxon Americans populated the northeastern coast of the North American continent, a struggle against Indians, Spaniards, and Frenchmen began. In this struggle the ideological construct of the racial inferiority of both Indians and blacks became pivotal. There was no space for accommodation or mutual tolerance. Indians were unworthy of the continent they occupied and blacks were beasts of labor that had to obey their white masters ...

In the eighteenth and nineteenth centuries, race continued to gain a hold on the imaginary and sociopolitical culture of the new nation that became known as the United States of America. Racist ideologies were deployed against the Native American peoples of its Midwestern and western prairies, the Mexican and Spanish peoples of the Southwest, and the Chinese who began migrating to San Francisco in the eighteenth century.

Race, in short, has been part of an ideology of conquest, subjugation, and subalternization, of destruction and decimation … In Anglo America, race crystallized in objective institutions, legal regulations, political dispensations, and cultural prescriptions, thereby becoming a social fact that refused to acknowledge its fictional character. Race was read as a biological fact, and as such, it became nature: ineluctable, irreversible, uncircumventable. Race became fate …

To conclude, the historical detour I provided above should allow us to appreciate the ways in which Hispanics are mystified and disoriented by the American urge to racialize everyone and everything. When we are sent looking for a Hispanic, we do not know what we are looking for. This is certainly a problem for both Hispanics and Americans. It is a problem for Hispanics because it makes it hard for us to posit our claims for justice—claims for redistribution, as Nancy Fraser calls them—on the basis of recognition claims. This is not to say that we do not need to, or cannot, make recognition claims. We certainly can and must. But these claims are and will be of a different sort than those we are accustomed to because of the polarized racial imaginary of American political culture. That one does not know—and really cannot know—what a Hispanic looks like from his or her purported visible identity is also a problem for Americans in general because here they are faced with a people who must be acknowledged, recognized, and granted certain rights. These rights, however, cannot be granted on appeals and claims that have anything to do with the United States' history of slavery and its endemic sexist Puritanism. Let me conclude by suggesting that, just as Latin Americans dismantled race through five hundred years of *mestizaje* and miscegenation, they are poised to contributed to the remaking and reconfiguration of America by dismantling its racial edifice, which has been as much auction block as confessional and penitential church.[3]

Three claims are especially important from this passage:

1. Hispanics are not a race but an ethnic group.
2. The concept of race in Latin America differs from that in the United States.
3. The Iberian (Spanish and Portuguese) encounter with the New World was shaped by a different worldview from that of Anglo-Saxons

in North America. Through Hispanics this worldview is entering American culture, giving them an important role to play in the evolution of American society.

Let us explore the first of these claims further.

3.2 Are Hispanics a race or an ethnic group?

If race isn't a meaningful concept (a possibility discussed in Chapter 1), then of course Hispanics aren't a race. But even if the concept of race is meaningful, there are problems in thinking of Hispanics as a race. Consider the following passage by Linda Alcoff:

> ### Race and Ethnicity
> The question of Latina/o identity's relationship to the conventional categories of race that have been historically dominant in the United States is a particularly vexing one. To put it straightforwardly, we simply don't fit. Racialized identities in the United States have long connoted homogeneity, easily visible identifying features, and biological heredity, but none of these characteristics apply to Latinas/os in the United States, nor even to any one national subset, such as Cuban Americans or Puerto Ricans. We are not homogeneous by "race," we are often not identifiable by visible features or even by names, and such issues as disease heredity that are often cited as the biologically relevant sign of race are inapplicable to such a heterogeneous group.[4]

Alcoff's point is that when we seek to understand the term "Latinas/os" (to use Alcoff's label) it is difficult to understand it by means of racial categories. The persons referred to as Latinas/os are diverse. Some are white, some black, some brown. Not only that, they speak different languages (such as Spanish, Portuguese, French, English) and have different religions. They also come from significantly different cultures (e.g, those from Brazil are rooted in Portuguese culture, those from Haiti in French culture, those from most Latin American countries in Spanish culture). They are heterogeneous, "racially" and otherwise.

So, even if race is a meaningful concept, it would be difficult to determine to what race Hispanics belong. It might be that they are so racially diverse that racial categories are unhelpful in trying to understand them as a group.

Another possibility, however, is that the concept of race has a different meaning in the Hispanic experience (as Mendieta suggests in the earlier passage) from what it has traditionally had. Still another possibility is that it can be given a different meaning from what it traditionally has had.

Note that here we are talking about the *meaning* of race. And we can distinguish between de facto meaning and prescribed meaning.

Theory Box 3A

De Facto and Prescriptive Meaning

De facto meaning: the literal or common-sense meaning of a term— what ordinary speakers of a language have in mind when they use it. Meaning in this sense is more or less fixed. It changes only gradually, if at all. If you observe a language closely, you can report what de facto meaning a term has and encapsulate it in a definition, as compilers of dictionaries do.

Prescriptive meaning: the meaning you think a term *should* have, even if that differs from its de facto meaning. You might propose a meaning for a term if it has no clear de facto meaning (which sometimes happens) and you want to give it one, or if you think, for social, political, or moral reasons, its meaning ought to be changed.

The idea of meaning can be represented in the following way:

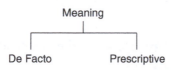

In these terms, claim (2) above might be represented as saying that *the de facto meaning of race* (or of the English word "race" and its equivalent in the various languages spoken in Latin America) in Latin America and the United States has differed. In the United States, its meaning has largely been determined by the European racial ideology that sees races as groups of persons distinguished by biologically determined essential properties (see

Chapter 1, Theory Box 1C, Section 1.6, on essential properties). In Latin America, it has been understood more broadly in terms of variable characteristics such as skin color but also in terms of characteristics definitive of class (largely economic and social status).

With regard to proposed meanings, some believe it's sometimes good to deliberately try to alter the meanings of certain terms. By so doing, they believe, important social causes, such as combating racism or sexism, can be promoted. (We sought to do this by recommending a meaning for the term "racist" in Chapter 1, Definition Box 1F, Section 1.3.) Another passage from Alcoff makes this clear with regard to the concept of race:

> Although racial ideology and practices of racialization seem to always carry within them some commitment to biological essentialism, perhaps the *meaning* of race is transformable. If race is going to be with us for some time to come, it might still be the case that race itself will alter in meaning, even before the perceptual practices of racialization can be done away with. It seems to me that this change in meaning is exactly what Paul Gilroy is attempting to chart ... in *The Black Atlantic*, as well as what some other African-American theorists are doing, such as Gooding-Williams, bell hooks, Lewis Gordon, and Patricia Williams. You will notice in their works an intentional use of the term *black* [a supposedly racial term] rather than *African-American* [a supposedly ethnic term]; ... But in their works, blackness has been decidedly de-essentialized and given a meaning that consists of historical experience, collective memory, and forms of cultural expression ... Only a semantic essentialist could argue that race can mean nothing but biological essentialism; in reality, this is not the way meaning works ... Perhaps we can help lift the meaning of race out of its status as an insult by uniting with the efforts of those ... who seek to give it a cultural meaning.[5]

Although we don't have space to assess their truth, it's important to distinguish the following claims:

1. Race has different de facto meanings in Latin American and the United States.
2. Within American society, race can be given a prescribed meaning, for example, in terms of historical experience, collective memory, and so on.
3. While Hispanics cannot plausibly be thought to constitute a race in biologically essentialist terms, they might nonetheless be thought to

constitute a race if race is given a different meaning from what it has in American society.

If ethnicity is understood in terms of cultural, linguistic, and religious commonalities, then to give race a cultural meaning would seem to be simply to fuse it with the concept of ethnicity. Indeed, the term *ethnorace* has been proposed for this purpose.[6] Although there's no consensus as to precisely how ethnorace should be understood, we'll define it as follows:

Definition Box 3A

Ethnorace
Ethnorace: A term for a group of people who have a common identity but can't accurately be characterized as either a race (however understood) or an ethnicity, though they share some of the characteristics often associated with each.

Although the analysis of these issues may be expected to continue for years to come, for our purposes we'll consider Hispanics an ethnorace rather than exclusively a race or an ethnic group, being mindful that there is no consensus on this topic.

3.3 Naming

We have been using the term "Hispanic." Alcoff uses the term "Latina/o." Mendieta in the earlier passage alternates between "Hispanic" and "Latino." Which is the appropriate term to use?

We need terms designating groups for ease of communication. Thus we speak of New Yorkers, Californians, British, Americans, Chinese, Protestants, and Catholics for easy reference to persons whose identities we are largely agreed upon. The same when we speak of Republicans or Democrats, Liberals or Tories, soldiers and sailors, citizens and noncitizens.

But when we come to terms for so-called racial, ethnic, and gender categories the problems become more complex. Not only is there the question of how to understand the relevant terms, there is also the question of which terms to use in the first place. Why is this important? Recalling the distinction between descriptive and emotive meaning (Theory Box 1A in

Chapter 1, Section 1.3), consider the following words for persons of various "racial" or ethnic identities:

Predominantly descriptive	Predominantly emotive
Italian	wop
Irish	mick
Mexican	spic
Jew	kike
Italian or Greek	dago
African American, black, negro	nigger
white, caucasian, anglo	honky, gringo
Vietnamese	geek, slope*

* Sometimes used by US soldiers during the Vietnam War.

The terms in the first column have predominantly what we earlier (Section 1.3) called descriptive meaning. They tend to express beliefs and to produce similar beliefs in the hearer. They are relatively neutral, in that they don't reflect moral judgments about the persons denoted. Those in the second column, however, although they share the descriptive meaning of their counterparts in the first column, have predominantly emotive meaning. They're pejorative terms and are typically insulting, disrespectful, and disparaging. They're used to express negative feelings or attitudes and to evoke the same in others.

The term "African American" has a core descriptive meaning: an American of African descent. The term "nigger" has the same descriptive meaning but also a strong emotive meaning—expressing contempt and disrespect, which predominates in most contexts. With regard to gender and issues of sexual orientation we find the same with words such as these:

Predominantly descriptive	Predominantly emotive
woman	broad, chick, babe, bimbo
homosexual	fag, queer

There are other more vulgar terms. They're not only offensive and disrespectful but are typically used precisely for that reason. Even a relatively uncontroversial term like "woman" is controversial to some, as it contains the word "man," and some feminists prefer "womyn" or "wimmin."

So we have the substantive moral, political, social, and legal questions surrounding issues like racism, sexism, sexual harassment, and affirmative action. But discussion requires language. We must use words. And words have origins, meanings, and associations. We cannot readily divest words of these characteristics, though their meanings and associations can often be altered over time. Because our words affect our attempts to communicate, which words to use in discussing issues like racism and sexism *itself* becomes an issue. This may be called a *meta-linguistic* question. Thus, it's important to distinguish:

> Primary Issues: Racism, Sexism, Sexual Harassment, Affirmative Action, etc.
> Meta-linguistic Issues: Those dealing with the proper terms with which to discuss primary issues.[7]

Meta-linguistic issues evolve from the primary issues and can be almost as controversial as the primary issues. For our present purposes, two specific meta-linguistic questions are especially important:

1. Which key terms should we use in discussing primary issues (racism, sexism, Hispanic/Latino issues, etc.)?
2. How should their meanings be defined or explicated?

A third question needs to be added. Its importance will become clear as we proceed:

3. Who should decide the answers to questions (1) and (2)?

3.4 What words to use and who should decide?

Let us begin with question (1). One concern has to do with the origin of the words in question. This is particularly true of words that refer to groups of persons.

Thus, for example, many Native Americans object to being called "Indians," a label originally applied to them by white Europeans.

Columbus, you recall, sailed in search of India. He thought he had found it when he reached North America. Accordingly, he mistakenly called the inhabitants of the new land "Indians"—a term that has persisted through the centuries. Even more specifically, the native Americans of the Six Nation Confederacy, the Haudenosaunee, are often called "Iroquois." But that term was used by the French, not by the Haudenosaunee themselves. Another term, "Negro," was first used by the Spanish and Portuguese in the sixteenth century to characterize the peoples of West Africa.[8] It wasn't a term those peoples used to describe themselves. Nor was it a term that African Americans chose to describe themselves. It was chosen by white people. Many African Americans prefer the term "black" or "African American" for self-reference.

Even with regard to a word like "sexism" there is controversy, as the following passage reveals:

Constructing Definitions

As Meaghan Morris ... notes, a dictionary may also render women invisible; the Australian *Macquarie dictionary* obliterates women's linguistic and political achievements through the way it constructs definitions and thus achieves what Morris calls "code control": *sexism* is defined as "the upholding or propagation of sexist attitudes," a *sexist attitude* one which "stereotypes a person according to gender or sexual preference, etc," and *feminism* as an "advocacy of equal rights and opportunities for women." As Morris points out, *sexism* was originally used by *women* attempting to construct a theory of patriarchy; the notion of stereotyping a "person" by virtue of holding certain "attitudes" obscures and almost makes nonsense of its original political meaning; by defining *feminism* in terms of its lowest common denominator, both current and historical distinctions among different feminist positions are eliminated.[9]

The point is that not only is it important to understand the issues bound up in racism, sexism, and the like. It's also important to understand the issues surrounding the choice of words used to discuss the issues, for those words can come with biases attached to them. We cannot easily detach them from those biases, if only because we're sometimes unaware of them. For this reason, one option is to look for words which don't have those biases, or don't have them to the same degree.

How does this apply to the issues involving Hispanics? Here we find that there are many terms one could use: *Hispanic, Latino, Latina, Latina/o, Hispanic-Latino, Latin-American, person of Latin American descent*, and so on. What is the most appropriate term by which to name the people to whom these terms apply?

There are two issues here. First, it's important to find terms that aren't laden with negative emotive meaning; otherwise, we risk perpetuating bias in the very language we use. Second, even if we restrict ourselves to terms that are as free of bias as possible (as, e.g., are the terms in the preceding paragraph), there is still the question of how those terms are to be understood. That, as we shall see, is a more complex issue than one might think.

First, let us begin with a *description* of the people. Here is one by an Hispanic philosopher Jorge J. E. Gracia:

Describing Hispanic/Latinos as a Group

Hispanics are the group of people comprised by the inhabitants of the Iberian peninsula after 1492 and what were to become the colonies of those countries after the encounter between Iberia and America took place, and by descendants of these people who live in other countries (e.g. the United States) but preserve some link to those people. It excludes the population of other countries in the world and the inhabitants of Iberia and Latin America before 1492 because, beginning in the year of the encounter, the Iberian countries and their colonies in America developed a web of historical connections which continues to this day and which separates these people from others.[10]

Gracia uses the term "Hispanic" to name the people described in the statement. Some people have reservations about that label. Consider the following by Suzanne Oboler:

Racializing Ethnic Identities?

In 1977 the U.S. Office of Management and Budget's Directive 15 created five racial/ethnic categories: white, Asian or Pacific Islander, black, American Indian or Alaskan native, and Hispanic. These ethnic labels are best described as "masterpieces of ambiguity." ... For the 1990 census, for example, "Hispanics" were defined in the following terms:

A person is of Spanish/Hispanic origin if the person's origin (ancestry) is Mexican, Mexican-Am., Chicano, Puerto Rican, Dominican, Ecuadoran, Guatemalan, Honduran, Nicaraguan, Peruvian, Salvadoran; from other Spanish-speaking countries of the Caribbean or Central or South America; or from Spain.

The effects of differentiating and, in effect, racializing the entire U.S. population through these ethnic categories have been contradictory. Undoubtedly it has allowed us to track the progress toward political inclusion of racial minorities, as well as of women, since the end of legal segregation. But it has simultaneously reinforced the belief in the superiority of whiteness and "white privilege," making explicit the continuing existence of a socioracial hierarchy in a society that historically, and to this day, proclaims its adherence to the belief in equality for all ...

In short, the official creation of these ethnic categories has ensured that, as in Latin America, everyone "knows his (or her) place" in U.S. society. And as in Latin America, the outcome is the impossibility of establishing an expanded community of equals in the United States ... [I]n the United States, the term *Hispanic*—as originally conceived by the state in the 1970s and currently understood—is first and foremost a bureaucratic invention, used for census data collection ...

The term *Hispanic*, like other ethnic labels, is here to stay. And from this point of view, the Hispanic (or Latino) experience and identity in the United States cannot be understood outside of the context of the relations that colonized citizens (such as the Puerto Ricans) and conquered peoples (such as sectors of the Chicano population) have historically had with the U.S. government. This context conflated race and nationality and, in 1977, allowed for the official designation of the ethnic label Hispanic which homogenized all people of Latin American descent ... [T]he label "Hispanic" marks all Latinos as culturally and socially inferior, as having "bad values" that are perceived to be related to their "foreign"—un-American—origins.[11]

Recall question (3) in the previous section: Who should answer questions (1) and (2) (regarding which terms should be used in discussing primary issues and how should they be defined)? With regard to the choice of terms, members of groups that have been discriminated against feel that, as a matter of principle, it's they who should decide by what "name" they shall be known. They consider naming a form of empowerment. This sometimes carries over to names of places as well. Thus, India chose to rename many of its major cities to dissociate itself from the residues of British rule. Bombay, for example, is now Mumbai, Madras is Chennai, Calcutta is Kolkata. Following the collapse of the Soviet Union, Russia renamed Leningrad as St. Petersburg and Stalingrad as Volgograd.

Even Hispanics disagree over what the preferred term should be. In the absence of a consensus on the issue among the persons denoted by the various terms ("Hispanics," "Latinos," "Latina/Latinos," etc.) we shall, for the sake of simplicity, continue to use the term "Hispanic." But be mindful that this is a disputed issue.

3.5 Can "Hispanic" be defined?

We now need to ask how the term "Hispanic" should be understood. What does it *mean* to call someone an Hispanic? How do we determine that meaning?

Much of traditional philosophy sought to understand the meanings of terms through definitions. This was characteristic of Socrates and Plato, who believed that to make headway in an inquiry, whether in ethics or politics or theory of knowledge, one first needed to be clear about the meanings of the terms one was using. And this meaning could best be established through definitions. Many of the so-called Socratic dialogues (written by Plato but in which Socrates is often the central character) involved a quest for meaning.

As represented in these dialogues, Socrates appeals to criteria for a correct definition. Consider the following passage, in which he seeks a definition of "piety" from a friend, Euthyphro, who is bent upon having his father prosecuted for murder and is convinced that what he's doing is the pious thing:

Socrates on Defining Piety
What I asked you, my friend, was, What is piety? And you have not explained it to me to my satisfaction ... Remember, then, I did not ask you to tell me one or two of all the many pious actions that there are; I want to know what is characteristic of piety which makes all pious actions pious ... My question, Euthyphro, was, What is piety? But it turns out that you have not explained to me the essential character of piety.[12]

Let's try to understand more precisely what sort of definition Socrates is seeking here. To do this it will be helpful to make use of some logical and philosophical distinctions.

Theory Box 3B

Denotation and Connotation

Language contains many group terms: dogs, cats, trees, humans, teams, games, and so on. With regard to these we may distinguish the following:

> **Denotation**: the particular things to which a term refers.
> The denotation of *dog* would include Spot, Lassie, Fido, Cerberus, etc.
> **Connotation**: the properties common to all the things to which a term refers.
> Thus dogs have in common such properties as that they have four legs (barring mishap), tails, and bark (possibly excepting basenjis).

We also need to recall again the distinctions made in Chapter 1 (Theory Box 1C, Section 1.6) between essential and accidental properties:

Essential Properties: Invariable properties that make up the intrinsic nature of what possesses them (i.e, that make a thing what it is). Thus being 3-sided would be an essential property of triangles.

Accidental Properties: All variable properties a thing possesses. Thus, being a college student is an accidental property of yours; you possess it now but will cease to possess it when you graduate.

Making use of these distinctions, we can formulate more precisely the kind of definition Socrates was seeking.

Theory Box 3C

Socratic Definition

A **Socratic definition** specifies:

- Properties common to all the things the term being defined denotes, that is, the term's connotation

- Properties unique to all the things the term denotes, that is, properties that distinguish them from other things
- Properties essential to the thing being defined; that is, properties that make it what it is

Socrates makes clear that he doesn't simply want a list of the things being defined. If you wanted to know the meaning of "president," it wouldn't suffice to have someone mention Washington, Lincoln, Jefferson, and so on. You would want to know, among other things, what it is they have in common (such as that they were all elected according to the constitutional processes of the United States). You would also want to know what distinguishes them from other elected officials (such as that they were required to be over the age of thirty-five when elected) and from other people generally (such as that they received at least 270 electoral votes in a general election). Assuming that you had specified *all* of their common and unique properties, you'd be able to identify any president of the United States. That is, you would have a *criterion* that would enable you to determine whether any person, living or dead, was (or had been) a president of the United States.

Would that be enough? Socrates would say no. Simply being able to identify instances of a thing being defined doesn't suffice to explain *what* that thing is. Let us take an example.

Suppose you don't know the meaning of the word "phenomenologist." Suppose someone proposes to define it for you. Suppose further (contrary to fact) that all phenomenologists and only phenomenologists wear red hats. The property of wearing a red hat would then be common to all phenomenologists and unique to phenomenologists. Citing that property would then meet the first two conditions of a Socratic definition. It would provide a criterion by which you could identify phenomenologists. If you walked around the streets (or, more promisingly, looked in universities or cafes), you could invariably pick out phenomenologists. But would this mean that you understood what a phenomenologist was? Not at all. You'd be able to identify them, but you wouldn't know what it was about them that made them phenomenologists. You wouldn't know what was essential to them.

Put more technically, Socrates is implicitly distinguishing between a *criterion* and *essential properties*. An essential property, as we have seen, is a property (or more often, a set of properties) that is invariably possessed by a thing and makes it what it is. A criterion, on the other hand, is a property or set of properties that enables you reliably to identify instances of a thing (whether or not you know what makes it what it is). Thus, in the preceding example, wearing a red hat would be a criterion of phenomenologists. It would enable you to identify them (again, on the assumption that all, and only, phenomenologists wear red hats). But it would be only an accidental property, not an essential property (phenomenologists would still be phenomenologists if they stopped wearing red hats).

Thus, Socrates requires that in addition to stating the common and unique properties of what is being defined, a good definition must state the essential properties as well.

The question, then, is whether the term "Hispanic" can be given a Socratic definition. There are reasons for doubting that it can. Hispanics, as we have seen, are a heterogeneous group. There are differences among them in size, shape, skin color, hair color, eye color, and other physical characteristics. There are also differences among them in language, religion, politics, culture, and ancestry. It's difficult, for that reason, to single out any properties that would be both necessary and sufficient to invariably identify persons as Hispanic. If one cannot do that, then the first two conditions of a Socratic definition cannot be met. And if the first two conditions aren't met, then the third, which is dependent upon them, also cannot be met. If that's the case, then we cannot define "Hispanic" in terms of essential properties. Hence we cannot give it a Socratic definition.

What are the implications of this? Let us represent them as follows:

1. There are no common and unique properties to all persons denoted by the term "Hispanic" (i.e, there is no logical connotation to the term).
2. A Socratic (or conventional) definition of a term is possible only if there are common and unique properties to all of the things denoted by the term.
3. Therefore: A Socratic (or conventional) definition of "Hispanic" isn't possible.
4. Therefore: Either there's no meaning to the term "Hispanic" or its meaning must be explainable other than by such a definition.

Suppose that the above reasoning is correct. Must we say that the term "Hispanic" has no meaning? Or can its meaning be explained other than through a definition?

The twentieth-century Austrian British philosopher Ludwig Wittgenstein (1889–1951) broke with the Socratic tradition of seeking precise definitions of terms. He maintained that some group words don't have common (and unique) properties. Hence there's no precise criterion by which to identify them and no essential nature of theirs to be revealed. The term "game" is an example. It doesn't appear that there are any common, unique, and essential properties shared by such disparate games as hop-scotch, chess, and football. Yet we understand the meaning of the term "game." If we want to explain that meaning, we need to examine the ways in which a term is *used.* John Dewey (1859–1952), a leader of American pragmatism, independently argued much the same thing. If we study how common words are used, we'll come to understand their meaning without worrying about giving them definitions.

Contemporary philosopher, Jorge J. E. Gracia (himself an Hispanic, as we've noted) applies this approach to understanding the term "Hispanic."

Understanding "Hispanic" Historically

The view that the effective use of names requires a property, or a set of properties, that can be identified has been effectively challenged in contemporary philosophy. This does not mean that there are no names whose use is justified by an essence. It means only that not all names are of the same sort and, therefore their use need not be justified in this way ... We can grant, then, that there are no common properties to all those people whom we wish to call Hispanics, and yet that does not mean that the use of the term is unjustified or meaningless. In general, my point is that there is a way to understand the concept of Hispanic that allows us to speak meaningfully of, and refer effectively to, Hispanics, even when the people named by it do not share any property in common at all times and places. More particularly, my thesis is that the concept of Hispanic should be understood historically, that is, as a concept that involves historical relations ... This group of people must be understood as forming a unit which goes beyond political, territorial, linguistic, cultural, racial, or genetic frontiers ... What ties them together, and separates them from others, is history and the particular events of that history rather than the consciousness of that history; a unique web of changing historical relations supplies their unity.

Obviously, historical relations tend to generate common properties, but such properties might not go beyond certain periods, regions, or subgroups of people. There can be unity without community. A may follow B, and B may follow C, and C may follow D, implying a connection between A and D even when A has nothing in common with D ...

> This is the kind of unity that I submit justifies the notion of Hispanic. We are speaking here of a group of people who have no common elements considered as a whole. Their unity is not a unity of commonality; it is a historical unity founded on relations. King John II of Portugal has nothing in common with me, but both of us are tied by a series of events that related us and separate us from Queen Elizabeth II and Martin Luther King. There is no need to find properties common to all Hispanics in order to classify them as Hispanics. What ties us is the same kind of thing that ties the members of a family, as Wittgenstein would say. There may not be any common properties to all of us, but nonetheless we belong to the same group because we are historically related, as a father is to a daughter, an aunt to a nephew, and grandparents to grandchildren.[13]

This provides an alternative to trying to define "Hispanic." It also provides an alternative to saying that the term has no meaning. According to this account, the term has a meaning but one that must be understood by reference to the historical context of the many peoples to whom the term refers. This, we may say, best represents the way in which the term is *used*.

Such an approach to meaning is challenging, though. It suggests that the meaning of a term like "Hispanic" cannot be conveyed in capsule form (like a definition). It requires some understanding of the history, culture, and social condition of the people to whom the term refers—along the lines, for example, in the earlier passage from Mendieta (Section 3.1).

It should be noted, however, that some Hispanics are impatient with the preoccupation with naming, even by other Hispanics. Consider the following statement by columnist Esther J. Cepeda:

> Hispanics are nothing less than all-American constructs. Ironically, though, it's a classification that's mostly meaningful to non-Hispanics in the United States ... White, Asian and black non-Hispanics call us Latino, Hispanic, the teeth-grinding "Latin," and sometimes even the cringe-inducing "Spanish." And if they're from California, they might whip out "Chicano" as well.
>
> Generally there's been a years-long (and incredibly tiresome) back-and-forth among people with Latin American heritage about whether they should be identified as "Latino" or "Hispanic." As of last

count—the Pew Research Center's Hispanic Trends Project reported on this phenomenon in 2012—a few of these people (21 percent, including me) were a minority-within-a-minority who identified as "American." [14]

What emerges from all of this is that to discuss the social issues of the day we must use language, and which language we use is—rightly or wrongly—itself an issue. We can ignore the issue, and use whatever words we want, in which case we risk offending and alienating many people; or we can use language that enables us, as nearly as possible, to discuss objectively the substantive issues without bias. One of those issue concerns anti-Hispanic bias and outright discrimination.

3.6 Immigration and anti-Hispanic bias

Bias is often harder to document than discrimination. Discrimination usually involves actual conduct: treating people prejudicially by comparison with treatment of members of other groups. Bias is reflected in attitudes, often in subtle ways. But a people's collective mind-set can become biased when they're encouraged to think disrespectfully of members of a particular group. There is evidence that this is happening in the United States as people come to think of Hispanics as "immigrants." In so doing, they identify them according to where they or their ancestors came from. Worse yet, they identify them as threats to our society and culture, which is predominantly white, Anglo-Protestant. The following passages highlight the issues. The first is from noted academic, Samuel P. Huntington, the second from now President Donald J. Trump, and the third another passage from Hispanic columnist Esther J. Cepeda:

In this new era, the single most immediate and most serious challenge to America's traditional [Anglo-Protestant] identity comes from the immense and continuing immigration from Latin America, especially from Mexico, and the fertility rates of these immigrants compared to black and white American natives. Americans like to boast of their past success in assimilating millions of immigrants into their society, culture, and politics. But Americans have tended to generalize about immigrants without distinguishing among them and have focused on the economic costs and benefits of immigration, ignoring its social and cultural consequences. As a result, they have overlooked the unique characteristics and problems posed by contemporary Hispanic immigration ... This reality poses a fundamental question: Will the United States remain a country with a single national language and a core Anglo-Protestant culture? By ignoring this question, Americans acquiesce to their eventual transformation into two peoples with two cultures (Anglo and Hispanic) and two languages (English and Spanish).[15]

* * *

When Mexico sends its people ... [t]hey're sending people that have lots of problems, and they're bringing those problems. They're bringing drugs. They're bringing crime. They're rapists ... It's coming from more than Mexico. It's coming from all over South and Latin America.[16]

* * *

As immigration from Latin America slows and Hispanics continue to marry and reproduce with people from other ethnicities and races—and generally stop being made to feel as though their ancestry is their defining characteristic—the big to-do about Hispanic Heritage Month will go the way of German-American Heritage Month ...

Among Pew's 2012 finding about Hispanic/Latino labeling was that most Latinos (69 percent vs. 29 percent) said that the more than 50 million Latinos in the U.S. have many different cultures rather than a common culture.

This is not exactly a recipe for uniting around a particular ethnic label—and that is as it should be. The promise of the melting pot is that from many we become one. And what are we living through if not a moment in the nation's history when cross-category understanding and unity will be a key ingredient to successfully moving forward?

Latinos aren't just a bundle of statistics. They are your doctors, lawyers, journalists, accountants, sports heroes, Silicon Valley entrepreneurs, rocket scientists and politicians.[17]

The issue of immigration in general is a larger one than we can go into in depth here. But we can identify from the above certain key issues that are important to understanding the problem. To begin with, there are factual issues. First, is it true that Hispanic immigration is increasing or is it, as Cepeda says, in fact decreasing from Latin America? Second, is there a trend toward two cultures (Hispanic and Anglo) as Huntington maintains, or a trend toward a richer and more complex single culture, as Cepeda maintains. In other words, is the metaphor of a melting pot still appropriate, or has it been rendered obsolete by a partitioning of America into two cultures? Third, is it true—as many have denied—that criminals, drug users, and rapists are being sent to America from Mexico, as Trump maintains? With the possible exception of the second, which may be in part a matter of judgment, these questions should admit of clear answers. They are questions of fact and susceptible of empirical confirmation or disconfirmation.

But apart from these factual questions, there are some normative—and ultimately moral—questions as well. First, would it be better for the American people if the country had essentially one culture grounded in the white, Anglo-Protestant values of its founders; or would it be better if it evolved into a blend of many cultural elements, religious, musical, artistic, culinary? Should the fact that certain values characterized the founders of the country dictate that those values be preserved indefinitely. Some of those values were worthy, such as a belief in democracy. But some of them weren't, such as the belief that women weren't deserving of the right to vote or blacks to be free.

As we've seen in discussing racism and sexism, one cannot derive a value from a fact without supporting argument (see Chapter 1, Theory Box 1D in Section 1.7). And even if one could argue from the fact

1. The founding fathers were overwhelmingly white, British, and Protestant.

to the judgment

2. Those represent the highest values.

one could not go from either (1) or (2) to the ought judgment

3. America ought to perpetuate and foster those values as part of its identity.

without further argument. To maintain that one can infer (3) directly from (1) would be to go from is to ought, as we have seen earlier. To maintain that one can go directly from (2) (or (1) and (2)) to (3) would be to go from value to ought, which as we have also seen would require further argument. Even if (2) were conceded, the perpetuation even of the highest values through a whole society might require the suppression of other emerging conceptions of the highest values. Violating the rights of those who hold those other values, which might turn out to be morally indefensible. Both inferences would be susceptible to the charge of committing the naturalistic fallacy.

In any event, framing these issues as "native" in the way Huntington does creates the impression that the early settlers were the first people to set foot on the North American continent. In so doing it ignores the history and diverse cultures of the native Americans who inhabited the continent long before 1492. Even if one were to concede that the values Huntington cites are the highest values (which is debatable), one would have to factor into the assessment of the costs of the implementation and fostering of those values throughout the whole of the present United States, and the costs of near-genocide against native Americans and the enslavement of millions of Africans. These were components of the creation of the culture Huntington extols.

However one resolves the question of bias and immigration, there are millions of Hispanics in the United States legally, and there are substantive issues of discrimination that they and the society at large face. Let us turn to some of the more serious of these.

3.7 Anti-Hispanic discrimination

The preceding linguistic considerations might seem to be of only theoretical interest. But the question of how to understand Hispanic identity is important to understanding the social and ethical problems Hispanics face.

If, for example, you believe that Hispanics are and have been discriminated against in American society, it's important that you be able to identity the particular individuals you are referring to. Similarly, if you believe that remedial measures for such discrimination (such as reparations or affirmative action) are warranted, then it's equally important that you be able to identify the persons who are entitled to such measures.

Few dispute that Hispanics are disadvantaged in American society. They're underrepresented in the political arena, have a higher poverty rate than whites, and are often handicapped by language. Being disadvantaged, per se, isn't tantamount to being discriminated against, of course. If one person devotes his or her life to writing poetry and another to making money, the fact that the former ends up disadvantaged financially by comparison with the latter doesn't mean that he's been discriminated against. But many believe that Hispanics are not only disadvantaged but also discriminated against as well; and that where they are not *currently* discriminated against, they suffer as a result of past discrimination. Younger Hispanics in particular feel they have been discriminated against, as this report documents:

> Half of all Hispanics, 52 percent, say they've experienced discrimination or were treated unfairly at some point in their life because of race or ethnicity. But such experiences are more often to be cited by Hispanics 18 to 29 years old, Pew [Research Center] found. In fact, 65 percent of Latinos in that age group told Pew they had experienced racism or discrimination. In contrast, just 35 percent of Hispanics 50 or older said the same. Hispanics are very similar to blacks in their attitudes on race relations. About six-in-10 Hispanics, 58 percent, say they are generally bad in the U.S. About 61 percent of blacks have that same belief and 45 percent of whites.[18]

One might also ask whether the discrimination Hispanics experience is as bad as that experienced by African Americans and women. Differing views on this issue are set forth in the following passages by Hispanic philosophers Jorge J. E. Gracia and J. Angelo Corlett. The first passage is from Gracia:

> ### Hispanics and Affirmative Action: Pro and Con
> In contrast with African Americans and women, the argument [for affirmative action] based on reparation does not seem to work for Hispanics for three reasons: (1) not all, or even most, Hispanics have suffered discrimination, (2) the degree of discrimination and abuse some have suffered never reached the levels suffered by African Americans or women, and (3) it is difficult to prove that the reason some Hispanics have suffered discrimination and abuse in the United States is because they are Hispanics. Hispanics have not been subjected to the kind of abuse to which African Americans and women have been subjected. Hispanics have never been slaves; we were not brought into this country against our will to work for others and be subservient to their whims; we were not deprived of our culture, language, religion, freedom, basic human rights, education, or dignity; and, unlike women, we have not, as a whole, played a secondary role in American society. Under these circumstances, reparation does not

seem justified. There is nothing, or not much, that must be given back to Hispanics as a group because it was taken away from us. And there is no harm done to us as a group that cries out for repair.[19]

* * *

Disagreeing with this assessment, J. Angelo Corlett reasons as follows:

Nonetheless, the history of Latinos in the United States is transparent on the matter of anti-Latino discrimination, whether it concerns the discriminatory practices against us in the U.S. military, the social relations that led to the zoot suit riots in East Los Angeles, current and long-standing negative attitudes of Anglos toward us, or any of numerous other examples. Whether in the form of ethnocentrically based anti-Latino cultural imperialism, institutional racism, or noninstitutional racism, evidence that we are discriminated against because we have been and are Latinos is plain. Anti-Latino racism is in principle no more difficult to demonstrate than it is to show that certain other ethnic groups have been discriminated against because of what they are, ethnically speaking. And this fact holds despite the unforgivable levels and kinds of harms committed against Native Americans and African Americans by the U.S. government and many of its citizens, making racism against these groups even more easily identifiable than anti-Latino racism. Thus not only have a majority of Latinos been discriminated against, they have been discriminated against *because* they are Latinos. Throughout the history of the United States, anti-Latino attitudes have often given rise to anti-Latino discrimination based on such attitudes . . .

It is obvious that African Americans have suffered significantly more than Latinos. But is it true that anti-Latino discrimination has never reached the levels of discrimination against women?

Gracia intimates that Latinos . . . have not been treated as poorly as women . . . in the United States. In reply to this position, it might be argued that although women (and men) of color have been treated rather poorly in the United States, even by Anglas [non-Hispanic white women] such as Susan B. Anthony and Louisa May Alcott, it is dubious to claim or imply that Anglas were, on average and as a group, treated more poorly than Latinos. Whatever role Anglas have played in U.S. society, Latinos have played an even *more* secondary role. In fact, Anglas in the United States were, and remain, among our more ardent oppressors, for many such women (as a class) were, and remain, members of a ruling class of Anglos that serves as an incessant source of racism. It seems naïve to think that such racism among Anglos would not extend in significant measure to us Latinos … it is true that many women are raped and abused by men. But then again, so are many Latinas. It is true that many women do not receive a fair wage for their labor, but this is even truer of Latinos (especially Latinas) as a group. It is true that in general women are disrespected in U.S. society, though in some ways they are placed on pedestals when it comes to standards of physical beauty. But the dominant society has never thought that brown is beautiful, unless, of course, the brown person in question has various Angla physical features that make her "acceptable" to Anglo eyes. Although Anglas suffer from psychological issues regarding their physical selves, this is typically based on the shape of their bodies. But Latinas suffer even more, for they suffer not only from being judged according to the shape of their bodies, but also from perceptions of themselves and others regarding the *color* of their bodies. This is a kind and degree of discrimination that Anglas have not experienced in U.S. society. In fact, this latter kind of suffering is experienced by Latino males as well. It goes without saying that perception of skin color is one way in which we cognizers tend to categorize one another, sometimes for racist purposes. Anglas hardly suffered from racism to the extent that we Latinos did. To suggest otherwise would do violence to a reading of U.S. history.[20]

These passages suggest that there are differences, even among Hispanics, on the questions: (1) whether most Hispanics have suffered discrimination in America, and (2) whether such discrimination as they have suffered has been as bad as that of women (and more specifically, of "Anglas," or non-Hispanic white women).

3.8 Hispanics and the problem of language

There appears to be a consensus that Hispanics haven't suffered nearly as much in America as African Americans. But Hispanics face a problem most African Americans don't. That problem is language. Many of them are native speakers of Spanish (or are from families in which Spanish is the first language). As such, they're disadvantaged in a society whose predominant language is English. The following report documents the problem:

Redefining Latino

Language and nativity are two of the starkest lines of demarcation, with Spanish the dominant language among many foreign-born Latinos, and English generally the choice of those born or reared in the United States by Hispanic parents. This dichotomy within the country's rapidly expanding Latino population presents a quandary for advertisers, political candidates and anyone else whose business it is to pitch products or policies to the Latino community: Which group are you pitching to, and what, besides language, are the differences between them? ...

In a major survey last year, the Pew Hispanic Center, a research organization in Washington, D.C., and the Kaiser Family Foundation found that, on questions of attitude and social issues, native and immigrant Latinos differed sharply, reflecting the prevalent sensibilities of either the United States or Latin America. On issues like divorce, abortion and homosexuality, for example, foreign-born respondents were much more conservative than native-born or American-reared Latinos, whose views were more in synch with those of non-Hispanic whites and blacks, the survey showed.

"A second-generation English-speaking Dominican in New York will have more in common with a second-generation English-speaking Mexican in Los Angeles than with a recently arrived Spanish-speaking Dominican in New York," the Pew Center's director, Roberto Suro, said ...

Yet, all Latinos share certain views that set them apart from African Americans and non-Hispanic whites. Most of them are willing to pay higher taxes for more government services, for example, compared to only 35 percent of non-Hispanic whites and 43 percent of African Americans, the Pew survey found.

But a cultural divide sometimes is found even within the same Latino household.

Take that of Vianni Gomez, an 18-year old Dominican who lives in Harlem with her parents, two younger brothers and grandmother. Although she moved here barely four years ago, she and her 15-year-old brother already speak mostly English to each other, even though her parents understand little English and their grandmother none at all.

The siblings also shun Spanish-language television for shows like "American Idol" and neighborhood clothing stores with names like "El Mundo" for Macy's.[21]

This gives rise to the question of whether recent immigrants should aspire to fluency in English (easy for the very young, but difficult for mature adults), or whether society should accommodate them by providing Spanish-language signs and directions and facilitating the establishment of Spanish-speaking radio and TV stations.

On one side, some argue that if people choose to come to this country, they should adopt its language and culture. The responsibility for change is theirs, not that of the host country. On the other side, it's argued that society has an obligation to provide equal opportunity for all peoples residing here. Providing bilingual instruction, or the means by which to acquire competence in English, is a necessary condition of doing that.

The quandary for many Hispanics themselves is that, not only are they alienated from the rest of American culture—and thereby disadvantaged—they are also, as the above article reports, divided from many of their fellow Hispanics as well. If they want to nurture and preserve Hispanic culture (or the various Hispanic cultures) within the broader American culture, they must cope with this division, not only within families, but within the Hispanic population as a whole.

3.9 Hispanics, school segregation, and distributive justice

Some have noted that there may be growing competition between Hispanics and blacks for financial resources and political representation. That is only one problem facing Hispanics. Another concerns school desegregation.

School segregation was legitimized by the Supreme Court ruling *Plessy v. Ferguson* in 1896. The rationale was that segregation was permissible so long as equality prevailed. "Separate but equal" was the goal. Decades of segregation revealed, however, that the system led to more separation than equality. In 1954, in *Brown v. Board of Education*, the Supreme Court ended legal segregation. A major effort to desegregate schools later began, principally through busing. Where do things stand today? The following report on a Harvard study answers that:

> According to a new study by the Civil Rights Project at Harvard University, black and Latino students are now more isolated from their white counterparts than they were three decades ago, before many of the overhauls from the civil rights movement had even begun to take hold.
>
> Nationally, the shift is a result of several factors: big increases in enrollment by black, Latino and Asian students; continuing white flight from the nation's urban centers; and the persistence of housing patterns that isolate racial and ethnic groups. But another big factor, the Harvard study found, has been the termination of dozens of court-ordered desegregation plans.
>
> Spurred by Supreme Court decisions at the start of the 1990's, lower courts have lifted desegregation orders in at least three dozen school districts in the last 10 years ... A chief principle in the voiding of these orders is one established by the Supreme Court a decade ago: that school districts can be considered successfully desegregated even if student racial imbalances due entirely to demographic factors, like where children live, continue to exist.
>
> Largely as a result, black students now typically go to schools where fewer than 31 percent of their classmates are white ... That is less contact than in 1970, a year before the Supreme Court authorized the busing that became a primary way of integrating schools.
>
> Latino students, who have rarely been a focus of desegregation efforts, now attend schools where whites account for only 29 percent of all students, compared with 45 percent three decades ago.[22]

Such segregation today differs from that prior to 1954. Current school segregation may be a by-product of overt discrimination, but it's not the direct result of such discrimination. So what is wrong with such segregation?

Some think there's nothing wrong with it. They say it's simply the outcome of choices people make about where to live. Those choices, to be sure, are influenced by income, employment, and social status. But that's how it's always been in society. Others worry that these seemingly free choices are, in fact, constrained; that people who are less affluent, or living in outright poverty, don't have the same options that others do. They say by allowing such segregation to continue, society perpetuates the creation of an underclass in America. Not only is that unfair to the persons affected, it's also bad for society as a whole. The ideal of a democratic society, they say, should be a community of equals. Keeping millions confined to a life of disadvantage prevents the attainment of that goal.

There are two issues here. One concerns the consequences of increasing school segregation for American society. Those who see this as the primary issue are probably tacitly accepting some form of Utilitarianism (see Chapter 1, Section 1.8). On this view, it is the value of the consequences of a practice or policy that determines whether it is right (or permissible); and in this case, it is the value of the consequences for American society as a whole, not just for the persons directly affected. The second issue concerns distributive justice.

Theory Box 3D

Distributive Justice

Distributive justice deals with fairness in the comparative treatment of persons or groups. It becomes an issue when there are benefits or burdens to be distributed and fewer benefits to go around than people would like or more burdens than people want to share. Benefits include material things like money or opportunities like jobs or education. Burdens can include taxes, jury service, and military service. A standard way of formulating a principle of distributive justice is:

From each (in sacrifices) according to_____;

To each (in benefits) according to_____.

This generates different conceptions of distributive justice depending upon how the blanks are filled in. A classic Marxist formulation we shall discuss in Chapter 8 says: From each according to ability; to each according to need.

The issue in the case of Hispanics (and African Americans as well) is whether largely segregated schools are unfair, hence unjust. Those who believe that segregated schools are not unjust maintain that if demographics, economic conditions, and free choice lead to such segregation, then so be it; no one has forced it upon blacks and Hispanics. If white children are forced to attend schools not of their choosing simply to advance the cause of desegregation, then it's they who are being discriminated against. Those who believe that segregated schools are unjust, consider quality education a benefit that should be distributed equally among all children in society; the opportunity for quality education should be extended equally to all. On this view, society should take further steps to ensure that schools become desegregated. The busing of children has been a major means to that end, but a highly controversial one at that.

It's possible that there is a tension between justice and utilitarianism on this issue. Some, for example, might concede that it's unfair (hence unjust) to white children to be bused to distant schools for the sake of racial and ethnic balance but believe, on utilitarian grounds, that it's for the good of society that it be done; that children will grow up more tolerant and aware of cultural differences if they associate with a diverse group of students in school than they would otherwise. Those who reason this way weigh the utilitarian, consequentialist consideration more heavily than that of justice. Those who oppose school desegregation might concede that it would promote a social good to have enforced school integration, but that such a good is outweighed by the unfairness (hence injustice) to white children who are deprived of the freedom to schools of their choice.

3.10 Conclusion

However much discrimination Hispanics have suffered, and apart from whether it's been as much as women and African Americans, they are and have been severely disadvantaged. And if a racially, ethnically, or sexually identifiable group is disadvantaged, it's relevant to ask what, if anything, should be done about it. For many, the answer to this question depends upon the cause of the disadvantage. If it's the result of discrimination, many feel that society should undertake remedial measures to offset the effects of that discrimination. If it owes to other factors, such as free choices, many think that it should not. In all three of the cases we have discussed this far—racism, sexism, and Hispanic issues—there is one especially difficult question: it's that of affirmative action. Given that African Americans, women, and Hispanics have been disadvantaged (whether or not to the same degree and whether or not exclusively through discrimination), the question that needs to be asked is: Should society implement affirmative action programs on their behalf? We'll take up this controversial question in the next chapter.

Study questions

1. What historical events shaped relations between the *United States and Mexico*? What bearing have those events had on the *immigration* of Hispanics to the United States?
2. Why is it difficult to settle whether Hispanics, as a group, constitute a *race* or an *ethnicity*? How does using the term *ethnorace* (Definition Box 3A) try to resolve the problem? Pg.95
3. What is the distinction between *de facto and prescriptive meanings* (Theory Box 3A)?
4. Why is so-called *Naming* an important issue for many peoples? What role does the distinction between *emotive* and *descriptive meaning* play in deciding how racial, ethnic, or cultural groups of people should be named?
5. What are the options in trying to determine who should decide what racial, ethnic, or cultural groups should be called (Section 3.4)?
6. What is a *Socratic Definition* (Theory Box 3C)? What alternative does Gracia propose to trying to define *Hispanic* (Section 3.5)?
7. What are some of the areas in which there is alleged *anti-Hispanic bias or discrimination* (Sections 3.6 and 3.7)?
8. Most Hispanic immigrants aren't *native speakers of English*. What problems does this create for their assimilation into American society?
9. What role does *distributive justice* (Theory Box 3D) play in understanding allegations of anti-Hispanic bias and discrimination?
10. Do you see parallels among *racism, sexism,* and *anti-Hispanic bias*?

Notes

1 "Negotiating Latina Identities," in Jorge J. E. Gracia and Pablo De Greiff (eds), *Hispanics/Latinos in the United States: Ethnicity, Race, and Rights* (New York: Routledge, 2000), p. 65.
2 Ashley Pettus, "End of the Melting Pot? The New Wave of Immigrants Presents New Challenges," *Harvard Magazine*, May/June 2007, p. 46.
3 Eduardo Mendieta, "The Making of New Peoples: Hispanizing Race," in Gracia and De Greiff (eds), *Hispanics/Latinos in the United States*, pp. 51–6.

4   Linda Martin Alcoff, "Is Latina/o Identity a Racial Identity?," in Gracia and De Greiff (eds), *Hispanics/Latinos in the United States*, p. 24.

5   Ibid., pp. 41f.; emphases in the original.

6   David Theo Goldberg, as cited in ibid., p. 42.

7   Obviously it is not all of the terms in language that raise issues. In English, for example, there is no controversy over the use of words like "the," "and," and the like. The controversy surrounds the use of key terms referring to groups of persons.

8   Ivan Hannaford, *Race: The History of an Idea in the West* (Washington, DC: The Woodrow Wilson Center Press, 1996), p. 210.

9   "Words on a Feminist Dictionary," by Cheris Kramarae and Paula Treichler, in Deborah Cameron (ed.), *The Feminist Critique of Language* (London: Routledge, 1990), p. 149.

10 Jorge J. E. Gracia, *Hispanic/Latino Identity: A Philosophical Perspective* (Oxford: Blackwell Publishers, Ltd., 2000), pp. 48f.

11 Suzanne Oboler, "It Must Be Fake!," in Gracia and De Greiff (eds), *Hispanics/Latinos in the United States*, pp. 132–4.

12 Plato, *Euthyphro*, Stephanus 6, 11.

13 Gracia, *Hispanic/Latino Identity*, pp. 48–50.

14 Esther J. Cepeda, "Put an End to Hispanic Heritage Month," Rochester *Democrat and Chronicle*, October 5, 2016.

15 Samuel P. Huntington, "The Hispanic Challenge," *Foreign Policy*, March–April 2004, p. 32. From Samuel P. Huntington, *Who Are We?* (New York: Simon & Schuster, Inc.

16 Donald J. Trump: 2015 announcement speeches of 2016 presidential hopefuls, June 16, 2015.

17 Columnist Esther J. Cepeda, Rochester *Democrat and Chronicle*, October 5, 2016. The final paragraph is from *Democrat and Chronicle*, June 22, 2016.

18 Suzanne Gamboa, "Majority of Young Latinos Say They've Experienced Discrimination: Report," http://www.NBCnews.com/news/latino/majority-young-latinos-say-they-ve-experienced-discrimination-report-n602556 (July 1, 2016).

19 Jorge J. E. Gracia, quoted in J. Angelo Corlett, "Latino Identity and Affirmative Action," in Gracia and De Greiff (eds), *Hispanics/Latinos in the United States*, p. 209.

20 Ibid., pp. 230–2.

21 Mireya Navarro, "Redefining 'Latino,' This Time in English: Language Divides Hispanic Culture in U.S," *The New York Times*, June 8, 2003.

22 *The New York Times*, January 21, 2003.

For more resources:

www.bloomsbury.com/holmes-introduction-to-applied-ethics

4

Affirmative Action, Diversity, and Reparations

Affirmative action programs remain controversial ... partly because the familiar arguments for and against them start from significantly different moral perspectives.[1]

Introduction

We've seen in the first three chapters some of the forms prejudice and discrimination can take. We've largely deferred the question of what may justifiably be done about it. When an action or practice is wrong, people obviously should stop doing it. But often that isn't enough. If you've been stealing money from your employer, you should stop. But you should also repay what you've stolen. With discrimination on the basis of race, sex, or ethnicity the effects can persist even if the practices stop, an issue we'll explore further in Section 4.6. In addition to discontinuing those practices, which society is attempting to do with varying degrees of success, there's the question of whether more should be done. In particular, should measures be taken to offset the effects of past discrimination? Here is where the issue of affirmative action arises. In this chapter we'll explore what affirmative action is, what its justification is alleged to be, and how it differs from diversity and reparations—other approaches to trying either to compensate for past injustice or promote a social good.

4.1 What is affirmative action?

Although there are strong feelings for and against affirmative action, there is no consensus as to precisely what it is. Various definitions have been proposed, of which the following are representative:

1 [A] policy of preferring qualified women and minority candidates who have been disadvantaged by past injustices over equally or more qualified white male candidates who have not been similarly disadvantaged.[2]

2. [P]ositive action by employers to ensure that minority groups are not discriminated against during recruitment or employment.[3]

3. [P]referential treatment toward women and minority applicants as practiced by employers, university admissions officers and government contractors…[4]

4. [T]he government policy to overcome the effects of past societal discrimination by allocating jobs and resources to members of specific groups, such as minorities and women.[5]

Notice the differences among these accounts. Number (1) makes reference to unspecified past injustices. The others don't. (1) and (3) speak of preferring or giving preferential treatment to certain persons. (2) and (4) don't. (2) and (4) make express reference to discrimination, (4) specifically to past discrimination. The others don't. These differences reflect changes in the thinking about affirmative action. To understand these changes, let us consider briefly the history of affirmative action. Then we'll return to the question of how to define it.

4.2 The evolution of affirmative action

Systematic racial discrimination was practiced in America after the freeing of the slaves in 1865. The following account details the discrimination in policies regarding housing.

The practices of the Federal Housing Authority exemplified governmental racism. For decades after its inception in 1934, the FHA, which insured mortgage loans, enshrined racial segregation as public policy. The agency set itself up as the protector of all-white neighborhoods, especially in the suburbs. According to urban planner Charles Abrams, the FHA's racial policies could "well have been culled from the Nuremberg Laws." Today white suburban youths continue to benefit from the past racist practices of this governmental agency. Not only will they inherit homes purchased with the FHA assistance, denied to blacks; they also enjoy racially privileged access to the expanding employment opportunities in all-white suburbs. In 1973, legal scholar Boris I. Bittker summed up governmental misconduct against blacks: "More than any other form of official misconduct, racial discrimination against blacks was systematic, unrelenting, authorized at the highest governmental levels, and practiced by large segments of the population." The role of government in practicing, protecting, and providing sanction for racism by private parties suffices to demonstrate the moral legitimacy of legally required compensation to blacks.[6]

Governmental agencies were part of the problem. Nonetheless, affirmative action grew out of a governmental response to racial discrimination. The term "affirmative action" was first used in 1961 by President John F. Kennedy in Executive Order 10925. The Order directed contractors receiving federal funds to "take affirmative action to ensure that applicants are employed ... without regard to race, creed, color, or national origin."[7] The aim was to end discrimination.[8]

The term was used again in the Civil Rights Act of 1964 prohibiting discrimination in employment on the basis of race, sex, religion, ethnicity, and so on. Title VII of the Act says in part:

Key Quote 4A

If the court finds that the respondent has intentionally engaged in or is intentionally engaging in an unlawful employment practice ... the court may ... order such affirmative action as may be appropriate, which may include, but is not limited to, reinstatement or hiring of employees, with or without back pay ... or any other equitable relief as the court deems appropriate.

Beyond merely prohibiting discrimination, the act allows courts to mandate "equitable relief" to remedy discrimination when an employer has practiced it. In so doing, affirmative action was extended to include remedial measures. Amendments in 1972—referred to as Title IX—extended the provisions of the act to education as well as employment.

A further dimension was added in a 1965 commencement address by President Lyndon B. Johnson at Howard University, in which he said:

Key Quote 4B

You do not take a person who for years has been hobbled by chains and liberate him, bring him up to the starting line of a race and then say, "You're free to compete with all the others," and still justly believe that you have been completely fair ... We seek not ... just equality as a right and a theory but equality as a fact and equality as a result.[9]

Although the term "affirmative action" isn't used here, the implication is that steps should be taken to offset the effects of past discrimination. Precisely what those steps should be wasn't clear. But the basic idea was that equal opportunity needed to be realized in fact, not just in principle.

Subsequently, in Executive Order 11246, Johnson stated that in addition to ending discrimination and providing equal opportunity, it was the policy of the Federal Government "to promote the full realization of equal employment opportunity through a positive, continuing program in each department and agency." The notion of a "positive, continuing program" implies going beyond just ending discrimination and providing remedies in particular instances.

While the Civil Rights Act prohibits discrimination and authorizes court-mandated measures to deal with it, affirmative action came to extend to voluntary measures as well.

Some voluntary measures were relatively uncontroversial. Few objected to colleges or businesses advertising to attract minority or female students or actively recruiting minorities in high schools. Such measures don't involve preferential treatment in hiring or admissions.

The problems have centered about cases that did seem to involve preferential treatment. Consider this landmark case. The University of California Medical School at Davis implemented a quota system, described here in part in the Supreme Court Case *University of California v. Bakke* (1978):

The Medical School of the University of California at Davis opened in 1968 with an entering class of 50 students. In 1971, the size of the entering class was increased to 100 students, a level at which it remains. No admissions program for disadvantaged or minority students existed when the school opened, and the first class contained three Asians but no blacks, no Mexican-Americans, and no American Indians. Over the next two years, the faculty devised a special admissions program to increase the representation of "disadvantaged" students in each medical school class. The special program consisted of a separate admissions system operating in coordination with the regular admissions process ...

The special admissions program operated with a separate committee, a majority of whom were members of minority groups. On the 1973 application form, candidates were asked to indicate whether they wished to be considered as "economically and/or educationally disadvantaged" applicants; on the 1974 form the question was whether they wished to be considered as members of a "minority group," which the medical school apparently viewed as "Blacks," "Chicanos," "Asians," and "American Indians." If these questions were answered affirmatively, the application was forwarded to the special admissions committee. No formal definition of "disadvantage" was ever produced, but the chairman of the special committee screened each application to see whether it reflected economic or educational deprivation. Having passed this initial hurdle, the applications then were rated by the special committee in a fashion similar to that used by the general admissions committee, except that special candidates did not have to meet the 2.5 grade point average cut-off applied to regular applicants ... The special committee then presented its top choices to the general admissions committee. The latter did not rate or compare the special candidates against the general applicants, but could reject recommended special candidates for failure to meet course requirements or other specific deficiencies. The special committee continued to recommend special applicants until a number prescribed by faculty vote were admitted. While the overall class size was still 50, the prescribed number was eight; in 1973 and 1974, when the class size had doubled to 100, the prescribed number of special admissions also doubled, to 16.

From the year of the increase in class size—1971—through 1974, the special program resulted in the admission of 21 black students, 30

> Mexican-Americans, and 12 Asians, for a total of 63 minority students. Over the same period, the regular admissions program produced one black, six Mexican-Americans, and 37 Asians, for a total of 44 minority students. Although disadvantaged whites applied to the special program in large numbers, none received an offer of admission through that process. Indeed, in 1974, at least, the special committee explicitly considered only "disadvantaged" special applicants who were members of one of the designated minority groups.

A white male, Allan Bakke, applied to the Davis Medical School in 1973 and 1974. Both times he was turned down, even though minority applicants with significantly lower scores than his were admitted under the special admissions program. Bakke challenged the University of California in the courts. The case eventually reached the Supreme Court, which issued a landmark 5-4 ruling in favor of Bakke. Written by Justice Lewis Powell, it read in part:

> In summary, it is evident that the Davis special admission program involves the use of an explicit racial classification never before countenanced by this Court. It tells applicants who are not Negro, Asian, or "Chicano" that they are totally excluded from a specific percentage of the seats in an entering class. No matter how strong their qualifications, quantitative and extracurricular, including their own potential for contribution to educational diversity, they are never afforded the chance to compete with applicants from the preferred groups for the special admission seats. At the same time, the preferred applicants have the opportunity to compete for every seat in the class.
>
> The fatal flaw in petitioner's [Davis Medical School's] preferential program is its disregard of individual rights as guaranteed by the Fourteenth Amendment. (Regents of the *University of California v. Bakke*. 438 U.S. 265 (1978))

The Bakke case closed the door to quotas but left open considering "race" and ethnicity as one factor among others. Thus many colleges and universities proceeded to make "race" and ethnicity factors in their admissions decisions—but not *decisive* factors of the sort ruled out by Bakke.

But in 1996 case, *Hopwood v. Texas*, a white female named Cheryl Hopwood (and others) alleged that the University of Texas Law School's affirmative action policies on behalf of African Americans and Mexican Americans discriminated against whites. A Federal Court agreed. It ruled against the university and barred the law school from using race *at all* in its admissions decisions.[10] The Supreme Court in *Bakke* had not prevented states from using race (and ethnicity) in admissions decisions, only from making it a decisive consideration. This ruling barred consideration of race altogether. In ballot initiatives, other states, such as California and Washington, also barred using race as a factor in admissions. Another white female, Abigail Fisher, later charged that the University of Texas at Austin's admissions policies for undergraduates (the Hopwood case dealt with the law school) discriminated against whites. In the second of two rulings on the case, the Supreme Court in 2016 ruled by a 4-3 vote (in Fisher II) that the University of Texas at Austin's use of race in the interest of diversity was constitutional. The Hopwood ruling was abrogated by the Supreme Court in a 2003 case, *Grutter v. Bollinger*, to be considered in Section 4.4.

The affirmative action programs in Texas colleges and universities were voluntary. No court had mandated them to remedy discrimination. And the programs were overt, in that their policies took race and ethnicity expressly into account in admissions.

Some schools then sought to try to preserve affirmative action by covert means. Consider the following report:

When a federal appeals court in New Orleans ruled in 1996 that the University of Texas Law School could not legally consider race in admitting students, lawyers at Rice University, a highly selective private college here, reluctantly decided that the ruling applied to it, too.

Almost overnight, the admissions officers at Rice stopped saying aloud the words "black," "African-American," "Latino," "Hispanic" or even "minority" in their deliberations. The next year, the proportion of black students admitted in the freshman class fell by half; the proportion of Hispanics fell by nearly a third.

The university feared that openly defying the federal court could cost it $45 million annually in federal aid, about 15 percent of its budget.

But like other colleges, Rice says it remains fiercely committed to having a diverse student body, so in the years since, it has developed creative, even sly ways to meet that goal and still obey the court. Thus the admissions committee, with an undisguised wink, has encouraged applicants to discuss "cultural traditions" in their essays, asked if they

> spoke English as a second language and taken note, albeit silently, of those identified as presidents of their black student associations.
>
> Those efforts, along with stepped-up recruiting at high schools with traditionally high minority populations, yielded a freshman class last year with a near-record composition of blacks and Hispanics ...
>
> The experience of Rice provides a preview of the subtle ways that life would most likely change inside the admissions offices of colleges like Yale, Princeton and Stanford should the Supreme Court decide to impose strict restrictions on affirmative action.[11]

Notice that Rice University is reported as saying that it's "fiercely committed" to having a *diverse* student body. It doesn't say that it is fiercely committed to compensating for past racial injustice. There is no reference to past injustices, much less to trying to compensate for them.

Following the *Bakke* decision, the rationale for voluntary affirmative action underwent a transformation. Initially the rationale was to end discrimination. Then it extended to redressing the wrongs of past discrimination. Finally, it came increasingly to be to promote diversity in education or in the workforce (or sometimes in society generally).

4.3 Diversity to the forefront

The basis for this turn to diversity was located within the *Bakke* case itself. Diversity was in fact one among several of the stated goals of affirmative action at the University of California.

> The fourth goal asserted by petitioner [the University of California] is the attainment of a diverse student body. This clearly is a constitutionally permissible goal for an institution of higher education. Academic freedom, though not a specifically enumerated constitutional right, long has been viewed as a special concern of the First Amendment. The freedom of a university to make its own judgments as to education includes the selection of its student body.

At the same time, the court held that quotas weren't a "necessary means" to achieving diversity. In support of this, it cited approvingly the program at Harvard College:

In recent years Harvard College has expanded the concept of diversity to include students from disadvantaged economic, racial and ethnic groups. Harvard College now recruits not only Californians or Louisianans but also Blacks and Chicanos and other minority students.

***

In practice, this new definition of diversity has meant that race has been a factor in some admission decisions. When the Committee on Admissions reviews the large middle group of applicants who are "admissible" and deemed capable of doing good work in their courses, the race of an applicant may tip the balance in his favor just as geographic origin or a life spent on a farm may tip the balance in other candidates' cases. A farm boy from Idaho can bring something to Harvard College that a Bostonian cannot offer. Similarly, a black student can usually bring something that a white person cannot offer.

Not only did colleges and universities jump on the diversity bandwagon, businesses and corporations did so as well. In addition to promoting social goals, diversity was deemed good for business, as these excerpts from a Microsoft ad make clear:

Valuing Diversity

This year, an incredible 800,000 skilled technology jobs in the United States will go unfilled because there are not enough qualified people to fill them ...

Although there is no quick fix, leaders in the high-tech industry, the academic community and government believe that continuing to expand diversity outreach efforts is a critical step toward addressing the shortage of skilled workers ...

A culturally diverse workforce provides companies with better decision-making based on multiple perspectives and varied approaches to product development. Not all cultures, for example, use technology in the same way. Understanding and factoring in such differences will enable companies to become more competitive in the global economy.

According to the most recent information available, women represented only 19 percent of science, engineering and technology workers in 1997, compared with their nearly 46 percent representation in the U.S. workforce as a whole. African Americans and Hispanics each made up about 3 percent of the science, engineering and technology workforce, while their representation in the workforce as a whole was 11 percent and 10 percent respectively. And according to other research, people with disabilities comprised 14 percent of the U.S. workforce but only 6 percent were in technical fields . . .

Diversity is one of the core values that define Microsoft's business practices and operating philosophy. To that end, Microsoft is working with a wide range of schools and organizations to increase technology training and educational opportunities for women and minorities. (*The New York Times*, November 27, 2000)

Whether or not valued as an end in itself, diversity has come to be seen by much of the business community as essential to profitability. This gives it an economic motivation, either instead of, or in addition to, a moral motivation. It also has been seen as promoting national security insofar as it is a goal in the armed forces. Indeed, affirmative action in the military is seen by some as a model for the rest of the country, as implied in the following report:

The core principle behind affirmative action is that excluding black people undermines civic harmony and runs counter to American ideals. This was evident in the case of the United States Army. After years of racial strife and rigorous segregation, it transformed itself into the most fully integrated organization yet seen in this country

The military during both World Wars consigned most black people to support jobs. The top brass commonly defended discrimination in racist terms, arguing that black men lacked the courage to fight or the intelligence to lead . . . One of the pivotal figures in the transformation in more recent years was Clifford Alexander, President Jimmy Carter's secretary of the Army. Early in his tenure, Mr. Alexander put a hold on a list of officers proposed for promotion to general. He was troubled, as he explained in a 1997 Op-Ed article, "because no black colonels had been promoted, even though many had achieved the rank and served with distinction."

The board that handled promotions was ordered to look at the records of eligible black colonels and to determine if they had been given lesser assessments or evaluated negatively by offers who were racially prejudiced. Once race-related blemishes were expunged, black colonels with otherwise sterling records emerged as strong candidates for promotion.

This decision was affirmative action in its purest, most elemental form ... Loaded terms such as "quotas" and "reverse discrimination" have made it all but impossible to see affirmative action as a constructive and vitally important policy for the United States ...

The typical Army base [today] is far more racially integrated than the average town or college campus.[12]

Having largely displaced racial justice as the rationale for affirmative action, diversity was starting to be represented as essential to education, the business world, national security, and even the flourishing of democracy.

4.4 The Supreme Court and the University of Michigan

The year 2003 saw landmark Supreme Court decisions involving the University of Michigan. In *Gratz v. Bollinger*, the court found unconstitutional the university's undergraduate admissions procedure. But in *Grutter v. Bollinger* it upheld the admissions procedure of the university's Law School. Both policies had used "race" (specifically, membership in an "underrepresented minority" group, defined as African American, Hispanic, or Native American) in their admissions decisions. And both had stressed diversity.

Michigan's undergraduate admissions program assigned 20 points (of 100 needed to guarantee admission) to minority applicants. The university contended that this was in keeping with the *Bakke* decision, because it allowed "race" to be a factor in admissions but didn't make it a decisive factor. The court ruled that the program nonetheless went too far:

To withstand our strict scrutiny analysis, respondents [the University] must demonstrate that the University's use of race in its current admission program employs "narrowly tailored measures that further compelling governmental interests." ... We find that the University's policy, which automatically distributes 20 points, or one-fifth of the points needed to guarantee admission, to every single "underrepresented minority" applicant solely because of race, is not narrowly tailored to achieve the interest in educational diversity that respondents claim justifies their program.

In *Bakke*, Justice Powell reiterated that "[p]referring members of any one group for no reason other than race or ethnic origin is discrimination for its own sake." 438 U.S., at 307. He then explained, however, that in his view it would be permissible for a university to employ an admissions program in which "race or ethnic background may be deemed a 'plus' in a particular applicant's file." *Id.*, at 317. He explained that such a program might allow for "[t]he file of a particular black applicant [to] be examined for his potential contribution to diversity without the factor of race being decisive when compared, for example, with that of an applicant identified as an Italian-American if the latter is thought to exhibit qualities more likely to promote beneficial educational pluralism." *Ibid.* Such a system, in Justice Powell's view, would be "flexible enough to consider all pertinent elements of diversity in light of the particular qualifications of each applicant." *Ibid.*

Justice Powell's opinion in *Bakke* emphasized the importance of considering each particular applicant as an individual, assessing all of the qualities that individual possesses, and in turn, evaluating that individual's ability to contribute to the unique setting of higher education. The admissions program Justice Powell described, however, did not contemplate that any single characteristic automatically ensured a specific and identifiable contribution to a university' diversity ...

The current LSA [University of Michigan's College of Literature, Science, and the Arts] policy does not provide such individualized consideration. The LSA's policy automatically distributes 20 points to every single applicant from an "underrepresented minority" group, as defined by the University. The only consideration that accompanies this distribution of points is a factual review of an application to determine whether an individual is a member of one of these minority groups. Moreover, unlike Justice Powell's example, where the race of a "particular black applicant" could be considered without being decisive, see *Bakke*, 438 U.S., at 317, the LSA's automatic distribution of 20 points has the effect of making "the factor of race ... decisive" for virtually every minimally qualified underrepresented minority applicant. *Ibid.* . . .

Nothing in Justice Powell's opinion in *Bakke* signaled that a university may employ whatever means it desires to achieve the stated goal of diversity without regard to the limits imposed by our strict scrutiny analysis.

We conclude, therefore, that because the University's use of race in its current freshman admissions policy is not narrowly tailored to achieve respondents' asserted compelling interest in diversity, the admissions policy violates the Equal Protection Clause of the Fourteenth Amendment. We further find that the admissions policy also violates Title VI [of the Civil Rights Act of 1964] and 42 U.S.C. 1981.

The University of Michigan Law School, on the other hand, didn't quantify the weight attached to race. Its procedures met with approval from a majority in the Supreme Court. The court's decision read in part:

The District Court heard extensive testimony from Professor Richard Lempert, who chaired the faculty committee that drafted the 1992 policy. Lempert emphasized that the Law School seeks students with diverse interests and backgrounds to enhance classroom discussion and the educational experience both inside and outside the classroom ... When asked about the policy's "commitment to racial and ethnic diversity with special reference to the inclusion of students from groups which have been historically discriminated against," Lempert explained that this language did not purport to remedy past discrimination, but rather to include students who may bring to the Law School a perspective different from that of members of groups which have not been the victims of such discrimination ...

Since this Court's splintered decision in *Bakke*, Justice Powell's opinion announcing the judgment of the Court has served as the touchstone for constitutional analysis of race-conscious admissions policies ...

Justice Powell approved the university's use of race to further only one interest: "the attainment of a diverse student body."

The Equal Protection Clause provides that no State shall "deny to any person within its jurisdiction the equal protection of the laws." U.D. Const., Amdt. 14, 2. Because the Fourteenth Amendment "protect[s] *persons*, not *groups*," all "governmental action based on race—a *group* classification long recognized as in most circumstances irrelevant and therefore prohibited—should be subjected to detailed judicial inquiry to ensure that the *personal* right to equal protection of the laws has not been infringed." ...

This means that such classifications are constitutional only if they are narrowly tailored to further compelling governmental interests ...

III

A

... Before this Court, as they have throughout this litigation, respondents [the Law School] assert only one justification for their use of race in the admissions process: obtaining "the educational benefits that flow from a diverse student body." ... In other words, the Law School asks us to recognize, in the context of higher education, a compelling state interest in student body diversity.

We first wish to dispel the notion that the Law School's argument has been foreclosed, either expressly or implicitly, by our affirmative-action cases decided since *Bakke*. It is true that some language in those opinion might be read to suggest that remedying past discrimination is the only permissible justification for race-based governmental action. ... But we have never held that the only governmental use of race that can survive strict scrutiny is remedying past discrimination. Nor, since *Bakke*, have we directly addressed the use of race in the context of public higher education. Today, we hold that the Law School has a compelling interest in attaining a diverse student body.

The Law School's educational judgment that such diversity is essential to its educational mission is one to which we defer ...

We have long recognized that, given the important purpose of public education and the expansive freedoms of speech and thought associated with the university environment, universities occupy a special niche in our constitutional tradition ... In announcing the principle of student body diversity as a compelling state interest, Justice Powell invoked our cases recognizing a constitutional dimension, grounded in the First Amendment, of educational autonomy: "The freedom of a university to make its own judgments as to education includes the selection of its student body." *Bakke, supra*, at 312. From this premise, Justice Powell reasoned that by claiming "the right to select those students who will contribute the most to the 'robust exchange of ideas,' " a university "seek[s] to achieve a goal that is of paramount importance in the fulfillment of its mission." ... Our conclusion that the Law School has a compelling interest in a diverse student body is informed by our view that attaining a diverse student body is at the heart of the Law School's proper institutional mission, and that "good faith" on the part of a university is "presumed" absent "a showing to the contrary." 438 U.S., at 318–319 ...

That a race-conscious admissions program does not operate as a quota does not, by itself, satisfy the requirement of individualized consideration. When using race as a "plus" factor in university admissions, a university's admissions program must remain flexible enough to ensure that each applicant is evaluated as an individual and not in a way that makes an applicant's race or ethnicity the defining feature of his or her application. The importance of this individualized consideration in the context of a race-conscious admissions program is paramount ...

Here the Law School engages in a highly individualized, holistic review of each applicant's file, giving serious consideration to all the ways an applicant might contribute to a diverse educational environment. The Law School affords this individualized consideration to applicants of all races. There is no policy, either *de jure* or *de facto*, of automatic acceptance or rejection based on any single "soft" variable. Unlike the program at issue in *Gratz v. Bollinger, ante,* the Law School awards no mechanical, predetermined diversity "bonuses" based on race or ethnicity ...

We are mindful, however, that "[a]core purpose of the Fourteenth Amendment was to do away with all governmentally imposed discrimination based on race." *Palmore v. Sidoti*, 466 U.S. 429, 432 (1984). Accordingly, race- conscious admissions policies must be limited in time. This requirement reflects that racial classifications, however compelling their goals, are potentially so dangerous that they may be employed no more broadly than the interest demands. Enshrining a permanent justification for racial preferences would offend this fundamental equal protection principle. We see no reason to exempt race-conscious admissions programs from the requirement that all governmental use of race must have a logical end point ...

In the context of higher education, the durational requirement can be met by sunset provisions in race-conscious admissions policies and periodic reviews to determine whether racial preferences are still necessary to achieve student body diversity ...

We take the Law School at its word that it would "like nothing better than to find a race-neutral admissions formula" and will terminate its race-conscious admissions program as soon as practicable ... It has been 25 years since Justice Powell first approved the use of race to further an interest in student body diversity in the context of public higher education. Since that time, the number of minority applicants with high grades and test scores has indeed increased ... We expect that 25 years from now the use of racial preferences will no longer be necessary to further the interest approved today.

IV

In summary, the Equal Protection Clause does not prohibit the Law School's narrowly tailored use of race in admissions decisions to further a compelling interest in obtaining the educational benefits that flow from a diverse student body. (*Gruter v. Bollinger* 539 U.S. 306 (2003))

In 2006 the state of Michigan banned affirmative action, understood as giving preferential treatment on the basis of race or gender in admissions at public institutions. The University of Michigan announced in 2007 it would comply with the new law. It thereby effectively ended its affirmative action program. In a 6-2 ruling in 2014, the Supreme Court upheld Michigan's ban on affirmative action.

Although affirmative action—narrowly conceived to use race-conscious admissions policies in the interest of diversity—has been ruled constitutional by the Supreme Court, states have the right to ban affirmative action in public universities if they choose. Eight states ban affirmative action: Arizona, California, Florida, Nebraska, New Hampshire, Michigan, Oklahoma, and Washington. The bans were by ballot in all except Florida, where it was by executive order of the governor, Jeb Bush.

4.5 Defining affirmative action

Against this background of its complex history, we're now in a position to define affirmative action:

Definition Box 4A

Affirmative Action: Voluntary or mandated measures (a) to end discrimination, (b) to compensate for past discrimination, or (c) to promote diversity (or all three).

We've seen that affirmative action may assume strong or weak forms. We may now define weak affirmative action as follows:

Definition Box 4B

Weak Affirmative Action: Measures short of preferential treatment on behalf of minorities and/or women in employment or education.

As stated earlier, weak affirmative action is relatively uncontroversial. Few object, for example, when colleges and universities advertise for faculty positions, saying that "women and minorities are especially encouraged to apply," or when they say, as some now do, that they are an "equal opportunity/affirmative action" employer and strongly encourage applications from candidates who would enhance the diversity of the university.

What is controversial is strong affirmative action, which we may define as follows:

Definition Box 4C

Strong Affirmative Action: Preferential treatment of minorities and/or women in education or employment (a) to compensate for present or past discrimination or (b) to promote diversity (or both).

Although affirmative action on behalf of minorities has received most of the legal attention, it's important to understand that it's frequently advocated and sometimes practiced on behalf of women as well.[13]

Against this background, we may schematize the various kinds of affirmative action in the following way:

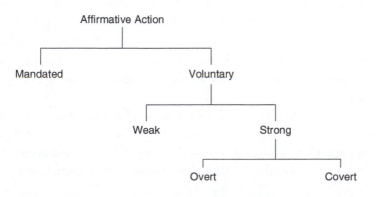

This shows the relationships of the many ideas encompassed by affirmative action. The most prominent aims that have been claimed for it are:

1. To end discrimination.
2. To compensate for past discrimination.
3. To promote equality.

Precisely what strong affirmative action means depends, as we shall see, upon how "preferential treatment" is understood. Since it's strong affirmative action that's most controversial, we shall concentrate on it. Unless otherwise noted, when speaking of affirmative action in what follows we shall mean *strong affirmative action*.

4.6 The moral problem

The legal standing of affirmative action in the United States may continue to evolve for years. *Court-mandated* affirmative action is permissible where discrimination has been proven. Voluntary affirmative action in admissions is permissible, at least for the time being (roughly the next 25 years, according to *Grutter v. Bollinger*), so long as it doesn't make use of quotas and is applied in an individualized, holistic way that takes full account of the individuality of applicants.

Our concern now is with the moral issues. Whatever the courts decide, a moral assessment of affirmative action may not coincide with the law. Let us begin by asking why the issue of affirmative action arises in the first place.

Imagine a racist society. Let's call it the Union of Racial Bigots. In it the racist majority has for centuries systematically oppressed a minority, depriving them of equal education, health care, nutrition, and so on. They've forced them to attend inferior schools, live in separate communities, and eat in separate restaurants. The majority controls the wealth of the country. From their ranks come the CEOs of the major corporations, the officers of the big banks, as well as doctors, lawyers, and educators. The police forces are made up of bigots, as are the judiciary and the legislature. Bigots dominate in every area of society.

Now suppose that, as though by the wave of a magic wand, the bigots awake one morning to find their souls cleansed of every trace of bigotry. They've miraculously become fair-minded, morally sensitive human beings. They're aghast at how they've treated the minority and immediately put an end to discrimination. To reflect this change of heart, they change the name of their country to the Republic of the Righteous.

If you were a member of the minority in the Union of Racial Bigots, you no doubt would be elated to find that discrimination had ended. But would you feel that you could now realize your potential on an equal footing with the former bigots? Surely not. For the wealth and power would still be in their hands. They would still own the property, control the banking and financial institutions, run the police forces, the hospitals, the better schools, and the colleges and universities. Elected officials would still be former oppressors, the political parties and electoral process still controlled by them. They're now decent human beings, but they still enjoy wealth, privilege, and power. Gross inequality would still exist.

If you, as a member of the minority, decide you'd like to go to a top university, you're now free to apply, whereas you wouldn't have been before. But since you've gone to inferior schools all your life, chances are you won't be competitive in the admissions process. Or you might like to run for political office, but you won't have the money to finance a campaign or the know-how to make your way in the political arena. You won't have millions of dollars inherited from your parents as will many of the former bigots. You're also free to apply for high-paying jobs with major corporations. But your lack of experience, skills, and training will put you out of the running in competition with well-educated members of the majority who have the technical skills and training.

The point is that *the effects of discrimination can survive beyond the end of the practice of discrimination*. Even if all racist beliefs, attitudes, and practices have disappeared, people who were severely disadvantaged in the Union of Racial Bigots will still be disadvantaged (though obviously less so) in the Republic of the Righteous. Since that disadvantage is undeserved, it seems unfair, hence unjust. Paradoxically, even a society made up of fair-minded and righteous individuals can still be pervaded by injustice. There can still be what in Chapter 1 (Section 1.2) we called "secondary racism."

4.7 Reparations?

Contemporary American society (and those in countries like Britain with substantial minorities) probably stands somewhere between the Union of Racial Bigots and the Republic of the Righteous. Gigantic strides toward racial justice have been made with the emancipation of the slaves, desegregation, and civil rights legislation. But prejudice and discrimination exist. And vast disparities in wealth and opportunity persist. There is, in short, still inequality linked to past discrimination against African Americans, Native Americans, Hispanics, and women.

What, if anything, should be done about this? Three questions arise here:

1. Ought we to try to offset past injustice and its continuing effects?
2. If so, how? (Specifically, is affirmative action the best way to do this?)
3. Is affirmative action itself unjust?

Regarding (1), some would say that eventually things will even out now that blatant discrimination has largely ended. Society owes nothing to minorities and women beyond ensuring that they're no longer discriminated against. The job of government is to provide for national security, the role of business is to make profits, and the mission of schools is to educate. It's not their business to promote social causes, however worthy. Others concede that eventually things might even out but that might take hundreds of years. Meanwhile people who have been oppressed will constitute an underclass, with higher rates of poverty and malnutrition, less desirable jobs, and political underrepresentation. Since it was a racist and sexist society that created this situation, they would say, it's society's responsibility to remedy it.

Whether we should try to offset past injustices depends, of course, upon whether we *can* offset them and by what means. This leads directly to question (2). What are the options when confronting past injustices? Are there alternatives to doing nothing?

One alternative is to give *reparations*. Reparations involve making restitution for past wrongs. A group that has wronged another can, for example, make a payment of money in compensation for the wrong done. There is a movement in the United States today seeking reparations in the amount of billions of dollars for African Americans for their enslavement. The following summarizes the case:

The Cost of Slavery

Marching across the South in 1865, Union soldiers seized up to 900,000 acres of "abandoned property." Some radical Northerners hoped to use this land to provide freed slaves with the now-legendary "40 acres and a mule" as restitution for slavery. Their hopes were obviously dashed. But the argument for reparations lives on nearly 140 years later.

While few doubt that slavery was a great wrong, the challenge before us is how to make things right through financial restitution. But just how would we devise a practical formula to determine who gets what?

Most assessments start with the notion of payment for lost wages. One research took 1860's prices for slaves as an estimate of their labor value and applied compound interest. The result: $2 trillion to $4 trillion. Six generations after slavery's demise, such approaches present serious difficulties. There are issues of what to do with whites (and blacks) who immigrated here after slavery ended. What about descendants of blacks who lived freely during the antebellum period? Does someone who is born to a white parent and a black parent cancel out? It would take Solomon to solve this.

Perhaps the issue needs to be looked at differently. One way is to recognize slavery as an institution upon which America's wealth was built. If we take this view, it is not important whether a white family arrived in 1700 or in 1965. If you wear cotton blue jeans, if you take out an insurance policy, if you buy from anyone who has a connection to the industries that were built on chattel labor, then you have benefited from slavery. Likewise, if you are black—regardless of when your ancestors arrived—you live with slavery's stigma.

Extending the reparations argument this broadly frees one to move beyond the issue of lost wages and seek out other factors on which to base a formula. If there were one statistic that captured the persistence of racial inequality, it would be net worth.

The typical white family enjoys a net worth that is more than eight times that of its black counterpart, according to the economist Edward Wolff . . .

This equity inequity is partly the result of the head start whites enjoy in accumulating and passing on assets. Some economists estimate that up to 80 percent of lifetime wealth accumulation results from gifts from earlier generations, ranging from the down payment on a home to a bequest by a parent. If the government used such net-worth inequality as a basis, and then factored in measures like population size, it could address reparations by transferring about 13 percent of white household wealth to blacks. A two-adult black family would receive an average reparation of about $35,000.

What would be the effect of wealth redistribution on such a vast scale? My own research—using national data to follow black and white adolescents into adulthood—shows that when we compare families with the same net worth, blacks are more likely to finish high school than whites and are equally likely to complete a bachelor's degree. Racial differences in welfare rates disappear. Thus, one generation after reparations were paid, racial gaps in education should close—eliminating the need for affirmative action.

The unpopularity of this radical plan would no doubt be unprecedented. There are also no guarantees that reparations would be a magic bullet for lingering racial problems. That said, it remains vital . . . to explore formulas and keep the reparations debate alive. It is important because each resulting dollar amount implies a theory of race, history and equal opportunity. That includes the figure implicit in our current policy—zero—which rests on the most absurd assumption of all: that slavery didn't matter.[14]

Is there a moral basis for reparations? A relevant consideration is brought to light by the twentieth-century British philosopher W. D. Ross (1877–1971). He held that if you have wronged someone, you have an obligation to rectify that wrong. He called this a duty of *reparation*. This, as often understood, is an obligation a wrongdoer has quite apart from the consequences of remedying the wrong. But the obligation is not an absolute one. It is what has been called a prima facie duty or obligation.

Theory Box 4A

Prima Facie Right, Wrong, and Obligatory
Judgments of right and wrong aren't always of the same strength. Sometimes acts are right in some respects but not in others. Let us therefore say that

Prima facie right (permissible): right in at least one respect.

Driving through an intersection when you have a green light is prima facie right. All other things being equal, you have the right of way. But if a child has wandered into the intersection, all other things aren't equal. The fact that you risk hitting the child more than offsets the fact that you have a green light. An act that is prima facie right might be **actually wrong** on balance.

Similarly, we may say that

> **Prima facie wrong: wrong in at least one respect.**
>
> Jay walking is wrong, all other things being equal, because it's ille-gal and may put your life at risk. But if you're across the street, and see that same child wander into the street, and you can dash across to save it, that's **actually right** on balance.
> And consider:
>
> **Prima facie obligatory: obligatory in at least one respect; i.e., obligatory all other things being equal.**
>
> You've promised to visit your grandmother at noon and on your way you witness an auto accident whose victims need assistance. You're the only one who can provide it. While you have a prima facie obliga-tion to visit your grandmother at noon (after all, you promised), none-theless other things aren't equal. Providing aid to the injured overrides that consideration. Your **actual duty** is to provide assistance.

If this is correct, we might apply it to groups as well as to individuals. If one group has wronged another, then, on the face of it, the first has a duty to the second to make restitution. Groups as well as individuals, it might be argued, have duties of reparation. Thus, given that whites enslaved African Americans (and seized the land of Native Americans), it would seem they have a duty of reparation to try to undo the effects of those wrongs. Although Britain abolished slavery in 1833, and other European countries at different times, it might be argued that they as well as the United States should share in reparations. We shall focus on the United States and on the question of reparations for African Americans.

But there are problems here. First, the individuals who would receive the reparations aren't the ones who suffered the wrong (at least in the case of slavery). Second, those who would pay for the reparations (through taxes) aren't the individuals who committed the wrongs.

That there is inequality and disadvantage in society doesn't in and of itself suffice to determine who, if anyone, is obligated to try to remedy it. Reparations in contemporary America would spread the cost over the whole of the present population and distribute the benefits over the whole of the present African American population. Since reparations presumably would be paid with tax money, and African Americans pay taxes, they would be receiving reparations with money they helped provide. White Americans, for their part, would be paying for the sins of their fathers.

4.8 Affirmative action distinguished from reparations

The other main alternative in answer to question (2) is affirmative action. Although affirmative action is sometimes taken to include the possibility of reparations, the two are usually distinguished (as they are in the above passage), and we shall do so in what follows. Affirmative action differs from reparations in some important ways.

First, reparations (at least as represented above) deals specifically with compensation for slavery, whereas affirmative action is usually thought to deal with the effects, not only of slavery, but of discrimination as well. And as we have seen, affirmative action can—when its rationale is to promote diversity—be unconnected in any direct way with past wrongs.

Second, for this reason affirmative action (unlike reparations, at least as envisioned in the article above), can be implemented on behalf of women and other ethnic minorities, such as Hispanics and Native Americans. The question of reparations could be raised in these other cases as well, but there has been no concerted movement to do so.

Third, one might think that affirmative action is justified without thinking that present persons are responsible for the past injustices in question. A duty of reparation arguably comes into existence when *you*, whether an individual or group, have done a wrong. A society would owe reparation only if *it* had done the wrong. Affirmative action, on the other hand (even when premised upon past wrongs as opposed to promoting of ends like diversity) might be a duty even if you (or today's society) haven't done the wrong. It's the *fact* of past injustice (and its continuing effects) that's the governing consideration, not necessarily who is responsible for the injustice.

Fourth, in affirmative action certain individuals are singled out to bear the costs of offsetting past wrongs and other individuals are singled out to receive the benefits.

Finally, and relatedly, affirmative action (and remember that we are speaking now of strong affirmative action) implies *preferential treatment* of individual members of groups that have suffered wrongs when they are competing with individual members of other groups. Because of this, some people who favor reparations might nonetheless object to affirmative action. Why?

This brings us to question (3). Just as the answer to question (1) depends in part upon what the options are—and hence leads naturally to question (2)—so also the answer to question (2) depends upon whether affirmative action itself is unfair, which leads naturally to question (3). In this way, the three questions are interconnected.

4.9 Justice for groups or for individuals?

Question (3) is a complicated one. Let's begin to deal with it by making some distinctions.

So long as we see the problem solely in terms of *groups*, we're operating with what may be called a "macro ethics," which takes a primary concern of ethics to be with the survival and well-being of groups. It can be contrasted with a "micro ethics."

Theory Box 4B

Micro Ethics and Macro Ethics
Micro ethics takes the primary concern of ethics to be the survival, well-being, and rights of individuals. **Macro ethics** takes the primary concern of ethics to be the survival, well-being, and rights of groups. The group can be the state, society, a religion, sex, race, or ethnicity.

Suppose that one group has long oppressed another. We've seen that, all other things being equal, it's plausible to say that the first group should compensate the second for wrong done. It's the *group* that owes the duty of reparation. But groups don't exist in the abstract. A group can act only insofar as individual members of the group act. And a group can be harmed only insofar as individual members of the group are harmed.

If we consider not only groups but also the individuals who make up groups, we see the complexities of affirmative action.

Affirmative action can be practiced on behalf of a group only insofar as individual members of that group are given preference in hiring or admissions over individual members of another group. (Remember we're speaking now of strong affirmative action—voluntary programs that give preferences.) Since competition for jobs or admission to college, graduate or professional school are goods, this raises a question of how these benefits are to be distributed. This is the question of distributive justice (see Theory Box 3D in Chapter 3, Section 3.9). It requires looking at the situations of individual members of groups when they compete for these goods. Since distributive justice also deals with the fairness in the imposition of burdens, it also comes into play when people are (say, for economic reasons) let go from jobs.

Contextualized in terms of contemporary American society, let's say that Group A stands for whites, Group B for blacks (or African Americans). In light of our discussion in Chapter 1, we won't assume that these groups stand for races; only that they represent groupings commonly recognized in ordinary discourse. With appropriate qualifications, what we say will apply to Hispanics, Native Americans, or women as well. And let's consider two members of groups A and B respectively, Jones and Smith.

Group A (white): Jones, individual member of A.
Group B (black): Smith, individual member of B.

Before continuing, it's important to avoid a misconception. Affirmative action doesn't mean favoring unqualified persons over qualified persons. It favors minorities or women only when they're qualified. But two kinds of controversial cases can arise: (1) those in which the minority and nonminority applicants are *equally qualified* and (2) those in which both are qualified but the nonminority candidate is *more highly qualified*.

Suppose we could measure qualifications on a scale of 1–10, with 1–5 representing unqualified, 6–10 representing qualified (and 10 being the highest qualified). And suppose Jones, a white, applies for admission to a college or university in competition with Smith, a black. Is it fair to give preference to Smith over Jones because Jones is a member of Group A? It's Group A that did the wrong but the individual, Jones, who stands to lose the job or admission. And it's Group B that suffered the wrong but the individual, Smith, who stands to benefit. Consider three scenarios.

First scenario: Jones (white) and Smith (black) have scores of 8. Both are well qualified. The position is given to Smith because of his membership in a minority group.

Second scenario: Jones scores 8 and Smith 7. Both are qualified but Jones is more highly qualified. The position is given to Smith because of his membership in a minority group.

Giving preference to minority candidates in either of these sorts of cases is controversial. But doing so in cases of the second sort is more controversial. Since distributive justice deals with fairness in the imposition of burdens as well as the conferring of benefits, we need to consider a third scenario, which is closely related to the first:

Third scenario: Jones and Smith are equally qualified and are employed at the same place and performing at an equally high level. But one of them has to be let go (say, for budgetary reasons). Jones is let go and Smith retained because of his membership in a minority group.

That cases of the first and third sorts are less controversial doesn't mean that they are uncontroversial. Consider the following case of two public school teachers, which illustrates the third scenario:

How Far Can Affirmative Action Plan Go?

Sharon Taxman and Debra Williams were hired to teach in the business department of the high school here on the same day 14 years ago. Over the years they both received strong evaluations, volunteered outside the classroom and were granted tenure at the same time—to the point where there was nothing at all separating their professional qualifications.

But in 1989, when the school board in this small, central New Jersey town [Piscataway] decided to lay off one member of the high school business staff, it did not hesitate. It fired Sharon Taxman because she was white, and kept Debra Williams because she was black ...

What has brought the case national attention is that the Piscataway school board chose Williams over Taxman not to reverse any past pattern of discriminatory hiring or even because blacks were underrepresented on the Piscataway High School staff. Rather it fired Taxman because board members felt a racially diverse teaching staff was a better teaching staff.

For those looking to clarify the often murky legal status of affirmative action, this case raises one of the principal unresolved issues surrounding affirmative action as clearly as if it were dreamed up for a law school civil rights class: Is it right for an employer to discriminate in favor of minorities even if that employer hasn't previously discriminated against them? ...

The case hinges on the legality of the guidelines issued by Piscataway, which includes, in addition to a general commitment to hiring more women and minorities, the following: "In all cases, the most qualified candidate will be recommended for appointment. However, when candidates appear to be of equal qualification, candidates meeting the criteria of the Affirmative Action program will be recommended." ...

Board members chose to keep Williams because she was the only black person on the nine-member business department staff, and they felt that providing a diverse group of teachers was an important part of providing a good education.[15]

Here the issue concerns the imposition of a burden (loss of a job), not the provision of a benefit (hiring for a job). Distributive justice, once again, concerns the allocation of burdens as well as benefits, and is raised in this case as well as in cases involving the awarding of a job (the same for admissions).

Notice also that in this case the issue is diversity. Promoting a diverse teaching faculty is the justification offered for retaining the black teacher, not the remedying of past discrimination by the school. There is no duty of reparation here, since the school district hasn't done a wrong.

But the principal feature of this case for our present purposes is that the two teachers were equally qualified. They were hired at the same time, given tenure at the same time and received equally good evaluations over the years. But one was let go because she was white, the other was retained because she was black.

Consider now a case of sort (2), in which a nonminority applicant for law school is turned down despite having higher qualifications by the standards used by the school (this is the case *Hopwood v. Texas* referred to in Section 4.2):

"Racial Discrimination or Righting Past Wrongs? White Woman Accuses Law School of Bias"

From Cheryl J. Hopwood's point of view, if overcoming past hardship was counted as a plus when applying to the University of Texas Law School, she should have been among the more qualified candidates.

Ms. Hopwood's father died when she was a girl and she was reared under difficult circumstances by her mother. She worked all through high school and put herself through both community college and the California State University at Sacramento, where she graduated with a 3.8 grade point average. Then, having become a Texas resident, she did well enough on the law school admissions test to get into a category of law school applicant that is almost automatically admitted at Texas.

But Cheryl Hopwood was not admitted, and she believes the reason is that she is white ...

According to the law school, its affirmative action policy works like this: Every one of roughly 4,000 applicants is assigned a Texas Index number, a combination of undergraduate grade point average and law school admissions test score. The numbers range from about 145 to 220. Under examination by plaintiffs' lawyers, law school officials acknowledged that blacks and Mexican-Americans are given something close to automatic admission at index numbers substantially below those of many whites who are rejected, including all four plaintiffs in the case.

The head of the law school's admissions committee, Stanley Johanson, admitted under question that no black or Mexican-American applicants who were state residents and had a Texas Index of 185 or higher were denied admission. Ms. Hopwood's index was 199 and the three other plaintiffs, white men, had 198.

Mr. Johanson also said that had Ms. Hopwood been black or Mexican-American she would "in all probability" have been accepted.

"Hopwood is the epitome of who is harmed by affirmative action," said Mr. Smith, a former state legislator. "If she had been black, she would have been admitted. Every black applicant that had her credentials got a $7,000 scholarship and free tuition." ...

"Are there white applicants who were not admitted who would have gotten in if they had been black?" asked Samuel Issacharoff, a law professor at the school and member of the legal team that argued the case. "The answer is clearly yes. That's the nature of a racial preference."

But, he said, while affirmative action is not "cost free," it is an essential tool to enable minorities to overcome a legacy of past discrimination.[16]

Cheryl Hopwood was rejected for admission, yet she had higher scores than some of those who were accepted. At issue here is denial of a *benefit* (admission to a quality law school, along with a scholarship and free tuition) rather than imposition of a burden (firing from a job), so the issue of distributive justice is raised in a different way. Those who were admitted with lower scores than Cheryl Hopwood were qualified applicants. It's just that she was more qualified.

Finally, notice that in this case the rationale offered by the law professor is not diversity but the importance of affirmative action to overcoming a "legacy of past discrimination." Recalling the different possible goals for affirmative action, two of the three goals are represented in these cases.

4.10 Is affirmative action unfair?

Let us try to understand further why these cases are controversial. We'll focus upon cases of sort (2), though most of what we say will apply to cases of sort (1) as well.

Let's now continue our focus upon individual members.

Consider first Smith, the black member of the minority in competition with Jones, a white member of the nonminority. First, Smith will not have suffered what was arguably the worst of the oppression of Group A, because that oppression (slavery) occurred before Smith was born. It may even be that Smith hasn't personally suffered discrimination in employment or education, if only because he or she is applying for a job or to college for the first time. It's possible also that Smith is from an affluent family and hence hasn't suffered the poverty and economic deprivation of many members of Group B. Smith, let us suppose, has also attended quality schools.

The point is that, while the *group* may have been severely oppressed historically, there will be some individual members of that group who have not, and who, furthermore, aren't disadvantaged economically and educationally.

The moral question raised by this is whether someone like Smith should be given preference over someone like Jones.

Let us focus now upon Jones, the white. Although a member of the oppressing Group A, Jones won't have been party to the worst of Group A's oppression of Group B because, like Smith, Jones wasn't alive at the time it took place. Jones couldn't have been a slaveholder and couldn't have benefited immediately and directly from slavery. Moreover, Jones (like Cheryl Hopwood in the above case) may have faced hardships that Smith didn't. Jones may have lost a parent early in life, had to overcome financial hardship, and may have attended inferior schools. Even if Group A on the whole is significantly better off than Group B—and better off in considerable part because of its oppression of Group B through slavery and discrimination—it doesn't follow that every member of Group A is better off than every member of Group B.

Should a particular individual, like Smith, be given preference over another individual, like Jones, in competition for a job (or for college or professional school admissions)? Group A has grievously wronged Group B. But Jones has not wronged Smith (or, let us suppose, anyone in Group B).

The matter is more complicated still. Remember that distributive justice involves the comparative treatment of individuals or groups. We have been comparing Jones and Smith. But let us add a third individual, Brown. Suppose Brown, like Jones, is white and hence a member of the oppressing Group A. But unlike Jones, Brown is (let us suppose) a white supremacist, who has supported discrimination at every turn and in addition has a big home, a good job, and a comfortable living. Brown doesn't need to enter the competition for jobs or college admissions. He's unaffected if fellow whites like Jones are bypassed for jobs or rejected for college.

If we compare Jones—not with Smith now, but with Brown—the question is: why should Jones be made to bear the burden of losing out in employment or education when people like Brown are not? Why should society expect only *certain* individuals to pay the price of trying to remedy past discrimination (or promote diversity), and not everyone?

The preceding merely hypothesizes that there will be some individuals who roughly fit the descriptions of Jones and Smith. It's not to prejudge how many there will be. With a little ingenuity, we could alter the descriptions of them to change our common-sense judgments of fairness. Suppose Smith is a hard-working, severely disadvantaged African American raised by a single parent, and Jones is a lazy and affluent white male who has enjoyed every luxury in life. Suppose Jones scored one-point higher on the relevant qualification index for a job or college admissions. Would it be fair to give preference to Smith under those circumstances? Would it be fair if they had identical scores? Many who are troubled by the comparisons in the preceding case might be less troubled in accepting affirmative action in this sort of case.

Since we're talking about the allocation of burdens and benefits, distributive justice is at issue in these cases. Questions of fairness arise both when we compare the treatment of Jones and Smith and when we compare the treatment of Jones and Brown.

Some would argue that we've left out an important dimension of this situation (at least as it applies to actual society). They would maintain that Smith *as a matter of fact* has suffered disadvantages from being black, whether or not he's from an affluent background. Racial discrimination is pervasive, they say. Even if you can't quantify the harms done, every single member of a minority group that has suffered racial or ethnic (or gender) discrimination is disadvantaged to some degree. By the same token, every single member of the oppressor group has benefited from the advantages of being a member of that group. And these benefits have come at the expense of the oppressed group (and within both groups, males will have benefited at the expense of females). So even if by more obvious criteria (wealth, education, etc.) Smith will have fared better than Jones, once the less visible effects of racism (and ethnic and gender discrimination) are factored in, Smith deserves preference.

Although the idea of affirmative action, as understood today, wasn't an issue in his time, Frederick Douglass, an escaped slave and friend of Susan B. Anthony, expressed views that some take to mean that he would have opposed affirmative action. The following is excerpted from a speech Douglass gave before the Massachusetts Anti-Slavery Society in Boston in 1865, in which he argued for giving blacks the right to vote:

What the Black Man Wants

I understand the anti-slavery societies of this country to be based on two principles—first, the freedom of the blacks of this country; and, second, the elevation of them. Let me not be misunderstood here. I am not asking for sympathy at the hands of abolitionists, sympathy at the hands of any. I think the American people are disposed often to be generous rather than just. I look over this country at the present time, and I see Educational Societies, Sanitary Commissions, Freedmen's Associations, and the like—all very good: but in regard to the colored people there is always more that is benevolent, I perceive, than just, manifested towards us. What I ask for the Negro is not benevolence, not pity, not sympathy, but simply *justice*. The American people have always been anxious to know what they shall do with us ... I have had but one answer from the beginning. Do nothing with us! Your doing with us has already played the mischief with us. Do nothing with us! If the apples will not remain on the tree of their own strength, if they are worm eaten at the core, if they are early ripe and disposed to fall, let them fall! I am not for tying or fastening them on the tree in any way, except by nature's plan, and if they will not stay there, let them fall. And if the Negro cannot stand on his own legs, let him fall also. All I ask is, give him a chance to stand on his own legs! Let him alone! ... your interference is doing him positive injury.[17]

Douglass in the above passage makes clear that, in his view, blacks want justice from society, not sympathy and not benevolence (the motivation to do good). Do-gooding, as much as it may salve the consciences of those who share responsibility for injustice, and as much as it may inflate the pride of the righteous, can be detrimental in its effects. That seems to be what Douglass has in mind. It should be said, however, that at the time of his speech, near the end of the Civil War and the freeing of the slaves, he may well have expected that blacks would thereafter be free to rise by their own intelligence, talent, and initiative. That turned out to be mistaken. After a brief period of relative freedom, systematic oppression soon was visited upon blacks, and didn't begin to be lifted until the mid-twentieth century, with the Supreme Court decision in *Brown v. Board of Education* (1954), ending school segregation, and the Civil Rights Act of 1964 (see Key Quote 4A).

Some people allege that Martin Luther King, Jr., might have agreed with Frederick Douglass on this issue. They cite his famous words:

Key Quote 4C

I have a dream my four little children will one day live in a nation where they will not be judged by the color of their skin, but by the content of their character.

The speech, delivered at the Lincoln Memorial, was part of the March on Washington for jobs and freedom. Affirmative action, as we have seen, hadn't yet evolved into anything like its present form. Yet in retrospect, some people believe that King would have opposed it, since, at least in its most controversial forms, it seems to give preferential treatment to minorities— that is, judging people by the color of their skin.

Responding to this view, King's widow, Coretta Scott King, wrote an op-ed piece detailing what she said was King's position:

Man of His Word
Who would have thought, 33 years after my husband, Martin Luther King, Jr., uttered those words that their meaning would be distorted by supporters of The California Civil Rights Initiative, which would eliminate affirmative action plans.

> My husband unequivocally supported such programs. He did indeed dream of a day when his children would be judged by the content of their character, instead of the color of their skin. But he often said that programs and reforms were needed to hasten the day when his dream of genuine equality of opportunity—reflected in reality, not just theory—would be fulfilled.
>
> In a 1965 interview, when Martin was asked about the fairness of the idea of affirmative action, he replied: "Can any fair-minded citizen deny that the Negro has been deprived? ... We have ample precedents for special compensatory programs, which are regarded as settlements. American Indians are still being paid for land in a settlement manner. Is not two centuries of labor which helped build this country, as real a commodity? And will you remember that America adopted a policy of special treatment for millions of veterans after the war—a program which cost far more than a policy of preferential treatment to rehabilitate the traditionally disadvantaged Negro would cost today."
>
> Those who say that affirmative action is no longer necessary rarely cite statistics to support their argument, for the evidence of continuing pervasive discrimination against minorities and women is overwhelming ...
>
> Like my husband, I strongly believe that affirmative action has merit, not only for promoting justice, but also for healing and unifying society.[18]

The California Civil Rights Initiative to which Coretta King refers was passed in 1996, and later upheld by the courts. It prohibits discrimination or preferential treatment on the basis of race, sex, ethnicity, and so on. It effectively ended affirmative action.

Notice that in apparent contrast to Frederick Douglass, Coretta King (and presumably her deceased husband, Martin Luther King, Jr.) saw affirmative action as a matter of justice, not merely benevolence. (Remember that there was no such thing as affirmative action in Douglass's time, so we're extrapolating from what he says.) And she saw it in addition as having the potential to heal and unify society, adding a consequentialist element to its justification as well as justice.

Some would argue that, appearances to the contrary notwithstanding, affirmative action on behalf of African Americans (and/or Hispanics, Native Americans, and women) isn't preferential treatment at all. It's simply a case of removing an unfair competitive disadvantage they suffer. Whites (and particularly white males) enjoy an undeserved competitive advantage because of past discrimination and arguably of more recent discrimination as well.[19] American society, according to this argument, reaped enormous economic prosperity from the labor of slaves, the displacement of Native Americans, and the underpaid labor of Hispanics. Every white person is a beneficiary of this injustice. And every white male is in addition the beneficiary of the subordination of women, who for years were deprived of the right to vote, to equal opportunity employment, and equal political representation. What appears to be reverse discrimination in the form of affirmative action is simply the removal of an injustice.

These last two considerations are difficult to evaluate; not because there isn't a large measure of truth to them (particularly the first), but because it's difficult to assess what that measure of truth is and how it's to be weighed against other considerations which may also have a measure of truth.

For example, while arguably every contemporary African American has suffered disadvantages from past slavery and discrimination, many of them probably have experienced benefits as well. There may be some individual African Americans today who enjoy a level of prosperity they otherwise wouldn't have if their ancestors hadn't been brought to this country as slaves. Their ancestors suffered grievously. But they (the current members of society) didn't. And all of us, they included, have no doubt benefited in various ways from the institution which caused that suffering. In the absence of highly detailed knowledge of a sort we rarely have, it's difficult to assess of any two individuals just how much each has been advantaged or disadvantaged by past injustices (unless, e.g., one has inherited wealth directly traceable to the slave trade). And if we cannot do that, it's difficult to say of any two individuals that to favor one because of membership in a group that has suffered enormously is simply to remove an unfair competitive disadvantage and not give preferential treatment. In some cases no doubt that's true; but in others not. If so, in the one, we treat one person unfairly; in the other, we treat the other person unfairly.

The point is that when we move from talking solely about groups to talking about individuals, the moral issues become much more complex.

4.11 Diversity or compensation for past injustices?

We have in the previous section considered affirmative action against the background of historic wrongs done to African Americans, Native

Americans, Hispanics, and women. But we saw earlier that the focus of affirmative action has largely turned to diversity. Where does diversity now fit into the picture?

If the emphasis is shifted from injustice in the past to the promotion of diversity in the future, the earlier three questions (in Section 4.7) don't seem to arise. Those questions begin with: (1) Ought we to try to offset past injustices and their continuing effects? If we shouldn't, then questions (2) and (3) (concerning how to do it and whether affirmative action is unjust) don't arise. The emphasis on diversity disconnects the issue of affirmative action from question (1) (even if one thinks that, in the last analysis, the need for greater diversity is caused by past discrimination).

If we take diversity to be a value in education or the workplace or society as a whole, the question is, why? And what constitutes diversity?

Critics of affirmative action raise this latter question. Singling out colleges and universities in particular, they argue that if diversity should be promoted, then because political conservatives allegedly are underrepresented on college and university faculties we should have affirmative action on behalf of them as well. Consider the following, written at the time the previously discussed University of Michigan cases were going to the Supreme Court:

Diversify Michigan with Conservatives

It is really a misunderstanding. Out in Ann Arbor ... the large-hearted and progressive-minded University of Michigan insists that its undergraduate and law school admissions policies do not actually involve racial preferences. Heaven forfend. The policies are diversity preferences.

Granted, African-American, Hispanic and Native-American undergraduate applicants get 20 points added to their scores (150 is the maximum possible) just for being members of their groups. And although the law school has a different way of weighting race, applicants from those three groups are much more likely to be admitted than other applicants with comparable academic credentials. However, the university says rewarding certain favored races and ethnic groups is just a means of promoting diversity ...

Now, given the university's insistence that its preferences are not about race but diversity, and given the fact that the only pertinent diversity in a university is diversity of thought, and given the fact that the university fancies itself exquisitely concerned with the excluded, therefore: its admissions policies should include preferential treatment for conservatives.

In Ann Arbor, which voted for George McGovern in 1972 and Walter Mondale in 1984, when each was losing 49 states, conservatives are scarce. This must grieve the university, which craves diversity and surely resents the accusation that academic institutions favor diversity in everything but thought.[20]

Even if the above may be more a way of putting down the diversity rationale for affirmative action than of seriously proposing affirmative action for conservatives, others seriously argue that American colleges and universities generally (and not just Michigan) need greater "intellectual inclusiveness" (i.e., greater balance of liberal and conservative political views). Apart from admissions policies, they argue for affirmative action in hiring. The following is an argument by philosopher Christina Hoff Sommers:

For More Balance on Campuses

Campus talks by "politically incorrect' speakers happen rarely; visits are resisted and almost never internally funded. When Camille Paglia, Andrew Sullivan, David Horowitz, or Linda Chavez do appear at a college, they are routinely heckled and sometimes threatened. The academy is now so inhospitable to free expression that conservatives buy advertisements in student newspapers. But most school newspapers won't print them. And papers that do are sometimes vandalized and the editors threatened.

The classical liberalism articulated by John Stuart Mill in his book "On Liberty" is no longer alive on campuses, having died of the very disease Mr. Mill warned of when he pointed out that ideas not freely and openly debated become "dead dogmas." Mill insisted that the intellectually free person must put himself in the "mental position of those who think differently" adding that dissident ideas are best understood "by hearing them from persons who actually believe them."

... David Horowitz's Center for the Study of Popular Culture has launched a "Campaign for Fairness and Inclusion in Higher Education." It calls for university officials to:

1. Establish a zero-tolerance policy for vandalizing newspapers or heckling speakers.

2. Conduct an inquiry into political bias in the allocation of student program funds, including speakers' fees, and seek ways to promote underrepresented perspectives.

3. Conduct an inquiry into political bias in the hiring process of faculty and administrators and seek ways to promote fairness toward—and inclusion of—underrepresented perspectives.

Were even one high-profile institution ... to adopt a firm policy of intellectual inclusiveness, that practice would quickly spread, and benighted students everywhere would soon see daylight.[21]

Sommers seems to *favor* affirmative action and to favor it on grounds of diversity. But she favors it for conservatives (or more specifically, on behalf of conservative perspectives). Whereas the University of Michigan's admissions procedures referred to "underrepresented minorities," she refers to "underrepresented perspectives." If we should seek diversity in the one area, why not in the other as well? And if we should seek diversity in these areas, why not in still others?

Extrapolating from this concern, we might ask whether we should seek greater diversity by increasing the representation of gay and lesbian, Islamic, pacifist, vegetarian, Marxist, socialist, communist, creationist, fascist, and white supremacist perspectives, as well as others that have ardent supporters but are underrepresented in campuses. Once diversity is disconnected from past injustice, the door swings wide open. And just as those who are disadvantaged by current affirmative action policies feel that it's now *they* who are being discriminated against, those who would be disadvantaged by affirmative action on behalf of underrepresented groups like the preceding would likely feel the same.

The above highlights a problem with disconnecting the concern with diversity from past injustice. Need diversity be so disconnected? Not necessarily. One could advocate diversity but only insofar as it is a means to overcoming inequality arising from historic injustice. To take diversity as an objective presupposes that it's now lacking. If it's now lacking, then there's an imbalance in the representation of certain groups. If so, it's relevant to ask why. What explains the imbalance? If lack of diversity involving certain groups has to do with discrimination, then there would be grounds for considering affirmative action to remedy the imbalance. But if it has nothing to do with discrimination, then there might be no justification for adopting affirmative action to promote that end. That there are few if any creationists on science faculties may be because creationism isn't generally considered a scientifically credible approach to evolution, and hence many people don't take it seriously. For that reason, few creationists even apply for faculty positions. It's possible—though this is speculative—that political conservatives in general prefer higher-paying careers in business, law, or politics than in academia, and for that reason relatively few of them even apply for academic positions. If that explained their disproportionately few numbers on college faculties, there might be no justification to make a concerted effort to redress that imbalance. A more problematic case concerns the perceived need on the part of some colleges to give preferential treatment in admissions to males. Because girls do better academically in high school than boys, to rely solely on the usual admissions standards results in a disproportionately high percentage of girls in entering freshman classes. But some schools consider something approximating a balance between males and females in the student body desirable. Giving preference to boys would be in the interests of diversity, but it would be unconnected with the boys having been discriminated against in the past.

If, on the other hand, the explanation of lack of diversity points to past discrimination, then pursuit of diversity is ultimately linked to past injustice after all. That the inequality owes to past injustice might, however, be only a necessary condition of its being a justified objective to pursue. There might still need to be another component of the justification. That component could be (as advocates of diversity maintain) to promote education or profitability or democracy (or some other social good). The objective would still be forward-looking, to achieve diversity in the future. But the rationale would look to the causes of the societal circumstance that makes racial, ethnic, and sexual diversity something to be desired. This would leave the door open to arguments for diversity for groups (say, gays and lesbians) who have suffered discrimination in the past. But it wouldn't open the door to arguments for diversity on behalf of all who might like to see their favored political, religious, or moral views more widely represented.

4.12 Conclusion

The arguments for affirmative action are either backward-looking, appealing to the wrongs of past discrimination, or forward-looking, appealing to the future good to be achieved by affirmative action policies. The backward-looking argument appeals to a duty of reparation, in which those responsible for a wrong have an obligation to remedy the wrong. This, as often understood, is an obligation a wrongdoer has quite apart from the consequences of remedying the wrong. But the obligation is not an absolute one. It is what has been called a prima facie duty or obligation.

At the same time, the fact that affirmative action would promote the social goods of equality or integration, either in particular institutions or in society at large would (assuming it to be true) make it prima facie right to institute affirmative action policies. If they would advance those social goods better than any other alternative (such as reparations, for example), then it would be prima facie obligatory to implement affirmative action policies. On either of these grounds (assuming that we do have duties of reparation and that we ought to promote social good), affirmative action would be prima facie right or even obligatory.

But are all other things equal? Here we encounter the objection to affirmative action. It would appear to many that *even if* an oppressor group has a duty of reparation to a group it has oppressed, and *even if* there should be a prima facie duty to promote social goods like equality and integration, still, to do so through affirmative action would be to do an injustice to the particular individuals who would be disadvantaged by the policies.

Jones, in our earlier example, hasn't practiced discrimination, and may even be an ardent supporter of racial, ethnic, or gender equality. It would seem unfair to disadvantage Jones (and those like Jones) in competition for jobs or admission seats against persons like Smith. Jones didn't commit the wrongs in question. As it is prima facie wrong not to try to offset past injustices, it is prima facie wrong to treat persons unfairly. Similarly, in comparing Jones with Brown (the racist beneficiary of past injustices), it would seem unfair, hence unjust, to place upon Jones (and those like Jones) the burden of redressing past group wrongs or the costs of achieving the social goods of equality or integration.

Almost certainly greater diversity and racial, ethnic, and gender equality would be good for society. Almost certainly to achieve it through affirmative action would be unfair to some individuals. How great the good would be, and how extensive the unfairness would be, we don't know. And even if we did, it might be difficult to say what is right. Morality provides no formula by which to judge with exactitude the weights of competing moral considerations of this sort when they conflict. This doesn't mean that there isn't ultimately a right or wrong to affirmative action. It does suggest, though, that at present it may be difficult to know with confidence what it is. Perhaps the best we can do is to follow legal decisions and cultivate a vocabulary and ethical framework within which to think deeply about these complex and still evolving issues.

Study questions

1. What role was assigned to *affirmative action* in the Civil Rights Act of 1964 (Key Quote 4A)?
2. What role was implied for affirmative action in the statement by President Lyndon Johnson (Key Quote 4B)?
3. What was the Supreme Court's main objection to the version of affirmative action under challenge in *University of California v. Bakke* 1978) (Section 4.2)?
4. What change in the rationale for affirmative action was brought about as a result of the Bakke case (Section 4.3)?
5. How does the text define affirmative action (Definition Box 4A, Section 4.5)? What are the *strong* and *weak* forms of affirmative action (Theory Boxes 4B and 4C)?
6. How is the moral (as opposed to the legal) problem of affirmative action illustrated by the case of the mythical Union of Racial Bigots and the Republic of the Righteous (Section 4.6)?
7. What are reparations? How do *reparations* differ from affirmative action as a way of responding to social injustice?
8. What are *prima facie* rightness, wrongness, and obligatoriness (Theory Box 4A, Section 4.7)?
9. Although the one lived before affirmative action, and the other when affirmative action was in its infancy, what different views of affirmative action are implied by Frederick Douglass and Martin Luther King, Jr. in the passages attributed to them in Section 4.10?
10. What different rationales for affirmative action are implied by the appeal to *diversity* and the appeal to the need to compensate for past injustice?

Notes

1   Thomas E. Hill, Jr., "The Message of Affirmative Action," in Steven M. Cahn (ed.), *The Affirmative Action Debate* (New York: Routledge, 1995), p. 169.
2   James P. Sterba, *Justice for Here and Now* (Cambridge: Cambridge University Press, 1998), p. 105.
3   *Oxford English Dictionary.*
4   Michael Weinstein, Editorial Observer, *The New York Times*, October 17, 2000.

5   Maidstone Mulenga, Rochester *Democrat and Chronicle*, January 19, 2003.

6   Gertrude Ezorsky, *Racism & Justice: The Case for Affirmative Action* (Ithaca, NY: Cornell University Press, 1991), pp. 74f.

7   See *Christian Science Monitor*, June 24, 2003.

8   Although ending current discrimination is less frequently cited nowadays as a justification for affirmative action, Barbara R. Bergmann maintains that "[t]he major justification for affirmative action in the workplace is its use as a systematic method of breaking down the current discrimination against African Americans and women." See "In Defense of Affirmative Action," in Steven M. Cahn (ed.), *The Affirmative Action Debate*, 2nd ed. (New York: Routledge, 2002), p. 148.

9   www.presidency.ucsb.edu/ws/?pid=27021.

10 Although the ruling applied directly to public institutions, it, in effect, held equally for private institutions as well, since nearly all of them are beneficiaries of federal funds which they risk losing if they defy such rulings. Thus, a private university can use practically any criteria it wants in admissions, but it does so at its own financial risk.

11 Jacques Steinberg, "Using Synonyms for Race, College Strives for Diversity," *The New York Times*, December 8, 2002.

12 Editorial Observer/Brent Staples, *The New York Times*, January 6, 2003.

13 Somewhat different characterizations of strong and weak affirmative action are given by Louis Pojman, "The Case against Affirmative Action," in James P. Sterba (ed.), *Morality in Practice*, 6th ed. (Belmont, CA: Wadsworth Publishing, 2001), p. 235. Sometimes strong affirmative action is defined as giving preference to minorities and women who are less qualified than those with whom they are competing. See Stephen Kershnar, "Strong Affirmative Action Programs at State Educational Institutions Cannot be Justified via Compensatory Justice," *Public Affairs Quarterly*, Vol. 11, No. 4, October 1997, 345–64.

14 Dalton Conley, *The New York Times*, February 15, 2003.

15 Malcolm Gladwell, *The Washington Post National Weekly Edition*, October 3–9, 1994.

16 *The New York Times*, July 13, 1994.

17 Frederick Douglass, Speech before the Massachusetts Anti-Slavery Society, Boston, April 1865. Not only was Douglass an abolitionist, he staunchly supported women's rights and spoke at the women's rights convention in Seneca Falls, New York, in 1848.

18 Coretta Scott King, *The New York Times*, November 3, 1996.

19 For discussions of closely related issues, see Mark van Roojen, "Affirmative Action, Non-consequentialism, and Responsibility for the Effects of Past Discrimination," *Public Affairs Quarterly*, Vol. 11, No. 3,

July 1997, 281–302; and George Sher, "Justifying Reverse Discrimination in Employment," *Philosophy & Public Affairs*, Vol. 4, No. 2, Winter 1975, 159–71.

20 George Will, Rochester *Democrat and Chronicle*, January 27, 2003.

21 Christina Hoff Sommers, *Christian Science Monitor*, May 6, 2002.

For more resources:

www.bloomsbury.com/holmes-introduction-to-applied-ethics

5

Sexual Harassment

I resent the women who bring sexual harassment suits and convince courts that we are as helpless and victimized as Melanie Wilkes in *Gone With the Wind*.

—Marianne M. Jennings[1]

In addition to being victims of the practice, working women have been subject to the social failure to recognize sexual harassment as an abuse at all. Tacitly, it has been both acceptable and taboo; acceptable for men to do, taboo for women to confront, even to themselves.

—Catherine A. MacKinnon[2]

Introduction

Sexual harassment is often confused with gender (or sex) harassment. It's also often confused with sexual misconduct in general and with sex discrimination. This is true of the legal treatment of sexual harassment as well. In this chapter we shall define "sexual harassment" and distinguish it from these other practices, and argue that it's wrong because it constitutes a violation of privacy. In so doing, we'll distinguish the different meanings the term has in social discourse. Finally, we shall give particular attention to the problem of sexual harassment in the university.

5.1 What is sexual harassment?

Virtually everyone agrees that sexual harassment is wrong. But, as with affirmative action, there is little agreement as to what precisely it is. Various definitions have been proposed. They include the following:

1. Sexual harassment, most broadly defined, refers to the unwanted imposition of sexual requirements in the context of a relationship of unequal power.[3]
2. Sexual harassment is the use of words, gestures, bodily actions or other means of verbal and nonverbal communication to insult, degrade, humiliate or otherwise dehumanize women.[4]
3. [S]exual harassment is defined as any action occurring within the workplace whereby women are treated as objects of the male sexual prerogative.[5]
4. Sexual harassment is best described as unsolicited nonreciprocal male behavior that asserts a woman's sex role over her function as worker.[6]
5. [Sexual harassment is] any form of sexual behavior by members of a dominant gender group towards members of a subordinate gender group whose typical effect is to cause members of the subordinate group to experience their powerlessness as a member of the group … In our society, it is men who are the dominant gender group, and so only men who can sexually harass.[7]
6. Unwelcome sexual advances, requests for sexual favors, and other verbal or physical conduct of a sexual nature constitute sexual harassment when (1) submission to such conduct is made either explicitly or implicitly a term or condition of an individual's employment, (2) submission to or rejection of such conduct by an individual issued as the basis for employment decisions affecting such individual, or (3) such conduct has the purpose or effect of unreasonably interfering with an individual's work performance or creating an intimidating, hostile, or offensive working environment.[8]
7. Sexual harassment ranges from sexual innuendo, to the creation of a hostile or intimidating environment, to coerced sexual relations. Examples of sexual harassment include:
   - sexually degrading words or gestures
   - offensive sexual graffiti, pictures, or cartoons
   - subtle pressure for sexual activity
   - leering or ogling
   - disparaging remarks to a person about his/her gender or clothing
   - unnecessary touching, patting, pinching, or brushing
   - stalking, telephone, and/or computer harassment
   - forced sexual contact including sexual assault, rape, or date rape[9]

Even a cursory review of such accounts reveals wide differences. Some (3, 4, 6) represent sexual harassment as occurring only in the workplace. Some (1, 5) represent it as occurring only in the context of unequal power. Some (2–5) view it as directed solely against women. Others (6, 7) don't say what sexual harassment is but instead give examples of what it supposedly is.

Unclarity about what sexual harassment is predictably results in confusion over which conduct constitutes sexual harassment. If sexual harassment is defined in such a way that it can occur only in the workplace, then a woman who experiences the identical behavior in some other setting has no recourse. Or if it is defined in such a way that only women can be victimized by it, then a man who experiences the same behavior that constitutes sexual harassment when directed against a woman has no grounds for complaint.

We shall take our clue from the English language. For anything to constitute sexual harassment, it must be *harassment*. What is harassment? According to the *Oxford English Dictionary*, to harass means: "To trouble or vex by repeated attacks." Harassment is repeated or persistent unwanted behavior. It can be directed against persons or groups because of race, ethnicity, religion, sex, physical appearance, sexual orientation, or virtually any other attributes. It can also be practiced by police, governments, and nations in a wide range of areas, including warfare. In all such cases it is *prima facie wrong* (see Theory Box 4A, Chapter 4, Section 4.7).

Sometimes it's maintained that harassment may consist of a single act, unrepeated.

Key Quote 5A

[S]ometimes people think that harassment has to be constant. It doesn't; it's a term of art in which once can be enough.[10]

This doesn't seem true. The offending behavior, to be sure, doesn't have to be constant, but it does have to be repeated. Otherwise a man who asked a woman out for a drink and was turned down because the request was unwanted would be guilty of sexual harassment even if he never repeated the request. Such a conclusion would trivialize sexual harassment and make sometime-harassers of virtually everyone.

A single instance of unwanted behavior may be wrong, but it doesn't constitute harassment; it must be repeated or persistent. Nor do actions that exceed a certain threshold of severity constitute harassment, even if they are repeated. The United States continually tracked and tried to sink German submarines during the Second World War. That was harassment. But the atomic bombing of Hiroshima wasn't harassment. It was of a different order of magnitude. In short, harassment is always a serious matter, but some harassment is more serious than others. Its seriousness depends in large part on the effect on the person or persons harassed. At one end of the scale, harassment may be no more than mildly bothersome; at the other end of the scale, it may be deeply upsetting or even traumatizing.

For conduct to constitute sexual harassment it must also be *sexual*. That means, at the minimum, showing sexual interest or having a sexual character. This, too, is denied by some accounts. It has been said, for example, that sexual harassment "is about male privilege and dominance, and it is not necessarily explicitly sexual: a woman carpenter on a job who is asked to clean the toilets and a wife who is hit by her husband because he doesn't like what she says are both experiencing sexual harassment."[11] Again, it has been said that in "the blue-collar work place there's often a real hostility to women. Men see women as invading a masculine environment. These are guys whose sexual harassment has nothing whatever to do with sex. They're trying to scare women off a male preserve."[12] Such accounts conflate sexual harassment with sex discrimination. The first quotation even conflates it with domestic violence. Whether sexual harassment is about male privilege and dominance we shall take up later. What seems clear (if we are to be guided by the English language) is that sexual harassment is not *by definition* about male privilege to the exclusion of sexual interest.

In light of these considerations, let us define "sexual harassment" as follows:

Definition Box 5A

Sexual Harassment: Repeated unwanted sexual attention.

"Unwanted" doesn't require that the behavior be harmful or even offensive, though sexual harassment is often that. It's enough that the person harassed doesn't like it and wants it stopped. Nor does it require that the behavior result in economic or social deprivation. Again, sexual harassment often does that, but it needn't. And sexual "attention" needn't always signify any expectation or even hope of sexual involvement with the person harassed. So-called street harassment—such as whistles by construction workers at women passers-by—isn't usually accompanied by such expectations. Nor need there be any intention on the part of the offender to harass. A person might not even know (at least for a time) that his behavior is unwanted; harassment might be the farthest thing from the mind of one whose lovestricken persistence alienates the object of his affections.

It's important that the adjective "sexual" be attached to "attention." Not every unwanted expression of friendly or even potentially romantic interest is sexual harassment. It's harassment if it persists, but it isn't *sexual* harassment. Suppose a man invites a woman to lunch to discuss their mutual interest in herbal medicine, and she doesn't care for his company and declines. If he repeatedly asks her to lunch and she continues to decline, he's harassing her, but it's not sexual harassment. There are many grounds other than sexual on which men and women interact. There are platonic (nonsexual) relationships between men and women as well as among gays and among lesbians. Not every unwelcome attempt to initiate such a relationship is sexual harassment.

One clear case of behavior that has been considered sexual harassment but doesn't depend upon the harasser having power over the victim is the sexual harassment of female physicians. Physicians typically are thought to have power over patients, who, at least in the medical setting, often feel vulnerable. Yet female physicians report sexual harassment at the hands of patients.

That victims of sexual harassment are almost always women shows that this is a society in which women generally lack power relative to men. For that reason, the discussion of sexual harassment in the context of the doctor-patient relationship has generally focused on the harassment of female patients by male doctors. Almost by definition, physicians hold a position of power and trust, which is accentuated by the patient's vulnerability.. . .

Female physicians share the power of their profession with their male counterparts, but they share with other women the vulnerability of their sex.. . .

More than three quarters of the women surveyed (77 percent, or 321 women) reported having been sexually harassed by a patient at least once during their career ... Among the common types of behavior thus reported were requests for genital examinations by patients

> who had no physical findings and displays of erections by patients before or during a physical examination. . . .
>
> The respondents indicated that they thought much abusive behavior results from the disinhibition associated with drug and alcohol use. Physicians reported being grabbed, fondled, and having their breasts brushed by intoxicated patients, particularly in emergency departments.[13]

Cases of this sort suggest that it's a mistake to assume that sexual harassment is always a case of a person in position of power harassing someone in a position of subordination. It's even more of a mistake to make such a relationship part of the definition of sexual harassment.

One borderline case concerns harassing behavior that has a sexual overlay but in fact expresses no sexual interest. A man might, for example, use sexual language solely for the purpose of demeaning women. Far from seeking any sexual involvement he may be deliberately distancing himself from them. Here the governing interest isn't sexual but, more likely, sexist or misogynistic. Such behavior is more accurately characterized as gender or sex harassment.

But some gender harassment has no sexual overtones to it. If a man in dealing with women calls them "broads" or refers to them as "ditsy," he's being disrespectful of them because of their gender. In doing so he may have no sexual interest in them and may not use sexual language in expressing himself. If the behavior is unwanted and repeated, that's enough for it to constitute harassment. But it's not enough for it to be sexual harassment. Matters are made confusing by the fact that people (as well as the media) often use the terms "sexual harassment" and "sex harassment" interchangeably. To try to minimize that confusion, we shall speak of *gender* harassment, which we may define as follows:

Definition Box 5B

Gender Harassment: Repeated unwanted behavior toward people because of their sex or gender.

Consider a case that made it to the courts:

To Eve Bruneau, entering sixth grade was like entering a different world: schoolboys she had played with at age 5, she said, now tormented her ... every day, boys in her class called her names, and they frequently shoved her, snapped her bra strap and spat on her, she said.

She said that her teacher and the school did nothing to stop the harassment. The teacher ... even made things worse, she said, by encouraging a "male-dominated" atmosphere in the classroom, decorating it like a hunting lodge, with deer antlers as coat hooks and gun magazines as reading material.

He segregated the class by sex for projects, she said, with girls working on environmental science and boys building six-foot rockets.

Miss Bruneau, now 14, says she is the victim of sexual harassment, and in the first such case in New York State, she is suing the South Kortright Central School District for monetary damages....

Miss Bruneau said the harassment left her depressed and made her grades suffer. Other girls had similar experiences, she said, but did not formally complain. But when a boy called her "ugly" and "dogfaced" and concluded with a profanity, Miss Bruneau sought help.[14]

The jury of six women and two men decided against the girl, Eve Bruneau, now 15 ... The jury foreman ... said afterward that jurors were sympathetic to the girl and that they agreed that the name calling and nasty tricks constituted some kind of harassment ... The lawyer for the district ... had argued that the boys who had tormented the girl were guilty of misbehavior, not sexual harassment.[15]

Whether or not one agrees with the verdict, this case brings out that not all harassment is sexual harassment. And though the article doesn't use the term "gender harassment," it's possible that the harassment the boys directed against the girl was because she was a girl and not because of sexual interest. Gender harassment can be as devastating as sexual harassment.

5.2 The potential for misunderstanding

Where conduct expresses sexual and/or romantic interest the matter is often complicated. Behavior that constitutes harassment is usually unwanted whenever it occurs. This is true, say, of racial, ethnic, or religious harassment. It is not as though some people feel bothered, demeaned, or frightened by repeated racial, ethnic, or religious abuse and others welcome it. Some of the behavior that constitutes sexual harassment, however, is sometimes welcomed. In fact, it's often encouraged and reciprocated. As a popular commentator on such matters writes:

Key Quote 5B

Courtship is best conducted, and romantic interest indicated … by hints, suggestions and little actions … That is why we have always had the gestures of interest—the lingering look, the hand laid on the other person's arm, the brushing together too often for it to seem an accident.[16]

This creates considerable potential for misunderstanding. Attention that's welcome from one person may be unwelcome from another. The lingering look may be perceived as a leer, the suggestion as an innuendo. And behavior that's acceptable in one context may be inappropriate in another. Inquiries about personal life that are the norm in a singles bar are out of place in a professor's office or a physician's examining room. And behavior that's acceptable in one culture may not be so in another. Accordingly, it has been said that "[t]here is so much variation in human behavior across cultures that behavior which may be sexual harassment in one need not be in another."[17]

So, while some behavior is harassing whomever it's directed against, much of the behavior that constitutes sexual harassment is not. Whether it's sexual is relative to the person engaging in the behavior; whether it's harassing is relative to the person affected (and sometimes to the broader social and cultural context). This means that whether an act is a case of sexual harassment can't be determined from an evaluatively neutral description of the behavior alone. It requires consideration of context. One must know the governing interest of the behavior and how it's received.

But it should be stressed that harassment isn't necessarily less serious just because it isn't *sexual* harassment or because it may be misperceived as sexual harassment when it's not.

Consider the following four situations:

I. A shows sexual interest in B.
1. A's attention is unwanted by B.
2. A knows the attention is unwanted by B.
3. A persists in the attention.

II. A shows sexual interest in B.
1. A's attention is unwanted by B.
2. A mistakenly thinks the attention is welcome.
3. A persists in the attention.

Case I is a clear case of sexual harassment. The governing interest is sexual and the unwanted behavior is repeated. Case II is still sexual harassment, even though A doesn't know that the behavior is unwelcome. This suggests that one can harass another person without intending to do so and even (as atypical as this may be) without knowing that one is doing so.

III. A shows friendly interest in B.
1. A's attention is unwanted by B.
2. B mistakenly thinks A's interest is sexual.
3. A persists in the attention.

Here the behavior isn't *sexual* harassment because it lacks the requisite sexual interest on A's part. But it's harassment. And it may—depending upon the circumstances—mistakenly be perceived by B as sexual harassment.

IV. A shows sexual interest in B.
1. A's attention is welcomed by B.
2. A knows the attention is welcome.
3. A persists in the attention.

Case IV is clearly not a case of sexual harassment, even though the behavior exhibited by A may be identical to the behavior exhibited by A in Case I. These examples suggest that to identify behavior as sexual harassment requires knowing something about the person engaging in the behavior, namely, what that person's governing interest is, and knowing something about the person experiencing the behavior, namely, whether the person finds it welcome or not.

We should now note that the A in the examples may be a man and B a woman or vice versa. Or A and B may both be women or both men. It's the nature of the interest, whether it's sexual or not, and how it's received, whether it's unwanted or not, that determines whether the conduct is sexual harassment, not the gender of the persons involved. That the most blatant cases of sexual harassment are those of men against women, and that some of the most damaging of such cases occur in the workplace doesn't make those aspects of sexual harassment part of its definition.

If the preceding is correct, sexual harassment doesn't, by definition, occur only in the context of unequal power; it isn't confined to the workplace; it doesn't extend to offensive nonsexual behavior; and it isn't experienced only by women.

5.3 Kinds of sexual harassment

To the extent there's confusion about what sexual harassment is there will likely be disagreement about why it's wrong. Often it's said to be wrong for one reason only, such as that it represents sex discrimination or is an expression of sexism (specifically, of the domination of women by men), or both. But this oversimplifies. Various considerations contribute to its wrongness, depending upon context.

Although our interest is primarily with the moral issues surrounding sexual harassment, evolving case law is instructive here. Title VII of the Civil Rights Act of 1964 (henceforth simply "Title VII") prohibits sex discrimination in the workplace (along with discrimination on the basis of race, religion, ethnicity, etc., as we have seen in Chapter 1). This prohibition was extended to educational institutions in Title IX of the 1972 Education Amendment.[18]

There have come to be recognized two principal kinds of sexual harassment actionable under these titles: (1) *quid pro quo harassment*, in which some job disadvantage (or the withholding of some benefit) is threatened for failure to comply with sexual overtures; and (2) *hostile environment harassment*, in which it is recognized that sexual harassment may create a hostile environment without necessarily resulting in any demonstrable job detriment.

In quid pro quo harassment one thing is offered for another. Thus if a job (or retention of a job or a raise in pay) is offered in exchange for sex, that's quid pro quo harassment. Or the proposed transaction might take the form of one thing (sex) being offered in exchange for a benefit (say, a raise), though here there's lacking the clear coercive character of the first case. Again, these cases would strictly constitute harassment only if the offers were unwanted and repeated.

So-called hostile environment harassment encompasses two kinds of cases. In one sort of case, sexual harassment itself *creates* a hostile environment. If, for example, a woman suffers sexual harassment at the hands of fellow workers, that may make the work environment an inhospitable place for her—a "hostile" environment—even if none of the workers has any authority over her. Quid pro quo harassment typically presupposes a power differential between the harasser and the harassed, as between a boss and a secretary. *Peer harassment* makes no such presupposition. It occurs between individuals, neither of whom has authority over the other. But an environment might be sexually inhospitable even to one who isn't targeted for sexual harassment. If a woman sees other women around her being sexually harassed, that may be sufficiently troubling to her as to make the work environment a "hostile" one for her, even if she isn't harassed herself. In these cases, sexual harassment creates the hostile environment.

In the other sort of case, a hostile environment is itself said to *constitute* sexual harassment. Consider the following two cases:

At a private university in the Northeast, in a library reading room frequented by students, is large painting … depicting an urban newsstand. One can see the cover of various publications, including Hustler and similar magazines.

A sophomore woman complains to the dean's office. She says the painting creates a hostile environment, promotes the degradation of women by portraying them as sex objects, and is antithetical to the school's sexual harassment policy. She wants the painting removed.[19]

* * *

Embarrassed? Scared? Don't think it really happened? Don't want to believe that it did. Whether you realize it or not, you may have been sexually harassed. It can happen anywhere, even in a place where you feel completely safe, such as [the] … Library.

According to [the] … director of … Security, sexual harassment occurs in the stacks of [the library] … in many forms. Most sexual harassment in the stacks seems to take the form of someone writing degrading messages or drawing lewd pictures on a desk, lingering in an area seemingly without reason, exposing himself or masturbating in the public areas. There is rarely contact between the perpetrator and victim.[20]

In the first case it isn't the actions of a particular individual that's said to constitute sexual harassment; it's a *state of affairs*—an environment that contains pictures or writing that one finds offensive. No one in particular is targeted. The person claiming sexual harassment might not even know, or be known by, those responsible for the painting. The same with regard to the graffiti in the second case. Only with regard to the exhibitionists in the second case is a specific individual directly responsible at the time the harassment allegedly occurs.

But sometimes the alleged offender and accuser are known to one another, and it's a specific act of the alleged offender that is said to create the hostile environment. Consider the following:

> As the religion professor delivers a lecture to his students at the Chicago Theological Seminary, a school official sits nearby with a tape recorder, a kind of word cop, in case the professor says anything sexually offensive.
>
> The 63-year-old professor … is being monitored after a sexual harassment ruling in a case that many scholars say illustrates the Orwellian consequences of stringent codes intended to enforce political and moral rectitude on campuses.
>
> In a discussion of the role of intent in sin, Professor Snyder recited a story from the Talmud, the writings that make up Jewish civil and religious law, about a man who falls off a roof, lands on a woman and accidentally has intercourse with her. The Talmud says he is innocent of sin, since the act was unintentional.
>
> A woman in the class was offended, not by the sexual theme but because she believed the story justified brutality toward women. She filed a complaint against Professor Snyder, an ordained minister who has used the Talmudic lesson in the classroom for more than 30 years.
>
> The university issued a formal reprimand and put notices in the mailboxes of every student and teacher at the school, telling them that Dr. Snyder had "engaged in verbal conduct of a sexual nature" that had the effect of "creating an intimidating, hostile or offensive" environment.[21]

Both quid pro quo harassment and hostile environment harassment were recognized by the Supreme Court in 1986. Both apply to colleges and universities as well as the workplace. Indeed, it has been alleged that the creation of a hostile academic environment "is the most widespread form of sexual harassment in the classroom."

A common view is that sexual harassment is sex discrimination and prohibited because sex discrimination is prohibited. This is suggested by the following passage quoting a lawyer for the Equal Employment Opportunity Commission (EEOC): " 'Even if an employer doesn't harass all women,' says a commission [EEOC] lawyer, 'if he harasses one woman sexually, he does so because she is a woman ... So the EEOC considers sexual harassment to be sex-based discrimination covered by Title VII.' "

5.4 Sexual harassment and sex discrimination

Is this correct that sexual harassment is sex discrimination? To evaluate this claim, it's important to note that Title VII of the Civil Rights Act of 1964 (see Section 4.2) protects *groups* defined by race, religion, sex, and so on. Thus, if one suffers discrimination in employment or education because of one's race—that is, simply because of one's membership in a racially defined group—that constitutes racial discrimination. If one suffers discrimination because of membership in a group defined by sex, that's sex discrimination.

This suggests a possible defense against the claim that sexual harassment is discrimination. It consists of arguing that if the alleged conduct wasn't directed against a protected group defined by sex (say, women as a group), then though it may have been sexual harassment, it wasn't discrimination. Rosemarie Tong summarizes the reasoning as follows:

> Since there is no sex discrimination unless a plaintiff can show that her personal injury contains a sufficient gender referent, a red-headed, large-breasted, sexually harassed woman employee must be able to explain why her employer has not harassed similarly situated blond, flat-chested women, if all he was interested in was *a woman* and not a specific kind of woman with red hair and large breasts. Supposedly, if she cannot explain this, she does not have cause to invoke Title VII.[22]

To this Tong observes: "But all this seems rather ludicrous. The sexually harassed red-haired or large-breasted woman does have an explanation for her employer's conduct: he would not be sexually harassing her were she a man or were she her employer's boss."

Elaborating this line of reasoning still further (but in connection with hostile environment claims), Anja Angelica Chan writes: "To satisfy this element of a hostile environment claims [that harassment be based on sex] a plaintiff must prove ... that she was harassed *because of* her gender. This element essentially requires the plaintiff to show that she would not have been subjected to harassment, or would not have experienced the conduct as offensive, *but for* the fact that she is a woman."[23] This reasoning applies to Title IX as well, hence to sexual harassment in educational institutions.

If one was harassed *because* she's a woman (i.e., her being a member of that group sufficed to make her a target), then her harassment was a case of sex discrimination. To establish that one has been harassed because she's a woman, it might seem enough to show (as Chan argues) that a woman who's been sexually harassed wouldn't have been harassed *but for* the fact she's a woman. Since this would seem to be true of virtually all cases of sexual harassment of women (except by bisexuals, where a woman might have been harassed even if she had been a man), sexual harassment of women would appear to be sex discrimination. Similarly, if to show that a man wouldn't have been sexually harassed but for the fact he's a man were sufficient to show that he was harassed because he was a man, that would show that sexual harassment of men is sex discrimination as well.

But on closer examination this reasoning is flawed. To see why, let us start at the beginning with the apparent reasoning underlying Title VII. Though Title VII protects men as well as women, since the preponderance of sexual harassment is against women, I shall frame the argument in those terms. The implicit reasoning in Title VII is as follows:

1. Sex is a protected category.

Therefore,

2. Discrimination based upon sex (i.e., sex discrimination) is prohibited.
3. Sexual harassment of women (other than by bisexuals) is discrimination based upon sex.

Therefore:

4. Sexual harassment of women is prohibited.

The question is whether this is a good argument. First we need to explain what a sound argument is.

Theory Box 5A

Valid and Sound Arguments

An argument is a set of propositions, one of which, the **conclusion**, is supported by the others, the **premises**. The following is an argument:

1. All dogs are animals.
2. Beagles are dogs.
3. Therefore: Beagles are animals.

The supporting propositions (1) and (2) are **premises**, (3) the **conclusion**.

A **valid argument** is one in which it's impossible for the premises to be true and the conclusion to be false; that is, if the premises are true, the conclusion *must* be true. If it's true that all dogs are animals and that beagles are dogs, it must be true that beagles are animals. So, the above is a valid argument.

A **sound argument** is a valid argument whose premises are true. It's true that all dogs are animals and that beagles are dogs. Therefore the above is a sound argument. A sound argument demonstrates the truth of its conclusion.

An argument needn't be sound to be a good argument. A sound argument is a valid argument, but there are few strictly valid arguments outside of philosophical and logical contexts. A good argument is one which, if it isn't sound, could readily be recast as a sound argument; that is, could be recast as a valid argument with true premises. Since a sound argument has true premises, and truth in many areas is a matter of probability, we may say further that an argument is a good argument if it's valid or can be shown to be valid and its premises can be judged to be true with a high degree of probability.

In light of this, let's examine the above argument regarding sexual harassment more closely. Actually, the above propositions constitute two arguments. (1) and (2) represent an argument, with (1) being the sole explicit premise and (2) being the conclusion. (2), (3), and (4) represent a second argument, with (2) and (3) being the premises and (4) the conclusion.

The first argument is unproblematic. Premise (1) is true by virtue of the provisions of the Civil Rights Act of 1964. If those provisions were made explicit and included as premises, it could be seen that the argument is valid and sound, and hence that its conclusion, (2), is true.

The second argument is also valid. If sex discrimination against women is prohibited, and sexual harassment of women is sex discrimination, then it must be true that sexual harassment of women is prohibited. Since premise (2) is true, the soundness of the argument depends upon whether premise (3) is true.

As best one can tell, the reasoning to establish (3) proceeds from premise (2) as follows:

2a. Whenever a woman is sexually harassed (other than by a bisexual), it's the case that she wouldn't have been harassed *but for* the fact she's a woman.
b. If one wouldn't have been sexually harassed *but for* the fact she's a woman, then she's been discriminated against *because* she's a woman.
c. If one is discriminated against *because* she's a woman, then that discrimination is based upon sex.

Therefore:

4. Sexual harassment of women (other than by bisexuals) is discrimination based upon sex (i.e., sex discrimination).

Premise (2b), however, is false, or at least can't be assumed to be true. 2b is a conditional proposition or statement.

Theory Box 5B

Conditional Propositions
A conditional proposition is an if-then compound of two propositions. An example would be: If Socrates is a man, then he is mortal.

The proposition following the "if" is the **antecedent**, the proposition following the "then," the **consequent**. A conditional proposition is often called a "conditional" for short.

If we separate the antecedent and the consequent of (2b), it can be seen to legitimize inferences of the following sort:

2b(i) (If) A would not have been *sexually harassed* but for the fact that she's a woman.

Therefore,

2b(ii)   (then) A has been *discriminated against* because she's a woman.

But such an inference would entail that a lesbian who sexually harassed another woman would be guilty of discriminating against women—not a logical impossibility, perhaps, but sufficiently odd to render the inference suspect. (2b) *presupposes* the very link between sexual harassment and sex discrimination that's at issue; hence it cannot—without independent support—be used to warrant that conclusion. That such support is unlikely to be forthcoming can be seen from the fact that 2b(i) doesn't even warrant an inference to

2b(i)' A has been sexually harassed *because* she is a woman,

and even less does it warrant an inference to 2b(ii). That is, the fact that a woman wouldn't have been sexually harassed but for the fact she's a woman doesn't even entail that she was sexually harassed *because* she's a woman, much less that she was *discriminated against* because she's a woman.

That a woman wouldn't have been harassed but for the fact she's a woman means only that her being a woman was a necessary condition of her being harassed. That she was harassed because she was a woman means her being a woman was a sufficient condition of her being harassed; that's the reason why she was harassed. And the second claim doesn't follow from the first. It implies, as the first does not, that, all things being equal, *any* person having the properties of a woman would also be harassed. The unsoundness of the inference can be seen from the fact that in any case in which one wouldn't have been sexually harassed but for the fact she's a woman, it will also be true that she wouldn't have been harassed but for the fact she's a human being. But it wouldn't follow from this that she was sexually harassed because she's a human being, which would make such harassment discrimination against humans.

If this is correct, it means that the argument under consideration isn't a good argument. Although the argument is valid, it isn't sound. Premise (3) is false (or at least hasn't been shown to be true). Sexual harassment per se isn't sex discrimination.[24] That, in turn, means that sexual harassment in general hasn't been shown to be prohibited by virtue of being sex discrimination. The standard view of sexual harassment as sex discrimination—even in legal cases—is mistaken. This, it should be emphasized, doesn't mean that sexual harassment is less serious than sex discrimination. It simply means that its wrongness isn't grounded in discrimination.

5.5 Sexual harassment and sexism

There is another outlook, however, that constitutes a challenge to the above conclusion. It views sexual harassment as wrong by virtue of being a manifestation of sexism, which might be true even if the reasoning considered in the previous section is faulty. It is suggested by the following three passages:

> Sexual harassment is an expression of sexism which reflects and reinforces the unequal power that exists between men and women in our patriarchal society. It's a part of a pattern of male-female interaction in which men routinely express their dominance over women.[25]
>
> * * *
>
> To be precise: "Economic power is to sexual harassment as physical force is to rape." And regarding Title IX, intellectual power is to gender harassment on the campus as economic power is to gender or sexual harassment in the workplace as physical force is to rape anywhere. Rape and harassment are abuses of power as well as expressions of male sexuality. The power that makes rape or harassment effective derives from the superior position that the rapist or harasser holds by virtue of his social position.[26]
>
> * * *
>
> Racial and sexual harassment, separately and together, promote inequality, violate oppressed groups, work to destroy their social standing and repute, and target them for discrimination from contempt to genocide ... They are no different in the severity of impact on victims or in the degree of damage they inflict on equality rights.[27]

In this view, sexual harassment isn't, as in our proposed definition, essentially a matter of sexuality. It is largely, or even in some views, exclusively, a matter of power; specifically, men's power over women in a sexist culture; a means (along with rape and pornography) by which men dominate women. As such, sexual harassment in its very nature is an expression of sexism. Since sex discrimination is inherent in the idea of sexism, sexual harassment, by virtue of that fact, is a form of sex discrimination. We might represent this reasoning as follows:

1. Sexual harassment is an expression of sexism.
2. Sexism by its nature entails sex discrimination.

Therefore,

3. Sexual harassment entails sex discrimination.

It's a mistake, in this view, to think of sexual harassment in terms of the behavior of this or that individual toward other individuals. It's a form of group oppression in which males collectively dominate females.

Premise (2) in this reasoning we may take to be true. Recall that in Chapter 2 (2.2) we defined "primary sexism" as the beliefs, attitudes, and practices of sexists. What a sexist is, we saw, could be defined in different ways, but a full-blown conception of a sexist we defined as: one who practices sex discrimination in the belief (a) that one sex is innately superior to the other, and (b) that the superior sex ought to dominate the inferior. Since sex discrimination is one of the hallmarks of sexism, we may assume (2) to be true.

The question is whether (1) is true. In Sections 5.1 and 5.4 we have argued that sexual harassment is not *by definition* sex discrimination. It might nonetheless *in fact* be sex discrimination. To illustrate the point, chess can be defined as: "a game of ancient origin for two played on a chessboard in which each player moves his chessmen according to fixed types of movements for each," etc. (*Webster's Third International Dictionary*). It's no part of the definition of chess that playing it is time-consuming. But *in fact* playing chess ("speed chess" aside) is time-consuming. Objects, events, and actions always have properties over and above those that define them. In more philosophical terms, as noted in Chapter 1 (Theory Box 1C, Section 1.6), things have accidental as well as essential properties.

Now, while sexual harassment can be practiced by sexists, it needn't be; nor need its practice be limited to sexists. Sexual harassment, recall, is repeated unwanted sexual attention. This can be shown by anyone, male or female, either toward members of the opposite sex or (in the case of gays and lesbians) toward members of the same sex. This doesn't preclude that those who engage in sexual harassment may be sexists; it simply leaves it open whether they are.

By the same token, just as those who engage in sexual harassment may, but need not, be sexists, sexists may, but need not, practice sexual harassment.

A man might believe that males are superior to females and yet not engage in sexual harassment. One stereotype of the sexist is a man who puts women "on a pedestal," treating them as delicate creatures who need to be cherished and cared for. It might be antithetical to his view of the proper relations between men and women that men should sexually harass women.

Nonetheless, sexual harassment might contribute to sex discrimination even when it's not (in individual cases) an instance of sex discrimination; that is, when its practitioners don't target all women but only those they find sexually attractive. In other words, sexual harassment could conceivably be so pervasive in some situations (say, in a particular workplace or classroom), and have such prejudicial effects, that even women who aren't themselves targeted by it are disadvantaged. The distress it might cause just by witnessing it could create a hostile environment for virtually all women in that context. It's arguable that this is true of women being molested in crowded areas, such as subways or trains, as the following article details:

On Tokyo's Packed Trains, Molesters Are Brazen

Kawasaki, Japan—Every morning, millions of Japanese brace for the ugly commuting hurly-burly: the train ride … "When men and women are packed together, squeezed onto a train, I think everybody has some kind of desire to touch someone else's body," said Mr Yamamoto, who says he belongs to a small clandestine, loosely organized molesters' group that meets occasionally to share tips and experiences. "If some were molesting on a train elsewhere in the world, they'd be accused of sexual harassment. It's unique to Japan that people put up with this."… It's the same throughout the Tokyo region … as nearly 15 million passengers shuffle through each day. And during the busy moments of pedestrian traffic, molesters, drunkards and pickpockets … often ruin a subway rider's underground experience … It is common for Japanese women to say they have been groped at least once on the trains, and molesting seems far more widespread in Tokyo than in New York.[28]

It should be noted that some locales in Japan began running women-only trains in 2001, and a number of other countries do the same. The point, however, is that sexual harassment, when it rises to the level of a social practice, if only in specific contexts, can have discriminatory effects even if the motivation behind the individual acts that constitute the practice may be sexual and have little to do with discrimination. A practice, in other words, may have a character that differs from that of the individual acts that make it up.

If this is correct, it would be too strong to say that sexual harassment by its nature entails sex discrimination, as premise (2) does. But a weaker claim might be true. That claim would be that pervasive, ongoing sexual harassment as a social practice could so disadvantage women as to constitute sex discrimination. Whether that is so would then be a factual issue, dependent upon the extent of sexual harassment and its effect upon all members of the sex against which it's primarily directed.

5.6 Sexual harassment, sexual misbehavior, and gender harassment

Before proceeding it will be useful to summarize the main conceptions of what sexual harassment is and their relationships to one another. The definition I have proposed holds that sexual harassment is any repeated unwanted sexual attention. But often sexual harassment is identified with virtually any sexual wrongdoing, including rape and assault, without regard to whether it constitutes harassment. From some of the examples we saw in Section 5.3, it's also clear that sexual harassment is sometimes used to stand, not only for actions and practices, but for states of affairs (such as a library reading room) containing sexual aspects to which some people take offense. And sexual harassment is sometimes taken more broadly still to extend to wrongdoing directed against groups defined by sex or gender as well as to environments that are hostile to members of specified groups. For ease of reference, let's gather these together:

Definition Box 5C

Definitions of Sexual Harassment

Sexual Harassment$_1$: Repeated unwanted sexual attention.
Sexual Harassment$_2$: Any sexual wrongdoing.
Sexual Harassment$_3$: 1. Any sexual wrongdoing and/or,

2. Any sexually hostile environment.
Sexual Harassment$_4$: 1. Any sexual wrongdoing and/or,

> 2. Any sexually hostile environment, and/or
> 3. Any gender (or sex) harassment, wrong-doing against or creation of a gender-hostile environment.

This helps to underscore the confusion in much of the discussion of sexual harassment. Some people take it broadly to stand for virtually any sexual wrongdoing, including violent crimes like rape, as well as any forms of gender harassment or discrimination. According to some of these accounts, sexual harassment has nothing to do with sex. Other accounts, as we have seen, say that a single occurrence of offending behavior constitutes sexual harassment. They are saying, in effect, that sexual harassment need have nothing to do with harassment.

The proposed definition of this text takes its clue from the meanings of the terms involved, and defines sexual harassment in such a way that it is harassment and must have a sexual component to it. This way of understanding sexual harassment distinguishes it from sexual violence, like rape and assault, as well as from states of affairs such as sexually hostile environments. According to *sexual harassment*$_1$, sexual harassment may *create* a hostile environment and undoubtedly often does. But this represents a causal connection between sexual harassment and the context in which it takes place. It presupposes that the behavior and the environment are two different things and should not be confused with one another.

5.7 Sexual harassment and privacy

Whether or not sexual harassment can be shown to be wrong by virtue of being sex discrimination, it can be seen to be wrong on the grounds that it violates privacy. Privacy (as we shall see in Chapter 11) is freedom from intrusion into areas of one's life that one hasn't explicitly or implicitly opened to others. Sexual harassment, by virtue of its sexual character and the fact that it is unwanted, is always such an intrusion. This makes it presumptively wrong, and virtually always actually wrong as well. If widely and systematically practiced (as it clearly is in some cultures, though not in all), it may also be associated with overt or covert sexism and contributory to sex discrimination as well. But even if it doesn't express sexism and contribute to sex discrimination, the fact that it violates privacy suffices to establish its presumptive wrongness.

5.8 Sexual harassment and the university

Much of the attention with regard to sexual harassment has shifted from the workplace to educational settings, particularly colleges and universities. The tendency has been to extend to the university the same thinking—largely imported from the law—that has come to govern the workplace. This is in keeping with a growing tendency to view universities on an economic model, where students pay, and faculty deliver a commodity called education. But learning isn't a commercial product, and education isn't the delivery of a product. Education is the encouragement of learning. The aim of colleges and universities should be to foster the conditions under which that can best take place.

Besides being an invasion of privacy and often harmful to those victimized by it, sexual harassment in a college or university is wrong because the harassment of any person or group for *any* reason—sexual, religious, ethnic, racial, and so on—jeopardizes the conditions under which learning can take place. This is true whether the harassment be peer harassment (say, of students by other students) or quid pro quo harassment (say, of students by professors). It should, if only for that reason, not be engaged in. But there are other reasons why sexual harassment is wrong in the university.

Sexual harassment of a student by a professor is a betrayal of trust on the part of the professor. A community of learning, unlike the workplace, isn't—or ought not to be—governed by economic motives, in which a pervasive quid pro quo set of values obtain. In the workplace, the employer often tries to extract the best from his employees, not because it is to their benefit to do so, but because it profits him. In the university, the central concern should be the enrichment and empowerment of the learner to continue the process of intellectual growth in the ways he or she personally deems best. This requires confidence on the part of students that professors—their guides in this enterprise—won't exploit the trust placed in them for their own ends. To harass a student in any way, including sexually, is to violate that trust.

The university setting, of course, is a minefield of potential problems in honoring this trust. In this respect it differs from most workplaces. The vast majority of students are young, single, and (many of them) sexually active; facts that create both opportunities and temptations for amorous relations between professors and students. These cannot all be dismissed as cases of lecherous 50-year-old male professors and 18-year-old ingénues. There are also worldly 22-year-old women and 28-year-old assistant professors (or occasionally professors and graduate students of roughly the same age). And these cases are more difficult. While some analyses of sexual harassment start from the assumption that all intimate relations between professors and students should be prohibited—and that even consensual relations constitute misconduct—that is a separate issue and would need consideration on its own. There have been some happy marriages of students and professors. Persons on both sides of that issue could be in agreement on sexual harassment and the reasons for its wrongness, and for that reason we won't take up that issue.

For better or worse, romantic and sometimes consensual sexual relationships develop within the university community. They occur between undergraduates and undergraduates, graduate students and undergraduates, faculty and graduate students, secretaries and students, faculty and secretaries, librarians and faculty, faculty and faculty, and sometimes between faculty and undergraduates. They have even been known to occur among administrators. This isn't to say that any or all of these are advisable or conscionable. Only that they occur and almost certainly will continue to do so. Sometimes they even result in marriages—occasionally even good ones. It's not unreasonable to assume that most of them begin with signals and subtle forms of behavior of the sorts referred to in Section 5.2, and only later grow into more assertive and declaratory behavior. This means that the possibilities for misunderstanding abound. It also means that the possibilities for intimidation and coercion abound. Faculty should be particularly mindful of this when dealing with students, and graduate students (in their capacity as teaching assistants) should be mindful of it in their dealing with undergraduates.

In any event, much of the sexual harassment in the university occurs among peers—among students, among professors, or among staff. Where there is no differential in power or authority, this constitutes *peer harassment* and normally doesn't fit the model of quid pro quo harassment. This doesn't, however, affect its wrongness. For peer harassment is still an invasion of privacy and still jeopardizes the conditions under which learning can best take place.

Peer harassment does, however, focus the issue of the responsibilities and obligations of a university. For it raises the question of the extent to which the university should monitor the nonacademic behavior of students. At a time when universities have moved away from the conception of the university as in loco parentis (surrogate parents), they must reconsider whether, or to what extent, they are to resume or expand that role—a decision complicated by the fact that threat of lawsuits under Federal law may be a severe constraint upon them.

Students are nearly all over eighteen, and many of them, especially graduate students, are over twenty-two as well. All things being equal, how they live and conduct their personal affairs is their business. While individual faculty members may be sought out for advice or counsel concerning various personal problems, the university doesn't routinely involve itself in such matters, and probably shouldn't (other than by providing counselors if students choose to go to them). If two students develop a relationship that turns sour, and one of them pursues the other (say, by phoning at all hours or appearing unexpectedly at the door pleading for one more chance), that's clearly harassment, arguably even sexual harassment. But it's the kind of problem that adults are normally expected to cope with on their own.

When, however, harassment occurs in the setting provided for learning and the conducting of affairs relating thereto (such as in the classroom or the library or around a department), and/or when it interferes with the ability of the person harassed to function comfortably and effectively in that setting, it becomes a proper concern of the university. Steps should then be taken to see that it stops, and that it's understood by the offender (and others, if necessary) why it's wrong. What exactly these steps should be may vary from case to case. Where possible, it is probably best if the matter is resolved directly between the parties (say, by discussion, or if that isn't feasible, by a letter from the person harassed to the harasser detailing what behavior is objectionable and asking that it cease; or through the mediation of a third person, perhaps a fellow student or faculty member). Victims of harassment may, however, feel unable to cope with the situation on their own, in which case the university should become directly involved. And if it should be unable to handle the situation informally, it should then proceed to implement fair and impartial judicial proceedings, followed by sanctions when warranted. That is, the goodwill and mutual respect of all members of the university community are best presumed until shown not to obtain; and it is best that the least damaging steps (to both parties) be taken that are consistent with a prompt and satisfactory resolution of the problem.

The preceding applies to cases in which sexual harassment has occurred and is known to have occurred. In those cases there's a victim and a perpetrator. Often these conditions aren't met. There may be cases in which it's alleged to have occurred but hasn't, or in which it has occurred but no one but the principals involved knows it. In those cases, all one can objectively say is that there's an accuser and an accused. Allowing for extraordinary cases of miscommunication in which an offender doesn't realize that his behavior is unwanted, there may even be cases in which the victim is the only one who knows it has occurred. The problems then are compounded further. To handle all of them adequately would require shifting from the God's-eye point of view of the preceding (where, *ex hypothesi*, one person is known to be victim, the other victimizer) to the point of view of third parties trying to adjudicate conflicting claims, often without benefit of adequate evidence.[29]

If sexual harassment is alleged but denied by the person alleged to have done the harassing, then one cannot properly speak of a victim and a perpetrator but only of an accuser and the accused. If there are witnesses and supporting evidence, the university can assess testimony and evidence and reach the conclusion to which they point. If there are no witnesses and no independent evidence, it may be confronted with nothing more than the conflicting testimony of two equally respected students. Short of looking deep into their eyes as they tell their respective stories, there may be no way of knowing precisely what the truth is. And if that's unavailing, and if students, like everyone else, should be presumed innocent unless proven guilty, there may be no recourse but to suspend judgment. That may sometimes mean that a guilty person goes scot-free, in which case of victim of sexual harassment will undergo the added distress of seeing a miscarriage of justice. But it may also mean that an innocent person wrongfully accused isn't himself victimized. Which of these is the case the university may be unable to tell.

Be that as it may, a university can nonetheless take steps to see that the chances of a recurrence of whatever it was that led to the initial accusation are minimized. That is, even if it not should be possible to make a finding with regard to the truth or falsity of the charges, it's possible to safeguard the well-being of the accuser in the event the charges are in fact (though not known to be) true. With a little good sense, it should be possible to do this in ways that aren't detrimental to the accused if the accused should in fact be (though not known to be) innocent. And it's important to do that as well. In short, a university's concern should extend equally to all of its students. It's important that victims of sexual harassment not be doubly victimized by being made to feel guilty about having sought help, or, worse yet, by being made to feel that they themselves are to blame. It's also important that innocent persons wrongly accused not be unjustly stigmatized as offenders.

There probably aren't any rules that are very helpful in this regard, as the whole matter is a case of highly imperfect procedural justice.

5.9 Conclusion

The best safeguard against sexual harassment even occurring in the first place, or if it does occur, against its leading to unnecessarily harmful consequences, is to educate both students and faculty (and staff) about what sexual harassment is and why it's wrong, and to foster a sense of community in which friendship, trust, caring, and mutual respect enable everyone to flourish in as relaxed and supportive an environment as possible. In the university, faculty in particular can help to do this. They can be open and available as friends and counselors or mediators when problems arise. And they can promote understanding and reconciliation when conflicts occur. But it's something for which everyone shares responsibility. Students can foster these conditions as well. They can help create a climate in which problems like sexual harassment don't arise, or if they do arise, are handled in ways that don't leave any of the persons involved feeling isolated and adrift. In short, the goodwill that a sense of community can generate, through women and men working cooperatively on an equal and respectful basis, is more likely in the long run to be effective in ending sexual harassment than threats and punishment.

Study questions

1. How does the text define *sexual harassment* (Definition Box 5A)? How does sexual harassment differ from *gender (or sex) harassment* (Definition Box 5B)?
2. What are the differences among *peer harassment, quid pro quo harassment* and *hostile environment harassment* (Section 5.3)?
3. What is a *valid argument*? What is a *sound argument* (Theory Box 5A)?
4. How does *sexual harassment* differ from *sex discrimination* (Section 5.4)?
5. What differences are there between *sexual harassment* and *sexism* (Section 5.5)?
6. The following are often confused with one another: *sexual harassment, sexual misbehavior*, and *gender harassment*. How does the text distinguish among them (Section 5.6)?

7. What are some of the different ways sexual harassment is understood (see Definition Box 5C)?
8. In what way might sexual harassment be thought to involve a *violation of privacy* (Section 5.7)?
9. In what ways does *sexual harassment in a college or university* setting raise issues that differ from those raised by *sexual harassment in the workplace* (Section 5.8)?
10. What does it mean for a college or university to play the role of *in loco parentis*?

Notes

1   Marianne M. Jennings, "The Extent of Sexual Harassment Is Exaggerated," in Louise I. Gerdes (ed.), *Sexual Harassment* (San Diego, CA: Greenhaven Press, 1999), p. 50.
2   Catherine A. MacKinnon, *Sexual Harassment of Working Women: A Case of Sex Discrimination* (New Haven: Yale University Press, 1979), p. 1.
3   Ibid.
4   A definition of the DC Rape Crisis Center, as found in Martha J. Langelan, *Back Off! How to Confront and Stop Sexual Harassment and Harassers* (New York: Simon & Schuster, 1993), p. 32.
5   Equal Employment Opportunity Commission (EEOC) Guidelines on Discrimination Because of Sex, 29, C.F.R. 1604.11.
6   Lin Farley, "Sexual Shakedown: The Sexual Harassment of Women on the Job," in Linda LeMoncheck and James Sterba (eds), *Sexual Harassment* (New York: Oxford University Press, 2001), p. 30.
7   Jan Crosthwait and Graham Priest, "The Definition of Sexual Harassment," in LeMoncheck and Sterba (eds), *Sexual Harassment*, p. 66.
8   EEOC Guidelines on Discrimination Because of Sex, 29 C.F.R. 1604.11.
9   From a University of Rochester publication, *Think Safe*, 2001, outlining campus security policies.
10 Catherine MacKinnon, *Feminism Unmodified: Discourses on Life and Law* (Cambridge, MA: Harvard University Press, 1987), p. 109.
11 Dena Taylor, Preface to Amber Coverdale Sumrall and Dena Taylor (eds), *Sexual Harassment: Women Speak Out* (Freedom, CA: The Crossing Press, 1992), p. vii.
12 Louise Fitzgerald, a psychologist, quoted in "Sexual Harassment: It's About Power, Not Sex," *The New York Times*, October 22, 1991.
13 Susan P. Phillips and Margaret S. Schneider, "Sexual Harassment of Female Doctors by Patients," *The New England Journal of Medicine*, December 23, 1993, 1936–7.

14 *The New York Times*, November 4, 1996.

15 *The New York Times*, November 22, 1996.

16 Judith Martin ("Miss Manners"), Rochester *Times-Union*, November 11, 1988.

17 Susan M. Dodds, Lucy Frost, Robert Pargetter, and Elizabeth W. Prior, "Sexual Harassment," *Social Theory and Practice*, Vol. 14, No. 2, Summer 1988, 122.

18 More specifically, the prohibition was extended to those programs in universities that receive federal funds. In 1987, in the Civil Rights Restorative Act, the prohibition of sex discrimination was extended to the whole of any educational institution any part of which was the beneficiary of federal aid.

19 Margot Slade, "Sexual Harassment: Stories from the Field," *The New York Times*, March 27, 1994.

20 As reported in the University of Rochester's *Campus Times*, February 15, 1996.

21 *The New York Times*, May 11, 1994.

22 Rosemarie Tong, *Women, Sex, and the Law* (Savage, MD: Rowman & Littlefield Publishers, Inc., 1984), p. 81; emphasis in the original.

23 Anja Angelica Chan, *Women and Sexual Harassment: A Practical Guide to the Legal Protections of Title VII and the Hostile Environment Claim* (New York: The Haworth Press, 1994), p. 9; emphases in the original.

24 If correct, this means that the standard view of sexual harassment as sex discrimination is mistaken. See, for example, MacKinnon, *Sexual Harassment of Working Women*.

25 June Larkin, *Sexual Harassment: High School Girls Speak Out* (Toronto: Second Story Press, 1994), p. 21.

26 Tong, *Women, Sex, and the Law*, p. 87.

27 Catherine A. MacKinnon, *Only Words* (Cambridge, MA: Harvard University Press, 1993), p. 56.

28 Sheryl WuDunn, *The New York Times*, December 17, 1995.

29 "Most sexual harassment cases in the university setting will involve personal testimony from both the complainants and the accused. Documentary evidence is generally non-existent or unavailable. Likewise, testimony from non-complaining witnesses may be inadmissible or may be of only circumstantial value." Walter B. Connolly, Jr., and Alison B. Marshall, "Sexual Harassment of University or College Students by Faculty Members," *Journal of College and University Law*, Vol. 15, No. 4, Spring 1989, 400.

For more resources:

www.bloomsbury.com/holmes-introduction-to-applied-ethics

Part II

Profit and the Plight of Others

6

Corporate Responsibility

The social responsibility of business is to increase its profits.

—Milton Friedman[1]

[C]orporations should be treated as full-fledged moral persons and hence ... they can have whatever privileges, rights, and duties as are, in the normal course of affairs, accorded to moral persons.

—Peter A. French[2]

Introduction

The actions of corporations have significant effects, not only upon the economy, but also upon the lives of individual persons in their home country and abroad. In this chapter we examine the question of whether corporations have moral responsibilities in addition to their quest for profits. We shall consider, first, what corporations are; second, what sorts of social responsibilities they might be alleged to have; and third, whether those who manage corporations have the qualifications to make the requisite moral judgments if corporations are deemed to have moral responsibilities.

6.1 The problem

Attitudes toward capitalism are curiously mixed. Most people in capitalist countries defend capitalism. At the same time, they often speak as though it were morally disreputable, governed by greed and selfishness. What accounts for this?

Part of the explanation probably lies in the fact that people often think there is little connection between capitalism and ethics. The conjunction of the ideas of business and ethics, in fact, occasions smiles, as though there were a fundamental incompatibility between the two. But need there be? This is the issue we shall explore. We shall ask: Ought corporations to act morally? More specifically, ought they to assume social responsibilities?

6.2 What are corporations?

Let us begin by considering the nature of corporations. They are a relatively recent development in social and economic history. Consider the following account from Thomas Donaldson's book *Corporations and Morality*:

> ## The Evolution of the Corporation
> Corporations, like the aims they pursue, come in a generous assortment. We associate the word "corporation" with General Motors or Volkswagen, but since the corporation's beginning it has been flexible enough to accommodate such organizations as the Church, nonprofit trade guilds, and local governments. Ask a modern lawyer for his definition of "corporation" and he will say it is that thing which can endure beyond the natural lives of its members, and which has incorporators who may sue and be sued as a unit and who are able to consign part of their property to the corporation for ventures of limited liability. These elementary characteristics, and especially the advantage of limited liability (whereby members are financially liable for corporate debts only up to the extent of their investment), are often taken as the *sine qua non* of corporate existence. Yet each of these characteristics was missing at one time or another in the corporation's history.
>
> Both ancient and modern corporations can be sorted using a few simple distinctions. First, they may be profit-making or non-profit-making. For example, Wedgewood Pottery, Ltd., and Lockheed, Inc., are chartered for the express purpose of making a profit, while the University of Chicago and the Carnegie Foundation are chartered for educational or philanthropic purposes. Second, they may be privately owned or owned, to varying degrees, by the government. In the United States private corporations are virtually the only type, while in Europe public corporations, such as Renault of France, are common. Third, they may be privately held corporations in which a select group owns all the outstanding shares of stock, or publicly held ones in which stock is traded among the general public. Most good-sized U.S. corporations are publicly held.

Finally, corporations may be divided into "productive" and "non-productive" organizations. A productive organization is any organization producing a good or service; this definition would include even non-corporations such as government agencies. Examples of corporations which qualify as productive organizations are numerous; in addition to the obvious—chemical, manufacturing, and assembly firms—there are law firms, counseling firms, and universities. Only habits of thought obscure our understanding that virtually every corporation is a productive organization. Even law firms produce wills and contracts; counseling firms produce advice; and universities produce degrees, sporting events, and sometimes knowledge. Examples of nonproductive organizations are extremely rare. They would include organizations existing merely to hold a patent or copyright, or to provide a tax shelter for their members.

When most of us hear the word "corporation," we think of giants such as Exxon, Coca-Cola, and A.T.&T. These are profit-making, publicly held corporations which also qualify as productive organizations. Such giants affect the depth and breadth of society and for this reason have special ethical significance. They resemble each other sufficiently to constitute a natural locus of study; their size is a common denominator. General Motors shares little else with Bob's Market, Inc., the corner grocery store, than the name "corporation." Although this book will refer to small corporations and nonprofit corporations from time to time, its primary target will be medium-to-large-sized, profit-making, modern corporations.

In 1819 Chief Justice Marshall gave his often quoted interpretation of the corporation: "A corporation," he said, "is an artificial being, invisible, intangible, and existing only in the contemplation of law. Being the mere creation of law, it possesses only those properties which the charter of its creation confers upon it, either expressly, or as incidental to its very existence." Marshall's definition postulates an abstract entity. It stresses the sense in which the corporation is a creation of the mind, existing only in the "contemplation of law," and this is unlike a rock, or a living person, since its very existence depends upon being recognized by human beings.

In the United States an organization attains the status of a "corporation" only through a formal act of government. With the passage of the Fourteenth Amendment to the Constitution, U.S. corporations acquired full status as abstract persons, complete with rights to life, liberty, and state citizenship. (Most U.S. corporations are citizens of the state of Delaware.) Although modern U.S. corporations do not possess certain features of personhood—i.e., they neither eat, require medical attention, nor vote—they are treated as persons in a multitude of ways: they must pay taxes, are liable for damages, can enter into legal agreements, and have the right to freedom of speech. Modern corporations are created by persons, but they are created in the image of their creators.

The roots of the corporation reach deep into the past, a past which is revealing about the modern corporation. Corporate theory has paralleled corporate reality, and both may be traced to early laws governing the conduct of groups which assigned responsibility not merely to individuals, but to collectives such as families and civic organizations. Even before these laws emerged, blood feuds were fought on the assumption that the clan, not the individual, was to blame; with the rise of group law, the prevailing assumptions about corporate wholeness could be formalized and legitimized. Sometimes this resulted in unusual prohibitions; for example Anglo-Saxon laws forbade the selling of certain group property on the grounds that it ultimately belonged to the immortal corporate collective. By the Middle Ages the group was regarded as having prime economic status. In Italy the "casa," or family business, not the individual, handled donations, taxes, fines, guild dues, entertainment, and the necessary bribes.

Corporate evolution occurred in four stages. The first, encompassing the Medieval period, gave the Church, the guild, and the borough corporate status, but failed to do so for purely profit-making associations. In each of the former organizations, a common factor besides economic self-interest united members. For the Church, it was religion; for the guild, similarity of trade; and for the borough, geographical proximity and shared political interests.

The second stage witnessed the rise of corporations whose members shared nothing besides the desire to make money. This occurred in the early sixteenth century, when European entrepreneurs organized to launch trading voyages to the East. Such corporations, however, were a far cry from modern ones. Instead of pooling their capital, members financed their voyages individually and used the corporation only to act as bearer for special trading rights. For example, a company might hold a special trading right with Russia, a right bestowed by the Czar and available only to corporate members. Liability, however, was left to individual members, so that when an entrepreneur's vessel sank or was robbed by pirates, he alone was required to pay creditors.

The third stage of corporate evolution ushered in the prototypes of modern corporations. Beginning in 1612 with the reconstitution of the East India Trading Company, this stage saw capital being pooled, power being placed in the hands of a governor and his committees, and liability being distributed among the stockholders. The products of these changes were the "great trading companies" of the seventeenth and eighteenth centuries: in addition to the East India Company, there were the Hudson Bay Company, La Compagnie des Indes, the Company of Adventurers of London Trading into Africa, and counterparts in Spain, Italy, Russia, and Germany. The motives behind the creation of these companies lay predominantly in considerations of economy of scale: boats were becoming bigger and more expensive, so that merely buying and outfitting them exceeded the resources of wealthy individuals. Similarly, losing such boats through storms or pirates could be ruinous to an individual. The solution was pooled capital and shared liability: the trademarks of the modern corporation.

The final stage is characterized by the gradual shedding of government restrictions upon corporate chartering procedures. From the seventeenth century through the first half of the nineteenth, prospective English corporations were required to apply to the Crown for charters. In the United States following the Revolutionary War they were required to apply to state governments ...

As corporations evolved, so did the moral problems they engendered. Society was prepared to cope morally with human persons, and to react to murder, fraud, and vice, but it was ill-prepared to cope with corporations. When, for example, an East India Company ship collided with another ship, who was liable? Was the company itself liable *only* for acts authorized in its charter, or for all acts undertaken by its agents? Were mental states relevant in the assessment of corporate punishment? Could the East India Company act with "malice" or "criminal intent"? The natural tendency was for corporate managers to pass liability off to the stockholders, but the tendency of stockholders was just the reverse. Both were able to come together through the policy of making the *corporation* liable, as distinct from managers or stockholders. Thus, the doctrine of the corporation as possessing its own moral and legal status, with limited financial liability for stockholders and managers, satisfied both camps.

If a corporation can be legally guilty, how should it be punished? This question acquired new overtones during the eighteenth and nineteenth centuries when European politicians inspired by the ideas of the Enlightenment moved to standardize policies of punishment. Instead of flogging one criminal and placing another in the stocks, they began to apply the same punishment to all, namely deprivation of liberty for varying time periods. But though corporations can lie, cheat, and steal just as individuals can, they cannot be thrown in jail. How, then, do they pay for their crimes?

Historically the form of punishment the courts hit upon was monetary. Instead of being deprived of liberty, corporations were deprived of money, in varying amounts depending on the severity of the crime. During the nineteenth and early twentieth centuries progressive steps were taken in the United States to expand the limits of corporate financial liability. By 1812, corporations were financially liable for acts instigated by documents bearing the corporate seal. By 1842 they were liable for any acts of corporate agents acting within the scope of their authority. And in 1862 they became liable for acts which contradicted company instructions in cases where the agent believed his act was in the interest of his employers.[3]

6.3 Liberal and conservative positions on corporate social responsibility

Both sides in the debate over corporate responsibility agree that corporations have responsibilities. They disagree only over what those responsibilities are. Some hold that a corporation's sole responsibility is to make a profit. Others hold that corporations *may* assume social responsibilities provided doing so doesn't jeopardize profits. Still others allow that corporations *ought* sometimes to assume social responsibilities, even at the expense of maximizing profits.

Let us make this clearer by formulating three principles by which to understand the approaches to the issue.

1. Corporations ought not to assume social responsibilities.
2. Corporations may (but aren't obligated to) assume social responsibilities
   a. when doing so is consistent with profit maximization; or
   b. even at the expense of profit maximization.
3. Corporations ought to assume social responsibilities:
   a. when doing so is consistent with, or in the interest of, profit maximization; or
   b. even at the expense of profit maximization.

What we may call the pure conservative position can be defined as the acceptance of (1). The pure liberal position can be defined as the acceptance 3(b). Qualified conservatism will be the acceptance of 2(a) and qualified liberalism the acceptance of either 2(b) or 3(a).

6.4 What is the basic obligation of corporations?

It's often assumed that the Liberal argues from a moral position and the Conservative from a nonmoral position. But this needn't be so. Each of the above positions can be held on either moral or nonmoral grounds. Each says only what corporations should (or may) do, not *why* they should do it or what *justifies* their doing it. Thus, the above need to be understood in terms of two more basic positions. The first, the nonmoral position, can be stated as follows:

NM: The sole obligation of corporations is to maximize profits.

This view is stated forcefully in the following passage by Milton Friedman (1912–2006), one of the twentieth century's leading defenders of capitalism:

Key Quote 6A

The view has been gaining widespread acceptance that corporate officials and labor leaders have a "social responsibility" that goes beyond serving the interest of their stockholders or members. This view shows a fundamental misconception of the character and nature of a free economy. In such an economy, there is one and only one social responsibility of business—to use its resources and engage in activities designed to increase its profits so long as it stays within the rules of the game.[4]

On the assumption that maximizing of profits isn't in itself a moral end, this implies that corporations have no moral obligations. The second basic position, which we may call the moral position, is as follows:

M: The basic (though not sole) obligation of corporations is always to act morally.

This second position leaves it open what morality specifically requires. It would sanction any of the Liberal and Conservative positions if they could be shown to be justified by the basic principles of morality. It's possible that Adam Smith (1723–90) had something like this in mind in a famous passage:

Key Quote 6B

Every individual is continuously exerting himself to find the most advantageous employment for whatever capital he can command. It is his own advantage, indeed, and not that of the society, which he has in view. But the study of his own advantage naturally, or rather necessarily, leads him to prefer that employment which is most advantageous to the society ... In this, as in many other cases, he is led by an invisible hand to promote an end which was no part of his intention.[5]

If one took the interest of society to be the end which ultimately justifies the pursuit of self-interest, then the justification of the pursuit of self-interest would ultimately be a moral one. It's perfectly consistent to say that people should promote a moral end like the greatest good for society but that the most effective means to that end is the pursuit by each person of his or her own interest. All that's required is the assumption—though a large one— that morality and self-interest coincide. This, however, isn't how Smith is usually understood. He's usually understood as saying that people are motivated by self-interest, and that in pursuing that interest they *happen* to promote a social good without intending to do so. What justifies them is their own self-interest.

6.5 Possible objections to corporate social responsibility

Do corporations have moral responsibilities (as the liberal says and the conservative denies)? It might seem evident that they do. But there are possible objections to this view. Let's take account of two.

The first objection contends that morality has no application to corporations at all. Corporations aren't persons, and morality applies only to persons. It's only conscious, rational beings whose behavior can be said to be right or wrong and who can have moral responsibilities and duties.

This objection makes an important point. That morality applies only to rational beings is true. But it doesn't follow that morality is inapplicable to corporations. All that follows is that we need to understand what it means to say that corporations have moral responsibilities. When we speak of corporations acting and making decisions, this can be understood to refer to the conduct of a corporation's officials acting as its agents. Corporations act only through the choices and decisions of individuals. There's no action that corporations can take that isn't translatable into actions by the appropriate agents of the corporations. If so, then corporations can fail to have moral responsibilities (or to warrant moral consideration) only if corporate managers, qua corporate managers, can fail to have moral responsibilities. And this they cannot do. Those agents are persons. No conduct of persons is immune from moral assessment (though mere behavior sometimes is, as when it's reflexive, deranged, or psychotic). But self-directed, uncoerced action—conduct in the fullest sense of the term—is always appraisable as right or wrong. Morality isn't a compartment of human affairs that one steps out of by passing through the door of an executive suite or by assuming public office or putting on a military uniform. It constrains us in all that we do.

The second objection concedes that corporations are governed by morality but maintains that it is a morality of a different sort than applies to individuals—a collective as opposed to a personal morality. Corporations can, on this second view, have responsibilities of the collective sort but not of the personal sort. This view is suggested by the following passage:

Key Quote 6C

The individual cannot be moral in independence. The modern business collectives force a collective morality ... [s]o individual morality must give place to a more robust or social type.[6]

By "individual" the authors mean primarily the shareholder. Their concern is with whether shareholders can invest in a morally responsible way. But we can adapt the point to include corporate executives and ask whether, as corporate executives, they're forced into a different morality than that which governs them in their capacity as ordinary persons.

We have seen in Chapter 4 (Theory Box 4B, Section 4.9) the distinction between macro ethics and micro ethics; that is, between ethical outlooks which emphasize the importance of collectivities (like states, societies, etc.) over individuals. While the collective morality of which Dewey and Tufts speak may not rise to the level of a macro ethics, it suggests that individuals, when they play certain roles in society, government, or business, may have different obligations than they would ordinarily have, and it's possible that sometimes those obligations conflict with their other obligations.

The following passage from Milton Friedman is important in this connection:

> Few trends could so thoroughly undermine the very foundations of our free society as the acceptance by corporate officials of a social responsibility other than to make as much money for their stockholders as possible. This is a fundamentally subversive doctrine. If businessmen do have a social responsibility other than making maximum profits for stockholders, how are they to know what it is? Can self-selected private individuals decide what the social interest is? Can they decide how great a burden they are justified in placing on themselves or their stockholders to serve that social interest? Is it tolerable that these public functions of taxation, expenditure, and control be exercised by the people who happen at the moment to be in charge of particular enterprises, chosen for those posts by strictly private groups? If businessmen are civil servants rather than the employees of their stockholders then in a democracy they will, sooner or later, be chosen by the public techniques of election and appointment.
>
> And long before this occurs, their decision-making power will have been taken away from them. A dramatic illustration was the cancellation of a steel price increase by U.S. Steel in April 1962 through the medium of a public display of anger by President Kennedy and threats of reprisals on levels ranging from anti-trust suits to examination of the tax reports of steel executives. This was a striking episode because of the public display of the vast powers concentrated in Washington. We were all made aware of how much of the power needed for a police state was already available. It illustrates the present point as well. If the price of steel is a public decision, as the doctrine of social responsibility declares, then it cannot be permitted to be made privately ...
> One topic in the area of social responsibility that I feel duty-bound to touch on, because it affects my own personal interests, has been the claim that business should contribute to the support of charitable activities and especially to universities. Such giving by corporations is an inappropriate use of corporate funds in a free-enterprise society.

> The corporation is an instrument of the stockholders who own it. If the corporation makes a contribution, it prevents the individual stockholder from himself deciding how he should dispose of his funds. With the corporation tax and the deductibility of contributions, stockholders may of course want the corporation to make a gift on their behalf, since this would enable them to make a larger gift. The best solution would be the abolition of the corporate tax. But so long as there is a corporate tax, there is no justification for permitting deductions for contributions to charitable and educational institutions. Such contributions should be, made by the individuals who are the ultimate owners of property in our society.
>
> People who urge extension of the deductibility of this kind of corporate contribution in the name of free enterprise are fundamentally working against their own interest. A major complaint made frequently against modern business is that it involves the separation of ownership and control—that the corporation has become a social institution that is a law unto itself, with irresponsible executives who do not serve the interests of their stockholders. This charge is not true. But the direction in which policy is now moving, of permitting corporations to make contributions for charitable purposes and allowing deductions for income tax, is a step in the direction of creating a true divorce between ownership and control and of undermining the basic nature and character of our society. It is a step away from an individualistic society and toward the corporate state.[7]

This passage could be read as saying that morality simply doesn't apply to corporations at all, which may be how Friedman intends it. If it's taken in this way, then it simply restates the first objection and is covered by what we said above about it. But even though Friedman doesn't say this, the passage is consistent with holding that there is a kind of morality that applies to corporations that is different from that which applies to individuals, a *collective morality* (as Dewey and Tufts call it in Key Quote 6C) as opposed to an *individual morality*. Let us clarify these.

Theory Box 6A

Individual Morality and Collective Morality
Individual morality: a morality intended to guide the conduct of individual persons in their relations to other individual persons.

Collective morality: a morality intended to guide the conduct of collectivities (states, societies, corporations, etc.) in their relations to individuals and other collectivities.

It's important to distinguish individual and collective morality from **micro** and **macro ethics** as defined earlier (Theory Box 4B, Chapter 4, Section 4.9). Individual and collective morality refer to the *entities* (individuals or groups) whose conduct is governed by morality, without regard to the values or obligations morality entails. The distinction between micro and macro ethics specifies what *within* morality is taken to be most important or the highest value, a concern for individuals or a concern for collectivities.

It's often assumed that the morality to which corporations are beholden sanctions conduct that's wrong according to individual morality. When there is such a conflict, the reasoning goes, collective morality supersedes individual morality.

A line of reasoning in support of this position runs as follows: we aren't the architects of the socioeconomic system in which we find ourselves. We're (usually) born into it. That system is given. Unless we move to another country or dedicate ourselves to a life of reform, we can only accept it. The most any of us can reasonably expect to do is to conduct ourselves responsibly in the working out of whatever plan of life we have chosen within that framework. A part of that plan may call for a career with a corporation, either because you like the money or the work or because you believe in the value of the institution and of the capitalist system as a whole. Be that as it may, you're not the creator of the duties and responsibilities attaching to the role you find yourself playing within the corporation or of those of the broader society of which it's a part. If in the course of managing a corporation or of implementing the decisions of those who do, your duties call for conduct which in some of your other capacities (citizen, neighbor, Christian, Jew, Muslim, etc.) would be adjudged wrong, you should allow the former to override the latter. Only in that way can you avoid obstructing the relatively smooth operation of the system which provides the setting for these other roles and makes the quality of life associated with them possible.

For example, if you head a large real estate development corporation, and you have a chance to buy up a heavily wooded tract of land that enhances the community, you might feel that your obligation to the corporation's shareholders to maximize profits supersedes any obligation to members of the community to preserve a valued woodland. You might feel, in other words, that the collective morality supposedly governing a corporation overrides the individual morality that might call for consideration of the persons in the community (either singly or collectively). Thus, in this view, we cannot but recognize two different, and at some points incongruent, moralities, and to allow the higher morality, the collective morality, to override the lower, the individual.

This argument, though forceful, fails to establish the need to recognize two moralities. That the best lives are possible only within a social context may be granted. Philosophers from Plato to the present have made the same point. But this doesn't establish the existence of two moralities, much less the supremacy of one over the other.

Whatever concrete moral judgments one holds with regard to the priorities of business and economic conduct vis-à-vis interpersonal conduct can be defended without assuming that there are two moralities. There are at least two reasons for saying this.

First, Friedman may be assuming (perhaps inadvertently) a consequentialist principle, to the effect that we ought to act in a way that is socially the most beneficial. Consequentialists are those who hold the ethical theory called consequentialism:

Theory Box 6B

Consequentialism and Nonconsequentialism
Consequentialism: Moral rightness is determined solely by the consequences of actions.

Nonconsequentialism: Any theory of morally right conduct that is not consequentialist.

    A. **Strong**: The consequences of acts are irrelevant to the determination of moral rightness.

    B. **Weak**: The consequences of acts are relevant to the determination of moral rightness but not decisive.

    Consequentialism is often used interchangeably with **utilitarianism** (see Theory Box 1E in Chapter 1), but the two should be distinguished. Utilitarianism is a consequentialist ethical theory, but not all consequentialist ethical theories are utilitarian. **Ethical Egoism** (the view that one ought always to maximize one's own personal good) would be a consequentialist theory that isn't utilitarian.

The Friedman passage could be read as advancing a moral argument against the assumption of social responsibilities by corporations: namely, that it would have bad consequences (the "destruction of the free-enterprise system" and, more broadly, "undermining of the basic nature and character of our society"). This would be a consequentialist argument, fully within the province of morality. Given the basic orientation of his theory, however, Friedman probably doesn't intend the passage to be taken in this way, that is, as reflecting a particular type of ethical theory.

Second, nonconsequentialists need only say that there are within morality conflicting prima facie obligations (see Chapter 4, Theory Box 4A, Section 4.7) and that these often confront the corporate executive. The problems they pose may be vexing. Indeed, corporate managers are often confronted with the interests of shareholders on one side, and those of employees and society (and perhaps other societies as well in the case of multinationals) on the other. But it doesn't advance our understanding of these dilemmas to think that they arise because of competing moralities. Whatever we may want to say on either side of this issue can be accommodated within the framework of a single morality.

If this is correct, then although both the Liberal and Conservative positions can be held on either moral or nonmoral grounds, only the moral ground can justify either position. This means that corporations do indeed have moral responsibilities. But what those responsibilities are, and specifically whether they include social responsibilities, remains open.

6.6 Which social responsibilities?

Social responsibilities may be internal or external. *Internal social responsibilities* are those to employees and shareholders. They pertain to such matters as hiring, promotions, working conditions, benefits, job training, profits, dividends, stock-splits, and so on. *External social responsibilities* are all those that aren't internal. They pertain to such things as racial and gender discrimination, affirmative action, pollution, depletion of natural resources, and urban decay. There are also alleged external responsibilities extending beyond our own society. These are important in assessing problems raised by multinational corporations, whose operations have direct consequences for persons in foreign countries.

Additionally, there are responsibilities related to social costs and those which aren't. Social costs have been defined as "all direct and indirect losses suffered by third persons or the general public as a result of private economic activities ... all those harmful consequences and damages which third persons or the community sustain as a result of the productive process."[8] Social costs would include losses resulting from pollution, destruction of wildlife habitats, relocation of corporations, and so forth. Nonsocial cost related responsibilities would include obligations to support charities, to contribute to universities, to promote diversity, or to open facilities to the public for recreational use. We can represent the interrelations among these distinction as follows:

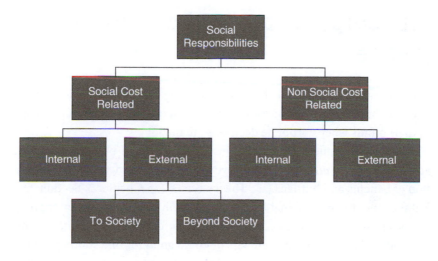

6.7 Non-maleficence

Whether or not corporations have an obligation to do good (*beneficence*) in the area of nonsocial cost related matters, it seems clear that they have an obligation not to do harm. That is, they have at least a prima facie *duty of non-maleficence* (see Theory Box 4A, Chapter 4, Section 4.7 on prima facie and actual duties). We all arguably have such a duty, corporation managers included. It's morally wrong, for example, for corporations to deceive the public into thinking that harmful drugs are beneficial or that defective cars are safe. It's also wrong for them knowingly to subject employees to detrimental working conditions. All of these are wrong whether or not in violation of any laws. Moreover, if corporations have a *duty of non-maleficence*, then it's plausible to maintain that they also have a duty when they've caused harm. Having caused harm creates a prima facie obligation to remedy that harm.

This doesn't mean that every conceivable harm is of sufficient importance to require remedy. Nor does it mean that it's possible to remedy all harms or even to calculate all harms. Nor does it mean that every corporate action with social costs is wrong; if that were so, little that corporations do would be justified. Many social costs are offset by sufficient benefits as to be justified on balance. What it does mean is that corporations have at least *some* social cost related responsibilities.

6.8 Corporations and distributive justice

Do corporations have social obligations deriving from considerations of justice? Ought corporate managers to have considerations of justice uppermost in their minds when corporate decisions are made?

It might be argued that to take justice seriously in business (or other areas) leads to absurdities. Distributive justice is concerned with the allocation of benefits and burdens (see Theory Box 3D in Chapter 3, Section 3.9). But it cannot be the case that if I confer a benefit upon one person or group I must always be prepared to do the same for others. That would make families unjust, because family members often do good for one another but not for members of other families. It would also make friendship unjust, because friends look out for one another in ways they don't for strangers. In the business world, it would seem to require that a corporation which opens a plant in one country (thereby, let us assume, conferring a benefit) acts unjustly if it fails to do the same for other countries.

This objection points up the need to qualify distributive justice. Questions of distributive justice don't arise when one is engaged in gratuitous benefactions—that is, in conferring of benefits in circumstances in which the beneficiary has no antecedent claim to the good. If I give five dollars to the first homeless person I meet, I don't act unjustly if I fail to do the same for the second and third. Questions of justice arise in connection with benefactions only when people are entitled to them; that is, when the potential beneficiaries have an antecedent claim to the good in question or a claim to share in the good *if* it is to be conferred upon others. Conversely, we may say that persons have a responsibility to assume a burden only if there's some antecedent obligation on their part to assume it. (Or there's an antecedent obligation to bear their fair share of the burden if it's to be imposed upon others.)

Children, for example, have a claim upon parents simply by virtue of being their children. Food and clothing are benefits to which they're entitled. If you're a parent, you're constrained by the requirements of justice in the distribution of such benefits. It would be unjust (or unfair, as we would more likely put it in this case) to feed one child but starve the other, or clothe one adequately but leave the other in rags. But you don't in the least act unjustly if you fail to feed and clothe your neighbor's children or children across town or across the country. (This isn't to say that you shouldn't have a moral concern for children in need wherever they may be; only that the concern isn't grounded in fairness by comparison with the way you treat your own children.) By virtue of being the children of different parents, they have claims upon their own parents, not upon you. If, on the other hand, you give one of your two children a gratuitous benefit—say, extra money for popcorn at the movies—then you act unfairly if you fail to do the same for the other. Even though neither has any antecedent claim to that particular benefit, each has, all things being equal, an equal claim *if* the benefit is to be conferred upon the other. (It should be added that if your neighbor's children have no claim to the entitled benefits you confer on your own children, they also have no responsibility to share in the burdens you may impose upon your children; you may ask your children to help with the dishes, clean their room, or rake leaves, but you have no grounds for expecting your neighbor's children to share in these chores.)

In short, questions of justice don't arise in all contexts of distributing benefits and burdens but in some only. They arise only with regard to the comparative treatment of certain relevantly specified classes of persons. We may take this to apply to corporations as well as to individuals.

6.9 Corporations and the making of moral judgments

With that in mind, let us note that the answer to our primary question about justice depends upon the answers to three more general questions. They are:

1. Should corporations make moral judgments of justice?
   a. About their own business operations?
   b. About their own society and government?
   c. About the societies and governments of other countries?
2. If so, what should they do about those judgments?
3. Who within corporations should make such judgments, and can it be expected that they will make them wisely?

Some corporations do make moral judgments, at least about our own society and government. And some of them act upon those judgments, at least to the extent of publicizing them. In a Supreme Court case, a Massachusetts law limiting the First Amendment rights of free speech for corporations to matters pertaining to their business operations was struck down. This enabled corporations to use corporate funds to publicize their views on a variety of social and political issues. So, corporations can (legally), and many do in fact, act upon moral and social judgments.

Should they do so? That depends in part upon the scope of the judgments and the competence of the persons making them. And that depends in turn at least partly upon the types of judgments being made. Three main candidates for types of moral judgments corporations might make are those of *utility*, *non-maleficence*, and *justice*. We've already seen that corporations arguably should be prepared to make judgments of non-maleficence. Considerations of utility are difficult to evaluate in the long run, since there's no cut-off point in the flow of consequences that enables one to be certain that all of the relevant outcomes have been considered. For that reason, and also because an outcome might be unjust even if it represents a greater good (hence is supported by considerations of utility), we shall focus primarily upon judgments of justice. We've already seen that corporations should be prepared to make judgments of non-maleficence. Let us now focus upon judgments of justice.

Because justice is a matter of the comparative treatment of persons, groups, or societies, to know whether someone has been treated unjustly it's not enough to know whether he or she has been harmed. One needs to know how he or she is treated by comparison with the way in which certain others are treated. A person who mistreats his children equally harms them but does them no injustice. One may also be done an injustice without being harmed. Depriving people of deserved benefits, though it may be just as wrong, nonetheless differs from harming them. If during the course of an ordinary day that has otherwise gone well, you've (unbeknownst to

you) been unfairly deprived of your share of an inheritance by the machi-
nations of a vengeful sibling, you've been done an injustice. But you're not
worse off than before, hence arguably haven't been harmed; you're simply
not better off.

If, therefore, a corporation is to judge the justice of its policies and operations, it must assess both their direct and their indirect consequences. It
must determine not only what benefits and burdens will fall to those most
immediately affected. It must also determine how such benefits and burdens
affect those persons vis-à-vis others who may be claimants of such benefits
(or proper bearers of the burdens), or who may rightly claim to share in
them if others do. Such assessment must be made in light of the character of
its distribution as gratuitous or entitled.

That a corporation chooses to establish a plant in a given country will
normally be a gratuitous benefit—assuming it's a benefit at all—to the
country. The corporation doesn't act unjustly if it fails to open a similar
plant in other countries. On the other hand, benefits like stock dividends
are clearly owed to a certain group of persons (viz., stockholders), and
considerations of distributive justice are relevant regarding distributions
within that class. Other cases are more problematic. When a corporation moves into a lesser developed country in search of cheap labor and
access to natural resources, is there an obligation to market the corporation's products in that country so far as possible, or to seek out and train
management personnel from among the country's citizens, or to reinvest
capital there rather than elsewhere? Each of these might be regarded as a
benefit. But is each a gratuitous benefit? Some would say so, arguing that
the benefit to the country of the presence of the corporation extends to
these other considerations as well. Others would say that the benefits are
non-gratuitous, and that the citizens of the country are entitled to them.
The point is that, particularly with regard to the operations of multinationals, the proper characterization of benefits and burdens may be difficult to
arrive at in the first place.

It matters little whether a corporation makes moral judgments of any
sort apart from whether, and in what ways, it proposes to act upon them. It
makes little difference what the answer to question (1) is (at the beginning
of this section) abstracted from the answer to question (2). Simply making
judgments and keeping them to oneself is of no consequence. Making them
and publicizing them is of some consequence. Making them and acting
upon them may be of considerable consequence. The third raises the most
difficult moral questions. So, the interesting question isn't simply *whether*

corporations should make judgments of distributive justice, but whether they should make them and act upon them.

With regard to its internal business operations, it seems clear that a corporation should both make and implement judgments of distributive justice. In this area a corporation cannot help acting in ways that raise questions of justice. They're part and parcel of the conduct of corporate affairs. Whether a corporation provides equal pay for equal work cannot be avoided, for example, nor can the question of whether to grant equal employment opportunities to persons irrespective of race or sex. This holds true whether we are talking about the corporation's home country or its dealings in other countries.

When we move to broader question of a corporation's possible judgments about the conduct of governments and the degree of justice they embody, the issue is more difficult. Yet even normal business operations might contribute to the perpetuation of injustice in those societies.

On the one hand, there are strong arguments for saying that corporations should make such judgments and assume the social responsibilities associated with them. Corporations wield enormous power. Their influence in trying to effect social reform is preferable to the violent upheavals that often result when reform is not forthcoming by peaceful means. If progressive social change can be furthered by a corporation's action, it's said, then by all means it should be supported. But the "if" in this judgment is a big one. For it's here that the issue is complicated by question (3) of those raised earlier, concerning who should make corporate moral judgments and the likelihood of their making sound judgments.

The range of possible interpretations of distributive justice is enormous. The problem isn't so much that principles of distributive justice aren't in operation in the societies of the world and in the practices of corporations. It's that the principles that are operating are often indefensible ones. Distributions can be made according to race, religion, class and so on. The problem is to implement correct principles. For corporate executives (the likeliest candidates for persons to actually make the judgments that guide corporations) to undertake a thorough and reasoned approach to distributive justice would require far greater understanding of ethical theory than most of them have. It would also require greater understanding of the governments and social orders in countries in which they do business. It's arguable that they would profit from greater understanding of ethics even in their handling of problems of justice in those areas in which such questions unavoidably arise.

It's relevant what persons in an affected society would want done. If a corporation's withdrawal would cripple a country's economy, the persons affected—even if they're lowest on the scale of beneficiaries of the economy in an unjust society—will undoubtedly suffer. So will those employed by the corporation. It's been said that in most third world countries multinationals "pay up to 100% higher wages than local companies (a fact testified by the International Labor Organization), and they provide hospitals, housing, and schools far more than do local companies. A job with an MNC is a plum."[9] To try to decide for such persons what is in their interest in the absence of firm knowledge of their preferences is presumptuous at best. Even in affluent countries like the United States, if a company or corporation moves its operations to another country, some people will lose jobs even if the overall economy of the country is little affected.

Even if it should be agreed that a particular principle of distributive justice is the correct one, and that according to it grave injustices exist within a society in which a corporation does business, simply establishing that fact doesn't in and of itself suffice to determine what should be done about it. Suppose a corporation wants to combat injustice within a host country. Is the most effective way to do that to withdraw altogether and thereby help undermine the country's economy? Or is it to remain and try to combat the injustice by instituting just practices that model a better way of treating people? The answers to such questions aren't easy to give in the abstract. They require knowledge of consequences of a sort it may be difficult to acquire. Moreover, the correct answers for one case might not be correct for another. This makes judgments of utility in connection with corporation's operations difficult to assess.

For a corporation to make and implement judgments of distributive justice in countries in which they do business may constitute a form of intervention in the internal affairs of those countries. This fact has broad implication for the conduct of foreign policy, as well as for domestic policy in analogous cases in which the society is one's own. There also is the question of a company's liability for human rights abuses that may take place in a country in which it does business. Consider the following ad on this topic from the National Foreign Trade Council, published in *The New York Times*, April 9, 2004:

The Business of Human Rights

Suppose a foreign country engages in human rights abuses against its own people. Should corporations that happen to do business there be held liable?

In 1990, a federal grand jury indicted a Mexican national, Humberto Alvarez-Machain, for participating in the torture of an agent with the Drug Enforcement Administration. As a result, the DEA devised a plan using Mexican nationals to apprehend him in his own country.

In court, the indicted Mexican proclaimed his innocence. Following his acquittal, he sued the United States and those who arrested him. Relying in part on a 200-year-old statutory provision, he argued that his human rights were violated because of his arrest ...

The so-called Alien Tort Provision is a single sentence in the judiciary Act of 1789. It says, "The district courts shall have original jurisdiction of any civil action by an alien for a tort only committed in violation of the law of nations or a treaty of the United States."

Although this case does not involve any corporation, the decision will likely have broad implications, both for foreign policy and for the international business community. That's because lawyers have begun to use the very provision at issue here to sue not only U.S. corporations but foreign corporations as well. In these suits, the lawyers seek monetary damages for alleged human rights abuses perpetrated—not by the companies, but by the foreign governments in whose countries the corporations operate.

The Court should use this case to reign in the use of this provision because ...

It interferes with foreign affairs—Suits relying on this provision often require U.S. courts to judge the conduct of foreign governments against their own citizens. Such cases thrust our courts into the position of establishing U.S. foreign policy—a task our Constitution assigns to the President and Congress.

It discourages foreign investment—These suits discourage companies from investing in the very countries where such investment can be an important diplomatic tool. In fact, the U.S. companies sued are often better able to promote human rights through their economic and social contributions than by packing up and leaving.

It permits suits against bystander companies—Many of these suits challenge conduct that U.S. corporations do not and cannot control. In fact, often the suits do not even allege that the company directly committed any human rights abuses. Instead, the companies often face legal action simply because they relied upon the foreign government's security services to protect their workers in dangerous, war-torn regions.

It is being misapplied—The provision was never intended to justify suits against U.S. companies. It was merely a "jurisdictional" provision that sought to steer suits involving piracy into federal courts. The First

Congress, hoping to avoid legal rulings that might embroil our new nation in a foreign controversy, did not want violations of the "law of nations" to be heard in a state forum. The provision, however, did not define what constituted a violation of the "law of nations." That task was left to the Congress and the Executive Branch as the Constitution mandated.

It permits U.S. courts to decide international law—The provision permits courts to decide what constitutes the "law of nations," and enables foreigners to sue companies for violations of "international agreements" to which the U.S. itself does not subscribe.

Most everyone agrees that governments engaging in human rights abuses should be ostracized and the abusers themselves prosecuted. But, distorting the Alien Tort Provision to permit suits against companies—which did not partake in any abuses—will not achieve that goal.[10]

The issue is whether corporate executives who haven't been elected by the citizenry at large, and who represent vested interests, should be encouraged to undertake interventionist actions in other countries and politically oriented actions within their own.

Those who urge that corporations go into the business of making moral judgments probably want them to make the *same* moral judgments they do. It can reasonably be assumed that if corporate executives make moral judgments in their capacity as corporate executives, the values that will prevail in the making and implementation of those judgments will be those of industrial capitalist society. If one wants corporations to make moral judgments, he must be prepared to see them make judgments of the sort that leading American banks did in the case of Chile, in which they helped to bring down an avowedly Marxist but democratically elected government by refusing it loans. Similar refusals helped to bring down the leftist Aristide government in Haiti in 2004. One might even suggest that corporations are less likely to do harm if they stay out of the business of making moral judgments, since the making of such judgments carries with it no guarantee that sound judgments will be made. The probability of corporations making such judgments must be a factor in determining whether they should be encouraged to do so.

6.10 Conclusion

We should distinguish between the ideal case in which corporations make all the right judgments and actual cases in which they don't. In actual cases, people with little or no expertise in moral matters direct the vast power of giant corporations. They can be assumed to hold a shared set of values that often conflict with those of societies whose laws and customs they may judge. It's not that the corporation as a vehicle for social change and moral reform doesn't need steering; it's that those who stand at the helm may not be the best ones to do the steering. The corporation isn't the sort of entity designed to act morally, any more than a tractor trailer is designed to pull a plow or a Cadillac to collect garbage. It can be used for that purpose. But if it is, one shouldn't be overly optimistic about the results. And such results as come about may be less good than if the corporation stuck mainly to the business of maximizing profits. In proportion as one increases its capacity to do good, one increases its capacity to do mischief.

If the effects of corporate activities are sometimes bad, they unquestionably are often good. It's possible that the aggregate good corporations do outweighs whatever injustice results from their operations. But another possibility which merits serious consideration is that the overall system which contains them is basically immoral and ought to be replaced. It's possible that corporations simply cannot effectively be reformed in the context of the values of the system of which they are a part. It is this question— whether capitalism or socialism or some other economic arrangement best answers to human needs—to which the question of corporate responsibility ultimately leads.

Study questions

1. How does the text define the *liberal* and *conservative* positions on the issue of corporate responsibility (Section 6.3)?
2. What does economist *Milton Friedman* take to be the basic *obligation of corporations* (Key Quote 6A)?
3. What, according to *Adam Smith*, is the role of *the "invisible hand"* in self-interested economic pursuits (Key Quote 6B)?
4. What *objections* might be made to the claim that corporations should assume moral responsibilities (Section 6.5)?
5. How does the distinction between *individual morality* and *collective morality* (Theory Box 6A) relate to the question of whether corporations should adopt moral responsibilities?

6. What is the distinction between *consequentialism* and *nonconsequentialism* in ethics (Theory Box 6B)? Which sort of theory seems to underlie Friedman's defense of the view that the sole obligation of corporations is to maximize profits?

7. How does the text argue that there is no need to postulate two moralities (individual and collective) in assessing the issue of corporate responsibility; that the assumption that there is *one morality* is all that is needed (Section 6.5)?

8. What is *non-maleficence*, and how does it bear upon the conduct of corporations?

9. How does the question of *distributive justice* inevitably arise in connection with the actions of corporations, both at home and abroad (Section 6.8)?

10. If corporations should assume moral responsibilities, *who should decide* what those responsibilities should be? What problems does trying to answer that question raise (Section 6.9)?

Notes

1 Milton Friedman, "The Social Responsibility of Business Is to Increase Its Profits," *The New York Times Magazine*, September 13, 1970.

2 Peter A. French, "Corporate Moral Agency," in Tom L. Beauchamp and Norman E. Bowie, *Ethical Theory and Business* (Englewood Cliffs, NJ: Prentice-Hall, Inc., 1979), p. 176.

3 Thomas Donaldson, *Corporations and Morality* (Englewood Cliffs, NJ: Prentice-Hall, Inc., 1982), pp. 2–6; emphasis in the original.

4 Milton Friedman, *Capitalism and Freedom* (Chicago: University of Chicago Press, 1962), p. 133.

5 Adam Smith, *Wealth of Nations* (1776), Bk V, Ch. 11 (Cannon ed., London, 1930), p. 421.

6 John Dewey and James H. Tufts, *Ethics* (New York: Henry Holt, 1908), p. 519.

7 Ibid., pp. 133–6.

8 K. William Kapp, *The Social Costs of Private Enterprise* (New York: Schocken Books, 1950), pp. 13f.

9 Jack Powelson, *Holistic Economics and Social Protest* (Wallingford, PA: Pendle Hill Publications, 1983), p. 24.

10 National Foreign Trade Council, 1625 K Street, NW Suite 200 Washington, DC 2006.

For more resources:

www.bloomsbury.com/holmes-introduction-to-applied-ethics

7

Poverty and World Hunger

There would be no poverty on earth if we made a sacred resolution that we would have no more than we need for our creature comforts.

—Gandhi[1]

Introduction

In this chapter we shall consider the nature of poverty and why some people choose to live in poverty despite the fact that, in general, it's bad. When people involuntarily find themselves in poverty, do others have an obligation to help relieve their condition? If so, do people individually have such an obligation or only collectively, as part of a social movement? We shall explore these questions, as well as the question whether attempts to remove poverty are futile.

7.1 What is poverty?

Although declining globally, poverty is widespread. It's seen by many as one of the major social and international problems of our time. Most of us feel we know poverty when we see it, but what precisely is it? The matter is more complex than might at first appear. Consider the following definition:

> Poverty: "lack or relative lack of money or material possessions." (*Webster's Third International Dictionary*)

According to this definition, you're poor if you lack money or material possessions. Few would dispute that. But the definition also implies that you're poor if you have a *relative* lack of money or material possessions. And this is questionable.

If you own a home and two cars and are worth $500,000 you aren't poor. But by comparison with someone who owns three homes and five cars and is worth $500 million you have a relative lack of money and possessions. There is great *inequality* between you. But inequality doesn't in itself signify poverty. Without specification of the relevant comparison group, "relative" lack of money or possessions tells us little.

Let us, instead, define poverty more simply:

Definition Box 7A

Poverty: Possession of little or no money and material goods.

According to this definition, poverty is an absolute (as opposed to a relative) lack of money or material possessions, meaning either a lack of *any* money or possessions (which is rare) or lack of all but a little money and a few possessions.

7.2 Is poverty necessarily bad?

Is poverty, understood in this way, bad? Most people think so. A survey of American college freshmen showed that 73.6 percent had as an objective to be very well off financially, that is, not only to avoid poverty, but to be affluent.[2] Most would probably share that goal. Poverty is associated with disease, hunger, malnutrition, and high crime rates. Some see it as the breeding ground of terrorism as well. These things are obviously bad. But is poverty *itself* necessarily bad? Not everyone thinks so.

Siddartha Gautama (the Buddha) was born a prince in sixth century BCE India, but he renounced wealth to lead a spiritual life of poverty, walking back and forth across India teaching the way to end human suffering. Socrates (470–399 BCE), at his trial, spoke of his poverty, saying he didn't care about making money but only about persuading people to think first of their mental and moral well-being. His attempt to do that by persistent and probing questioning of his fellow Athenians led to his being charged with corrupting the youth of Athens (among other things) and being sentenced to death. Jesus also chose a life of poverty, spreading teachings that likewise led to his death. The same in the twentieth century with Mahatma Gandhi (1869–1948). Some Jain monks in India today renounce *all* material possessions—even clothing. They walk about naked, living off contributions of food from villagers. In their view, nonpossession, as they call it, is essential to living nonviolently, deepening spiritual awareness and minimizing the costs they impose upon other forms of life. Henry David Thoreau (1817–62), who retreated to the woods to live a life of simplicity, about which he wrote in his book *Walden*, expressed the spirit of this outlook:

> Most of the luxuries, and many of the so-called comforts of life, are not only not indispensable, but positive hindrances to the elevation of mankind. With respect to luxuries and comforts, the wisest have ever lived a more simple and meager life than the poor. The ancient philosophers, Chinese, Hindu, Persian and Greek, were a class than which none has been poorer in outward riches, none so rich in inward ... None can be an impartial or wise observer of human life but from the vantage ground of what *we* should call voluntary poverty.[3]

So, some people value poverty and voluntarily choose it. They see it as a better way to live.

Some go even further than this. They not only think poverty is good, they think it *ought* to be chosen. They believe, as Gandhi did, that it's wrong to live with more than you need so long as there are others in dire need. We're obligated to forego affluence in our own lives in order to help others. Gandhi even thought that Western culture, with its emphasis upon accumulating material possessions, should be resisted (at least by Indians) in favor of the traditions and simplicity of life as it had endured for centuries in Indian villages.

But isn't there a contradiction here? On the one hand, some people advocate a simple life devoid of all but a few material possessions: a life that many (particularly Westerners) would consider one of impoverishment. At the same time, they would urge upon us a sense of obligation to relieve the poverty of others. Why? If poverty is good, as at least some people think, why try to pull people out of it? Why not, rather, teach them the advantages of poverty and encourage them to accept it?

To answer this, let us return to the definition of poverty. It speaks of lack of money or material possessions. One can live without *ownership* of wealth and material goods. But obviously one can't live without *having* (or having access to) material goods, such as food, clothing, and shelter. If you lived alone on a remote, previously undiscovered island with a warm climate, bountiful food, and clean water, you would own nothing; ownership is a legal concept that wouldn't apply in such isolation. But you'd have available to you the material necessities of life. You'd need only pick fruit from a tree when hungry, drink from a spring when thirsty, and step into a nearby cave when in need of shelter. The Chinese philosopher Lao Tzu, in the *Tao Te Ching*, speaks of the supreme virtue, and includes in it, "having and not possessing."

The point is that having material things is essential to life; owning them isn't. Newborns own nothing (beyond rattles, pacifiers, and stuffed animals), but they're cared for. Priests and nuns take a vow of poverty and renounce all but the minimum of material possessions. They lack money and goods in the sense that they don't *own* them. But they have access to them; food, clothing, and shelter—the necessities of life—are provided for them by the church. They have medical care, transportation when needed, and the support of a community of persons likewise committed to the church. In short, they personally have little in the way of money and material possessions, but they're provided for by an institution that has considerable money and material possessions.

Gandhi's point is that so long as we have more than we need we should sacrifice some of what we have to help others. Notice the emphasis here is upon need. People who lack money or possessions aren't necessarily in need; as we've seen, they may nonetheless have the necessities of life, as do priests, nuns, and Jain monks. What is bad is to be deprived of the necessities of life—of the conditions of decent human existence. Millions of people are so deprived. They're not only poor, they're destitute.

One of the necessities of life is food. One can be poor and still have plenty of food to eat. But poverty often brings with it an acute lack of food. That's one of the worst of the possible consequences of poverty. And it's a condition that millions face in the contemporary world, as the following report documents:

20 Million Face Famine in a "World of Plenty"

In a world filled with excess food, 20 million people are on the brink of famine, including 1.4 million children at imminent risk of death. In the face of such grim numbers, a stark question confronts the world's most powerful: Why in 2017 can't they avert such a seemingly archaic and preventable catastrophe?[4]

As we've said, people living in poverty can have sufficient food, though often they don't. When they don't, they're hungry; when their hunger is severe, they're famished; and when their lives are at risk from shortage of food, they're starving. An individual can be famished, but only a whole people or region can experience famine; it's a condition of extended extreme shortage of food.

Definition Box 7B

Famine
Famine is a rare and specific state. It is declared after three specific criteria are met: when one in five households in a certain area face extreme food shortages; more than 30 percent of the population is acutely malnourished; and at least two people for every 10,000 die each day.[5]

People who voluntarily choose a life of poverty don't choose to starve. Adequate food is required even for the simple life that individuals like Socrates, Jesus, Thoreau, Gandhi, or Mother Teresa choose; they simply forego many of the material goods and comforts of life that most people desire.

This suggests that we should recognize a condition beyond poverty, that of destitution. Let us define it as follows:

Definition Box 7C

Destitution
Destitution: Being deprived of what is necessary for a minimally decent human life.

One can be poor without being destitute. Although some people voluntarily choose poverty, no one (with the possible exception of ascetics) chooses destitution. Yet poverty and destitution often go together. Many—perhaps most—of the millions who live in poverty today are destitute. They live in dire poverty, which often includes inadequate food. When poverty, famine, and destitution occur together, the consequences can be catastrophic. When people speak of poverty as a world problem, they usually have in mind, not the voluntary poverty of a Gandhi or Mother Teresa, but extreme poverty, a state of destitution, one that often involves a shortage of food as well as other necessities of life.

Put in other terms, we may distinguish *needs* and *wants*. Most of us want many things (e.g., cell phones, trendy clothes, trips abroad) beyond our needs. Lack of these things doesn't signify poverty. All of us, however, need nourishment, clothing, clean water, and shelter. Without them we perish. Even with them in insufficient supply we cannot live well. When speaking of world poverty as a moral problem, we mean that millions of people world-wide live in dire poverty—not by choice but by necessity—a condition in which the essentials of a good life are in inadequate supply.

Even vast wealth isn't necessarily good. You may own five luxury cars, three estates, and be worth $100 million, but if someone cuts off your water supply (and you're unable to buy water or travel to where it can be found), you'll die. Your wealth will count for nothing. And it will count for nothing if you are thrown into solitary confinement for life with no access to your money; or, worse yet, placed under the guillotine, as happened to many of the aristocracy during the French Revolution. There are, in short, circum-stances in which wealth is no better than poverty. There are even circum-stances in which it's worse than poverty. If Gandhi and Thoreau are correct, even if you manage to preserve your life and luxury, you risk going through life spiritually impoverished. And if Jesus is correct, your prospects of going to heaven are about as good as those of getting a camel through the eye of a needle.

We may conclude that wealth isn't necessarily good (since some people renounce it and claim to find their lives better for having done so). But per-haps it's good most of the time, and it's certainly definitely valued by most people. Poverty, by the same token, isn't necessarily bad (since some people choose it and believe their lives better for having done so). It's nonetheless bad most of the time. It not only prevents people from living the best lives of which they're capable, it also prevents them from living even minimally satisfactory lives.

7.3 How serious a problem is poverty?

That there's widespread poverty is indisputable, but its extent, severity, and causes are disputed. These are factual, not moral, issues, but they're relevant to assessing the moral issues. Let us consider some of the diversity of opinion here. Consider the following analysis of poverty in the United States:

On the Gap between the Rich and the Poor
The "official" measure of poverty used by the U.S. Census Bureau was developed in the 1960s and was originally based on the cost of an adequate diet; specifically, having a money income less than three times the cost of a minimally adequate diet for a family of a given size. Although initially adjusted each year for changes in the cost of the diet plan, poverty thresholds today are recalculated based on price inflation using the Consumer Price Index.

Official poverty is based on money income before taxes. It does not include capital gains and nontax benefits, such as public housing, Medicaid, and food stamps. The threshold for a family of four in 2002 was $18,556. If a family's money income falls below the established threshold, then all members of the family are classified as poor.

Using these criteria to estimate the number of people suffering in poor living conditions has some serious shortcomings ... For example, current living conditions depend not only on current income, but also on past income and expected future income. The poor may also benefit from private transfers from charities and relatives, alimony, or unreported income from sources other than wages or salaries (welfare recipients have an incentive to underreport income). One more shortcoming is that noncash benefits are not figured in when calculating poverty rates. Thus, providing the less fortunate with government housing, food stamps, Medicaid, education, etc. would not lift a single one of them out of official poverty.

Although many may be below the official threshold, the poverty rate peaked in 1983 and has been falling since ... This would seem to be a positive development.

Using consumption rather than some definition of income as the standard may be more appropriate, since poor families typically spend more than their reported income on consumption. According to the 2001 Consumer Expenditure Survey published by the Bureau of Labor Statistics, the lowest income quintile had an income before taxes of $7,946, but annual expenditures of $18,883. Only the fourth and fifth income quintiles had higher incomes before taxes than annual expenditures ...

Although the poor spend more than they earn, that does not reflect how they live. The basic goods that all people need to purchase are food, clothing, and shelter. People who cannot afford these basics could be said to be living in genuinely poor conditions. One way to gauge this is to compare what people living in official poverty spent on these necessities over time. Economist Michael Cox and business reporter Richard Aim found that among households below the poverty line, spending on food, clothing, and shelter in 1995 amounted to 37 percent of their consumption, compared with 52 percent in 1975, 57 percent in 1950, and 75 percent in 1920. As the poor spent less and less on basics, they had more discretionary money to spend on consumption goods such as washers and dryers, microwave ovens, VCRs, etc... . [B]y 1994, poor households were just as likely to possess certain conveniences as the average household did two decades earlier.

Another way to gauge how people live is to measure well-being. Some types of shortfalls in material well-being are far less common than income poverty. For example, according to U.S. Census Bureau data, 7.5 percent of households in poverty sometimes or often did not have enough of the food they wanted, 13.2 percent missed rent or mortgage payments, and 14.1 percent had a member who needed to visit a doctor or hospital but did not go.

Finally, if we are to avoid the mistaken impression that the same people remain trapped at the bottom of the income distribution, remember that people in the lowest quintile often move into higher quintiles over time ...

Social critics confuse the distinction between official poverty and living in poor conditions and argue that greater income inequality increases the misery of the poor. But the data show that the poverty rate is falling, and that those in poverty do not necessarily live in misery. The poor tend to be better off than the rich were a century ago, and better off than they were a couple of decades ago. These trends would seem to be positive developments—despite growing income inequality.[6]

Compare the preceding analysis with the following report, excerpted from a detailed set of statistics compiled by the US government:

Key Quote 7A

Poverty in the United States

- The official poverty rate in 2015 was 13.5 percent.
- In 2015, there were 43.1 million people in poverty.
- The 2015 poverty rate was 1.0 percentage point higher than in 2007, the year before the most recent recession.
- Between 2014 and 2015 ... the poverty rate for children under age 18 dropped ... from 21.1 percent to 19.7 percent. Rates for people aged 18 to 64 dropped ... from 13.5 percent to 12.4 percent. Poverty rates for people aged 65 and older decreased ... from 10.0 percent to 8.8 percent.[7]

The preceding deals with poverty in the United States. Let us now consider an account of hunger worldwide:

1. **Some 795 million people** in the world do not have enough food to lead a healthy active life ...
2. The vast majority of the world's hungry people **live in developing countries**, where 12.9 percent of the population is undernourished.
3. Asia is the continent with the most hungry people—two thirds of the total. The percentage in southern Asia has fallen in recent years but in western Asia it has increased slightly.
4. Sub-Saharan Africa is the region with the highest *prevalence* (percentage of population) of hunger ...
5. Poor nutrition causes **nearly half (45%) of deaths** in children under five—3.1 million children each year.
6. One out of six children—roughly 100 million—in developing countries is **underweight**.
7. One in four of the world's **children are stunted**. In developing countries the proportion can rise to one in three.
8. If **women** farmers had the same access to resources as men, the number of hungry in the world could be **reduced by up to 150 million**.

9. 66 million primary school-age **children attend classes hungry** across the developing world, with 23 million in Africa alone.
10. WFP calculates that US$3.2 billion **is needed per year to reach all 66 million hungry school-age children**. (World Food Programme (wfp.org))

Statistics on poverty and world hunger are controversial, and accounts vary. But what isn't questionable is that millions of people live in poverty, and that millions, particularly children, are undernourished worldwide. Whatever the precise figures, the moral question of what can and should be done about poverty stands out.

7.4 Are we individually obligated to fight world poverty?

Analyses like the preceding make clear that the extent and severity of poverty—both in the United States and worldwide—are disputed. But that there is widespread poverty is indisputable. We don't have space to deal with both poverty in the United States and worldwide poverty, so we shall focus primarily upon worldwide poverty. Let us formulate the moral issue by means of two questions:

1. Do we, individually, have a moral obligation to try to alleviate world poverty?
2. Do we, collectively (as a community, society, or nation), have an obligation to try to alleviate world poverty?

One might answer either question with a Yes or No, but the questions raise somewhat different issues. Let us begin with the first.

Many Christians believe we, individually, have an obligation to help the poor, as derived from the example and message of Jesus in the commandment to love. Muslims are under an express obligation, according to the Koran, to given alms to the poor. Religion aside, some argue for such an obligation on purely philosophical grounds. Consider the following passage from philosopher Peter Singer:

The Singer Solution to World Poverty

In the Brazilian film "Central Station," Dora is a retired schoolteacher who makes ends meet by sitting at the station writing letters for illiterate people. Suddenly she has an opportunity to pocket $1,000. All she has to do is persuade a homeless 9-year-old boy to follow her to an address she has been given (She is told he will be adopted by wealthy foreigners.). She delivers the boy, gets the money, spends some of it on a television set and settles down to enjoy her new acquisition. Her neighbor spoils the fun, however, by telling her that the boy was too old to be adopted—he will be killed and his organs sold for transplantation. Perhaps Dora knew this all along, but after her neighbor's plain speaking, she spends a troubled night. In the morning Dora resolves to take the boy back.

Suppose Dora had told her neighbor that it is a tough world, other people have nice new TV's too, and if selling the kid is the only way she can get one, well, he was only a street kid. She would then have become, in the eyes of the audience, a monster. She redeems herself only by being prepared to bear considerable risks to save the boy.

At the end of the move, in cinemas in the affluent nations of the world, people who would have been quick to condemn Dora if she had not rescued the boy go home to places far more comfortable than her apartment. In fact, the average family in the United States spends almost one-third of its income on things that are no more necessary to them than Dora's new TV was to her. Going out to nice restaurants, buying new clothes because the old ones are no longer stylish, vacationing at beach resorts—so much of our income is spent on things not essential to the preservation of our lives and health. Donated to one of a number of charitable agencies, that money could mean the difference between life and death for children in need.

All of which raises a question: In the end, what is the ethical distinction between a Brazilian who sells a homeless child to organ peddlers and an American who already has a TV and upgrades to a better one—knowing that the money could be donated to an organization that would use it to save the lives of kids in need ... But one doesn't need to embrace my utilitarian ethic to see that, at the very least, there is a troubling incongruity in being so quick to condemn Dora for taking the child to organ peddlers while, at the same time, not regarding the American consumer's behavior as raising a serious moral issue.[8]

Singer speaks here of the plight of children, but his point applies to world poverty generally. If he's correct, it would not just be nice if we individually sought to relieve poverty; we have an obligation to do so—it would be wrong not to. Why? Singer's reasoning is set forth in an earlier work:

I begin with the assumption that suffering and death from lack of food, shelter, and medical care are bad. I think most people will agree about this ...

My next point is this: if it is in our power to prevent something bad from happening, without thereby sacrificing anything of comparable moral importance, we ought, morally, to do it. By "without sacrificing anything of comparable moral importance" I mean without causing anything else comparably bad to happen, or doing something that is wrong in itself, or failing to promote some moral good, comparable in significance to the bad thing that we can prevent. This principle seems almost as uncontroversial as the last one. It requires us only to prevent what is bad, and not to promote what is good, and it requires this of us only when we can do it without sacrificing anything that is, from the moral point of view, comparably important. I could even ... qualify the point so as to make it: if it is in our power to prevent something very bad from happening, without thereby sacrificing anything morally significant, we ought, morally, to do it. An application of this principle would be as follows: if I am walking past a shallow pond and see a child drowning in it, I ought to wade in and pull the child out. This will mean getting my clothes muddy, but this is insignificant, while the death of the child would presumably be a very bad thing.

The uncontroversial appearance of the principle just stated is deceptive. If it were acted upon, even in its qualified form, our lives, our society, and our world would be fundamentally changed. For the principle takes, firstly, no account of proximity or distance. It makes no moral difference whether the person I can help is a neighbor's child ten yards from me or a Bengali whose name I shall never know, ten thousand miles away. Secondly, the principle makes no distinction between cases in which I am the only person who could possibly do anything and cases in which I am just one among millions in the same position.

I do not think I need to say much in defense of the refusal to take proximity and distance into account. The fact that person is physically near to us, so that we have personal contact with him, may make it more likely that we *shall* assist him, but this does not show that we *ought* to help him rather than another who happens to be further away. If we accept any principle of impartiality, universalizability, equality, or whatever, we cannot discriminate against someone merely because he is far away from us … Admittedly, it is possible that we are in a better position to judge what needs to be done to help a person near to us than one far away, and perhaps also provide the assistance we judge to be necessary. If this were the case, it would be a reason for helping those near to us first. This may once have been a justification for being more concerned with the poor in one's own town than with famine victims in India. Unfortunately for those who like to keep their moral responsibilities limited, instant communication and swift transportation have changed the situation. From the moral point of view, the development of the world into a "global village" has made an important … difference to our moral situation. Expert observers and supervisors, sent out by famine relief organizations or permanently stationed in famine-prone areas, can direct our aid to a refugee in Bengal almost as effectively as we could get it to someone in our own block. There would seem, therefore, to be no possible justification for discriminating on geographical grounds …

One objection to the position I have taken might be simply that it is too drastic a revision of our moral scheme. People do not ordinarily judge in the way I have suggested they should. Most people reserve their moral condemnation for those who violate some moral norm, such as the norm against taking another person's property. They do not condemn those who indulge in luxury instead of giving to famine relief. But given that I did not set out to present a morally neutral description of the way people make moral judgments, the way people do in fact judge has nothing to do with the validity of my conclusion. My conclusion follows from the principle which I advanced earlier, and unless that principle is rejected, or the arguments shown to be unsound, I think the conclusion must stand, however strange it appears.[9]

Let us examine this reasoning more closely. We can begin by noting that Singer's argument rests upon the following principle:

P: If it is in our power to prevent something bad from happening without sacrificing anything of comparable moral importance, then we ought to do so.

Since we each presumably have it within our power to relieve the suffering of some of those living in poverty without sacrificing anything of comparable moral significance, Singer thinks we ought to do so. In terms of our earlier distinction between needs and wants, if some of us can sacrifice some of the things we want in order to help provide for the needs of others, we should do so, providing the sacrifice isn't of anything comparable to the bad (as represented by poverty and hunger) we're trying to alleviate. That is, we're obligated to sacrifice, but not to the point that we ourselves are poor and hungry.

In case some should think that this principle demands too much, Singer proposes a modified principle:

MP: If it is in our power to prevent something bad from happening without sacrificing *anything* morally significant, we ought to do so.

The first principle, P, would require that we take steps to prevent the bad from happening up to the point at which the cost of the remedy (itself a bad, in that it would require sacrifice of time and money and many things we want) became comparable to the original bad. That is, there's a comparative judgment involved. Suppose we could measure badness on a scale in which the cost of the proposed remedy is measured against the initial bad.

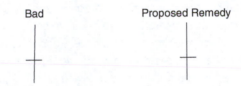

If we compare the initial bad (say, starvation of those living in poverty) and the cost of the remedy, then we are obligated to pay that cost up to (but not beyond) the point at which the remedy equals the initial bad.

The second principle, MP, however, would demand much less of us. Assume that the initial bad is the same, it would require only that we institute the remedy up to the point at which anything of moral significance (however that's defined) is sacrificed. The situation would look like this:

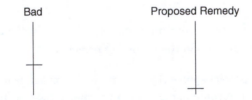

This would require less of us than principle P. Many actions we'd be obligated to perform according to P we wouldn't be obligated to perform according to

MP. For example, P might require that we forego new cars, vacations abroad, and homeownership in order to alleviate world poverty. We might even have to forego one meal a day. MP, on the other hand, might require only that we forego upgrading our TV or iPhone.

Both P and MP are consequentialist principles (see Theory Box 6B, Chapter 6, Section 6.5). They require that we look at the consequences of actions to assess their rightness or wrongness. But they require not that we promote positive good in the world, but only that we remove some bad (pain or suffering). That is, they're minimalist consequentialist principles. At this point it's important to understand the difference between non-maleficence and beneficence. (It'll be helpful to remind you in the process of consequentialism as defined in Theory Box 6A.)

Theory Box 7A

Non-Maleficence and Beneficence
Consequentialism: Moral rightness is determined solely by the consequences of actions.

> **Non-maleficence**: one ought to do no harm.
> **Beneficence**: one ought to do good.

    a. One ought to alleviate suffering.
    b. One ought to do good beyond alleviating suffering.

Both non-maleficence and beneficence would have us look to the consequences of our actions, first, to see that we don't cause harm, second, to see that we do some positive good. But if we seek to do good, we might either limit our effort to trying to alleviate suffering or try to promote good beyond that.

Both non-maleficence and beneficence relate to the Golden Rule. That rule has both negative and positive formulations. In Confucianism we find a negative formulation:

Key Quote 7B

Negative Golden Rule
Do not do unto others what you would not have them do unto you.

Although it doesn't speak expressly of harm, a reasonable interpretation of this principle is that we ought not to harm others, since we wouldn't want them to harm us. But in Christianity there is a different formulation:

Key Quote 7C

Positive Golden Rule
Do unto others as you would have them do unto you.

This doesn't speak specifically of good, but it may be interpreted to mean that we ought to do good for others, if we would have them do good for us.[10] Put simply, we may think that we ought to do good in the world.

But if we accept the positive golden rule, how much good ought we to do for others beyond the alleviation of suffering? And do we have an *obligation* to go beyond the alleviation of suffering?

Some people are uncomfortable with the suggestion that we should do good for others. People who dedicate themselves to doing good for others are sometimes disparagingly called Do-gooders, which implies self-righteous meddling. As Thoreau said:

Key Quote 7D

If I knew for a certainty that a man was coming to my house with the conscious design of doing me good, I should run for my life.[11]

But it would be difficult to charge the Gandhis and Mother Teresas of the world with being Do-gooders in the sense Thoreau had in mind. And Thoreau does urge those who choose such a life to persevere, even though he doesn't choose that life himself.

Some would argue that, even if we don't have an obligation to do good in the sense implied by the positive Golden Rule, we do have an obligation not to cause harm, as the negative Golden Rule implies. But further, they would maintain that we have an obligation at least to try to remove what is bad in the world. That is the place to start. While it might be good if poor people had TVs, cell phones, designer clothes, and cars, it's more important that their hunger, malnutrition, and disease first be alleviated. This is the idea behind both of Singer's principles. They differ only in how much we must be prepared to sacrifice to remove the suffering of others. Nothing in either principle clearly requires that we go beyond that.

7.5 Are we collectively obligated to fight world poverty?

Let's now turn to question (2), whether we collectively have an obligation to aid the poor. Some people question whether large-scale efforts to relieve poverty are effective. Others argue that they are actually counterproductive.

Grounds for questioning anti-poverty efforts at the social and international level are provided by the following report:

The West Helps, and Harms, as Southern Africa Seeks Food
Throughout Malawi, there are an estimated 3.3 million people … too poor to buy food, living on monthly distributions from international aid organizations.

But, say critics, the problem of terrible poverty will not be solved with handouts.

Rich donors—the US, the European Union, and Japan, in particular— would be doing much more good in the long term if they concentrated on trade, instead of aid, goes the argument.

Critics also say that the large farm subsidies paid by wealthy countries to their own farmers hurt farmers in developing countries. The subsidized farmers can flood the market and sell their goods for less than it costs to grow them; the governments make up the difference. Poor farmers can't compete with such low prices, keeping them out of international markets, and keeping their countries from gaining economically.

According to the World Trade Organization, rich countries gave $57 billion in development aid in 2001 but paid more than $350 billion to their own farmers. World Bank figures suggest that giving developing countries more access to rich markets could earn them about $150 billion a year …

In a recent report, Oxfam illustrates the damage being done by subsidies by looking at handouts given by the EU to sugar farmers in

Europe. These farmers then produce surpluses, which flood the world market at artificially low prices.

Meanwhile, South Africa, Malawi, Swaziland, and Zambia—all low-cost sugar producers—are unable to tap potential markets in North America or the Middle East because they are outbid by the subsidized European producers, according to the Oxfam report.

"This means that an agricultural commodity that could play a real part in poverty alleviation in Southern Africa does not do so," the Oxfam report said. "European consumers are paying to destroy livelihoods in some of the world's poorest countries."[12]

The preceding report raises serious questions about whether some of the collective efforts to relieve world poverty are doing more harm than good. An even more serious challenge is set forth in the following argument by Garret Hardin:

Environmentalists use the metaphor of the earth as a "spaceship" in trying to persuade countries, industries and people to stop; wasting and polluting our natural resources. Since we all share life on this planet, they argue, no single person or institution has the right to destroy, waste, or use more than a fair share of its resources.

But does everyone on earth have an equal right to an equal share of its resources? The spaceship metaphor can be dangerous when used by misguided idealists to justify suicidal policies for sharing our resources through uncontrolled immigration and foreign aid. In their enthusiastic but unrealistic generosity, they confuse the ethics of a spaceship with those of a lifeboat ... Metaphorically each rich nation can be seen as a lifeboat full of comparatively rich people. In the ocean outside each lifeboat swim the poor of the world, who would like to get in, or at least to share some of the wealth. What should the lifeboat passengers do?

First, we must recognize the limited capacity of any lifeboat. For example, a nation's land has a limited capacity to support a population and ... in some ways we have already exceeded the carrying capacity of our land.

Adrift in a Moral Sea

So here we sit, say fifty people in our lifeboat. To be generous, let us assume it has room for ten more, making a total capacity of sixty.

Suppose the fifty of us in the lifeboat see 100 others swimming in the water outside, begging for admission to our boat or for handouts. We have several options: we may be tempted to live by the Christian ideal of being "our brother's keeper," or by the Marxist ideal of "to each according to his needs." Since the needs of all in the water are the same, and since they can all be seen as "our brothers," we could take them all into our boat, making a total of 150 in a boat designed for sixty. The boat swamps, everyone drowns. Complete justice, complete catastrophe.

Since the boat has an unused excess capacity of ten more passengers, we could admit just ten more to it. But which ten do we let in? How do we choose? Do we pick the best ten, the neediest ten, "first come, first served"? And what do we say to the ninety we exclude? If we do let an extra ten into our lifeboat, we will have lost our "safety factor," an engineering principle of critical importance. For example, if we don't leave room for excess capacity as a safety factor in our country's agriculture, a new plant disease or a bad change in the weather could have disastrous consequences.

Suppose we decide to preserve our small safety factor and admit no more to the lifeboat. Our survival is then possible, although we shall have to be constantly on guard against boarding parties.

While this last solution clearly offers the only means of our survival, it is morally abhorrent to many people. Some say they feel guilty about their good luck. My reply is simple: "Get out and yield your place to others." This may solve the problem of the guilt-ridden person's conscience, but it does not change the ethics of the life-boat. The needy person to whom the guilt-ridden person yields his place will not himself feel guilty about his good luck. If he did, he would not climb aboard. The net result of conscience-stricken people giving up their unjustly held seats is the elimination of that sort of conscience from the lifeboat.

That is the basic metaphor within which we must work out our solutions . . .

The harsh ethics of the lifeboat becomes even harsher when we consider the reproductive differences between the rich nations and the poor nations. The people inside the lifeboats are doubling in numbers every eighty-seven years; those swimming around outside are doubling, on the average, every thirty-five years, more than twice as fast as the rich. And since the world's resources are dwindling, the difference in prosperity between the rich and the poor can only increase . . . In sharing with "each according to his needs," we must recognize that needs are determined by population size, which is determined by the rate of reproduction, which at present is regarded as a sovereign right of every nation, poor or not. This being so, the philanthropic load created by the sharing ethic ... can only increase.

The Tragedy of the Commons

The fundamental error of spaceship ethics, and the sharing it requires, is that it leads to what I call "the tragedy of the commons." Under a system of private property, the men who own property recognize their responsibility to care for it, for if they don't they will eventually suffer. A farmer, for instance, will allow no more cattle in a pasture than its carrying capacity justifies. If he overloads it, erosion sets in, weeds take over, and he loses the use of the pasture.

If a pasture becomes a commons open to all, the right of each to use it may not be matched by a corresponding responsibility to protect it. Asking everyone to use it with discretion will hardly do, for the considerate herdsman who refrains from overloading the commons suffers more than a selfish one who says his needs are greater. If everyone would restrain himself, all would be well; but it takes only one less than everyone to ruin a system of voluntary restraint. In a crowded world of less than perfect human beings, mutual ruin is inevitable if there are no controls. This is the tragedy of the commons.

One of the major tasks of education today should be the creation of such an acute awareness of the dangers of the commons that people will recognize its many varieties. For the example, the air and water have become polluted because they are treated as commons. Further growth in the population or per capita conversion of natural resources into pollutants will only make the problem worse. The same holds true for the fish of the oceans. Fishing fleets have nearly disappeared in many parts of the world, technological improvements in the art of fishing are hastening the day of complete ruin. Only the replacement of the system of the commons with a responsible system of control will save the land, air, water and oceanic fisheries.

Learning the Hard Way

What happens if some organizations or countries budget for accidents and others do not? If each country is solely responsible for its own well-being, poorly managed ones will suffer. But they can learn from experience. They may mend their ways, and learn to budget for infrequent but certain emergencies ...

"But it isn't their fault!" Some kindhearted liberals argue. "How can we blame the poor people who are caught in an emergency? Why must they suffer for the sins of their governments?" the concept of blame is simply not relevant here. The real question is, what are the operational consequences of establishing a world food bank? ... Some countries will deposit food in the world food bank, and others will withdraw it. There will be almost no overlap. As a result of such solutions to food shortage emergencies, the poor countries will not learn to mend their ways, and will suffer progressively greater emergencies as their populations grow.[13]

Let's examine this reasoning more closely. Hardin's argument, like Singer's, is consequentialist. But whereas Singer focuses upon individuals taking upon themselves an obligation to help the poor, Hardin focuses primarily upon whether we collectively have an obligation to fight poverty, specifically through the state. It's the wealthy *nations*, after all, that are in the lifeboat in his metaphor, even if it's individual persons (or perhaps poorer nations) struggling in the water around them. And much, though not all of his analysis, is focused upon collective efforts by governments—such as by means of a World Food Bank—to alleviate poverty. And it is other nations or their governments who may "learn from experience" and perhaps "mend their ways" if they suffer as a result of their policies. The implication is that poor countries themselves are, at least in part, responsible for their plight.

Singer's consequentialism is rooted in utilitarianism (see Theory Box 1E, Chapter 1, Section 1.8), whereas Hardin's is rooted in national egoism. His analysis elevates the good of one's own nation above that of others. Keeping one's own nation afloat is the principal goal.

Even if one questions Hardin's dire prediction of the catastrophic consequences of an all-out war on world poverty (the sinking of the wealthy nations without helping the poor), it is always relevant to question the effectiveness of collective efforts to help the poor. Consider the following report:

World Bank Challenged: Are the Poor Really Helped?
Wealthy nations and international organizations, including the World Bank, spend more than $55 billion annually to better the lot of the

world's 2.7 billion poor people. Yet they have scant evidence that the myriad projects they finance have made any real difference, many economists say.

That important fact has left some critics of the World Bank, the largest financier of antipoverty programs in developing countries, dissatisfied, and they have begun throwing down an essential challenge. It is not enough, they say, just to measure how many miles of roads are built, schools constructed or microcredit loans provided. You must also measure whether those investments actually help poor people live longer, more prosperous lives ...

A small band of development economists, who a year ago founded the Poverty Action Lab at the Massachusetts Institute of Technology, have become influential advocates for randomized evaluations as the best way to answer that question ...

The Poverty Action Lab scholars have made startling discoveries in their own randomized evaluations.

Adding an extra teacher to classrooms in rural India did not improve children's test scores. But hiring high-school graduates who were paid only $10 to $15 a month to give remedial tutoring to groups of lagging students in a Bombay slum markedly improved reading and math skills.

A series of education experiments in Kenya found that providing poor students with free uniforms or a simple porridge breakfast substantially increased attendance. But giving them drugs to treat the intestinal worms that infect more than a quarter of the world's population was more cost effective, at a price tag of only $3.50 for each extra year of schooling achieved. Healthier children are more likely to go to school. "You can't answer the general question: Does aid work?" said Esther Duflo, an economist and co-founder of the Poverty Action Lab. "You have to go project by project and accumulate the evidence."[14]

If world poverty is increasing in absolute numbers (even if decreasing in some areas, and decreasing percentage-wise), it's fair to ask whether current programs are effective. This is a factual, not a moral question. It may be that there aren't even agreed-upon criteria by which to measure reliably whether policies are effective. In that case, we simply may not at present be able to resolve the factual issue. (One might raise the same question about efforts to help the poor domestically, though that isn't our main concern at the moment.)

7.6 Are efforts to fight poverty futile under present socioeconomic conditions?

It's possible, however, that Singer and Hardin are arguing at cross-purposes. They may both be correct, if properly understood. It's possible that collective efforts to help the poor through nations or governments are counterproductive and even doomed to fail, as Hardin maintains. At the same time, it may be that efforts by *individuals*, as Singer stresses—either personally or through nongovernmental agencies—are or would be effective. This possibility cannot be discounted. In other words, it's possible that both Singer and Hardin are correct, given their assumptions and the different ways in which they frame their analyses.

But what if Hardin is correct and Singer wrong? Does that mean that it's fruitless to aid the poor? Not necessarily. There's another possibility, one whose consequences are more far-reaching.

It's suggested by another passage from Thoreau, though he doesn't expand upon it:

> ## Key Quote 7E
>
> There are a thousand hacking at the branches of evil to one who is striking at the root, and it may be that he who bestows the largest amount of time and money on the needy is doing the most by his mode of life to produce the misery which he strives in vain to relieve.[15]

It could be that even the sort of effort envisaged by Singer wouldn't suffice to materially alleviate the plight of the poor worldwide. But the reason may not be, as Hardin intimates, that poor nations don't manage themselves well. It may be that the broader socioeconomic system (or "mode of life" as Thoreau puts it) of which we're a part undercuts individual as well as collective efforts. That is, it may be that both Singer and Hardin have missed the mark. Perhaps the problem is with advanced industrial society itself. Perhaps neither individual nor collective efforts will avail so long as the system remains intact. This possibility, too, must be considered. The following report invites reflection on that question:

If Poor Get Richer, Does World See Progress?
In Shanghai this month [January 2004], bicyclists found themselves banned from certain portions of main thoroughfares. By next year, this ubiquitous two-wheel mode of transportation will have been kicked off such roads altogether. Why? To make way for all the new cars—11,000 more every week—pouring onto Chinese streets and highways.

A sure sign of growing affluence in the developing world? Without a doubt. A consumer trend portending a better world? That depends on one's point of view.

"Rising consumption has helped meet basic needs and create jobs," says Christopher Flavin, president of the Worldwatch Institute, a Washington, DC, think tank. "But as we enter a new century, this unprecedented consumer appetite is undermining the natural systems we all depend on, and making it even harder for the world's poor to meet their basic needs." …

But there are troubling indicators … say Worldwatch researchers:

- Damage to forests, wetlands, ocean fisheries, and other natural areas as resources are used and pollution created.
- Indications that increased consumption doesn't necessarily mean a better quality of life. In the United States, for example, average personal income more than doubled between 1957 and 2002. There now are more cars than licensed drivers, and the typical house is 38 percent bigger than it was in 1975, even though fewer people live in it. But when asked to rate how they feel about their lives, the same portion of Americans as a generation ago—only about one-third—describe themselves as "very happy."
- Growing disparities between rich and poor. More than 1 billion people still do not have reasonable access to safe drinking water. More than twice that number live without basic sanitation. (It's estimated that hunger and malnutrition could be eliminated globally for less than is spent on pet food in Europe and the US; universal literacy could be achieved for one-third of what is spent annually on perfumes.)[16]

The message of the above passage is that overconsumption on the part of the affluent people of the world stands in the way of alleviating world poverty. The passage also implies that making the poor rich wouldn't be a solution to the broader problem of promoting greater happiness in the world; it would simply expand the aggregate of people who aren't very happy. John Ruskin (1819–1900), a nineteenth-century British writer, saw the problem as requiring a change in mind-set; a recognition that the accumulation of wealth entails a corresponding deprivation to others, and that only individual, not public, effort can change this state of affairs. As he writes in "Unto This Last":

> Note, finally, that all effectual advancement towards … true felicity of the human race must be by individual, not public effort. That your neighbor should, or should not, remain content with *his* position, is not your business; but it is very much your business to remain content with your own … We need examples of people who, leaving Heaven to decide whether they are to rise in the world, decide for themselves that they will be happy in it, and have resolved to seek—not greater wealth, but simpler pleasure; not higher fortune, but deeper felicity; making the first of possessions, self-possession; and honoring themselves in the harmless pride and calm pursuits of peace.
>
> Of which lowly peace it is written that "justice and peace ha e kissed each other"; and that the fruit of justice is "sown in peace of them that make peace"; not "peace-makers" in the common understanding—reconcilers of quarrels; (though that function also follows on the greater one) but peace-Creators; Givers of Calm.[17]

7.7 Conclusion

It may be that the problem, as Thoreau and Gandhi maintain, is with the affluent mode of life to which we in advanced industrial societies like Britain and the United States are accustomed. Without a change in that mode of life, efforts to help the poor—whether along the individualist lines of Singer or the collectivist lines criticized by Hardin—are destined to fail. Perhaps we need to rethink our whole way of life. Perhaps if happiness isn't enhanced by increased consumption, as the above article intimates, and as some psychologists maintain, then why pursue affluence, particularly if to do so may undermine the efforts to alleviate world poverty?

On the other hand, some would say that the problem isn't with advanced industrial society so much as it's with advanced industrial *capitalist* society. Only if we understand the inherent flaws in that socioeconomic system will we be able to deal effectively with problems like world poverty. We've discussed in Chapter 6 the issues involved in the profit-motive of capitalism.

We shall examine in Chapter 10 some of the issues raised by the factory farming of animals, which is also governed by profit maximization. It's possible that neither individual nor collective efforts, nor a change in a people's mode of life, will help so long as the socioeconomic context in which those changes take place remains unchanged. That context is one of capitalism. These concerns bring us to the debate between capitalism and socialism in our next chapter.

Study questions

1. What are the differences among *poverty*, *famine*, and *destitution* (Sections 7.1 and 7.2)?
2. Why do some people choose poverty? Does the fact that it's sometimes voluntary mean that it's not necessarily bad?
3. What are duties of *non-maleficence* and *beneficence* (Theory Box 7A)?
4. What principle does *Singer* appeal to (Section 7.4) in arguing that we individually have an obligation to combat poverty?
5. What is the modified version of the principle Singer appeals to?
6. What are the positive and negative versions of *the golden rule* (Section 7.4)?
7. What is Garret Harden's argument regarding *"lifeboat ethics"* (Section 7.5)? In this metaphor, what is the lifeboat, who is in the lifeboat, and who is in the surrounding water?
8. What, according to Harden, is the *Tragedy of the Commons*?
9. How do *Singer and Harden's arguments* illustrate the differences between individual and collective efforts to fight world poverty?
10. What grounds might there be for thinking that collective efforts to fight world poverty might be futile (Section 7.6)?

Notes

1 From Raghavan Iyer (ed.), *The Moral and Political Writings of Mahatma Gandhi*, Vol. 2 (Oxford: Clarendon Press, 1986), p. 167.
2 As reported in *The Christian Science Monitor*, January 31, 2005.

3 Henry David Thoreau, *Walden*, in Carl Bode (ed.), *Thoreau* (New York: The Viking Press, 1964), pp. 269, 270; emphasis in the original.

4 *The New York Times*, February 23, 2017.

5 *The New York Times*, February 23, 2017.

6 Young Back Choi, *On the Gap between the Rich and the Poor* (Great Barrington, MA: American Institute for Economic Research, Economic Education Bulletin, Vol. XLIV No. 1, January 2004, 25–7.

7 United States Census Bureau, Report Number: P60-256, September 13, 2016.

8 Peter Singer, "The Singer Solution to World Poverty," *The New York Times Magazine*, September 5, 1999.

9 From Peter Singer, "Famine, Affluence, and Morality," *Philosophy and Public Affairs*, Vol. 1, No. 3, Spring 1972; emphasis in the original.

10 We shall not take up the many problems some see with these principles, such as those dealing with masochists, who might want others to do to them what those others wouldn't want done to them.

11 Thoreau, *Walden*.

12 *The Christian Science Monitor*, November 13, 2002.

13 Garrett Hardin, "Lifeboat Ethics: The Case against Helping the Poor," *Psychology Today Magazine*, 1974.

14 *The New York Times*, July 28, 2004.

15 Thoreau, *Walden*, p. 330.

16 "If Poor Get Richer, Does World See Progress?" *The Christian Science Monitor*, January 22, 2004.

17 John Ruskin, "Unto This Last," *Ruskin's Works*, Vol. 6 (Boston: Aldine Book Publishing Company, n.d.), pp. 224–5.

For more resources:

www.bloomsbury.com/holmes-introduction-to-applied-ethics

8

Capitalism, Socialism, and Economic Justice

Capitalism ... is outrageously unjust: it requires a continuing maldistribution of wealth in order to exist.

—Michael Harrington[1]

Another striking fact ... is that capitalism leads to less inequality than alternative systems of organization and that the development of capitalism has greatly lessened the extent of inequality.

—Milton Friedman[2]

Introduction

In this chapter, we shall explore the natures of capitalism and socialism. In so doing we shall, first, define the two; second, examine their differing views on liberty, equality, and human rights; third, detail the Marxist critique of capitalism; and, finally, consider the competing conceptions of distributive justice they represent.

8.1 What are capitalism and socialism?

With the Bolshevik Revolution in Russia in 1917, the world's largest nation became communist: The Union of Soviet Socialist Republics (USSR). From the end of the Second World War until the collapse of the Soviet Union in 1991, the Cold War between the United States and the USSR dominated the international scene. Each perceived the other as a military and economic threat. Their competing economic systems—capitalism and socialism— were central to this rivalry.

Although the Cold War was often represented as a contest between capitalism and communism, that was misleading. Capitalism is an economic system, communism an *ideology*. An ideology is an all-encompassing socioeconomic-historical (and sometimes racial and cultural) perspective on the world. Communism and fascism are ideologies. Capitalism and socialism are economic systems. Socialism was instituted in the USSR following the Bolshevik Revolution, in China following the 1949 communist revolution there, and in Cuba following the 1959 Castro-led revolution. According to Marx, socialism is but an intermediate stage between capitalism and communism.

As economic systems, capitalism and socialism contrast with political systems (like democracy, dictatorship, and monarchy) as well as with ideologies like communism and fascism. Although capitalism is often confused with democracy and socialism with communism, they should be distinguished. We shall define them as follows:

Definition Box 8A

Capitalism: A competitive economic system with private ownership of the means of production, which are used for profit.
Socialism: A cooperative economic system with public ownership of the means of production, which are used for the benefit of all.

These definitions represent the core notions of capitalism and socialism, but they need elaboration. Socialism, in particular, stands for many different things as represented by supporters and critics alike. Let us clarify some of the key components of these theories.

In capitalism, private ownership means ownership by individuals, either singly or collectively (as, e.g., by shareholders in corporations). It extends to shops, stores, companies, factories, farms, land, raw materials, money, financial institutions and the means of transportation, and exchange. These constitute the means of production. And they all represent wealth. And wealth is capital. In the words of economist Thomas Piketty:

> ## Key Quote 8A
>
> **Capital: All forms of wealth that individuals (or groups of individuals) can own and that can be transferred or traded through the market on a permanent basis.**[3]

Capitalism as an economic system represents the private ownership and use for profit of capital (in this broad sense) in any or all of its forms.

Many accounts of socialism leave unanswered precisely what *public ownership* means, as well as who's to determine how that ownership serves the interest of the people. Public ownership of the means of production might mean ownership by any of the following:

1. the state or government;
2. the people in name, but controlled or administered by the state or government;
3. the people, specifically (a) the workers or (b) the community.

Ownership or management of the means of production by the state is often referred to as *state socialism*. But it could equally be called *state capitalism*, as it is by Lenin, because control of the economy is out of the hands of the workers. Socialism stands in clearest contrast with capitalism if it involves ownership of the means of production by the workers or the community. How precisely that would work—that is, who would manage or administer those assets, and how they would be chosen for that role—isn't altogether clear. But according to *democratic socialism*, those issues would be settled by democratic processes.

In any event, *equality* is one of the aims of socialism, however understood, as is evident in the following passage.

> In the economic world of goods and services, equality and democracy are again central. In socialist society, all persons have a fundamental and equal right to food, clothing, shelter, education, useful work, leisure, medical care, and old age support. It is a primitive goal of socialism to ensure, for all persons in the society, that each of these basic needs be satisfied.[4]

Sometimes advocacy of equal rights of the sort Freeman mentions is taken by itself to constitute socialism. But that effectively makes socialism basically a moral theory about rights rather than an economic theory. Some think that such rights can be honored within the capitalist system, provided it enacts appropriate programs for social welfare. Whether that's feasible is an issue that divides liberals and conservatives. But it leads paradoxically to the possibility that socialism (if understood as a moral theory about rights) could exist within capitalism.

In short, not all socialists accept the idea of *state socialism* (complete control of the economy by the state) that communist regimes like the USSR and China adopted. Rather, they support *democratic socialism*, in which the means of production (e.g., factories) are publicly or socially owned under a democratic political system. They reject the authoritarian governments formed following the communist revolutions in Russia, China, and Cuba in which there was tight government ownership or control of the economy. It should be said again, however, that the forms of state socialism adopted in those countries don't represent communism as envisioned by Marx; socialism, for Marx, was but an intermediate stage between capitalism and communism.

The above definitions represent what might be considered pure forms of capitalism and socialism. In practice, many societies have mixed economies, combining considerable private ownership of the means of production (which capitalists favor) with substantial social welfare programs (which socialists favor). This brings competing values into conflict, *liberty* and *equality*. Let us see how.

Capitalism requires that people be free to compete with one another economically. This means that the political system of which the economy is a part must give people considerable liberty. In practice, this means democracy. (One could imagine a dictatorship allowing that kind of freedom to economic activity, but dictatorships tend to limit freedom in social, political, and economic ways.) On the other hand, if one values equality, as socialists do, there must be some limit to the freedom of some people to amass enormous wealth at the expense of others.

If you cannot have both maximum liberty and full equality at the same time, should liberty be valued over equality or equality over liberty? Answers to this question divide socialists and capitalists. Socialists criticize capitalists for the inequalities in wealth capitalism produces, and capitalists criticize socialists for the restrictions on liberty they believe socialism entails. In short, unconstrained capitalism leads to inequality in wealth; restraints on capitalism entail restrictions on liberty. These issues not only divide socialists and capitalists, they also divide liberals and conservatives in mixed economies. Liberals tend to support an essentially capitalist economy but one that promotes social welfare and minimizes inequality, which typically requires government involvement in the economy to provide appropriate benefits to the needy. Conservatives tend to reject such programs as government intrusion into the economy at taxpayer expense, which they see as limiting economic freedom and destabilizing a free market.

Although capitalism and socialism are economic rather than political systems, they're divided by political and ethical questions surrounding the nature of liberty and the extent to which it may justifiably be limited. To better understand this, let us clarify three central concepts that are often confused with one another: freedom, liberty, and rights. After that we'll return to the issue of equality and liberty.

8.2 Freedom, liberty, and rights

Freedom, in most general terms, is absence of constraint. *Absolute freedom* would be lack of all constraints, which only a god could have. Even if a god were all powerful (*omnipotent*), he could fail to achieve his ends if he lacked knowledge of how to do so. And even if he were all knowing (*omniscient*), he could fail to achieve his ends if he lacked the power to do so. So, any being, including a god, has absolute freedom only if he or she is both omnipotent and omniscient.

We humans, however, have only *conditional freedom*, because we're limited in both power and knowledge. We're constrained, first of all, by the natural environment and by our own physical and mental limitations. We can't fly by flapping our arms or leap tall buildings in a single bound. Nor can we know precisely what the stock market will do on a given day. We're also constrained by the actions of others; the ball-carrier in football has eleven men on the other team trying to stop him from reaching the goal line.

We'd have *complete freedom* (though not absolute freedom) if we were unconstrained by others, which rarely happens to most of us. We live in society and interact with others, and that limits our freedom. We'd have complete freedom if we lived on an otherwise deserted island, where our only limitations would be the natural environment and our own intelligence and strength; where we could do as we pleased without breaking laws or being interfered with by others. We'd be in a *state of nature*.

Add one other person to such an island and your freedom is limited. You couldn't stand or sit where that person was standing or sitting, because two physical objects can't occupy the same place at the same time. Your freedom to pursue your interests might be limited. If you like to watch the sunset atop a particular rock and one evening you find the other person sitting there, your freedom is limited. You could sit elsewhere, or ask him or her to move, or try to push him off the rock; you have a problem you wouldn't have but for the presence of the other person. Add ten or one hundred or one thousand people to the island and your freedom will be limited still further. Each would be constrained by the equal freedom of the others. Freedom limited by others where there's no law we may call *natural freedom*.

The nineteenth-century philosopher, anthropologist, and sociologist Herbert Spencer (1820–1903) formulated a principle that captures the condition of those living in such a state of nature:

Key Quote 8B

Every man is free to do that which he will, provided he infringes not the equal freedom of any other man.[5]

Most of us, however, live under conditions of *incomplete freedom*: freedom limited by others, individually or collectively, by custom, practice, or law.

Natural liberty is absence of legal constraints, in which one is free to do whatever is possible when others have equal freedom. If you infringe the freedom of your fellow island-inhabitants—or they infringe upon yours—you have a problem. You can't all sit on the same rock or pick the same coconuts at the same time. Laws have developed to minimize such problems. They seek to regulate everyone's behavior. *Liberty* is freedom defined by reference to law. Law consists of prohibitions (say, against stealing and drunk driving) and requirements (say, to pay taxes or get a license to fish). *Civil liberty* is freedom to do whatever isn't prohibited by law and not to do whatever isn't required by law.

Thus, freedom has the following structure:

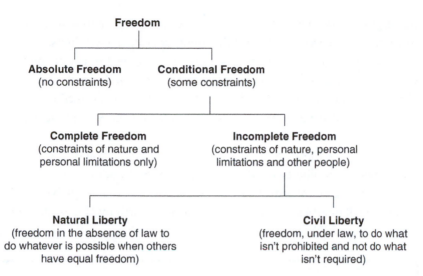

There are no laws in countries like America and Britain prohibiting you from dyeing your hair any color you want. You're free (at liberty) to do so. There are laws requiring that you wear clothes but no laws requiring that you wear any particular clothes. You're free to wear virtually whatever you want. You're free to listen to whatever music you like, get a tattoo or travel where you want within the country. These are among your civil liberties. *Civil rights*, we might add, aren't liberties but legal entitlements (either to be free of interference in certain areas of one's life or to receive certain benefits).

Because laws vary from society to society, and civil liberties are relative to laws, civil liberties also vary from society to society. For example, in Afghanistan and Saudi Arabia women are required to wear headscarves, whereas in France and Belgium and certain localities in other European countries the wearing of such scarves is prohibited. In Britain and America they're neither required nor prohibited.

Where do rights come in? *Human rights* are moral rights, as we saw in Chapter 1, Section 1.9, and as we'll explain more fully in Theory Box 8A. *Legal rights* are specific legal entitlements to receive certain benefits or be free of interference or discrimination in the exercise of your freedom (liberties). They single out freedoms that are deemed important. You're at liberty to dye your hair orange or put ketchup on your eggs, though no one thinks these are sufficiently important to require laws entitling you to do them. But expressing your opinions, voting, worshipping, assembling for peaceful protest, or being free of discrimination in employment or education are freedoms deemed important to the functioning of a free society. Societies that aspire to maximal justifiable freedom enact specific entitlements to the freedoms they represent. These entitlements are called "civil rights."

Civil liberties and *civil rights* exist only in the context of law. If you lived where there were no laws, you'd have complete freedom (or natural freedom if others were living there too) but not the specific sort of freedom we call liberty. (Early Patriots in America called themselves the Sons of Liberty not the Sons of Freedom.) And if there were no laws, then you'd also have no civil rights, since those are entitlements conferred upon you by law.

Although civil liberties and civil rights are legal notions, many believe that they have a moral justification. A moral principle that might be taken to underlie civil liberties is a principle of justice set forth by philosopher John Rawls (1921–2002):

Key Quote 8C

Each person is to have an equal right to the most extensive basic liberty compatible with a similar liberty for others.[6]

This resembles the principle stated earlier from Herbert Spencer (Key Quote 8B), but we'll take this principle (as Rawls seems to intend it) to be a normative principle which Spencer's may not have been. As a normative principle, it has the force of:

Each person *ought* to have an equal right to the most extensive basic liberty compatible with a similar liberty for others.

Rawls speaks of persons having a *right* to liberty, whereas we have spoken of legal rights as a subcategory of liberties singled-out for special guarantees. But we might say that (at least in a free society) there is a *general civil right* that encompasses civil liberties. It is the right, ceteris paribus, to do whatever isn't prohibited by law and to refrain from doing whatever isn't required by law. We might say, then (though we're departing from Rawls here), that civil liberties are protected by this general civil right, even though not all liberties are singled out for protection by specific civil rights (in the way the right to free speech is, for example). Someone would violate your general civil right if he tried to prevent you from getting a tattoo (which the law doesn't prevent you from doing) even though there's no specific civil right entitling people to get tattoos.

8.3 Human rights

The above suggests a possible moral basis for civil liberties in the idea of moral rights, specifically so-called human rights or natural rights. We've discussed this in connection with racism in Chapter 1, Section 1.9. Let us elaborate.[7]

Theory Box 8A

Human Rights
Let us say that a right is a **human right** if and only if:

(1) It's possessed by all persons simply by virtue of their being human.
(2) It's possessed by all persons equally and at all times.

A third condition makes explicit what is implicit in the first two:

(3) It's (a) independent of law, (b) independent of one's position, social status, or role in society or state; and (c) independent of whether it's honored or respected by others.

A human right isn't conferred by anyone. It's not like a driver's license, which a government must issue in order for you to have it. And no government can take it away, the way your driver's license can be taken away. Governments or other individuals or groups can violate your human rights, but they can't cause you not to have them. In fact, the violation of your rights presupposes that you have them.

The above tells us what makes a right a human right, but it doesn't tell us which rights are human rights. If there are human rights, they're moral entitlements possessed by everyone. But what sorts of entitlements are they? Here there's disagreement, but they generally represent entitlements of one or the other, or both, of two sorts:

Theory Box 8B

Positive and Negative Human Rights
Rights represent entitlements:

1. to noninterference in certain areas of one's life; and/or
2. to certain benefits.

Entitlements of the first sort are **negative rights** (or autonomy rights, since they are essential to the exercise of autonomy). Entitlements of the second sort are **positive rights** (or provident rights, since they require that others provide benefits to you).

Rights can be either legal or moral. Constitutionally guaranteed rights, such as the right to freedom of expression, are negative legal rights, prohibiting interference in the expression of political, religious, and other views. The right to unemployment benefits is a positive legal right, conferring benefits on the unemployed. During the Cold War, the United States and the USSR differed over human rights, with the United States criticizing the Soviets for failing to honor negative human rights, such as freedom of speech, association, and religion, and the Soviets criticizing the United States for failing to honor positive human rights, such as rights to medical care, education, employment, and pensions.

In the United States, civil rights are generally negative. They protect people against interference in various areas of their lives. But some are positive, such as a right to a trial by a jury of one's peers. These civil rights, specified by law, may be thought to be justified ultimately by the corresponding human rights. If there are human rights, and it's known what they are, then governments can if they choose pattern legal rights after those moral rights.

Different societies provide individuals with varying degrees of liberty. How much depends upon how extensively the lives of their citizens are regulated by laws. No government can control every aspect of people's lives, but totalitarian regimes leave only a small area in which people are free to do as they please. Even personal appearance and attire may be regulated, as they are in some contexts. (The Taliban in Afghanistan expect men to wear beards and women to wear burqas.)

8.4 Anarchism, libertarianism, conservatism, and liberalism

We've said that capitalism and socialism are economic systems as opposed to political systems. But economic systems exist in social contexts that include some sort of political system. For that reason, much of the debate over capitalism and socialism centers in issues pertaining to political theory, specifically over how much control government may legitimately exercise over citizens. Let's try to understand this further by clarifying the main types of political theory according to their answers to two questions:

1. Is the state morally justified in limiting individual freedoms?
2. If so, **(a)** to what extent?
      (b) and in what ways?
A. Anarchism answers the first question:
   1. No

Since the second question is relevant only if one answers the first question with a Yes, the anarchist doesn't answer the second. All governments, by their nature, restrict individual freedom in some way or the other. To answer No to question (1) is tantamount to saying that no government is morally legitimate, which is what Anarchism claims.

B. Libertarianism says in answer to these questions:
   1. Yes.
   2. **(a)** Minimally.
      (b) Only in ways necessary for security (preservation of life, liberty, and property).

Political conservatism and political liberalism ("conservatism" and "liberalism" for short) don't lend themselves to quite such simple summary. But generally they answer these questions as follows:

C. Conservatism:
   1. Yes.
   2. **(a)** Minimally in the economic sphere.
      (b) Variably on other issues (e.g., minimal taxation, limitations on immigration and rights to unionize).
D. Liberalism:
   1. Yes.
   2. **(a)** Substantially in the economic sphere (e.g., regulation of monopolies).
      (b) Variably on other issues (but typically supporting rights to unionize and strike and taxation to support welfare, unemployment benefits, medical care).

To avoid possible confusion, we should note that libertarianism, political conservatism, and political liberalism are all descended from liberalism of a broader sort, what we may call *philosophical liberalism*. Philosophical liberalism is a relatively recent development historically. It supports individualism, human rights, democracy, and free enterprise.

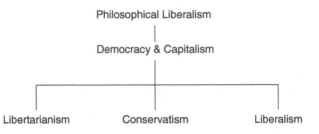

So, while there are sharp difference among libertarians, conservatives, and liberals in the contemporary political domain, all three have a common heritage in philosophical liberalism.

These political positions need to be distinguished from types of government such as democracy, dictatorship, monarchy, oligarchy, and so on, which as we've seen need to be distinguished from ideologies, such as communism and fascism. Finally, each should be distinguished from economic systems such as capitalism and socialism. As observed earlier, people sometimes speak of capitalism and communism as though they were theories on the same footing, which they're not.

Against the background of the above discussion of rights and political theories, let's now return to the conflict between liberty and equality that divides defenders of capitalism and socialism.

8.5 Liberty and equality

The political and economic realms are intimately connected, since the form of government and the freedom it gives to economic activity are major determinants of the character of society as a whole. Moreover, the degree of economic freedom in a society is important to understanding the tension between two values, those of *liberty* and *equality*.

If liberty is more highly valued, and there is unfettered economic activity, some people amass large fortunes. Since most do not, *inequality* is generated. Consider the following account of disparities in income in the United States.

Key Quote 8D

Income Inequality
In the United States, *income inequality,* or the gap between the rich and everyone else, has been growing markedly, by every major statistical measure, for some 30 years. Income disparities have become so pronounced that America's top 10 percent now average nearly nine times as much income as the bottom 90 percent. Americans in the top 1 percent tower stunningly higher. They average over 38 times more income than the bottom 90 percent. But that gap pales in comparison to the divide between the nation's top 0.1 percent and everyone else. Americans at this lofty level are taking in 184 times the income of the bottom 90 percent.[8]

Inequality doesn't exist only within countries; it exists among countries as well. The following is a report on the number of superrich (i.e., billionaires) in different countries of the world:

The Changing Face of the Superrich (2015)

According to Forbes, there were 1,826 billionaires across the globe in 2015, controlling approximately $7.05 trillion. By far, the world's billionaire population is most heavily concentrated in the US, which boasts 30.2 percent of the total (about 551).

Developed areas such as the US and Europe have long controlled the bulk of the world's wealth. However, extreme wealth in developing economies has grown rapidly in the past two decades. China, for instance, is now home to 9.2 percent of the world's billionaires. Economists Caroline Freund and Sarah Oliver analyzed 20 years of Forbes data to provide a snapshot of wealth around the world in their 2016 report, "The Origins of the Superrich: The Billionaire Characteristics Database." ... the kind of wealth varies from region to region. In Russia, it's dominated by political connections and resources (Russia is rich in natural resources including oil). In many European countries, inherited wealth is still the norm, as it was in most of the world for centuries. But in recent decades, wealth has been "increasingly self-made, even in the advanced countries," according to Freund and Oliver. In the US, company founders make up the largest group of billionaires (nearly a third). That's even truer in emerging markets. Virtually all of China's billionaires are self-made, largely because there wasn't any wealth to inherit in that region just a few decades ago.[9]

Not all of the inequalities are accountable entirely to capitalism. Some of the countries with big increases in billionaires, such as China, are essentially state socialist economies. But the loosening of government control there in recent decades has opened the door for some individuals to acquire vast fortunes.

On the other hand, if equality is valued more highly than liberty, then liberty (in the form of freedom to engage in unfettered economic activity) needs to be limited to keep people from getting too much wealth; either that, or measures, such as taxation, need to be implemented to redistribute wealth more equitably once it's been acquired. In either case, less liberty is the result.

We've dealt with liberty in the preceding section. Let's now turn to equality. To understand equality it's necessary to understand inequality. There would be no concern for equality in capitalist societies if there weren't substantial inequality. How does inequality develop? The simple answer is that some people derive greater profit from their economic activities than do others. Defenders of capitalism say that's because some people work harder and show greater initiative than others. Critics say that explains some inequality but doesn't explain the vast fortunes of billionaires, which are possible only in a system in which oppression and exploitation keep millions down while a few prosper almost beyond comprehension.

Key Quote 8E

Just 8 people now have the same wealth as the poorest 3.6 billion. (January 15, 2017, by Oxfam)

This raises the question of how profits arise. Is it by hard work, ambition, and persistence? Or is it by wheeling and dealing, cheating when you can, and paying workers as little as you can get by with?

As tempting as it may be to explain things in this simple way, it's not the way usually used by Marx, the principal exponent of communism (along with Frederick Engels and later Vladimir Lenin). His explanation of the origin of profit is part of his critique of capitalism. Let us consider his view, insofar as it provides a theoretical explanation of the ultimate source of inequality in society.

8.6 Marxism

Karl Marx (1818–83), a German philosopher who spent much of his life in England, was strongly influenced by the rise in science, the Darwinian theory of evolution, and the industrialization of Europe, particularly in England. Along with his collaborator Frederick Engels (1820–95), he believed that a proper understanding of society and the human condition was possible only by understanding the economic conditions under which social and political systems evolve.

Such an objective analysis, Marx thought, required understanding what he called the *mode of production*, which consists of productive forces (persons and the tools and machines they use) and relations of production (the relations among persons involved in economic transactions). The relations among persons are the principal economic relations. By understanding them, Marx thought, one could trace the development of socioeconomic systems. Their development is governed by what Marx calls dialectical laws.

Marx derives the concept of *dialectic* from another nineteenth-century German philosopher Hegel (1770–1831), who framed his conception of dialectic according to the triad:

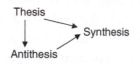

For Hegel, dialectic applies to thoughts and concepts—the immaterial world. Thus, to understand the concept of *being* (a thesis), one has to understand its opposite, *nothingness* (its antithesis). The concept of *becoming* (i.e., the process of emerging out of nothing) then represents a synthesis of being and nothingness. One needs the first two concepts to understand the third.

Marxists—particularly Marx's collaborator Engels—apply dialectic to the material realm, which they believe is the only reality there is. In nature, dialectic is at work when a seed of grain (thesis) develops into a plant (antithesis) and the plant grows and generates more seeds (synthesis). Fully to understand these processes, we need to recognize the following *laws of dialectic*:

1. Transformation from quantity to quality.

When sufficient quantitative changes characterize something, qualitative changes occur. Heat water to a certain temperature (a quantitative change) and it's transformed into steam (a qualitative change). Cool water below a certain temperature (a quantitative change) and it becomes ice (a qualitative change).

2. Negation of the negation.

When an acorn grows, it's destroyed (negated) and something related but distinct from it—namely, an oak tree—comes into existence. When the tree eventually dies (is negated), there is a negation of the negation.

3. Interpenetration of opposites.

Marxists, like the pragmatists after them, reject sharp distinctions among dualisms. To common sense day and night are opposites; the distinction between them is clear. But what about twilight? Is it day or night? There's no definitive answer to this; one can say either with equal plausibility. Day and night blend together during that period, as one shades into the other. So, there isn't a sharp distinction between them after all.

Of greater consequence, life and death seem clearly to be opposites, and until recently there was thought to be a sharp distinction between them. But as we shall see in Chapter 13, advances in medical technology give rise to circumstances in which there is no consensus whether a person is dead or alive. Thus, people speak of "brain death" when there's no brain activity but the body otherwise still functions; or of higher brain death, when there's no cognitive capacity, which is controlled by the higher brain, but the lower brain (controlling functions of the body like respiration) still operates. In some controversial cases, some people want life support removed because they believe the person is effectively dead, and others want it retained because they believe the person is still alive. Life and death, one might say, are intermingled in these cases. There is, in Marxist terms, an interpenetration of opposites.

8.7 Historical materialism

Marx thought that dialectical laws operate in the social sphere as well as in the natural order. This he called historical materialism. By a proper understanding of these laws, he thought, we can explain how socioeco-nomic systems have evolved and why capitalism will eventually be replaced by socialism:

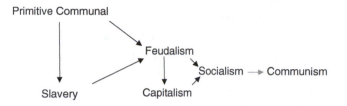

Primitive communal societies represent a thesis, which generates slave societies as its antithesis. Feudalism is a synthesis of the two. But feudalism itself becomes a thesis relative to the evolution of capitalism (its antithesis), and eventually socialism evolves as a synthesis of feudalism and capitalism. Contradictions within the earlier systems, primitive communal, slavery, feu-dalism, and so on, which led to their eventual negation and the appearance of the next higher stage, don't exist within socialism, and it will of its own eventuate in communism.

There isn't space to detail the reasoning by which capitalism is thought to be the natural evolutionary product of historical materialism. But we need to look more closely at what it is about capitalism that leads Marxists to predict that it will be superseded by socialism. This will provide a key to understanding the notion of profit, hence of inequality in society.

Here the laws of dialectic come into play. Remember the interpene-tration of opposites. Capitalism by its very nature generates opposites, according to Marx. They represent what he calls "contradictions." A prin-cipal contradiction is the tension between monopoly and competition. As commercial enterprises (stores, businesses, corporations) prosper, they tend to expand. As they do, they're able to buy out smaller enterprises (or force them out of business altogether). In the process (because there are fewer businesses putting out the same product or services) competi-tion is diminished. Thus, as nationwide booksellers become successful, they crowd out small bookstores; as supermarkets expand, they drive out neighborhood grocery stores; as restaurant chains flourish, they drive out local restaurants; as factory farms take over, they drive out family farms. If one auto maker were overwhelmingly successful, it would eventually be the only auto maker; it would have a complete monopoly, and there would be no competition. But competition is supposedly the heart of capitalism. It provides the incentive for people to strive to do better than others, the motivation for innovation, which leads to progress. The capitalist system would cease to exist if there were complete monopolies in the production of autos, shoes, computers, software, books, TVs, and so on. To try to prevent this, capitalist societies (like the United States) pass anti-trust laws against monopoly that are meant to preserve competition. But that involves governmental intrusion into the economic sphere. It restricts the freedom of people to engage in unfettered economic transactions. And *that*, in a different way (from the tendency of monopolies to emerge), is against the spirit of capitalism.

Another contradiction is the tension between classes. Capitalism gives rise to a distinction between capitalists (the owners of the means of production), called the *bourgeoisie*, and workers (those wielding the instruments of production), called the *proletariat*. Those who own the mines, factories, and stores need people to work in them. And it profits the owners to pay workers as little as they can and still maintain an effective workforce. For their part, the workers relentlessly seek higher pay, which diminishes the profits of the bourgeoisie. The two classes, bourgeoisie and proletariat, become in tension with one another. The workers try to form unions to maximize their bargaining power. Management typically opposes unions so as to be able to maximize profits. Strikes occur, sometimes accompanied by violence. Liberals want government to intervene and recognize unions and the right to strike. Conservatives want government to stay out of the economic realm in this way. Since the bourgeoisie and the proletariat represent classes, class struggle evolves.

Another contradiction arises between *wealth* and *poverty*. This represents inequality. The story behind this is more complex. It requires understanding what Marx calls "surplus value."

8.8 Surplus value

Economic transactions involve exchanges, whether of money, goods, services, or property. According to Marx, there must be some way to determine when exchanges are fair, that is, when equals are exchanged for equals. If you exchange a bicycle for a football, how do you know the exchange is fair, since the two things are radically different? To answer that requires explaining what gives things value, and that in turn requires identifying what the things exchanged have in common. The one salient feature they have in common is the *human labor* it takes to produce them. The amount of labor embodied (as it were) in a thing determines its value. It takes more labor to produce a car than a cow. You need only pasture, hay, and shelter to raise a cow but a factory and hundreds of workers to manufacture a car. A car is worth more than a cow because it takes more labor to produce it. All things being equal, you wouldn't exchange a car for a cow. In monetary terms, that's why a car costs more than a cow. Both a cow and a car cost more than an apple because the amount of labor embodied in them is more than the labor embodied in the apple (which—at least if it's wild—requires little more than to be picked). A blade of grass is virtually worthless, because most people can have one by just bending over and plucking it from the ground. Thoreau put much the same point in broader terms:

Key Quote 8F

[T]he cost of a thing is the amount of what I will call life which is required to be exchanged for it, immediately or in the long run.[10]

In Thoreau's terms, if you want a car that costs $20,000, then you'll have to devote a certain portion of your life to earning the money to pay for it. You're, in effect, exchanging a part of your life for the car. In the process, you're foregoing all of the other things you might have done with the time it takes you to acquire the money. The same with TVs, expensive clothing, and houses.

People buy and sell cows, cars, and apples. In so doing, they enter into economic transactions, which are exchanges of one sort or another. The various things bought and sold are *commodities*. If you own cows, cars, or apples you can enter into such transactions. They constitute wealth, as we saw in Key Quote 8A (Section 8.1). If you have enough of them you can make a good living. With ambition, hard work, and luck you may even become rich. You can open car dealerships, raise thousands of cattle, or cultivate apple orchards. Some people become billionaires.

But suppose you own nothing, not even a car or a cow. You have nothing to sell. How do you survive? You could beg or steal, but suppose you're honest and have pride. Even though you have no objects to sell or exchange, there's still one thing you can sell: it's your capacity to work (what Marx calls *labor power*). Each of us has certain mental and physical capacities. If we put them to work for others in exchange for money, we're then selling those capacities; we're selling our labor power. And we sell it for a certain amount of money and for a certain amount of time each day (or week or month). A part of us—our mental and physical capacities—itself becomes a *commodity*. If you own nothing, you have no choice but to sell this part of yourself.

But human mental and physical capacities also have a value. To work for eight hours requires that you've had a certain amount of nourishment, shelter, clothing, and health. Those things represent a certain amount of human labor that is embodied in you (someone had to grow the food that sustains you for the eight hours you work, manufacture the clothing you wear, build the shelter that protects you, etc.). Your capacity to work for eight hours embodies a certain amount of human labor no less than the car, the cow, and the apple. That determines its value.

Suppose now that the capitalist (the owner of the private property— the auto manufacturer, the cattle rancher, or the apple grower) pays you exactly what your labor power is worth for eight hours. Then you haven't been cheated. Equals have been exchanged for equals. You've received an amount of money equivalent to the value of the human labor "embodied" in your labor power. You're a free agent, not a slave. You voluntarily enter into this economic transaction, and you're paid what your labor power is worth. Marx puts this as follows:

> This sphere ... within whose boundaries the sale and purchase of labour-power goes on, is in fact a very Eden of the innate rights of man. There alone rule Freedom, Equality, Property and Bentham [a nineteenth-century British utilitarian philosopher]. Freedom, because both buyer and seller of a commodity, say of labour-power, are constrained only by their own free will. They contract as free agents, and the agreement they come to, is but the form in which they give legal expression to their common will. Equality, because each enters into relation with the other, as with a simple owner of commodities, and they exchange equivalent for equivalent. Property, because each disposes of only what is his own. And Bentham, because each looks only to himself. The only force that brings them together is the selfishness, the gain and the private interests of each.[11]

But there's a catch in all of this. Labor-power is unique among commodities. When put to use by the capitalist, it's capable of generating more value than it embodies. Assume the monetary value of the labor-power you sell to the capitalist for eight hours is $80. He then owns your labor-power to do with as he pleases for eight hours (or, more charitably, as per your understanding when you agreed to work for him). But remember that value consists of the human labor embodied in a thing. So when you work—whether milking cows, picking apples, or fitting parts together on an assembly line in a factory—you're transmitting value to the product of your work. A certain amount of human labor—your labor—becomes embodied in the product. Suppose that by the end of eight hours your labor-power has generated $100 worth of value, which is $20 more than the employer had to pay you. This is what Marx calls *surplus value*. And it's the capitalist's to keep. He paid you what your labor-power was worth. He exchanged equals for equals, so there was no unfairness in the transaction. It was simply his good fortune that when he put our labor-power to use it generated extra value. That, for him, constitutes *profit*. It's what capitalists strive for, the motive that drives capitalism. Each capitalist competes with others to maximize profits. It has been said (as we saw in Chapter 6) that the only responsibility corporations have is to maximize profits.

Some do better at maximizing profits than others, of course. Some businesses expand and become more and more profitable, others contract and go out of business. That's the way competition works. In the process, some individuals amass enormous fortunes while others struggle to make ends meet. Still others become poor. According to Marx, as more and more wealth becomes concentrated in the hands of fewer and fewer people, more and more workers (the proletarians) sink into poverty. The tension between these "opposites"—wealth and poverty—grows. Finally, this quantitative change (you can measure material wealth quantitatively) results in a qualitative change, and the capitalist system is transformed into something else. That something else is socialism. Marx thought the workers would become increasingly oppressed to the point where they revolt and overthrow the capitalists. (He allows that this might occur without revolution in Britain and America.) When workers take over the economy, public ownership of the means of production replaces private ownership, and socialism replaces capitalism. Socialism is the evolutionary product of the forces operating within capitalism itself and, more broadly, of the dialectical laws operating throughout history.

Here we need to consider another dimension of socialism. Recall our definition:

Socialism: A cooperative economic system with public ownership of the means of production, which are used for the benefit of all.

The phrase "for the benefit of all" means that wealth generated by economic activity must be shared by all of society. When there are no longer private individuals owning the factories, farms, and oil wells, there must be some way to distribute the earnings from those enterprises. If that's to be done fairly, it means that socialism requires a principle of *distributive justice*.

Theory Box 8C

Distributive Justice
A principle of fairness for the distribution of benefits and burdens. (See Theory Box 3D in Chapter 3, Section 3.9 for a more detailed account.)

When there are benefits or burdens to be distributed among two or more people, the question of fairness comes into play. If you have one piece of cake (a good or benefit) and two hungry children, there's a question of how to divide it fairly. If there are leaves to be raked (a burden) and two reluctant children, there's a question of how to assign that chore.

Similarly, if there's public ownership of the means of production (and we're not concerned now with whether ownership is by the state or by the workers or by the community) there has to be some way of distributing the benefits of production. Marxists believe that with public ownership, production will increase dramatically. Initially, in the socialistic stage after capitalism has been replaced, the following principle of distributive justice will be realized:

Definition Box 8B

Marxian Conception of Socialist Justice
**From each according to his work;
to each according to need.**

That will represent socialism. But as production increases there will be ample goods for all, and a different principle will go into effect:

Definition Box 8C

The Marxist Principle of Justice
**From each according to ability;
to each according to need.**

This principle could be fully realized only when socialism has evolved into communism, which it will as productivity increases, and the state withers away because it's no longer needed. People will be treated equally. They'll be expected to contribute to society according to their abilities—their strength, intelligence, talent, and creativity—and they'll receive according to their needs. Since there'll be no private ownership of the means of production, no individuals will profit at the expense of others. Whereas in previous systems there were sharp divisions between slaves and slave owners, landholders and serfs, and bourgeoisie and proletarians, under communism it's believed there will be equality. No individuals will acquire vast fortunes while others live in poverty. There will be a classless society.

8.9 A capitalist conception of distributive justice

Capitalists reject the Marxist analysis, particularly the socialist emphasis on equality. Let us consider first a critique of the Marxist principle of distributive justice by Ayn Rand, one of capitalism's most ardent supporters. In the following passage from her novel *Atlas Shrugged*, she describes the consequences for a fictional company of trying to implement the Marxist principle. After that, we'll look at a defense of a capitalist principle of distributive justice.

*"From Each According to his Ability,
To each According to his Need."*

This is the story of what happened at the Twentieth Century Motor Company, which put the above slogan into practice—as told by one of the survivors.

"Well there was something that happened at that plant where I worked for twenty years. It was when the old man died and his heirs took over ... they brought a new plan to run the factory. They let us vote on it, too, and everybody—almost everybody—voted for it ... The plan was that everybody in the factory would work according to his ability, but would be paid according to his need ...

"Hadn't we always been told that this was righteous and just? Well, maybe there's some excuse for what we did at that meeting. Still, we voted for the plan—and what we got, we had it coming to us ... what is it that hell is supposed to be? Evil—plain, naked, smirking evil, isn't it? Well, that's what we saw and helped to make ...

"We're all one big family, they told us, we're all in this together. But you don't all stand working an acetylene torch ten hours a day—together, and you don't all get a bellyache—together. What's whose ability and which of whose needs comes first? When it's all one pot, you can't let any man decide what his own needs are, can you? If you did, he might claim that he needs a yacht—and if his feelings are all you have to go by, he might prove it, too. Why not? If it's not right for me to own a car until I've worked myself into a hospital ward, earning a car for every loafer and every naked savage on earth—why can't he demand a yacht from me, too, if I still have the ability not to have collapsed? ... Well, anyway, it was decided that nobody had the right to judge his own need or ability. We *voted* on it ... How else could it be done? Do you care to think what would happen at such a meeting? It took us just one meeting to discover that we had become beggars—rotten, whining, sniveling beggars, all of us, because no man could claim his pay as his rightful earning, he had not rights and no earning, his work didn't belong to him, it belonged to 'the family,' and they owed him nothing in return, and the only claim he had on them was his 'need' ...

"What was it they'd always told us about the vicious competition of the profit system, where men had to compete for who'd do a better job than his fellows? Vicious, wasn't it? Well, they should have seen what it was like when we all had to compete with one another for who'd do the worst job possible ... But there was nothing else for us to do except to fake unfitness. The one accusation we feared was to be suspected of ability. Ability was like a mortgage on you that you could never pay off. And what was there to work for? You know that your basic pittance would be given to you anyway, whether you worked or not ...

"Do you see what we saw? We saw that we'd been given a law to live by, a *moral* law, they called it, which punished those who observe it—for observing it. The more you tried to live up to it, the more you suffered; the more you cheated it, the bigger reward you got ...

"Yet this was the moral law that the professors and leaders and thinkers had wanted to establish all over the earth. If this is what it did in a single small town where we all knew one another, do you care to think what it would do on a world scale? Do you care to imagine what it would be like, if you had to live and to work, when you're tied to all the disasters and all the malingering of the globe? To work—and whenever any men failed anywhere, it's you who would have to make up for it. To work—with no chance to rise, with your meals and your clothes and your home and your pleasure depending on any swindle, any famine, any pestilence anywhere on earth. To work—with no chance for an extra ration, till the Cambodians have been fed and the Patagonians have been sent through college ... And *this* is the moral law to accept? *This*—a moral ideal?"[12]

The preceding passage from Ayn Rand details what she supposes would be the disastrous consequences of trying to implement a Marxist conception of distributive justice. It doesn't in itself offer an alternative principle. For that, let us now consider a passage from another leading defender of capitalism, Milton Friedman (1912–2006), whose views we discussed in Chapter 6.

Suppose there are four Robinson Crusoes, independently marooned on four islands in the same neighborhood. One happened to land on a large and fruitful island which enables him to live easily and well. The others happened to land on tiny and rather barren islands from which they can barely scratch a living. One day, they discover the existence of one another. Of course, it would be generous of the Crusoe on the large island if he invited the others to join him and share its wealth. But suppose he does not. Would the other three be justified in joining forces and compelling him to share his wealth with them? Many a reader will be tempted to say yes. But before yielding to this temptation, consider precisely the same situation in different guise. Suppose you and three friends are walking along the street and you happen to spy and retrieve a $20 bill on the pavement. It would be generous of you, of course, if you were to divide it equally with them, or at least blow them to a drink. But suppose you do not. Would the other three be justified in joining forces and compelling you to share the $20 equally with them? I suspect most readers will be tempted to say no. And on further reflection, they may even conclude that the generous course of action is not itself clearly the "right" one. Are we prepared to urge on ourselves or our fellows that any person whose wealth exceeds the average of all persons in the world should immediately dispose of the excess by distributing it equally to all the rest of the world's inhabitants?[13]

Friedman speaks here of inequalities resulting from chance. But the same holds true of those resulting from individual effort and initiative. Let's consider his formulation of a capitalist principle of distributive justice[14]:

Definition Box 8D

A Capitalist Principle of Distributive Justice
To each according to what he, and the instruments he owns, produces.

In this view, people are entitled to receive the products of their own efforts, augmented, as the case may be, by what they own. Thus if a person makes shoes in his basement and sells them out of his home, he's entitled to what he earns. If he prospers and is able to build a shoe factory and hire 100 employees and produce thousands of shoes a year, he's entitled to that profit as well. If he becomes a millionaire, and his neighbor who mows lawns for a living doesn't, that's as it should be.

Notice that there's one point of agreement between Friedman and Marx. Both agree that a person is entitled to the fruits of his labor. Where they differ is that Friedman includes an entitlement to the fruits of his labor magnified by the use of what he owns, where ownership here means not personal property (e.g., furniture and the clothes on his back), but real property—which, economically translates into the means of production. One is entitled, on Friedman's view, to own land, tools, machinery, factories of the sort used to produce commodities. These will include food, clothing, houses—things that are essential for survival. For socialists, the means of production are to be owned by the public (or the community or the workers), not by private individuals. No one, in their view, should have to work for others, in the sense of producing by his own labor things that others then own and can sell for profit. Here the notion of freedom, discussed earlier, becomes relevant. Friedman sees the capitalist principle of distributive justice as grounded in freedom. If we value freedom, and want to see it exemplified fully in the economic realm, then we have to allow people to exercise initiative in creating and marketing commodities in open competition with others. The person who makes better shoes than another will be more successful. If the other person's shoes are shoddy, he'll go out of business, which is as it should be. Because some people will be successful beyond their wildest dreams and others will fail miserably, there will result marked inequalities in wealth in society. But that, too, is as it should be. It's the outcome of the operation of a free, democratic system. No central authority (a dictator or government) says who should have what and then allots wealth according to a formula. Even if that formula should be an egalitarian one—in which the authority tries to see to it that everyone has approximately equal wealth—it's still wrong. It denies people's liberty. It prevents them from being rewarded by their own initiative, ingenuity, and hard work. Whereas Marxists say that the worker is alienated from his labor because the fruits of his labor are owned by someone else, capitalists say that a regime that tries to enforce a socialist conception of equality deprives capitalists of the fruits of their labor (augmented by the instruments they own). Both see a limitation of individual autonomy, though in different ways.

Capitalists emphasize not only freedom, but also self-interest. The two, of course, are connected. In emphasizing freedom, capitalists stress that each person should be free to pursue his economic self-interest without restriction by others—particularly without the constraints of law. And that's a good thing. Contrary to what one would expect, everyone profits. As Friedman says:

Another striking fact, contrary to popular conception, is that capitalism leads to less inequality than alternative systems of organization and that the development of capitalism has greatly lessened the extent of inequality ... The chief characteristic of progress and development [under capitalism] over the past century is that it has freed the masses from backbreaking toil and has made available to them products and services that were formerly the monopoly of the upper classes, without in any corresponding way expanding the products and services available to the wealthy. Medicine aside, the advances in technology have for the most part simply made available to the masses of the people luxuries that were always available in one form or another to the truly wealthy. Modern plumbing, central heating, automobiles, television, radio, to cite just a few examples, provide conveniences to the masses equivalent to those that the wealthy could always get by the use of servants, entertainers, and so on.[15]

That the masses have allegedly prospered under capitalism doesn't mean that capitalists aim to better the masses (except, perhaps, insofar as it's in their self-interest to have people prosper so that they have more money to buy their products). Rather, it simply happens, as an unintended by-product of the operation of the capitalist system. As we saw earlier in Chapter 6 (Section 6.4), the eighteenth-century philosopher Adam Smith wrote that "[e]very individual intends only his own gain, and he is in this, as in so many other cases, led by an invisible hand to promote an end which was no part of his intention."[16] That end is the common good. No one aims at it. But it's in fact achieved, as though by the workings of an invisible hand, when everyone aims only at his own self-interest. So, the profit motive reigns supreme. Each seeks to maximize his self-interest through free and open competition. And virtually everyone—at least everyone who deserves to—miraculously gains from it.

There is at work here a principle that is more basic than the principle of capitalist justice cited by Friedman. It's what John Rawls calls *pure procedural justice*. Pure procedural justice (PPJ) obtains when a fair process operates. Then the outcome of such a process will be fair (or just) no matter what it is; no matter, that is, whether the outcome involves an unequal distribution of benefits. A game of poker approximates PPJ. You cannot specify in advance of playing a game of poker who should end up with how much money. You have to play the game and see. And so long as the game is played fairly (and of course so long as everyone is voluntarily playing, knows the risks, and so on), then the outcome is fair no matter what it is. If one person is a big winner and another a big loser, no injustice is involved. The loser has no right to claim part of the winner's money.

Analogously, defenders of capitalism reason as though they believe a capitalist system, so long as it is open and fair (under a democratic system, with just laws, and equal freedom for everyone, etc.), yields just outcomes whatever they may be—even if great inequalities result, and some people amass vast fortunes while others, who haven't made the same use of their freedom, live in poverty. No central authority has singled out some for preferential treatment over others. No one has been discriminated against. The system has provided an impersonal way of making distributions, and so long as the system is fair, the distributions are fair.

8.10 "Contradictions" within capitalism?

Thus far we've been speaking in relatively abstract terms about socialism and capitalism. Let's focus a little more specifically on issues that arise in the practice of capitalism as exemplified in the United States. Recall the two "opposites" that Marxists allege to be in tension with one another within capitalism: monopoly versus competition and wealth versus poverty. How does a capitalist society try to deal with the first problem? Consider the following news analysis.

One of the principal boasts of American policymakers has been that they found just the right balance between economic regulation and deregulation to maximize innovation and economic growth. But a recent string of crises and scandals—topped off by the Nov. 1 decision in the supposedly landmark Microsoft antitrust case—has called into question whether the government yet has the balance right … With the Microsoft decision, the hope was that the government could use antitrust laws to limit the natural tendency in high-tech markets for one company to achieve a monopoly or near-monopoly … The browser war that originally sparked the case is long since over, with Netscape, the competition to Microsoft's Internet Explorer, owning less than 5 percent of the market. And although Microsoft will have to abide by several dozen "thou shalts" and "thou shalt nots" that will be difficult and time-consuming to enforce, the company is bigger, richer and every bit as dominant in the industry as it was five years ago … The legal and economic thinking behind the Microsoft case was that the software industry tends toward monopoly because of the huge efficiencies of scale that accrue to the company that jumps into an early lead in any category of product … When it brought the Microsoft case, the government acknowledged that the software company had achieved its monopoly legally, but had engaged in illegal behavior trying to protect itself against competition in such technologies as the Web browser. The government also argues that because such monopolies develop so quickly, it was imperative that the government step in early to prevent the monopolist from squashing nascent technologies and extending its dominance to adjacent markets.[17]

What this indicates is that when the tendency toward monopoly becomes too strong, governmental intervention is required to constrain the monopolist and try to ensure competition. This requires a complicated array of governmental regulations. But to the extent the government regulates the economy, the system edges farther and farther away from pure, laissez-faire capitalism, because regulation limits the freedom of people and companies to engage in unfettered economic activity. Economic growth on the part of some businesses is, in fact, deliberately stifled in the interests of encouraging and supporting competition.

Let's now consider the second problem, the tension between wealth and poverty. There are actually two dimensions to this problem: the contrast between wealth and poverty within society and the contrast internationally, among countries. We shall for the present concentrate upon the discrepancies in wealth within American society.

The nature of the problem isn't difficult to define. When people are materially disadvantaged, they're limited in their autonomy—their capacity to live their lives as they choose. If there are no laws prohibiting them from living their lives as they choose, then this material disadvantage represents a limitation of their civil liberties. (Remember that we defined civil liberties as the freedom to do whatever isn't prohibited by law, or not to do whatever isn't required by law.) In this case, no one stands at the door to colleges and universities—or country clubs, luxury hotels, and fine restaurants—and says to the poor that they can't enter. It's just that they can't afford to. However it has happened, these people are poor, and poverty limits their freedom. Marxists see their plight, of course, as the result of capitalist exploitation—or at least as a by-product of that exploitation. (Although, as we've seen, Marx thinks that exploitation doesn't have to be appealed to in order to explain surplus value, he believes that in fact exploitation by capitalists abounds.) Others see the problem not so much as out-and-out exploitation as one of *marginalization*—the creation of an underclass by the workings of the capitalist system; people the system of labor cannot or will not use. Iris Young identifies the following groups as among such an underclass in American society[18]:

1. The racially marked
2. The elderly
3. The unemployed (laid-off)
4. Unemployed youths who can't find jobs
5. Many single-mothers and their children
6. Many of the mentally and physically disabled
7. American Indians

How is a capitalist society to deal with this problem? A principal method in the United States is through welfare, a system of public assistance in which tax dollars are used to benefit the most needy. Such "Welfare Capitalism," as it is called, is controversial. Critics argue that it takes money from some to give to others, hence represents a violation of individual rights. (Remember Friedman's principle. If a person is entitled to what he and the instruments he owns produces—i.e., to the wealth acquired thereby—then governmental intervention to take some of that wealth and give it to others is an infringement of that entitlement.) Even some who don't object to the government using tax dollars to benefit the needy criticize the welfare system as a bloated bureaucracy whose operation is demeaning to those it's designed to help by creating dependency and depriving them of self-respect.

Another way of dealing with the problem is by specifying a minimum wage. The federal government and most states set a standard minimum wage that all workers must be paid. The idea is to prevent workers from being exploited. Wages should be low enough that businesses can afford the labor necessary to keep them in operation but high enough that workers are encouraged to take such jobs. This program is designed to ensure that those at the bottom of the workforce are able to get by. Presumably they'll be encouraged to move on to higher paying jobs. Critics argue that the minimum wage is still too high to enable small businesses to hire people it otherwise would. In particular, they say, many of the young who would be hired for menial tasks if there weren't a minimum wage go unemployed because of the law. Critics and supporters thus disagree over the consequences of increasing—or even having—minimum wages.

8.11 Conclusion

With communism in retreat worldwide since the collapse of the Soviet Union, it's often supposed that socialism—even though it's not identical with communism—is essentially on the way out as well. That may or may not be. But the issues dividing capitalism and socialism remain. And even if the Soviet experiment in socialism was a failure, it's unclear that the Marxist critique of capitalism has ever been adequately met by capitalism's defenders. Short of a sustained theoretical analysis of the issues raised by socialists, combined with an empirical analysis of the inherent tendencies within capitalism—and an analysis of whether those tendencies are essential or accidental features of capitalist systems—it would be difficult to reach any consensus on the merits of the two systems. The upshot is that in the economic realm the ideals of liberty and equality remain in conflict.

Study questions

1. What are the definitions of *capitalism* and *socialism* (Definition Box 8A)?
2. What is *state socialism* (Section 8.1)?
3. What is *capital* (Key Quote 8A)?
4. What are human rights (Theory Box 8A)? What is the difference between *positive rights* and *negative rights*?
5. How does *liberty*, highly valued by capitalists, appear to conflict with *equality*, highly valued by socialists (Section 8.5)?
6. What do Marxists mean by *historical materialism* (Section 8.7)?
7. How, according to Marx, does *surplus value* come into existence? Why does he think that, at least in theory, it doesn't involve any injustice (Section 8.8)?
8. What is the *Marxist principle of distributive justice* (Definition Box 8C)? How does it differ from what Marx takes to be the *socialist principle* of distributive justice (Definition Box 8B)?
9. What is Friedman's *capitalist principle of justice* (Definition Box 8D)?
10. What are two of the *"contradictions"* Marx thinks inevitably develop within capitalism and will contribute to collapse?

Notes

1   Michael Harrington, *The Twilight of Capitalism* (New York: Simon and Schuster, 1976), p. 320.
2   Milton Friedman, *Capitalism and Freedom* (Chicago: University of Chicago Press, 1962), p. 169.

3 Thomas Piketty, *Capital in the Twenty-First Century* (Cambridge, Harvard University Press, 2014), p. 46.

4 Harold Freeman, *Toward Socialism in America* (Cambridge, MA: Schenkman Publishing Company, 1979), p. 119.

5 Herbert Spencer. *Principles of Ethics*, II, p. 46.

6 John Rawls, *Theory of Justice* (Cambridge: Harvard University Press, 1971), p. 60.

7 I have adapted this account from one provided by Richard Wasserstrom, "Rights, Human Rights, and Racial Discrimination," *Journal of Philosophy*, Vol. 61, 1964.

8 http://inequality.org/income-inequality/ Figures for 2014. A Project of the Institute for Policy Studies.

9 "The Changing Face of the Superrich," Schuyler Velasco, *The Christian Science Monitor Weekly*, October 17, 2016.

10 Thoreau, *Walden*, p. 286.

11 Karl Marx, *Capital*, Vol. 1 (New York: International Publishers, 1967), p. 176.

12 Ayn Rand, *For the New Intellectual: The Philosophy of Ayn Rand* (New York: The New American Library, 1961), pp. 101–107, 113; emphases in the original.

13 Friedman, *Capitalism and Freedom*, p. 165.

14 Ibid., p. 161f.

15 Ibid., p. 169.

16 Adam Smith, *Wealth of Nations* (1776), Bk. V, Ch. II (Cannon ed., London, 1930), p. 421.

17 Steven Pearlstein, "Competition vs. Regulation: The Microsoft Ruling Shows How Hard It Is to Rein in a Monopoly," *The Washington Post National Weekly Edition*, November 11–17, 2002.

18 See Iris Young, *Justice and the Politics of Difference* (Princeton: Princeton University Press, 1990).

For more resources:

www.bloomsbury.com/holmes-introduction-to-applied-ethics

Part III

Animals and the Environment

9

Environmental Ethics

What would the world be, once bereft
Of wet and of wildness? Let them be left,
O Let them be left, wildness and wet;
Long live the weeds and the wilderness yet.

—Gerard Manley Hopkins[1]

Introduction

In this chapter we shall outline the various ethical perspectives on environmental ethics. These include anthropocentrism, sentientism, and biocentrism. We'll then distinguish intrinsic and extrinsic value, and consider an argument for saying that nature as a whole has intrinsic value, hence deserves basic moral consideration. After considering an anthropocentric challenge to such an approach, we'll conclude by looking at the foreseeable as well as the intended effects of major dam projects in countries like China and India.

9.1 Why care about the environment?

The environment provides us with air, water, and food, without which we cannot live. If we care about living, we unavoidably care about the environment. As the early environmentalist puts it in characterizing what he calls "land ethic"[2]:

Key Quote 9A

"All ethics so far evolved rest upon a single premise: that the individual is a member of a community of interdependent parts …

> The land ethic simply enlarges the boundaries of the community to include soils, waters, plants, and animals, or collectively: the land." (Aldo Leopold)

The problems arise when we ask how much we should care about the environment and precisely why. These are ethical questions with social and political dimensions.

9.2 Basic and derivative moral consideration

Our interest will be with whether the environment warrants moral consideration. If something warrants moral consideration, it's always relevant to ask whether our conduct toward it is morally right or wrong, good or bad. But moral consideration can be basic or derivative.

Theory Box 9A

Basic and Derivative Moral Consideration
Basic moral consideration (BMC): concern for something (living or nonliving) for its own sake, usually because it's thought to have interests, rights, or value.
Derivative moral consideration (DMC): concern for something for the sake of something else (e.g., because it is useful to human beings). DMC is usually thought to be grounded in a thing's instrumental value, as a means to human ends.

Concern for the environment that arises from our concern for ourselves is derivative. It presupposes the environment's usefulness to us for survival, well-being, or happiness. Consideration we give to the environment for this reason is DMC.

But should we also be concerned for the environment for its own sake; that is, apart from or in addition to the concern that derives from our concern for ourselves? If so, then it warrants BMC as well as DMC.

Virtually no one denies that we should give the environment DMC. Global warming, for example (assuming that it's real, which some people deny), affects all life on the planet and can't fail to be of concern if humanity is to survive long term. The only question on that issue concerns how much consideration we should give it and what that means in practical terms for actions and policies. Those are difficult practical issues, and the need to address them is clear. The difficult moral question concerns BMC.

9.3 Who or what warrants basic moral consideration?

There are many possible answers to the question of what warrants BMC. Different moral positions are distinguishable according to which recipients they specify. These moral positions include (though are not limited to) the following:

Type of Moral Position	Recipients of BMC
Anthropocentrism	Human beings
Sentientism	Sentient beings
Biocentrism	Living things
Ecocentrism	All of nature

9.4 Anthropocentrism

According to anthropocentrism, the only entities deserving of BMC are humans.

Definition Box 9A

Anthropocentrism
The view that human beings are the most important entities in the universe and for that reason are the only ones warranting basic moral consideration (BMC).

If you give BMC only to yourself, you're an *egoistic anthropocentrist*. If you hold that certain individuals or groups (e.g., a particular race, gender, religion, or country), and only those, warrant BMC, then you're a *selective anthropocentrist*. Some racists and extreme nationalists are no doubt selective anthropocentrists in this sense, providing they don't believe in divinities of some sort. If you believe that every human being warrants BMC irrespective of race, gender, nationality, or social status, then you're a *universal anthropocentrist*. A related moral theory would give BMC to all rational beings, whether they are human or not, but on the admittedly questionable assumption that humans are the only rational beings, we won't consider that here.

Giving BMC only to yourself, as the egoist does, doesn't necessarily preclude giving DMC to other persons or things. Whether it does so will depend upon whether you think that a moral concern for yourself requires taking into account how your conduct affects other persons, other sentient beings, and so on. The same is true of the selective and universal anthropocentrists, the sentientist, and the biocentrist; that is, each could in principle extend DMC to each of the entities to which the others give BMC. The point is that these moral perspectives only specify different theoretical positions and don't indicate what judgments each of these perspectives leads to in particular cases. To ascertain that, we'd need to know what further beliefs the holder of the perspective has.

In the following passage, William F. Baxter defends an anthropocentric position. At times the position seems to be egoistic, at other times universalistic. In any event, he believes that the relevant criteria for evaluating environmental issues are grounded in a regard for humans.

People or Penguins?

Recently scientists have informed us that use of DDT in food production is causing damage to the penguin population ... The scientific fact is often asserted as if the correct implication—that we must stop agricultural use of DDT—followed from the mere statement of the fact of penguin damage. But plainly it does not follow if my criteria are employed.

My criteria are oriented to people, not penguins. Damage to penguins, or sugar pines, or geological marvels is, without more, simply irrelevant. One must go further, by my criteria, and say: Penguins are important because people enjoy seeing them walk about rocks; and furthermore, the well-being of people would be less impaired by halting use of DDT than by giving up penguins. In short, my observations about environmental problems will be people-oriented ... I have no interest in preserving penguins for their own sake.

It may be said by way of objection to this position, that it is very selfish of people to act as if each person represented one unit of importance and nothing else was of any importance. It is undeniably selfish. Nevertheless I think it is the only tenable starting place for analysis for several reasons. First, no other position corresponds to the way most people really think and act—i.e., corresponds to reality.

Second, this attitude does not portend any massive destruction of nonhuman flora and fauna, for people depend on them in many obvious ways, and they will be preserved because and to the degree that humans do depend on them.

Third, what is good for humans is, in many respects, good for penguins and pine trees—clean air for example . . .

Fourth, I do not know how we could administer any other system. Our decisions are either private or collective. Insofar as Mr. Jones is free to act privately, he may give such preferences as he wishes to other forms of life: he may feed birds in winter and do with less himself, and he may even decline to resist an advancing polar bear on the ground that the bear's appetite is more important than those portions of himself that the bear may choose to eat. In short my basic premise does not rule out private altruism to competing life-forms . . .

Questions of *ought* are unique to the human mind and world—they are meaningless as applied to a nonhuman situation. I reject the proposition that we *ought* to respect the "balance of nature" or to "preserve the environment" unless the reason for doing so, express or implied, is the benefit of man.[3]

In this view, only humans—whether considered individually or collectively—warrant BMC. Animals and nonliving aspects of nature warrant only DMC (though individuals making "private" as opposed to collective decisions may extend BMC to them).

Baxter makes an important claim in his concluding paragraph. He says that "[q]uestions of *ought* are unique to the human mind and world—they are meaningless as applied to a nonhuman situation." Presumably the second part of the sentence is meant to follow from the first. Let us break them down into two separate sentences, as follows:

1. Questions of *ought* are unique to the human mind and world.
2. Questions of *ought* are meaningless as applied to a nonhuman situation.

These may be considered an argument, or at least the rudiments of an argument, with (1) as the premise and (2) as the conclusion. (See Theory Box 5A in Chapter 5, Section 5.4 on what makes an argument.) (1) implies that morality is unique to humans.

Leaving aside religious assumptions and the possibility of extraterrestrial rational life, (1) is no doubt true. We don't say that wolves are wrong to eat lambs or that tornados are wrong to level trailer-parks. It's not true, however, with regard to concepts like "good" and "bad." We can say quite intelligibly that "Hurricane Irma was bad for Florida" or that "The 2011 tsunami to hit Japan was a terrible tragedy." In the context of Baxter's argument, (2) seems to mean that moral concepts are meaningless if applied to nonhuman situations. More specifically, (2) seems to mean that:

2a. We humans cannot meaningfully apply moral concepts to nonhuman things, living or nonliving.

But if this is how (2) is to be understood, then the argument is a non-sequitur. It doesn't follow from the fact that morality is unique to humans that humans cannot apply moral concepts to nonhumans. If I say "It's wrong to torture animals," whether you agree with me or not what I say isn't meaningless. That we could intelligibly discuss the morality of inflicting gratuitous pain on animals shows that the claim is meaningful.

So, either (2) is false or at best partially true. Either way, it hasn't been shown to follow from (1) in a sense that precludes our making moral judgments about both living and nonliving nonhuman things. If it's possible for (1) to be true and (2) false, then the argument isn't valid, hence isn't sound.

Baxter's argument aside, there appears to be no good reason to suppose that just because morality may be unique to humans we can't make moral judgments about our behavior toward the nonhuman realm. Therefore there's no bar (on those grounds) to giving BMC to nonhuman things. This doesn't show that sentientism, biocentrism, or ecocentrism are correct; it only shows that they can't be dismissed for the reason Baxter gives.

9.5 Sentientism

Sentientism extends BMC to all sentient beings, such as higher animals, as well as to humans. But it withholds it from lower forms of life and nonliving things.

Definition Box 9B

Sentientism
The view that all sentient beings, and only sentient beings, warrant basic moral consideration (BMC).

Sentient beings are conscious beings that are aware of feeling pleasure and pain. As Plato points out in his dialogue *Philebus*, a being like a clam might feel pleasure and pain but not be conscious of it. Whether that's possible or not, the fact that beings consciously experience pleasure and pain is thought by sentientists to suffice to give them interests and perhaps intrinsic value and rights, and therefore to warrant their receiving BMC.

A Sentientist Perspective
Rights protect what are hypothesized as the fundamental interests of human beings from cavalier encroachment by the common good—such interests as speech, assembly, belief, property, privacy, freedom from torture, and so forth. But those animals who are conscious also have fundamental interests arising out of *their* biologically given natures (or *teloi*), the infringement upon which matters greatly to them, and the fulfillment of which is central to their lives. Hence, I deduce the notion of animal rights from our common moral theory and practice and attempt to show that conceptually, at least, it is a deduction from the moral framework of the status quo rather than a major revision therein. Moral concern for individual animals follows from the hitherto ignored presence of morally relevant characteristics, primarily sentience, in animals. As a result, I am comfortable in attributing what Immanuel Kant called "intrinsic value," not merely use value, to animals if we attribute it to people.[4]

If pleasure is intrinsically good and pain intrinsically bad, as is widely believed, it's clear that we're capable of harming sentient beings as well as doing good for them. Since doing good and causing harm are relevant moral considerations, it's clear that it's intelligible to speak of right and wrong ways of treating sentient beings. Whether in addition to that we should say that sentient beings—animals in particular—have rights, interests, and intrinsic value, as the above passage suggests, is a further question. But those further questions, as interesting and important as they are, aren't necessary to establishing that we should give at least some BMC to sentient beings.

9.6 Biocentrism

Biocentrism doesn't stop with extending BMC to beings capable of experiencing pleasure and pain. It extends BMC to all living things (including plants and microscopic organisms which are generally thought not to be sentient). Biocentrism isn't always distinguished clearly from ecocentrism, but we'll distinguish it from ecocentrism by taking it to extend BMC to the *biotic community* (i.e., all living things).

Definition Box 9C

Biocentrism
The view that all living things without exception warrant some measure of basic moral consideration (BMC).

One might hold that the biotic community as a collective entity warrants BMC, but one might also hold that subgroups within that collectivity, such as plants and animals, warrant BMC. One might say, further, that each and every individual within those subgroups (e.g., particular humans, dogs, cats, mice, fleas, and mosquitoes) also warrants BMC. Consider the following passage:

Respect for Nature
The beliefs that form the core of the biocentric outlook are four in number:

1. The belief that humans are members of the Earth's Community of Life in the same sense and on the same terms in which other living things are members of that Community.
2. The belief that the human species, along with all other species, are integral elements in a system of interdependence such that the survival of each living thing, as well as its chances of faring well or poorly, is determined not only by the physical conditions of its environment but also by its relations to other living things.

3. The belief that all organisms are teleological centers of life in the sense that each is a unique individual pursuing its own good in its own way.
4. The belief that humans are not inherently superior to other living things.[5]

In the passage above, philosopher Paul Taylor sees acceptance of the four beliefs he enumerates as providing the basis for an ethical perspective of respect toward the world and living things. Some contend that life is so interconnected that we cannot consistently value our own lives and refuse to value other forms of life. Some Jain monks in India wear masks so as not to inadvertently breathe in (thus harming) flying insects. They also carry small brooms with which to whisk away insects they might otherwise step on. As the reputed founder of Jainism is quoted as saying:

Key Quote 9B

You are that which you intend to hit, injure, insult, torment, persecute, torture, enslave or kill. (Mahavira)

Most people, on the other hand (certainly in Western societies like Britain and the United States), think nothing of killing insects. In fact, they go to considerable expense to eliminate them from their homes and lawns, as farmers do in buying pesticides to try to protect their crops.

The Jain perspective on nature, unknown to most Westerners, is expressed in the following:

The Jain Declaration On Nature

The Jain tradition which enthroned the philosophy of ecological harmony and non-violence as its lodestar flourished for centuries side-by-side with other schools of thought in ancient India. It formed a vital part of the mainstream of ancient Indian life, contributing greatly to its philosophical, artistic and political heritage. During certain periods of Indian history, many ruling elites as well as large sections of the population were Jains, followers of the *Jinas* (Spiritual Victors).

The ecological philosophy of Jainism which flows from its spiritual quest has always been central to its ethics, aesthetics, art, literature, economics and politics. It is represented in all its glory by the 24 *Jinas* or *Tirthankaras* (Path-finders) ... whose example and teachings have been its living legacy through the millenia.

Although the ten million Jains estimated to live in modern India constitute a tiny fraction of its population, the message and motifs of the Jain perspective, its reverence for life in all forms, its commitment to the progress of human civilization and to the preservation of the natural environment continues to have a profound and pervasive influence on Indian life and outlook.

In the twentieth century, the most vibrant and illustrious example of Jain influence was that of Mahatma Gandhi, acclaimed as the Father of the Nation. Gandhi's friend, Shrimad Rajchandra, was a Jain. The two great men corresponded, until Rajchandra's death, on issues of faith and ethics. The central Jain teaching of *ahimsa* (non-violence) was the guiding principle of Gandhi's civil disobedience in the cause of freedom and social equality. His ecological philosophy found apt expression in his observation that the greatest work of humanity could not match the smallest wonder of nature.

I. The Jain Teachings

1. Ahimsa (non-violence)

The Jain ecological philosophy is virtually synonymous with the principle of *ahimsa* (non-violence) which runs through the Jain tradition like a golden thread.

"*Ahimsa parmo dharmah*" (Non-violence is the supreme religion).

Mahavira, the 24th and last *Tinhankara* (Path-finder) of this era, who lived 2500 years ago in north India consolidated the basic Jain teachings of peace, harmony and renunciation taught two centuries earlier by the *Tinhankara* Parshva, and for thousands of years previously by the 22 other *Tirthankaras* of this era, beginning with Adinatha Rishabha. Mahavira threw new light on the perennial quest of the soul with the truth and discipline of *ahimsa*. He said:

"There is nothing so small and subtle as the atom nor any element so vast as space. Similarly, there is no quality of soul more subtle than non-violence and no virtue of spirit greater than reverence for life."

Ahimsa is a principle that Jains teach and practise not only towards human beings but towards all nature. It is an unequivocal teaching that is at once ancient and contemporary. The scriptures tell us:

"All the Arhats (Venerable Ones) of the past, present and future discourse, counsel, proclaim, propound and prescribe thus in unison: Do not injure, abuse, oppress, enslave, insult, torment, torture or kill any creature or living being."

In this strife-torn world of hatred and hostilities, aggression and aggrandisement, and of unscrupulous and unbridled exploitation and consumerism, the Jain perspective finds the evil of violence writ large.

The teaching of *ahimsa* refers not only to wars and visible physical acts of violence but to violence in the hearts and minds of human beings, their lack of concern and compassion for their fellow humans and for the natural world. Ancient Jain texts explain that violence (*himsa*) is not defined by actual harm, for this may be unintentional. *It* is the intention to harm, the absence of compassion, that makes action violent. Without violent thought there could be no violent actions. When violence enters our thoughts, we remember *Tirthankara* Mahavira's words:

"You are that which you intend to hit, injure, insult, torment, persecute, torture, enslave or kill."

2. *Parasparopagraho jivanam* (interdependence)
Mahavira proclaimed a profound truth for all times to come when he said:

"One who neglects or disregards the existence of earth, air, fire, water and vegetation disregards his own existence which is entwined with them."

Jain cosmology recognises the fundamental natural phenomenon of symbiosis or mutual dependence, which forms the basis of the modern-day science of ecology. It is relevant to recall that the term "ecology" was coined in the latter half of the nineteenth century from the Greek word *oikos,* meaning "home," a place to which one returns. Ecology is the branch of biology which deals with the relationships of organisms to their surroundings and to other organisms.

The ancient Jain scriptural aphorism *Parasparopagraho jivanam* (All life is bound together by mutual support and interdependence) is refreshingly contemporary in its premise and perspective. It defines the scope of modern ecology while extending it further to a more spacious "home." It means that all aspects of nature belong together and are bound in a physical as well as a metaphysical relationship. Life is viewed as a gift of togetherness, accommodation and assistance in a universe teeming with interdependent constituents . . .

III. *The Jain Code of Conduct*

1. The five *vratas* (vows)
The five *vratas* (vows) in the Jain code of conduct are:

- non-violence in thought, word and deed,
- to seek and speak the truth,
- to behave honestly and never to take anything by force or theft,
- to practise restraint and chastity in thought, word and deed,
- to practise non-acquisitiveness.

The vow of *ahimsa* is the first and pivotal vow. The other vows may be viewed as aspects of *ahimsa* which together form an integrated code of conduct in the individual's quest for equanimity and the three jewels (*ratna-traya*) of right faith, right knowledge and right conduct.

The vows are undertaken at an austere and exacting level by the monks and nuns and are then called *maha-vratas* (great vows). They are undertaken at a more moderate and flexible level by householders and called the *anu-vratas* ("atomic" or basic vows).

Underlying the Jain code of conduct is the emphatic assertion of individual responsibility towards one and all. Indeed, the entire universe is the forum of one's own conscience. The code is profoundly ecological in its secular thrust and its practical consequences.

2. Kindness to animals
The transgressions against the vow of non-violence include all forms of cruelty to animals and human beings. Many centuries ago, Jains condemned as evil the common practice of animal sacrifice to the gods. It is generally forbidden to keep animals in captivity, to whip, mutilate or overload them or to deprive them of adequate food and drink. The injunction is modified in respect of domestic animals to the extent that they may be roped or even whipped occasionally but always mercifully with due consideration and without anger.

3. Vegetarianism
Except for allowing themselves a judicious use of one-sensed life in the form of vegetables, Jains would not consciously take any life for food or sport. As a community they are strict vegetarians, consuming neither meat, fish nor eggs. They confine themselves to vegetable and milk products

4. Self-restraint and the avoidance of waste

By taking the basic vows, the Jain laity endeavor to live a life of moderation and restraint and to practice a measure of abstinence and austerity. They must not procreate indiscriminately lest they overburden the universe and its resources. Regular periods of fasting for self-purification are encouraged.

In their use of the earth's resources Jains take their cue from "the bee [that] sucks honey in the blossoms of a tree without hurting the blossom" and strengthens itself. Wants should be reduced, desires curbed and consumption levels kept within reasonable limits. Using any resource beyond one's needs and misuse of any part of nature is considered a form of theft. Indeed, the Jain faith goes one radical step further and declares unequivocally that waste and creating pollution are acts of violence.[6]

As evident from the above manifesto, the Jains take all forms of life seriously, and try to respect those forms as nearly as possible.

It's interesting to reflect upon how lower forms of life might view us, if they could think and express themselves. A whimsical perspective of this sort—but one that contains a serious message—is contained in the following passage. A journalist in the 1920s wrote a regular column which he represented as the writings of a cockroach, named Archie, who would type out messages on the journalist's typewriter at night. Here is one of Archie's messages, reflecting upon the conduct of humans and its effect on the environment. Because it takes two hands to create caps on a typewriter, Archie could write only in lowercase as he jumped from key to key.

what the ants are saying

dear boss i was talking with an ant
the other day
and he handed me a lot of
gossip which ants the world around
are chewing over among themselves
i pass it on to you
in the hope that you may relay it to other
human beings and hurt their feelings with it
no insect likes human beings
and if you think you can see why
the only reason i tolerate you is because

you seem less human to me than most of them
here is what the ants are saying
it wont be long now it wont be long
man is making deserts of the earth
it wont be long now
before man will have used it up
so that nothing but ants
and centipedes and scorpions
can find a living on it
man has oppressed us for a million years
but he goes on steadily
cutting the ground from under
his own feet making deserts deserts deserts
we ants remember
and have it all recorded
in our tribal lore
when gobi was a paradise
swarming with men and rich
in human prosperity
it is a desert now and the home
of scorpions ants and centipedes
what man calls civilization
always results in deserts
man is never on the square
he uses up the fat and greenery of the earth
each generation wastes a little more
of the future with greed and lust for riches
north Africa was once a garden spot
and then came carthage and rome
and despoiled the storehouse
and now you have sahara
sahara ants and centipedes
toltecs and aztecs had a mighty
civilization on this continent
but they robbed the soil and wasted nature
and now you have deserts scorpions ants and centipedes
and the deserts of the near east
followed egypt and babylon and assyria
and persia and rome and the turk
the ant is the inheritor of tamerlane

and the scorpion succeeds the caesars
america was once a paradise
of timberland and stream
but it is dying because of the greed
and money lust of a thousand little kings
who slashed the timber all to hell
and would not be controlled
and changed the climate
and stole the rainfall from posterity
and it wont be long now
it wont be long
till everything is desert
from the alleghenies to the rockies
the deserts are coming
the deserts are spreading
the springs and streams are drying up
one day the mississippi itself
will be a bed of sand
ants and scorpions and centipedes
shall inherit the earth
men talk of money and industry
of hard times and recoveries
of finance and economics
but the ants wait and the scorpions wait
for while men talk they are making deserts all the time
getting the world ready for the conquering ant
drought and erosion and desert
because men cannot learn
rainfall passing off in flood and freshet
and carrying good soil with it
because there are no longer forests
to withhold the water in the
billion meticulations of the roots
it wont be long now it won't be long
till earth is barren as the moon
and sapless as a mumbled bone
dear boss i relay this information
without any fear that humanity
will take warning and reform
archy[7]

Whether ants and scorpions and centipedes will inherit the earth, as Archie surmises, there's no question but what humankind must have is a concern for nature. What is probably most problematic is whether BMC should extend to the whole of nature as well as to parts of it. This is philosophically the more interesting and difficult question.

9.7 Does nature as a whole warrant basic moral consideration?

By the whole of nature, we mean all there is: the universe in its entirety. The universe in its entirety consists of both living and nonliving things. So far as we know, only a small part of the universe directly affects us, namely, the conditions on planet Earth, or perhaps those of the solar system. Often when we speak of nature, we refer more narrowly to our earth and its surrounding environment. This narrower focus is all that one needs to consider in discussing most of the practical issues in environmental ethics (e.g., air and water pollution), but the broader focus (relating to the universe as a whole) is relevant to the deeper philosophical issues.

A common view is that nature exists to be controlled and used by human beings. Philosopher John Dewey (1859–1952) expressed this view when he wrote:

> Greek and medieval science formed an art of accepting things as they are … Modern experimental science is an art of control … [N]ature as it already exists ceases to be something which must be accepted and submitted to, endured or enjoyed, just as it is. It is now something to be modified, to be intentionally controlled. It is material to act upon so as to transform it into new objects which better answer our needs.[8]

Much of industrial development in capitalist and socialist countries alike has proceeded largely in this spirit: trying to control nature for human purposes. Native Americans, on the other hand, had a different conception of nature from the one Europeans brought with them.

Native American Beliefs as a Foundation for Environmental Consciousness

Although they varied significantly between different cultures, Native American relationships with the natural world tended to preserve biological integrity within natural communities, and did so over a significant period of historical time. These cultures engage in relationships of mutual respect, reciprocity, and caring with an Earth and fellow beings as alive and self-conscious as human beings. Such relationships were reflected and perpetuated by cultural elements including religious belief and ceremonial ritual . . .

In contrast, invading Europeans brought with them cultures that practiced relationships of subjugation and domination, even hatred, of European lands. They made little attempt to live *with* their natural communities, but rather altered them wholesale. The impoverishment of the ecological communities of sixteenth and seventeenth-century Europe was so great that, in contrast, early settlers of the New World found what they described as either a marvelous paradise or a horrendous wilderness, but certainly something completely outside their experience.

Native American cultures had adapted their needs to the capacities of natural communities; the new inhabitants, freshly out of Europe, adapted natural communities to meet their needs. The differences between these two approaches have had profound impacts on the diversity and functioning of natural communities in North America . . .

. . . Native American writers focus on the wonders of the land. Standing Bear, a Lakota Sioux, wrote that native Americans felt a special joy and wonder for all the elements and changes of season which characterized the land. They felt that they held the spirit of the land within themselves, and so they met and experienced the elements and seasons rather than retreating from them. For Standing Bear and the Lakota, the Earth was so full of life and beings that they never actually felt alone.

[A] very central belief which seems consistent across many native American cultures [is] that the Earth is a living, conscious being that must be treated with respect and loving care. The Earth may be referred to as Mother, or Grandmother, and these are quite literal terms, for the Earth is the source, the mother of all living beings, including human beings. Black Elk, a Lakota, asked, "Is not the sky a father and the earth a mother and are not all living things with feet and wings or roots their children." The Earth, and those who reside upon her, take their sacredness from that part of the Great Spirit which resides in all living beings.[9]

Does nature in this sense warrant BMC? One might think so if one believes in God and believes that God created all things. One might think we should have reverence for all things because they've been created by God.

Such a view presupposes faith in God and will be unconvincing to those who don't have such faith. Since we cannot here take up the question whether such faith is warranted, let's look to other possible grounds for assigning BMC to nature.

One might think that nature has rights. But even though many people believe that animals have rights, only a few hold that the whole of nature has rights. Yet the view that natural objects have rights has been defended.

Legal Rights for Natural Objects

It is not inevitable, nor is it wise, that natural objects should have no rights to seek redress in their own behalf. It is no answer to say that streams and forests cannot have standing because streams and forests cannot speak. Corporations cannot speak either; nor can states, estates, infants, incompetents, municipalities, or universities. Lawyers speak for them, as they customarily do for the ordinary citizen with legal problems. One ought, I think, to handle the legal problems of natural objects as one does the problems of legal incompetents—human beings who have become vegetable. If a human being shows signs of becoming senile and has affairs that he is de jure incompetent to manage, those concerned with his well being make such a showing to the court, and someone is designated by the court with the authority to manage the incompetent's affairs . . .

On a parity of reasoning we should have a system in which, when a friend of a natural object perceives it to be endangered, he can apply to a court for the creation of a guardianship . . .

The potential "friends" that such a statutory scheme would require will hardly be lacking. The Sierra Club, Environmental Defense Fund, Friends of the Earth, Natural Resources Defense Counsel, and the Izaak Walton League are just some of the many groups which have manifested unflagging dedication to the environment and which are becoming increasingly capable of marshalling the requisite technical experts and lawyers.[10]

This view defends the idea that natural objects may have legal rights. Although we shall not explore the issue, with appropriate modifications similar reasoning could be used to argue that natural objects have moral rights.

The principal ground for assigning BMC to something is that it has rights, interests, or value. While we cannot take up all of these possibilities, let's ask whether nature as a whole has intrinsic value. Some believe that it does:

Does Nature as a Whole Have Intrinsic Value?

The well-being and flourishing of human and nonhuman Life on Earth have value in themselves (synonyms: intrinsic value, inherent value). These values are independent of the usefulness of the nonhuman world for human purposes . . .

This formulation refers to the biosphere, or more accurately, to the ecosphere as a whole. This includes individuals, species, populations, habitat, as well as human and nonhuman cultures . . . The term "life" is used here in a more comprehensive nontechnical way to refer also to what biologists classify as "nonliving"; rivers (watersheds), landscapes, ecosystems . . . "The presence of inherent value in a natural object is independent of any awareness, interest, or appreciation of it by a conscious being."[11]

9.8 An argument for giving nature basic moral consideration

Here it will be useful to frame our discussion around a possible argument, which goes as follows:

1. Persons have intrinsic value.
2. If persons have intrinsic value, then nature has intrinsic value.
3. Therefore: nature has intrinsic value.
4. Whatever has intrinsic value warrants BMC.
5. Therefore: Nature warrants BMC.

The argument is valid, so whether it's also sound depends on whether the premises are true (see Chapter 5, Theory Box 5A, Section 5.4 on validity). Let's assume that premises (1) and (4) are true. Both could be questioned, but each has a fair measure of plausibility. Each (properly understood) would probably be widely accepted.

The key premise, for our purposes, is (2). Many would agree that persons have intrinsic value, but most would probably deny that nature does. Is there anything to be said in defense of premise (2)?

Let's return, for a moment, to the religious view. Suppose there's a God and that nature is God's creation. Suppose further that the biblical account is correct, that after creating the universe, God "saw everything that he had made, and behold, it *was* very good" (Gen. 1:31). It's commonly held in Christianity that God created only good, not evil. (This doesn't mean that there's no evil in the world; only that the explanation for it must be in terms of something other than God, e.g., free choice of the human will.)

If the whole of nature is good, we need to ask whether it's intrinsically good or extrinsically good.

Theory Box 9B

Intrinsic and Extrinsic Value
Intrinsic value: Value dependent solely upon the intrinsic nature of what has value.
Extrinsic value: Value that isn't intrinsic (i.e., that depends at least in part upon the relationship of what has value to other things).

One might think that nature is only extrinsically good on the grounds that it serves God's purposes. If its value consists in the fact that it serves some divine plan of God beyond our comprehension, then its value is instrumental—that is, outside of itself and its intrinsic nature. Even so, it seems *possible* that God's creation is intrinsically good and not merely extrinsically good. If it weren't possible, then God wouldn't be omnipotent (all powerful), because there would be something God couldn't do, namely, create a universe that's intrinsically good. So, if God is a supreme and perfect being, nature may be intrinsically good. This doesn't mean that it is intrinsically good; only that it may be (if there's a God and nature is God's creation).

If nature should be intrinsically good, then (given our understanding of intrinsic value) it's good in and of itself, quite apart from its relationship to anything else—even to God. This mean that once God has created the universe, its value resides in itself, quite apart from God.

Consider two identical universes, one created by God, the other not. If the first is intrinsically good, then it's difficult to see how the second can fail to be intrinsically good as well.

Theory Box 9C

The Universalizability of Judgments of Intrinsic Value
Recall the principle of universalizability from Chapter 1, Theory Box 1F, Section 1.10. It says:

   U: Persons ought to be treated similarly unless there are morally relevant dissimilarities between them.

   This principle demands consistency in our moral judgments about persons. But we might expect consistency in our value judgments (i.e., judgments about good and bad), as well. In particular, we might expect consistency in our judgments of intrinsic value. Let's call this a principle of universalizability of intrinsic value, or UIV for short:

   UIV: If something has intrinsic value, then anything identical to it in intrinsic nature must have the same intrinsic value.

This means that whether or not one believes in God, we can understand how nature might be intrinsically good. If there's a God, and God could create a universe that has intrinsic value, then even if there's no God but the universe (however it came into existence) is identical to one that God could have created and which would have had intrinsic value, then (given UIV) the universe that presently exists has intrinsic value.[12]

This take us only so far, however, toward understanding how premise (2) might be true. Skeptics will rightly point out that there are all kinds of things in nature that can't plausibly be thought to be intrinsically good: rocks, mud, molecules, and mold.

But much of what makes us up can't plausibly be thought to have intrinsic value either, such as kidneys, livers, and bladders. They have value, to be sure, but it's extrinsic value; as means to the proper functioning of the body. But they're part of something (as we're assuming) which does have intrinsic value, a human being. The fact that something is intrinsically good doesn't preclude its having parts that aren't intrinsically good or are even bad. Qualities such as kindness, compassion, sympathy, love, and virtue arguably are intrinsically good. Their presence might account for the intrinsic value of us humans, despite the fact that humans contain as parts things like toenails that seem to be neither intrinsically good nor bad (though they're extrinsically good for protecting the tops of toes) and other qualities, such as selfishness, thoughtlessness and sometimes cruelty that arguably are intrinsically bad. So, the fact that nature contains many things that don't have intrinsic value doesn't preclude the possibility that nature as a whole may have intrinsic value.

It may seem paradoxical that a human being can have intrinsic value even if, quantitatively speaking, most of the parts that make it up don't. Similarly, it may seem paradoxical that nature as a whole might have intrinsic value even if, quantitatively speaking, most of the parts that make it up don't have intrinsic value either.

There is a useful principle one might appeal to here. It was proposed by British philosopher G. E. Moore (1873–1958).[13] It is called the Principle of Organic Unities:

Theory Box 9D

Principle of Organic Unities
The intrinsic value of a whole may be more or less than the sum of the intrinsic values of its parts.

If one accepts this principle, one can make sense of saying that humans have intrinsic value despite the fact that most of what makes us up (in physical, biological terms) does not. So long as there are some qualities of humans (such as kindness and compassion) that are intrinsically good, those may offset the other parts that aren't intrinsically good. In the same way, it may be that nature as a whole has intrinsic value *if* humans have intrinsic value. Humans are a part of nature. Because of them there is kindness, compassion, sympathy, love, virtue, and righteousness in the world (qualities that arguably are intrinsically good). And it may be that these qualities—which are as much a part of nature as the physical properties of things—offset and outweigh the aspects of nature which aren't intrinsically good. This, to be sure, doesn't establish *that* nature is intrinsically good, but it opens the door to thinking that it may be, and provides the beginnings of an explanation why. And it suggests that there may be as good reason to believe that nature is intrinsically good as to believe that humans are intrinsically good. And if nature as a whole has intrinsic value, then (by premise (4)), it warrants BMC.

9.9 An anthropocentric challenge

Anthropocentrism is probably the biggest challenge to biocentrism and eco-centrism. Many (perhaps most) people think that humans come first and that other forms of life warrant only DMC. Those other forms of life are there to be used (though not necessarily abused) by us. The following is from libertarian philosopher Jan Narveson.

For Free Market Environmentalism
In a free market, individuals own and may do what they want with things, without fear of interference by others. Free market society is *consensual* society; exchanges occur only when owners believe they would be better off from them, compared with any other use they could make of their resources ... The free market philosophy's proposed moral rule for everything is: "No force or fraud, except to protect or compensate victims of force or fraud." On environmental matters, then, it is: "Do not use force against persons' utilizations of the environment, except by way of this rule."

One's environment is the rest of the world outside of oneself—the nonhuman part, for present purposes. What do we do about nature? My answer is the classic one: anything is free to take anything not already taken by anyone else. This is effected simply by commencing to use it—say, by working on it. This classic view is shared by ordinary people, but denied by many philosophers, who think that the environment is *everybody's*, and that the central control over it is essential . . .

Pollutions are side effects of otherwise voluntary interactions, on people who didn't ask for them and don't want them. Polluted air or water has stuff in it that the breather or drinker disvalues; it stinks or it makes him sick. Some impurities affect health, some affect taste; both are evils, of different kinds. And frequently there must be trade-offs: manure makes the crops grow better, but it stinks. Each individual farmer decides whether he'd rather have the crops than the smell. But suppose the manure makes the neighbors' air smell worse? What are the rights and wrongs of this? They own their lungs; you insert things they don't want into them, violating their property rights. In principle, then, the free market view says, they may sue. But will they in fact? That depends on two things: how much they dislike it; and how much benefit they get from it (I omit litigation costs.) Lower food prices made possible by your greater production may provide all the compensation desired, until smell free fertilizers come along . . .

Pollution problems exist, of course. But they are always confined to particular groups of people, and usually to relatively small groups. What matters, for any given person, is whether that person is affected, and how much, and whether there are benefits derived from the pollutions that he prefers to the costs of cleanup. In all the currently popular cases, the benefits win.

Consider garbage, which in almost all of North America is handled by public agencies, and the frequent subject of newspaper diatribes about how the planet will ere long succumb to garbage unless we do something, and so forth. On this basis, people are required to spend hours sorting their garbage into two or *n* distinct varieties, each handled separately, with compulsory recycling—at four times the cost of unsorted garbage, not counting time lost. There would be no talk of a general garbage problem if we allowed those things to be handled rationally, on the free market. There it would be a private business. Garbage companies would charge by the bag, giving people an incentive to minimize garbage production ... Is garbage disposal a looming environmental disaster, as we are told? Not at all. the fact is that it is quite trivial on the global landscape. All of the garbage that will be produced in North America in the entire 21st century would fit in a square landfill 9 miles on a side and 300 feet deep—1/40,000 of the land surface of the United States. Some "disaster"! And of course, within that century better technologies will emerge anyway. Extensive recycling now is a waster of time and money.[14]

The above passage says that pollution problems are always confined "to particular groups of people, and usually to relatively small groups." At least one case in which this is particularly true is that of the Eskimos (Inuit) and the effects of global warming.

Eskimos Seek to Recast Global Warming as a Rights Issue

The Eskimos, or Inuit, about 155,000 seal-hunting peoples scattered around the Arctic, plan to seek a ruling from the Inter-American Commission on Human Rights that the United States, by contributing substantially to global warming, is threatening their existence.

The Inuit plan is part of a broader shift in the debate over human-caused climate change evident among participants in the 20th round of international talks taking place in Buenos Aires aimed at averting dangerous human interference with the climate system . . .

Representatives of poor countries and communities—from the Arctic fringes to the atolls of the tropics to the flanks of the Himalayas—say they are imperiled by rising temperatures and seas through no fault of their own. They are casting the issue as no longer simply an environmental problem but as an assault on their basic human rights . . .

Such a petition could have decent prospects now that industrial countries, including the United States, have concluded in recent reports and studies that warming linked to heat-trapping smoke-stack and tailpipe emissions is contributing to bringing environmental changes in the Arctic, a number of experts said.

Last month, an assessment of Arctic climate change by 300 scientists for the eight countries with Arctic territory, including the United States, concluded that "human influences" are now the dominant factor [in global warming] . . .

If the Inuit effort succeeds, it could lead to an eventual stream of litigation, somewhat akin to lawsuits against tobacco companies, legal experts said.

The two-week convention . . . is the latest session on two climate treaties: the 1992 framework convention on climate change and the Kyoto Protocol, an addendum that . . . for the first time requires most industrialized countries to curb such emissions.

The United States has signed both pacts and is bound by the 1992 treaty, which requires no emissions cuts. But the Bush administration opposes the mandatory Kyoto treaty, saying it could harm the economy and unfairly excuses big developing countries from obligations.[15]

When it comes to the extinction of species, anthropocentrism believes this should be assessed in terms of its impact upon humans. Some believe that the problem has been overstated and that, in any event, there's relatively little benefit to humans from the maintenance of wild systems.

The anthropocentric perspective, as we've seen, has selective and universal versions. The universal dimension says that *all* humans—whether individually or collectively—warrant BMC. The selective version holds only that *some* humans—whether individually or collectively—warrant BMC. (One might maintain, e.g., that only one's own country—and therefore the citizens in it—warrant BMC.) We shall consider the universal version.

9.10 Intended and foreseeable consequences of environmental impacts

Two issues are particularly important here: first, concerning environmental impacts that are unintended but *foreseeable*: second concerning environmental impacts that are *intended*. Pollution isn't an intended effect of business and industrial practices, but it's a foreseeable effect of some of them.

Dams are deliberate attempts to alter and control the natural environment. (Picking a flower alters the environment, too, but not so far as we know in a major way.) Pollution receives a great deal of attention in our society (and is dealt with in the preceding selections by Baxter and Narveson). The environmental impact of dams receives little attention in countries like America and Britain, but it's a big issue in some countries that are striving to become major powers.

Two of the major dams of the world are in Asia: in China, the Three Gorges Dam, more than a mile and a quarter wide, on the Yangtze River; in India, the more than 3,000 dams proposed for the Narmada River. The dams are displacing thousands of villagers, possibly millions. The dams represent deliberate efforts to control a major aspect of nature, the flow of two large rivers. Their intended social benefits are great: power, control of floods, more accessible drinking water and irrigation for farming. But the costs to some people are also great: the loss of their homes, villages, and in some cases, livelihood. Despite promises of compensation, many of these people—often among the poorest in their societies—don't want to move. Yet they are forced to.

This is an issue that can be of central concern to both anthropocentrists and sentientists, biocentrists and ecocentrists—though for somewhat different reasons in each case.

The case of the Narmada project is illustrative. There has been a concerted nonviolent movement opposing the plans for the largest of the dams. From the anthropocentric standpoint, the issue is clear: displacement of some (though possibly millions) for the social good of hundreds of millions—indeed for the whole of India. Quite apart from judgments about the intrinsic value of nature, the moral issue stands. For whatever interventions we make on this scale in nature inevitably have consequences for humans.

A supporter of the protests against the Narmada project is the Indian writer Arundhati Roy. She sees the issues as involving the abuse of governmental power, in disregard of the well-being of those most affected by the projects, the villagers who are being displaced.

Listen to the Nonviolent Poor

On May 20 [2002], activists of the Narmada Bachao Andolan (NBA), the Save the Narmada Movement against Big Dams, began an indefinite fast in Bhopal. They fasted longer than Gandhi did on any of his fasts during India's freedom struggle.

Their demands are more modest than his ever were. They are protesting against the Madhya Pradesh government's forcible eviction of more than 1,000 Adivasi (indigenous) families to make way for the Maan Dam on the Narmada River. All they're asking is that the government ... implement its own policy of providing land to those being displaced by the Maan Dam ... At the end of 30 days, the activists called off the fast, having wrested a meager concession from the government—the setting up of a committee to "look into" the complaints. In India they kill us with committees ...

The NBA believes that big dams are obsolete. It believes there are more democratic, more local, more economically viable and environmentally sustainable ways of generating electricity and managing water systems. It is demanding more modernity, not less. It is demanding more democracy, not less ...

In the 21st century, the connections among religious fundamentalism, nuclear nationalism, and the pauperization of whole populations because of corporate globalization are becoming impossible to ignore ... As for the rest of us—concerned citizens, peace activists, and the like—it's not enough to sing songs about giving peace a chance. Doing everything we can to support movements like the Narmada Bachao Andolan is how we give peace a chance. This is the real war against terror.[16]

9.11 Conclusion

Everyone, without exception, has a stake in the well-being of the environment. This stake has often been lost sight of in the rush to control nature and turn it to human ends. But it's possible to enlarge one's perspective to give moral consideration to nature, whether that consideration be BMC or DMC. The theoretical issues—for example, whether nature as a whole has intrinsic value—are complex. But the practical issues can be understood and discussed without resolving all of the theoretical issues. If one assumes that all life, human and nonhuman, is interconnected, so that serious changes to one will impact the other, then the door is open to a convergence of the views of anthropocentrists and nonanthropocentrists. For the important issue, in the last analysis, is whether we give moral consideration to nonhuman things, whether that consideration be basic or derivative.

The nonhumans whose treatment occasions some of the greatest concern, of course, are animals. So we shall take up the moral question of the treatment of animals in the next chapter.

Study questions

1. What are *basic* and *derivative moral considerations* (Theory Box 9A)?
2. What are *anthropocentrism* (Definition Box 9A), *sentientism* (Definition Box 9B), and *biocentrism* (Definition Box 9C)?
3, What is *Baxter's argument* (Section 9.4) to try to show that moral concepts don't apply to nonhuman situations? What is the text's critique of that argument?
4. What is the connection between *ecological philosophy* and *nonviolence* (*ahimsa*) in the Jain Declaration on Nature (Section 9.8)?
5. How do *native American beliefs* about nature differ from those of the *Europeans* who settled America (Section 9.7)?
6. What does it mean for something to have *intrinsic value* (Theory Box 9B)? What does it mean for something to have *extrinsic value*?
7. What is the argument the text provides for showing the possibility that *nature as a whole* might have intrinsic value (Section 9.8)?
8. What is the *principle of organic unities* (Theory Box 9D)? What role does it play in the argument mentioned in question (7)?
9. What is the anthropocentric challenge presented in the argument for "*free market environmentalism*" (Section 9.9)?
10. What is the connection between *environmentalism* and *world poverty* claimed in the passage entitled "Listen to the Nonviolent Poor" (Section 9.10)?

Notes

1 From "Inversnaid," in Oscar Williams (ed.), *Immortal Poems of the English Language* (New York: Pocket Books, Inc., 1953), p. 460.

2 Quoted from Michael Boylan (ed.), *Environmental Ethics* (Upper Saddle River, NJ: Prentice-Hall, 2001), p. 43.

3 From William F. Baxter, *People or Penguins: The Case for Optimal Pollution* (New York: Columbia University Press, 1974), pp. 2–4; emphasis in the original.

4 Bernard E. Rollin, *Problems of International Justice*, Steven Luper-Foy (ed.) (Boulder, CO: Westview, 1988), p. 128; emphasis in the original.

5 From Paul Taylor, "Respect for Nature: A Theory of Environmental Ethics," in Boylan, *Environmental Ethics*, p. 249.

6 L. M. Singhvi, *The Jain Declaration on Nature*, presented to His Royal Highness Prince Philip, president of the WorldWide Fund for Nature (WWF) International on October 23, 1990. No publisher or date.

7 Don Marquis, *The Lives and Times of Archy and Mehitabel* (Garden City, NJ: Doubleday, Page, and Co., 1927), pp. 475–7.

8 John Dewey, *Quest for Certainty* (New York: G.P. Putnam's Sons, 1960), p. 100.

9 Annie L. Booth and Harvey M. Jacobs, from "Ties That Bind: Native American Beliefs as a Foundation for Environmental Consciousness," *Environmental Ethics*, Vol. 12, No. 1, 1990, 28f.; emphasis in the original.

10 Christopher D. Stone, from "Should Trees Have Standing? Toward Legal Rights for Natural Objects," 45 *Southern California Law Review*, 1972, 450–501.

11 Basic principles of deep ecology as set forth by George Sessions and Arne Naess and as published by Bill Devall and George Sessions in *Deep Ecology: Living as if Nature Mattered* (Salt Lake City: Gibbs M. Smith, Inc., Peregrine Smith Books, 1985), pp. 69f.

12 I've adapted this principle of the universalizability of judgments of intrinsic value from an analysis given in G. E. Moore, *Philosophical Studies* (New York: Harcourt, Brace & Co., Inc., 1922), p. 265.

13 G. E. Moore, *Principia Ethica* (Cambridge: University Press, 1956), p. 184.

14 Jan Narveson. Reprinted from *The Ag Bioethics Forum*, Vol. 6, No. 2, November 1994, 2–5; emphases in the original.

15 *The New York Times International*, December 15, 2004.

16 From Arundhati Roy, "Listen to the Nonviolent Poor," *The Christian Science Monitor*, July 5, 2002.

For more resources:

www.bloomsbury.com/holmes-introduction-to-applied-ethics

10

Moral Consideration for Animals

No humane being, past the thoughtless age of boyhood, will wantonly murder any creature, which holds its life by the same tenure that he does.

—Thoreau[1]

Introduction

This chapter explores the ethical issues that arise in connection with our treatment of animals. Should we give animals moral consideration, and if so, how much? Do we discriminate against animals when we use them for food, profit, and sport? Is it morally justifiable to eat animals, experiment on them and hunt them for sport? So-called speciesism answers yes. Animal rights and welfare advocates generally answer no. In this chapter, we'll set forth the basic moral considerations relevant to answering these questions.

10.1 Basic and derivative moral consideration

We don't give moral consideration to stones. We step on them, throw them, or kick them as we please. We do give moral consideration to humans. There are right and wrong ways of treating them.

What about animals? Are they like humans or more like stones—or somewhere in between? Do they have rights, and are there right and wrong ways of treating them?

Notice what is at issue here. We often give moral consideration to animals insofar as our treatment of them has consequences for humans. If your chicken strays into my yard and I kill it and eat it for dinner, I've done something wrong. But some people would say that's simply because it was *your* chicken. I destroyed something that belonged to you. You were wronged, not the chicken.

Whether animals deserve moral consideration in this sense isn't controversial. Anyone can agree that, all things being equal, it's wrong to harm, kill, or mistreat animals that belong to others without their owner's permission. The consideration animals warrant in this sense is *derivative moral consideration (DMC)* (see Theory Box 9A, Chapter 9, Section 9.2). It's consideration for animals based ultimately upon consideration for humans, not for animals themselves. What concerns us is whether animals deserve moral consideration *for their own sakes*—apart from the consequences for humans of how we treat them. This is *basic moral consideration (BMC).*

If we confine, kill, eat, or experiment upon animals, need we consider whether what we are doing is morally right or wrong beyond its consequences for humans? Is there anything about animals (unlike stones) that requires that we give them BMC?

There are two questions here: (1) Ought we to give animals BMC? (2) If so, how much (e.g., do they have rights on a par with humans)?

For practical purposes, (2) is the central question. Few people (in our society, at least) would deny that animals deserve *some* BMC. Most would say, for example, that it's wrong to torture animals for the fun of it. That wrongness doesn't depend upon how such treatment affects humans. Torturing animals is wrong even if some people enjoy doing it. But many would say that BMC extends only so far; while we shouldn't inflict gratuitous pain upon animals, we can cause them pain insofar as that's unavoidable in using them for legitimate human purposes. In this view, scientific research would be a legitimate human purpose; torture would not. Let us call such consideration *minimal* BMC. Such moral consideration wouldn't depend on the consequences of the treatment for humans, so it would be BMC. But it would be minimally limited by what is necessary to achieve legitimate human purposes.

Contrasted with minimal BMC is what we may call *maximal* BMC: moral consideration, comparable to what we give humans. Maximal BMC would, of course, allow for respects in which animals differ from humans and in which animal species differ from one another. Thus, we wouldn't expect to make and keep promises to cows, because they're unable to comprehend the concept of a promise. But this is no different from the way in which we treat some humans (e.g., the newborn or the irreversibly comatose) who likewise have no concept of a promise. And, according to maximal BMC, we might give different moral consideration to chimpanzees than to, say, clams by virtue of their having more highly developed nervous systems.

The key question, then, concerns (2). *How much* BMC do animals warrant? Is the BMC owed to animals minimal—that is, limited by what's necessary to achieve human ends? Or is it maximal—that is, comparable to the BMC owed to humans? Or is it somewhere in between? Many people who think it's wrong to use animals for food or experimentation nonetheless think it's permissible to own animals as pets. Maximal BMC would prohibit that, because we cannot legitimately own human beings. So we may speak of *significant BMC* to allow for BMC that goes beyond minimal BMC but falls short of maximal BMC. Consider two areas of concern.

The first involves food. Because we need to eat to survive, most people consider using animals for food a legitimate human end, even though doing so causes animals pain, suffering, and death. That can't be helped. Animals could be euthanized painlessly, but most aren't; factory farming requires efficiency in order to maximize profits, and that would be sacrificed if animals were given carefully managed individual deaths. In any event, they need to be killed to be eaten, whatever care they've received prior to being killed. What we shouldn't do—according to those who accord animals minimal BMC—is to cause them pain *beyond* what's necessary to using them for food. If, on the other hand, we owe animals maximal BMC, then we're limited in what we may consider legitimate human ends in the first place. In this view, if we wouldn't eat humans, then we shouldn't eat animals either.

The second involves experimentation. We use experimentation to seek cures for disease, expand scientific knowledge, and improve products which companies sell for profit. But we don't consider it legitimate to experiment upon humans against their will as a means to these ends. If we extend only minimal BMC to animals, then we may use them for experimentation but only so long as we don't cause them pain beyond what's necessary to achieve our research ends. On the other hand, if we extend maximal BMC to animals, then—because it would not be legitimate to experiment upon humans against their will even to find cures for diseases—it is not legitimate to experiment upon animals for this purpose either. We shall discuss experimentation in 10.6 and vegetarianism in 10.11.

10.2 Speciesism

Animal advocates (as we shall call those who argue for at least significant BMC for animals) focus upon two claims. The first is that animals have rights. The second is that animals are *sentient* (capable of sensation, specifically of experiencing pleasure, pain, and suffering). The possession of either or both of these properties, they say, requires that animals be given basic moral consideration. First a point of terminology:

Theory Box 10A

Biologically, humans are animals (specifically, mammals). Strictly, then, the issue concerns the treatment of nonhuman animals by human animals. But the terms "humans" and "animals" are commonly used to characterize human and nonhuman animals respectively, and we shall for convenience use these terms. Although animals include vertebrates (e.g., fish, birds, mammals) and invertebrates (e.g., worms, snails, clams), most discussions of the ethical treatment of animals focus upon vertebrates. We shall for the most part do so as well.

Second, a point about the scope of our inquiry. Animals are treated somewhat differently in various cultures and contexts. Some people (e.g., in polar regions where crops won't grow) need to hunt to survive. Others (e.g., if they can't afford machinery) rely on animals as beasts of burden in agriculture. These differing contexts raise differing moral issues. We shall focus upon the treatment of animals in advanced societies such as those in Britain and America, in which the first of these is not true and the second is rarely true any longer.

Some people contend that our treatment of animals is akin to racism and sexism. In racism and sexism, certain groups are treated prejudicially by comparison with the treatment of other groups. Here we can ask whether animals, *as a group*, are treated prejudicially by comparison with the ways in which we treat humans. The view that they are has sometimes been called speciesism (an obvious comparison with racism and sexism). Let us define "speciesism" as follows:

Definition Box 10A

Speciesism: The beliefs, attitudes, and practices of speciesists.

This, then (as in the analogous cases of racism and sexism), requires an understanding of what a "speciesist" is. So let us define that notion as follows:

> **Definition Box 10B**
>
> **Speciesist: One who practices or approves of discrimination against animals in the belief (a) that humans are innately superior to animals, and (b) that humans ought to dominate animals.**

The Bible (Gen. 1:26) says that God gives man dominion over the animals, which suggests that humans should dominate animals (though some translations say simply that man has stewardship over animals, which may mean that we should care for them, not necessarily dominate them).

Many who denounce racism and sexism readily embrace speciesism. They think, quite simply, that we humans are superior to animals and therefore may use them for our purposes. This doesn't mean that they condone causing animals unnecessary pain or suffering. A few do that, but most don't. They think, rather, that animals are there for us to use for food, fun, sport, and profit or the advancement of knowledge. As long as we don't inflict unnecessary pain, we may do with them as we please. We may treat them kindly, if we choose, but we needn't do so. We may kill them for food, research, or sport. And we may kill them if we tire of them as pets or they make a nuisance of themselves by eating our flowers (as deer commonly do) or raiding our dumpsters (as bears commonly do).

Notice that speciesists don't necessarily hold that animals warrant *no* BMC. They might do that but they needn't. They may say that such consideration as they warrant precludes inflicting unnecessary pain in using them for human purposes. That is, speciesists may say that animals warrant only minimal BMC.

10.3 Animals and discrimination

Although one might ask whether questions of right and wrong arise in general in connection with our treatment of animals, we might ask more specifically how our treatment of animals compares with our treatment of humans. This highlights the question of fairness or justice in a way in which simply asking whether our treatment of animals raises questions of right and wrong doesn't.

Do we (meaning, humans collectively) discriminate against animals? Discrimination implies a comparative judgment. Do we treat animals prejudicially by comparison with the way in which we treat fellow humans? We will take a look at some common activities wherein we use animals for our purposes.

10.4 Hunting

Let us begin with deer hunting, one of the most popular forms of hunting. Deer hunting is a major sport in America, with hunters killing 250,000–300,000 deer each year. (In the process, some cows and other hunters are accidentally killed as well.)

Some killing is done to control the deer population. Feeding stations are set and marksmen kill the deer as they come to feed. This, strictly speaking, isn't hunting. Some regulation of hunting, however, is done with a view to controlling the deer population. Such considerations as the duration of the season for which licenses are granted, and the sex of the deer—whether they are does or bucks—that are allowed to be killed are taken into account.

Most hunting, however, is for sport, that is, for enjoyment. For the most part, it's done in the wild, though some of it's done on so-called deer farms, where deer (and sometimes other animals like boars) are fenced in, usually in large areas where it takes at least some effort to find them, and hunters pay to shoot them. Even though deer that are killed are often eaten (with venison considered a treat by many), the primary motivation isn't to obtain food. One can buy meat at the nearest supermarket more easily than trek for hours in the woods stalking deer. The primary motivation is the experience of killing. For many, there is pleasure in killing as part of a hunt. For at least a few, however, it is much more than that. It's a spiritual experience. Consider the following article:

Killing with Kindness?

Mr. James's love affair with deer hunting belies the fact that almost nothing about it is what it was even a few years ago. And despite the rhapsodic narrative he can weave on a morning's hunt about the adventures of years past, he is also part of a vanguard of hunters trying to transform the sport. In small, determined bands they are preaching a new mantra of ethics and ecology—that hunting must be about more than killing, and that the killing must above all be as pain-less and cruelty-free as possible if hunting is to survive.

"No one wants to see a deer gut-shot," Mr. James said.

Whether hunting should survive—and whether an overlay of eth-ics and responsibility can overcome the objections that many people have to killing animals for recreation and food—is another question. But there is little disagreement among scientists, hunters and ordinary residents across the region that the relationship between humans and deer—and by extension, hunters say, between predator and prey—is being renegotiated . . .

The partnership [Deer Management Partnership] is led by a 51-year-old Quaker minister's son named Bill Badgley, who rejected his family's pacifist philosophy to take up hunting as a teenager and now preaches a combination of ethics, ecology and anatomy that he calls "the future of hunting." Members must pass a rigorous marksman-ship exam proving that they can kill a deer at various distances with a single shot to the lungs, which can bring death in as little as 10 sec-onds from the enormous blood loss . . .

Defining a quality experience, hunters say, is hard. Some talk about the intangible, almost mystical element they seek from their time in the woods, or the life-and-death moment of power in pulling the trigger or releasing the arrow. Some . . . admit to the thrill of the kill. Others describe a connection to the world that comes in no other way—the difference, as one hunter put it, between being a participant in nature and being a mere observer.

In some ways, the Deer Management Partnership redefines what it means to hunt at all. Mr. Badgley said that for him, hunting is a spiritual experience. He cradles the head of every deer he kills as a sign of respect. The group also completely rejects the trophy buck as a holdover of hunting's past. Deer populations are best controlled by killing does, not bucks, and the new breed of hunters, they say, must be population managers first and foremost . . .

There's both a sadness and a hope to deer hunting on this new terrain. The old spirit of hunting was animated by a sense of freedom, hunters say—the sense of being in the wild, without rules. The new hunter's world, especially in groups like the partnership, is all about rules. The question of what is natural—both for human beings and for deer—comes up again and again.

Wally John, a retired state employee who was hunting with Mr. James on a recent morning—though not a member of the partnership—said he thought that deer who live without predators

> were in fact being denied a part of their nature. Deer, he said, are at the peak of their powers of observation and awareness when they are evading danger—every sense is alive, he said, just as their evolutionary past intended.
>
> "When you take a deer at those times, you're besting him in his own environment—you're respecting it," Mr. John said. "When you buy meat at the grocery store, you're not."[2]

There is for many hunters excitement to hunting, a thrill that comes from the kill. Without it the experience wouldn't be the same. One could go through virtually all of the steps of a hunt: packing the SUV, picking up friends, trekking stealthily through the woods, and waiting patiently near deer trails. But rather than carry a gun one could carry a camera. At the moment of truth, one could snap the deer's picture rather than killing it. This, most hunters will tell you, wouldn't be the same. Something about squeezing that trigger with a deer in your sights gives the experience meaning. Some hunters report getting a rush from killing. Even the killing must be done a certain way. Hunters could tranquilize deer with dart guns then kill them at point blank range. That way the deer wouldn't suffer. They wouldn't run off wounded, as they often do, before succumbing to blood loss. But most hunters wouldn't consider that the same. Killing a healthy animal in its natural habitat and at the height of its powers is essential. Whether the excitement that comes from the kill derives from a primordial instinct in the genetic makeup of humans (mostly males), or from the fact that it represents a departure from the routine of civilized life—or is some combination of these and other motives—we don't know. The fact is that many people enjoy hunting. This is why hunting is called a sport.

We don't hunt humans. It would be more of a challenge if we did, particularly if the hunted had guns with which to shoot back. But it would be wrong. We can't justifiably kill people for sport. The challenge of doing so provided the plot of a short story entitled "The Most Dangerous Game," by Richard Connell. A wealthy European sportsman, a general who had become bored with hunting, contrives to hunt humans who shipwreck by chance or his design on his Caribbean island. The following passage describes his conversation with a renowned young hunter who has ended up on the island (and whom he is eventually to hunt). It conveys with brutal honesty one perspective on hunting. In it the young man, Rainsford, learns the awful truth:

> "Hunting was beginning to bore me! And hunting, remember, had been my life. I have heard that in America business men often go to pieces when they give up the business that has been their life."
>
> "Yes, that's so," said Rainsford.
>
> The general smiled. "I had no wish to go to pieces," he said ... "So," continued the general, "I asked myself why the hunt no longer fascinated me. You are much younger than I am, Mr. Rainsford, and have not hunted as much, but you can perhaps guess the answer."
>
> "What was it?"
>
> "Simply this: hunting had ceased to be what you call 'a sporting proposition.' It had become too easy. I always got my quarry ... It came to me as an inspiration what I must do," the general went on.
>
> "And that was?"
>
> "... I had to invent a new animal to hunt," he said ... So I bought this island, built this house, and here I do my hunting . . ."
>
> "But the animal, General Zaroff?"
>
> "Oh," said the general, "it supplies me with the most exciting hunting in the world. No other hunting compares with it for an instant. Every day I hunt, and I never grow bored now, for I have a quarry with which I can match my wits . . ."
>
> "But no animal can reason," objected Rainsford.
>
> "My dear fellow," said the general, "there is one that can."
>
> "But you can't mean—" gasped Rainsford.
>
> "And why not?"
>
> "I can't believe you are serious, General Zaroff. This is a grisly joke."
>
> "Why should I not be serious? I am speaking of hunting."
>
> "Hunting? General Zaroff, what you speak of is murder."[3]

Gladiators in ancient Rome fought one another, often to the death. But as slaves or captives they didn't do it for sport, as General Zaroff does in the above story. They were compelled to for the enjoyment of spectators. In hunting animals for sport we treat them prejudicially by comparison with the way we treat humans. To hunt and kill humans for sport is murder, as Rainsford proclaims in the story. Hence we discriminate against animals. This doesn't necessarily mean that hunting is wrong. It might be argued that some forms of discrimination are justified. But it does mean that the justification must be provided.

10.5 Eating animals

Most people eat meat from habit or because they like the taste. If asked, they often say it is for the protein. In any event, eating meat is well-established in tradition: turkey at Thanksgiving, goose at Christmas, grilled burgers on the 4th of July, and hot dogs at ball games. In the United States alone, 45 million turkeys bite the dust at Thanksgiving. People get pleasure from the taste of meat. Insofar as pleasure is good, their lives—other things being equal—are presumably enhanced by eating meat. That is a relevant moral consideration.

With the possible exception of people who live in regions where fruit, nuts, and vegetables cannot be grown, however, meat isn't necessary for a healthful diet. Sufficient protein can be derived from vegetables, eggs, soy and dairy products, and beans and rice. People eat meat basically because they like it.

Eating of animals isn't the central issue, of course. When animals are eaten, they're already dead. Few would object if people in advanced societies gathered up road kill each day and cooked it up to be eaten. What is problematic (beyond health issues in the overconsumption of meat) is the *treatment* of animals in the course of preparing them to be eaten. And here the contrast with our treatment of humans is obvious. We don't eat humans, even though we could get protein from doing so. We might even acquire a taste for humans, too. Not only is it wrong to eat humans, it would also be wrong to confine them against their will, fatten them, and slaughter them to be consumed. In doing this to animals we treat them prejudicially by comparison with the way we treat humans.

10.6 Experimenting on animals

Animals are experimented on for scientific, educational, and commercial purposes. Millions of frogs, mice, and rats are dissected in educational and research settings. Many scientists say that certain medical advances—such as the development of vaccines—wouldn't be possible without research on animals. It's our lives or theirs.

In human experimentation, informed consent is required. Animals can't consent (though one could leave their cages open at night to see whether they choose to stay). Animals don't survive in the majority of experiments upon them. They're either killed in the course of the procedure or die later as a result. Humans rarely do. And their death is never the expected outcome of experimentation on them (excepting some of the involuntary experimentation on prisoners done by the Nazis during the Second World War). Involuntary experimentation on humans is considered abhorrent.

If we consider owning, hunting, eating, and experimenting upon animals, the evidence seems clear. We kill animals for fun, food, and profit. We own animals. We perform lethal experiments upon them. We put them in zoos to look at, and watch them in circuses for our entertainment. We don't do these things to humans. Often (as in the case of show dogs and race horses), the special treatment accorded animals is designed to make them better serve human ends. They're bred and trained to run, trot, and jump on command. Some pets, to be sure, are pampered and cared for more than most humans; they're practically surrogate children. They get special diets, regular grooming, and expensive burials. They remain, however, the property of humans.

It seems clear that we treat animals as a group prejudicially by comparison with the way we treat humans. Hence we discriminate against them. Once again, this doesn't necessarily mean that it is wrong. We kill bacteria to help control disease, and we might say (though it would be odd to do so) that we discriminate against bacteria. But few would call that wrong. Discrimination against persons is wrong. Is discrimination against animals wrong?

10.7 Ought we to dominate animals?

Each of the above forms of discrimination also represents a form of domination. Such domination is practiced in virtually all parts of the world. Does this show that it's right? By itself it doesn't. Let us see why. Consider the following three propositions:

1. Humans in fact dominate animals.
2. Humans are innately superior to animals.
3. Humans ought to dominate animals.

Proposition (1) states a *fact*. Proposition (2) expresses a *value*. To say that humans are innately superior to animals means that we are naturally *better*, that is, more good. Proposition (3) expresses an *ought* judgment, which we may here take to be a moral judgment. So there are three relationships involved here: first, between *fact/value*; second between *fact/ought* (philosophers often represent this as the relationship between "is" and "ought"); and third, between *value/ought*. See Theory Box 1D in Chapter 1, Section 1.7, for an analysis of these distinctions in connection with racism.

Many philosophers have argued that we can't legitimately infer value judgments or ought judgments directly from factual statements. One needs to produce further reasons. Thus if I say that

1. Drugs are desired (factual statement).

I can't simply conclude that

2. Drugs are good (value judgment).

By the same token, I can't conclude from the fact that

3. Men have dominated women historically (fact).

that

4. Men are innately superior to women (value judgment).

Nor from the factual statement (3) or the value judgment (4) can I legitimately conclude

5. Men ought to dominate women (ought judgment).

Those who contend that men are naturally superior and ought to dominate women have to do more than just say that in fact men dominate women (which they undeniably do in many societies and have done historically almost universally). They have to give reasons to *show* that men are superior and ought to dominate women.

Similarly, from the indisputable fact that humans do dominate animals, reasons must be given why this establishes that humans are naturally superior to animals. And reasons must be given why those two considerations, even if they were true, *show* that humans ought to dominate animals.

10.8 Are humans innately superior to animals?

What are the criteria of superiority? Size? Strength? Speed? Eyesight? Hearing? Sense of smell? Longevity? Whales are bigger than humans, elephants stronger, cheetahs faster. Fish swim better, hawks see better, dogs hear better, and tortoises live longer. Monkeys have better balance, cats, keener night vision. Birds can fly (unaided); bats navigate by radar. Few humans could build a bird's nest with the skill of a robin. None can track a rabbit by scent. With regard to virtually every respect, there is some animal species that is superior to humans in that respect, except one. That's intelligence. Humans appear to have superior intelligence (though some researchers think that animals like dolphins and chimpanzees may be nearly as intelligent as humans). Through intelligence, humans have devised machines that can outperform animals in tests of speed, strength, or endurance. Though we cannot explore this possibility here, it could be that there are different forms of intelligence, and that in some of these forms animals surpass human. Elephants and squirrels, for example, are thought to have extraordinary memories. Cheetahs possess unusual abilities to make instantaneous geometrical calculations of angles in pursuit of prey.

The question isn't, however, simply whether humans are superior to animals in one respect. Probably every animal species is superior (or equal) to all others in some respect. The question is whether they are superior overall.

Does superiority in intelligence make humans superior overall? Does it, for example, outweigh longevity? For all of our intelligence, we humans live only about 70-some years on average (and much less in some societies). Some tortoises can live a couple hundred years. Should there be an all-out nuclear war, humankind could conceivably be virtually eliminated by radiation. Not so cockroaches, who can survive vastly higher doses. Why does intelligence outweigh longevity or survivability?

Key Quote 10A

It has certainly been true in the past that what we call intelligence and scientific discovery have conveyed a survival advantage. It is not so clear that this is still the case: our scientific discoveries may destroy us all.[4]

Let us examine more closely the value of intelligence.

A judgment of superiority, as we have seen, is a *value judgment*. To say that we're superior to animals says that we're better, of greater value. To say that we're naturally (or innately) superior to animals is to say that we're naturally *better*—that we are, as it were, more good. As we saw in Section 9.8, a thing can be said to be good either intrinsically or extrinsically. Let us look again at

> **Theory Box 9B**
>
> **Intrinsic Value**: Value dependent solely upon the nature of what has value.
> **Extrinsic Value**: Value that isn't intrinsic (i.e., that depends at least in part upon the relationship of what has value to other things).

In these terms, we can ask whether the value of intelligence is intrinsic or extrinsic. Some philosophers have thought that it's intrinsic. But that isn't obvious. If a person has great intelligence but doesn't use it, it is hard to see what value it has. If he or she sits around all day, doesn't develop any skills or talents or acquire an education, the intelligence would lie dormant. In a practical sense, that person would be no better off than someone of lower intelligence.

Worse yet, such a person might be thought not to be fully rational. Immanuel Kant (1724–1804) held that, as rational beings, we have a duty to develop our talents and capacities—that is, to use our intelligence. That is what a perfectly rational being would do. Failure to do so, he thought, represents an imperfection in our rationality. It also signifies violation of a moral duty to ourselves, since most of the goals we want to achieve in life require skills, training, and education. Failure to use reason to fulfill our purposes (since it would obstruct the achievement of things we want) would be contrary to such a duty.

It would seem, therefore, that most, if not all, of the value of intelligence is extrinsic. If you were stranded on a deserted island, your intelligence would be of little value if you didn't use it to find food, shelter, and security and to devise ways to signal passing ships or planes to rescue you. The main value of intelligence clearly is extrinsic, even if it has some intrinsic value. It's instrumental to achieving our purposes.

10.9 What extrinsic value does human intelligence have?

For humans collectively, intelligence has led to language, invention, science and technology, and countless ways of controlling and manipulating the environment for human ends. It has also led to the establishment of government, laws, schools, hospitals, and universities. None of these exists in nature. They are products of human intelligence. Art, music, literature, and dance are also expressions of human intelligence. Virtually all of these are considered good. Intelligence can be said to have extrinsic value by virtue of having produced them. Although animals can communicate, and some have complex social organization, they either haven't produced these other values or haven't done so (as in the case of communication and manipulation of the environment) to the same degree, at least as nearly as we can tell.

Does the fact that human intelligence has extraordinarily high extrinsic value in these ways offset the many other ways in which animals are superior to humans? In other words, does it make humans superior overall to animals?

In reflecting upon that question, we should also consider some of the other products of human intelligence. Let us consider the following passage from Mark Twain, who in his satirical way makes an important point.

Who Is Superior?

During several centuries hundreds of heretics were burned at the stake every year because their religious opinions were not satisfactory to the Roman Church.

In all ages the savages of all lands have made the slaughtering of their neighboring brothers and enslaving of their women and children the common business of their lives.

Hypocrisy, envy, malice, cruelty, vengefulness, seduction, rape, robbery, swindling, arson, bigamy, adultery, and the oppression and humiliation of the poor and the helpless in all ways have been and still are more or less common among both civilized and uncivilized peoples of the earth.

For many centuries "the common brotherhood of man" has been urged—on Sundays—and "patriotism" on Sundays and weekdays both. Yet patriotism *contemplates the opposite of a common brotherhood.*

Women's equality with man has never been conceded by any people, ancient or modern, civilized or savage

I have been studying the traits and dispositions of the "lower animals" (so-called), and contrasting them with the traits and dispositions of man. I find the result humiliating to me. For it obliges me to renounce my allegiance to the Darwinian theory of the Ascent of Man from the

Lower Animals; since it now seems plain to me that that theory ought to be vacated in favor of a new and truer one, this new and truer one to be named the Descent of Man from the Higher Animals . . .

The higher animals engage in individual fights, but never in organized masses. Man is the only animal that deals in that atrocity of atrocities, War. He is the only one that gathers his brethren about him and goes forth in cold blood and with calm pulse to exterminate his kind. He is the only animal that for sordid wages will march out ... and help to slaughter strangers of his own species who have done him no harm and with whom he has no quarrel.

Man is the only animal that robs his helpless fellow of his country—takes possession of it and drives him out of it or destroys him. Man has done this in all the ages. There is not an acre of ground on the globe that is in possession of its rightful owner, or that has not been taken away from owner after owner, cycle after cycle, by force and bloodshed.[5]

Though he doesn't use the word, Twain's philosophically interesting point—whether or not one agrees with all of the rest—is that humans are responsible for the creation of *evil*. Leaving aside the question of God and supernatural beings (like Satan), there would be no evil in the world but for humans. Let us see why.

It's important to distinguish evil from what is merely bad. A toothache is bad, but it isn't evil. Droughts, hurricanes, and floods are bad, but they aren't evil. Evil is the product of human minds. Without the malicious intentions and motives of conscious, rational beings, there would be no evil. In light of that, let us define evil as follows:

Definition Box 10C

Evil: intentionally causing, or taking pleasure in, the undeserved and unjustified suffering of others for its own sake.

Twain speaks of the hypocrisy, envy, malice, cruelty, and vengefulness of humans. We should include torture, terrorism, war, genocide, racism, sexism, anti-Semitism, oppression, and injustice. We humans have enslaved millions, killed tens of millions in war, destroyed whole cities in a flash. We have created concentration camps and systematically exterminated millions. We have devised diabolically sophisticated instruments of torture. We have degraded the environment in ways that adversely affect ourselves and other forms of life as well. In the worst case, we could conceivably kill ourselves off—and higher forms of animal life as well—in an all-out nuclear war. Human intelligence is capable of this as well as producing the good things enumerated earlier. However else they are characterized—and whether or not they can be justified—these things are bad. Whether they all constitute evil, in the sense defined, is another question. Much of the harm, suffering, and death humans cause is done from good motives and without malicious intentions. Be that as it may, evil and enormous suffering are products of human intelligence.

The evil and the bad that humans do must be weighed in the scales as well as the good in reflecting upon whether humans are naturally superior to animals by virtue of possessing intelligence. It may be that we are, but that judgment—though at first it may seem obvious—is far from evident. The most we can say with confidence is that we're superior to animals in some respects, and they are superior to us in some respects.

10.10   Do animals have rights?

The second key proposition in the definition of speciesism is that humans ought to (or may permissibly) dominate animals. We have seen in Section 10.7 that one can't conclude simply from the fact that humans do dominate animals that they ought to or may justifiably do so. Let us examine that proposition, considered as a moral judgment.

To review briefly: just as it doesn't follow directly from the fact that humans dominate animals that they ought to do so, it doesn't follow directly from the value judgment that humans are superior to animals that they ought to dominate animals. That is, just as one cannot go directly from *fact* to *value*, or from *fact* to *ought*, so one cannot go directly from *value* to *ought*. I may agree that a Mercedes is a good car, but it doesn't follow that I ought to buy one. I can readily accept the value judgment without accepting the ought judgment. In other words, even if it could be shown conclusively that we are naturally superior to animals, it wouldn't follow from that alone that we ought to dominate them. One would still have to give further reasons to support that conclusion. One might think, for example, that if we are superior to animals, we ought to care for them, not dominate them. Adults are superior to infants in most respects (though they're arguably not as cute, generous, and trusting), but we don't think for that reason that adults should dominate children rather than love and care for them.

Thus, even if animal advocates acknowledge that humans are superior to animals, they haven't, thereby, conceded that it's permissible for humans to discriminate against animals. On the other side, even if speciesists concede that humans discriminate against animals, they haven't, thereby, conceded that it's wrong to do so. They may say it's wrong to discriminate against humans but not wrong to discriminate against animals.

Speciesists might argue that discrimination against animals is permissible because they contend animals don't have rights. Rights, they may say, belong only to rational beings; those capable of membership in a moral community. This excludes animals. Hence there is no violation of rights when we kill animals or use them for food, profit, or sport. It's prejudicial treatment of them, to be sure, but it's not wrong.

Some animal advocates contend that animals do have rights. Others concede that they don't but say that doesn't matter. They say animals (at least higher animals) are sentient (see Section 10.2). And that suffices to establish that there are right and wrong ways of treating them, quite apart from comparison with how we treat humans.

Let us look at two views on the issue of whether animals have rights, both by philosophers. The first argues that animals do have rights, the second that they don't.

The Case for Animal Rights
by Tom Regan

I regard myself as an advocate of animal rights—as a part of the animal rights movement. That movement, as I conceive it, is committed to a number of goals, including:

- the total abolition of the use of animals in science;
- the total dissolution of commercial animal agriculture;
- the total elimination of commercial and sport hunting and trapping.

There are, I know, people who profess to believe in animal rights but do not avow these goals. Factory farming, they say, is wrong—it violates animals' rights—but traditional animal agriculture is all right. Toxicity tests of cosmetics on animals violate their rights, but important medical research—cancer research, for example—does not. The clubbing of baby seals is abhorrent, but not the harvesting of adult seals. I used to think I understood this reasoning. Not any more. You don't change unjust institutions by tidying them up.

What's wrong—fundamentally wrong—with the way animals are treated isn't the details that vary from case to case. It's the whole system. The forlornness of the veal calf is pathetic, heart wrenching; the pulsing pain of the chimp with electrodes planted deep in her brain is repulsive; the slow, tortuous death of the racoon caught in the leg-hold trap is agonizing. But what is wrong isn't the pain, isn't the suffering, isn't the deprivation. These compound what's wrong. Sometimes—often—they make it much, much worse. But they are not the fundamental wrong.

The fundamental wrong is the system that allows us to view animals as *our resources*, here for *us*—to be eaten, or surgically manipulated, or exploited for sport or money. Once we accept this view of animals—as our resources—the rest is as predictable as it is regrettable. Why worry about their loneliness, their pain, their death? Since animals exist for us, to benefit us in one way or another, what harms them really doesn't matter—or matters only if it starts to bother us, makes us feel a trifle uneasy when we eat our veal escalope, for example. So, yes, let us get veal calves out of solitary confinement, give them more space, a little straw, a few companions. But let us keep our veal escalope.

But a little straw, more space and a few companions won't eliminate—won't even touch—the basic wrong that attaches to our viewing and treating these animals as our resources. A veal calf killed to be eaten after living in close confinement is viewed and treated in this way: but so, too, is another who is raised (as they say) "more humanely." To right the wrong of our treatment of farm animals requires more than making rearing methods 'more humane'; it requires the total dissolution of commercial animal agriculture . . .

What to do? Where to begin? ... Suppose we consider that you and I, for example, do have value as individuals—what we'll call *inherent value*. To say we have such value is to say that we are something more than, something different from, mere receptacles. Moreover, to ensure that we do not pave the way for such injustices as slavery or sexual discrimination, we must believe that all who have inherent value have it equally, regardless of their sex, race, religion, birthplace and so on. Similarly to be discarded as irrelevant are one's talents or skills, intelligence and wealth, personality or pathology, whether one is loved and admired or despised and loathed. The genius and the retarded child, the prince and the pauper, the brain surgeon and the fruit vendor, Mother Teresa and the most unscrupulous used-car salesman—all have inherent value, all possess it equally, and all have an equal right to be treated with respect, to be treated in ways that do not reduce them to the status of things, as if they existed as resources for others. My value as an individual is independent of my usefulness to you. Yours is not dependent on your usefulness to me. For either of us to treat the other in ways that fail to show respect for the other's independent value is to act immorally, to violate the individual's rights.

Some of the rational virtues of this view—what I call the rights view—should be evident ... For example, the rights view *in principle* denies the moral tolerability of any and all forms of racial, sexual or social discrimination; and ... this view *in principle* denies that we can justify good results by using evil means that violate an individual's rights—denies, for example, that it could be moral to kill my Aunt Bea to harvest beneficial consequences for others. That would be to sanction the disrespectful treatment of the individual in the name of the social good, something the rights view will not—categorically will not—ever allow.

The rights view, I believe, is rationally the most satisfactory moral theory. It surpasses all other theories in the degree to which it illuminates and explains the foundation of our duties to one another—the domain of human morality. On this score it has the best reasons, the best arguments, on its side. Of course, if it were possible to show that only human beings are included within its scope, then a person like myself, who believes in animal rights, would be obliged to look elsewhere.

But attempts to limit its scope to humans only can be shown to be rationally defective. Animals, it is true, lack many of the abilities humans possess. They can't read, do higher mathematics, build a bookcase or make *baba ghanoush*. Neither can many human beings, however, and yet we don't (and shouldn't) say that they (these humans) therefore have less inherent value, less of a right to be treated with respect, than do others. It is the *similarities* between those human beings who most clearly, most non-controversially have such value (the people reading this, for example), not our differences, that matter most. And the really crucial, the basic similarity is simply this: we are each of us the experiencing subject of a life, a conscious creature having an individual welfare that has importance to us whatever our usefulness to others. We want and prefer things, believe and feel things, recall and expect things. And all these dimensions of our life, including our pleasure and pain, our enjoyment and suffering, our satisfaction and frustration, our continued existence or our untimely death—all make a difference to the quality of our life as lived, as experienced, by us as individuals. As the same is true of those animals that concern us (the ones that are eaten and trapped, for example), they too must be viewed as the experiencing subjects of a life, with inherent value of their own.

Some there are who resist the idea that animals have inherent value. 'Only humans have such value,' they profess. How might this narrow view be defended? Shall we say that only humans have the requisite intelligence, or autonomy, or reason? But there are many, many humans who fail to meet these standards and yet are reasonably viewed as having value above and beyond their usefulness to others. Shall we claim that only humans belong to the right species, the species *Homo sapiens*? But this is blatant speciesism. Will it be said, then, that all—and only—humans have immortal souls? Then our opponents have their work cut out for them. I am myself not ill-disposed to the proposition that there are immortal souls. Personally, I profoundly hope I have one. But I would not want to rest my position on a controversial ethical issue on the even more controversial question about who or what has an immortal soul. That is to dig one's hole deeper, not to climb out. Rationally, it is better to resolve moral issues without making more controversial assumptions than are needed. The question of who has inherent value is such a question, one that is resolved more rationally without the introduction of the idea of immortal souls than by its use.

Well, perhaps some will say that animals have some inherent value, only less than we have. Once again, however, attempts to defend this view can be shown to lack rational justification. What could be the basis of our having more inherent value than animals? Their lack of reason, or autonomy, or intellect? Only if we are willing to make the same judgement in the case of humans who are similarly deficient. But it is not true that such humans—the retarded child, for example, or the mentally deranged—have less inherent value than you or I. Neither, then, can we rationally sustain the view that animals like them in being the experiencing subjects of a life have less inherent value. *All* who have inherent value have it *equally*, whether they be human animals or not.

Inherent value, then, belongs equally to those who are the experiencing subjects of a life. Whether it belongs to others—to rocks

and rivers, trees and glaciers, for example—we do not know and
may never know. But neither do we need to know, if we are to make
the case for animal rights. We do not need to know, for example,
how many people are eligible to vote in the next presidential election before we can know whether I am. Similarly, we do not need to
know how many individuals have inherent value before we can know
that some do. When it comes to the case for animal rights, then,
what we need to know is whether the animals that, in our culture,
are routinely eaten, hunted and used in our laboratories, for example, are like us in being subjects of a life. And we do know this. We
do know that many—literally billions and billions—of these animals
are the subjects of a life in the sense explained and so have inherent value if we do. And since, in order to arrive at the best theory
of our duties to one another, we must recognize our equal inherent
value as individuals, reason—not sentiment, not emotion—reason
compels us to recognize the equal inherent value of these animals
and, with this, their equal right to be treated with respect.[6]

* * *[7]

The Case for the Use of Animals in Biomedical Research

by Carl Cohen

Why Animals Have No Rights

A right, properly understood, is a claim, or potential claim, that one
party may exercise against another. The target against whom such
a claim may be registered can be a single person, a group, a community, or (perhaps) all humankind. The content of rights claims also
varies greatly: repayment of loans, nondiscrimination by employers,
noninterference by the state, and so on. To comprehend any genu-
ine right fully, therefore, we must know *who* holds the right, *against
whom* it is held, and *to what* it is a right.

Alternative sources of rights add complexity. Some rights are
grounded in constitution and law (e.g., the right of an accused to trial
by jury); some rights are moral but give no legal claims (e.g., my right
to your keeping the promise you gave me); and some rights (e.g.,
against theft or assault) are rooted both in morals and in law.

The differing targets, contents, and sources of rights, and their inevitable conflict, together weave a tangled web. Notwithstanding all such complications, this much is clear about rights in general: they are in every case claims, or potential claims, within a community of moral agents. Rights arise, and can be intelligibly defended, only among beings who actually do, or can, make moral claims against one another. Whatever else rights may be, therefore, they are necessarily human; their possessors are persons, human beings.

The attributes of human beings from which this moral capability arises have been described variously by philosophers, both ancient and modern: the inner consciousness of a free will (Saint Augustine); the grasp, by human reason, of the binding character of moral law (Saint Thomas); the self-conscious participation of human beings in an objective ethical order (Hegel); human membership in an organic moral community (Bradley); the development of the human self through the consciousness of other moral selves (Mead); and the underivative, intuitive cognition of the rightness of an action (Prichard). Most influential has been Immanuel Kant's emphasis on the universal human possession of a uniquely moral will and the autonomy its use entails. Humans confront choices that are purely moral; humans—but certainly not dogs or mice—lay down moral laws, for others and for themselves. Human beings are self-legislative, morally *auto-nomous*.

Animals (that is, nonhuman animals, the ordinary sense of that word) lack this capacity for free moral judgment. They are not beings of a kind capable of exercising or responding to moral claims. Animals therefore have no rights, and they can have none. This is the core of the argument about the alleged rights of animals. The holders of rights must have the capacity to comprehend rules of duty, governing all including themselves. In applying such rules, the holders of rights must recognize possible conflicts between what is in their own interest and what is just. Only in a community of beings capable of self-restricting moral judgments can the concept of a right be correctly invoked.

Humans have such moral capacities. They are in this sense self-legislative, are members of communities governed by moral rules, and do possess rights. Animals do not have such moral capacities. They are not morally self-legislative, cannot possibly be members of a truly moral community, and therefore cannot possess rights. In conducting research on animal subjects, therefore, we do not violate their rights, because they have none to violate.

To animate life, even in its simplest forms, we give a certain natural reverence. But the possession of rights presupposes a moral status not attained by the vast majority of living things. We must not infer, therefore, that a live being has, simply in being alive, a "right" to its life. The assertion that all animals, only because they are alive and have interests, also possess the "right to life" is an abuse of that phrase, and wholly without warrant.

It does not follow from this, however, that we are morally free to do anything we please to animals. Certainly not. In our dealings with animals, as in our dealings with other human beings, we have obligations that do not arise from claims against us based on rights. Rights entail obligations, but many of the things one ought to do are in no way tied to another's entitlement. Rights and obligations are not reciprocals of one another, and it is a serious mistake to suppose that they are.

Illustrations are helpful. Obligations may arise from internal commitments made: physicians have obligations to their patients not grounded merely in their patients' rights. Teachers have such obligations to their students, shepherds to their dogs, and cowboys to their horses. Obligations may arise from differences of status: adults owe special care when playing with young children, and children owe special care when playing with young pets. Obligations may arise from special relationships: the payment of my son's college tuition is something to which he may have no right, although it may be my obligation to bear the burden if I reasonably can; my dog has no right to daily exercise and veterinary care, but I do have the obligation to provide these things for her. Obligations may arise from particular acts or circumstances: one may be obliged to another for a special kindness done, or obliged to put an animal out of its misery in view of its condition—although neither the human benefactor nor the dying animal may have had a claim of right.

Plainly, the grounds of our obligations to humans and to animals are manifold, and cannot be formulated simply. Some hold that there is a general obligation to do no gratuitous harm to sentient creatures (the principle of nonmaleficence); some hold that there is a general obligation to do good to sentient creatures when that is reasonably within one's power (the principle of beneficence). In our dealings with animals, few will deny that we are at least obliged to act humanely—that is, to treat them with the decency and concern that we owe, as sensitive human beings, to other sentient creatures. To treat animals humanely, however, is not to treat them as humans or as the holders of rights.

A common objection, which deserves a response, may be paraphrased as follows:

If having rights requires being able to make moral claims, to grasp and apply moral laws, then many humans—the brain-damaged, the comatose, the senile—who plainly lack those capacities must be without rights. But that is absurd. This proves [the critic concludes] that rights do not depend on the presence of moral capacities.

This objection fails; it mistakenly treats an essential feature of humanity as though it were a screen for sorting humans. The capacity for moral judgment that distinguishes humans from animals is not a test to be administered to human beings one by one. Persons who are unable, because of some disability, to perform the full moral functions natural to human beings are certainly not for that reason ejected from the moral community. The issue is one of kind. Humans are of such a kind that they may be the subject of experiments only with their voluntary consent. The choices they make freely must be respected. Animals are of such a kind that it is impossible for them, in principle, to give or withhold voluntary consent or to make a moral choice. What humans retain when disabled, animals have never had.

A second objection, also often made, may be paraphrased as follows:

Capacities will not succeed in distinguishing humans from the other animals. Animals also reason; animals also communicate with one another; animals also care passionately for their young; animals also exhibit desires and preferences. Features of moral relevance— rationality, interdependence, and love—are not exhibited uniquely by human beings. Therefore [this critic concludes], there can be no solid moral distinction between humans and other animals.

This criticism misses the central point. It is not the ability to communicate or to reason, or dependence on one another, or care for the young, or the exhibition of preference, or any such behavior that marks the critical divide. Analogies between human families and those of monkeys, or between human communities and those of wolves, and the like, are entirely beside the point. Patterns of conduct are not at issue. Animals do indeed exhibit remarkable behavior at times. Conditioning, fear, instinct, and intelligence all contribute to species survival. Membership in a community of moral agents nevertheless remains impossible for them. Actors subject to moral judgment must be capable of grasping the generality of an ethical premise in a practical syllogism. Humans act immorally often enough, but only they—never wolves or monkeys—can discern, by applying some moral rule to the facts of a case, that a given act ought or ought not to be performed. The moral restraints imposed by humans on themselves are thus highly abstract and are often in conflict with the self-interest of the agent. Communal behavior among animals, even when most intelligent and most endearing, does not approach autonomous morality in this fundamental sense.

Genuinely moral acts have an internal as well as an external dimension. Thus, in law, an act can be criminal only when the guilty deed, the *actus reus*, is done with a guilty mind, *mens rea*. No animal can ever commit a crime; bringing animals to criminal trial is the mark of primitive ignorance. The claims of moral right are similarly inapplicable to them. Does a lion have a right to eat a baby zebra? Does a baby zebra have a right not to be eaten? Such questions, mistakenly invoking the concept of right where it does not belong, do not make good sense. Those who condemn bio-medical research because it violates "animal rights" commit the same blunder.

In Defense of "Speciesism"

Abandoning reliance on animal rights, some critics resort instead to animal sentience—their feelings of pain and distress. We ought to desist from the imposition of pain insofar as we can. Since all or nearly all experimentation on animals does impose pain and could be readily forgone, say these critics, it should be stopped. The ends sought may be worthy, but those ends do not justify imposing agonies on humans, and by animals the agonies are felt no less. The laboratory use of animals (these critics conclude) must therefore be ended—or at least very sharply curtailed.

Argument of this variety is essentially utilitarian, often expressly so; it is based on the calculation of the net product, in pains and pleasures, resulting from experiments on animals. Jeremy Bentham, comparing horses and dogs with other sentient creatures, is thus commonly quoted: "The question is not, Can they reason? nor Can they talk? but, Can they suffer?"

Animals certainly can suffer and surely ought not to be made to suffer needlessly. But in inferring, from these uncontroversial premises, that biomedical research causing animal distress is largely (or wholly) wrong, the critic commits two serious errors.

The first error is the assumption, often explicitly defended, that all sentient animals have equal moral standing. Between a dog and a human being, according to this view, there is no moral difference; hence the pains suffered by dogs must be weighed no differently from the pains suffered by humans. To deny such equality, according to this critic, is to give unjust preference to one species over another; it is "speciesism." The most influential statement of this moral equality of species was made by Peter Singer:

The racist violates the principle of equality by giving greater weight to the interests of members of his own race when there is a clash between their interests and the interests of those of another race. The sexist violates the principle of equality by favoring the interests of his own sex. Similarly the speciesist allows the interests of his own species to override the greater interests of members of other species. The pattern is identical in each case.

This argument is worse than unsound; it is atrocious. It draws an offensive moral conclusion from a deliberately devised verbal parallelism that is utterly specious. Racism has no rational ground whatever. Differing degrees of respect or concern for humans for no other reason than that they are members of different races is an injustice totally without foundation in the nature of the races themselves. Racists, even if acting on the basis of mistaken factual beliefs, do grave moral wrong precisely because there is no morally relevant distinction among the races. The supposition of such differences has led to outright horror. The same is true of the sexes, neither sex being entitled by right to greater respect or concern than the other. No dispute here.

Between species of animate life, however—between (for example) humans on the one hand and cats or rats on the other—the morally relevant differences are enormous, and almost universally appreciated. Humans engage in moral reflection; humans are morally autonomous; humans are members of moral communities, recognizing just claims against their own interest. Human beings do have rights; theirs is a moral status very different from that of cats or rats.

I am a speciesist. Speciesism is not merely plausible; it is essential for right conduct, because those who will not make the morally relevant distinctions among species are almost certain, in consequence, to misapprehend their true obligations. The analogy between speciesism and racism is insidious. Every sensitive moral judgment requires that the differing natures of the beings to whom obligations are owed be considered. If all forms of animate life—or vertebrate animal life—must be treated equally, and if therefore in evaluating a research program the pains of a rodent count equally with the pains of a human, we are forced to conclude (1) that neither humans nor rodents possess rights, or (2) that rodents possess all the rights that humans possess. Both alternatives are absurd. Yet one or the other must be swallowed if the moral equality of all species is to be defended.

Humans owe to other humans a degree of moral regard that cannot be owed to animals. Some humans take on the obligation to support and heal others, both humans and animals, as a principal duty in their lives; the fulfillment of that duty may require the sacrifice of many animals. If biomedical investigators abandon the effective pursuit of their professional objectives because they are convinced that they may not do to animals what the service of humans requires, they will fail, objectively, to do their duty. Refusing to recognize the moral differences among species is a sure path to calamity. (The largest animal rights group in the country is People for the Ethical Treatment of Animals; its codirector, Ingrid Newkirk, calls research using animal subjects "fascism" and "supremacism." "Animal liberationists do not separate out the *human* animal," she says, "so there is no rational basis for saying that a human being has special rights. A rat is a pig is a dog is a boy. They're all mammals.")

Those who claim to base their objection to the use of animals in biomedical research on their reckoning of the net pleasures and pains produced make a second error, equally grave. Even if it were true—as it is surely not—that the pains of all animate beings must be counted equally, a cogent utilitarian calculation requires that we weigh all the consequences of the use, and of the nonuse, of animals in laboratory research. Critics relying (however mistakenly) on animal rights may claim to ignore the beneficial results of such research, rights being trump cards to which interest and advantage must give way. But an argument that is explicitly framed in terms of interest and benefit for all over the long run must attend also to the disadvantageous consequences of not using animals in research, and to all the achievements attained and attainable only through their use. The sum of the benefits of their use is utterly beyond quantification. The elimination of horrible disease, the increase of longevity, the avoidance of great pain, the saving of lives, and the improvement of the quality of lives (for humans and for animals) achieved through research using animals is so incalculably great that the argument of these critics, systematically pursued, establishes not their conclusion but its reverse: to refrain from using animals in biomedical research is, on utilitarian grounds, morally wrong.

When balancing the pleasures and pains resulting from the use of animals in research, we must not fail to place on the scales the terrible pains that would have resulted, would be suffered now, and would long continue had animals not been used. Every disease eliminated, every vaccine developed, every method of pain relief devised, every surgical procedure invented, every prosthetic device implanted—indeed, virtually every modern medical therapy is due, in part or in whole, to experimentation using animals. Nor may we ignore, in the balancing process, the predictable gains in human (and animal) well-being that are probably achievable in the future but that will not be achieved if the decision is made now to desist from such research or to curtail it.

Medical investigators are seldom insensitive to the distress their work may cause animal subjects. Opponents of research using animals are frequently insensitive to the cruelty of the results of the restrictions they would impose. Untold numbers of human beings—real persons, although not now identifiable—would suffer grievously as the consequence of this well-meaning but shortsighted tenderness. If the morally relevant differences between humans and animals are borne in mind, and if all relevant considerations are weighed, the calculation of long-term consequences must give overwhelming support for biomedical research using animals.[8]

Whether or not animals have rights, many of them (vertebrates and perhaps invertebrates as well) clearly feel pain. They're sentient. That's true of most of the animals whose treatment is in question in the debate over extending moral consideration to animals. And many of the ways humans treat animals cause them pain, suffering, and death.

Some speciesists would say that, even so, those ways of treating animals are morally justified. They're justified even if animals are sentient and have rights. The value of animals to humans justifies overriding their rights and inflicting pain and suffering upon them.

This way of reasoning has a utilitarian underpinning to it. Utilitarianism (recall Theory Box 1E in Chapter 1, Section 1.8) holds that rightness is determined by what maximizes value. The reasons utilitarian thinking may be thought to override the well-being of animals are twofold.

First, even if animals have rights, it may be thought that the well-being of humans overrides those rights. That is, rights may be considered absolute or prima facie:

Theory Box 10B

Prima Facie and Absolute Rights
A right is **prima facie** if, and only if, it should be honored, all other things being equal (i.e., if the right is not overridden by other moral considerations).
A right is **absolute** if, and only if, it should be honored irrespective of any other considerations, moral or nonmoral.

If rights are absolute (or imprescriptible) they may not be overridden. Any violation of an absolute right is wrong. But if a right is merely prima facie, there may be offsetting moral considerations that justify violating the right. Thus, if a right to life is absolute, then it's wrong to violate that right under any circumstances. If it's merely prima facie, then one might violate that right, say, to defend oneself or to prevent a deadly assault on someone else. If one thinks that promoting a greater good for humans requires violating the rights of some animals, then there is a conflict between *utility* and *rights*. If one thinks, furthermore, that when there is such a conflict utility outweighs rights (at least in the case of animals), then one could concede that animals have rights and still feel justified in discriminating against them for human ends.

Second, if animals don't have rights—and if the issue of right or wrong in their treatment is thought to depend solely upon the value of the consequences of such treatment—it might be thought that the value for humans of using animals for food and experimentation is so great that it outweighs the pain to animals. The alleviation of human suffering through advances in medical research that supposedly require experimentation upon animals is more important than the unavoidable pain caused to animals.

Animal advocates may challenge the first argument by maintaining that if rights and utility conflict in the case of the treatment of animals, it is rights that should take precedence. Just as we cannot justify harming particular individuals for the sake of a greater good to others, we cannot do so with regard to animals. Their rights are too important. They may reply to the second argument by contending that even if animals don't have rights, they do experience pain and the amount of pain that humans inflict upon animals outweighs the good that humans derive from dominating them. The issue then would hinge upon one's assessment of how much good humans derive from dominating animals, and whether that good outweighs the suffering caused to animals.

To assess this issue fully would require a fuller treatment of the grounds for making judgments of value than we have space to go into here. It would require asking whether or not we can quantify good and pain in ways that would allow us to confidently make such utilitarian calculations. Further, it would require asking whether pain and suffering caused to animals weighs equally with pain and suffering caused to humans. For example, does the pleasure that millions of people get from eating meat outweigh the pain of the millions of animals killed yearly for that purpose? One might come out with different assessments depending upon the mode of treatment of animals in question. One might, for example, quite consistently argue that the pain caused to animals outweighs the pleasures humans get from hunting and eating meat, but that the benefit to humans from research and experimentation upon animals outweighs the pain to animals. In that case, utilitarian reasoning might justify some forms of discrimination against animals but not others.

Further complicating matters in the assessment of the utilitarian way of thinking is the fact that the utility of certain ways of treating animals might vary from society to society. We indicated earlier that we were confining our attention to a society like ours, in which people don't have to hunt for food and rarely need to rely on animals as beasts of burden. But in some societies people depend upon animals in these ways. And it might well be that one's utilitarian calculations of the cost to animals versus the benefits to humans would differ in those societies from what they would be for a society like ours.

10.11 Vegetarianism

Few issues (excepting abortion) elicit stronger reactions from people than does vegetarianism. Let us consider why some people are vegetarians. A broad, philosophical view is expressed by Francis Moore Lappé:

Key Quote 10B

For many people, the relationship of indigenous North American peoples to the animals they hunted suggest the possibility that human beings can develop humility, awe, and awareness of ourselves within the ever-renewing chain of life and death. Others, discovering as I have that human beings need eat no flesh to be healthy, understandably arrive at a different point. Why inflict any death that is unnecessary to sustaining life?[9]

Religion aside, there are three principal reasons why people are vegetarians, consisting of the following beliefs:

1. Vegetarianism is a healthier diet.
2. Meat-eating causes unnecessary suffering to animals.
3. Meat-eating is harmful globally because it contributes to climate change and inefficient use of the earth's resources.

Regarding (1), whether or not a vegetarian diet is better from a health standpoint is controversial. The evidence is clear, however, that it's not detrimental. People worry about getting enough protein, but nutritionists say ample protein can be obtained from plant (including fruit, beans, soy, etc.) and dairy sources. The American Dietetic Association (ADA) reports:

It is the position of the American Dietetic Association that appropriately planned vegetarian diets, including total vegetarian or vegan diets, are healthful, nutritionally adequate, and may provide health benefits in the prevention and treatment of certain diseases. Well-planned vegetarian diets are appropriate for all individuals during all stages of the life cycle, including pregnancy, lactation, infancy, childhood, and adolescence, and for athletes.

Vegetarian diets are often associated with a number of health advantages, including lower blood cholesterol levels, lower risk of heart disease, lower blood pressure levels, and lower risk of hypertension and type 2 diabetes. Vegetarians tend to have a lower body mass index (BMI) and lower overall cancer rates.[10]

In any event, choice of a healthful diet is a personal matter and doesn't raise the more important ethical questions. How food is produced does. Seafood is an important source of protein and needs to be discussed in any thorough examination of vegetarianism, but we shall focus on the use of land animals for food. While meat consumption is unnecessary to good health, it's absolutely necessary to the profits of factory farms. Of the meat eaten by people in societies like Britain and the United States, 99 percent is produced by factory farms. Many people think of farms as bucolic settings, with cows grazing contentedly in green pastures, Farmer Brown milking them in the evening, and tousled-haired children gathering eggs laid here and there by clucking hens running free. But except for a tiny percentage of farms this is a false image. Consider the following passages discussing, first, the conditions of factory-farmed chickens, then those of pigs, and finally, the slaughter of cows.

Chickens

It's hard to get one's head around the magnitude of 33,000 birds [chickens] in one room. You don't have to see it for yourself, or even do the math, to understand that things are packed pretty tight. In its Animal Welfare Guidelines, the National Chicken Council indicates an appropriate stocking density to be eight-tenths of a square foot per bird ... Try to picture it ... Find a piece of printer paper and imagine a full-grown bird shaped something like a football with legs standing on it. Imagine 33,000 of these rectangles in a grid ... Now enclose the grid with windowless walls and put a ceiling on top. Run in automated (drug-laced) fee, water, heating, and ventilation systems. This is a farm ... The muscles and fat tissues of the newly engineered broiler birds [chickens for eating as opposed to laying eggs] grow significantly faster than their bones, leading to deformities and disease. Somewhere between 1 and 4 percent of the birds will die writhing in convulsions from sudden death syndrome, a condition virtually unknown outside of factory farms. Another factory-farm-induced condition in which excess fluids fill the body cavity, ascites, kills even more (5 percent of birds globally) ... Needless to say, jamming deformed, drugged, overstressed birds together in a filthy, waste-coated room is not very healthy. Beyond deformities, eye damage, blindness, bacterial infections of bones, slipped vertebrae, paralysis, internal bleeding, anemia, slipped tendons, twisted lower legs and necks, respiratory diseases, and weakened immune systems are frequent and long-standing problems on factory farms.

Pigs

[F]actory farmed piglets often will be injected with iron because of the likelihood that the rapid growth and intensive breeding of their mother has left her milk deficient. Within ten days males have their testicles torn out, again without pain relief. This time the purpose is to alter the taste of the meat—consumers in America currently prefer the taste of castrated animals ... The weaned pigs will then be forced into thick wire cases—"nurseries." These cages are stacked one on top of the other, and feces and urine fall from higher cages onto the animals below. Growers will keep piglets in these cages as long as possible before moving them to their final destination: cramped pens. The pens are deliberately overcrowded because, as one industry magazine says, "overcrowding pigs pays." ... Piglets that don't grow fast enough—the runts—are a drain on resources and so have no place on the farm. Picked up by their hind legs, they are swung and then bashed headfirst onto the concrete floor. This common practice is called "thumping." "We've thumped as many as 120 in one day," said a worker from a Missouri farm.

Cattle

At a typical slaughter facility, cattle are led through a chute into a knocking box—usually a large cylindrical hold through which the head pokes. The stun operator, or "knocker," presses a large pneumatic gun between the cow's eyes. A steel bolt shoots into the cow's skull and then retracts back into the gun, usually rendering the animal unconscious or causing death. Sometimes the bolt only dazes the animal, which either remains conscious or later wakes up as it is being "processed." The effectiveness of the knocking gun depends on its manufacture and maintenance ... the effectiveness of knocking is also reduced because some plant managers believe the animals can become "too dead" and therefore, because their hearts are not pumping, bleed out too slowly or insufficiently ... As a result, some plants deliberately choose less-effective knocking methods ... Let us say what we mean: animals are bled, skinned, and dismembered while conscious. It happens all the time, and the industry and the government knows it.[11]

Regarding (3), in global economic and environmental terms, it's said that far more protein can be produced per acre by growing plant foods and consuming them directly than by growing food for cattle, then raising, killing and eating the cattle for protein.

As important as (1) and (3) are, it's (2) that raises issues most directly relevant to our present concern, the treatment of animals.

As noted earlier, people like the taste of meat. Eating meat gives them pleasure. But if nutritionists are correct that eating meat is unnecessary to a healthy diet, then eating meat is unnecessary. And if eating meat is unnecessary, then the pain and suffering caused to animals in raising them for that purpose is unnecessary. If so, then the stark fact is that most people (again excepting those relative few who must eat meat to survive) unnecessarily derive daily pleasure at the of pain and suffering to animals. Can that be morally justified?

In terms of our earlier discussion, the practice of factory-farming—and indeed of all farming that raises meat for consumption—clearly constitutes systematic discrimination against animals. If it would be deplorable to treat human beings in those ways, then the treatment of animals by comparison is discrimination.

So the ultimate question regarding meat-eating is whether the systematic discrimination against animals is justified by the pleasure humans get from eating meat and by the profit some people get from factory-farming.

10.12 Conclusion

We've seen that the basic question is whether animals deserve BMC, and if so, whether they deserve minimal or significant BMC (or, of course, some gradation between these two). Animals clearly warrant BMC if they have rights, especially if those rights should be on a par with the rights possessed by humans. But it's controversial whether they have rights. They may still warrant BMC, however, even if they have no rights. They would warrant BMC simply by virtue of the fact that they are sentient. (If only higher animals are deemed sentient, then it would be only they who warrant BMC on these grounds.)

Speciesists maintain that humans are naturally superior to animals and may justifiably dominate them. We saw that the judgment of superiority (a value judgment) is difficult to substantiate. Humans are clearly superior to animals in intelligence, but in virtually every other respect there are animals who in that respect are superior to humans. But even if it's granted that humans are naturally superior, that doesn't suffice to justify the judgment that humans ought to dominate animals (any more than the fact that humans traditionally have dominated animals suffices to justify continued human domination of animals). Further reasons need to be given to justify discrimination against animals. Here the issue turns principally upon one's assessment of whether if animals have rights, those rights are on a par with those possessed by humans; and if they don't have rights, whether the benefit to humans from discrimination against animals outweighs the pain caused to animals by that discrimination.

Study questions

1. The text claims that animals clearly warrant derivative moral consideration. What would it mean for animals to warrant *basic moral consideration* as well (Section 10.1)?
2. What is *speciesism* (Definition Box 10A)? What is a *speciesist* (Definition Box 10B)?
3. What kinds of considerations are relevant to deciding whether humans *discriminate against animals* (Section 10.3)?
4. How do the distinctions between *fact/value* and *value/ought* enter into the argument to show that humans ought to dominate animals (Section 10.7)?
5. What is Mark Twain's satirical argument to show that animals are superior to humans (Section 10.9)?
6. How does the text define *evil* (Definition Box 10C)? Do you agree with the text that evil is a product of human intelligence?
7. What are the main points of Regan's argument (Section 10.10) that *animals have rights*?
8. What argument does Cohen present *against the claim that animals have rights* (Section 10.10)?
9. What is Cohen's argument for speciesism?
10. What are the three main grounds on which *vegetarianism* can be defended (Section 10.11)?

Notes

1   Henry David Thoreau, *Walden*, in Carl Bode (ed.), *The Portable Thoreau* (New York: The Viking Press, 1964), p. 459.
2   Kirk Johnson, *The New York Times*, December 2, 2002.
3   Richard Connell, "The Most Dangerous Game," in *Prentice Hall Literature* (Englewood Cliffs, NJ: Prentice Hall, 1991), p. 21.

4 Stephen Hawking, *A Brief History of Time* (1988), chapter 1.

5 Mark Twain, *Letters from the Earth*, Bernard DeVoto (ed.) (New York: Harper & Row, Publishers, 1974), pp. 176, 179; emphasis in the original.

6 Tom Regan, "The Radical Egalitarian Case for Animal Rights," in Peter Singer (ed.), *In Defense of Animals* (Oxford: Basil Blackwell, Inc., 1985), pp. 13–15.

7 Ibid.; emphases in the original.

8 From Carl Cohen, "The Case for the Use of Animals in Biomedical Research," *The New England Journal of Medicine*, Vol. 315, October 2, 1986, 865–8; emphases in the original.

9 Francis Moore Lappé, *Diet for a Small Planet* (New York: Ballantine Books, 1991), p. xxviii.

10 ADA, "Vegetarian Diets," Position Statement, *Journal of the American Dietetic Association*, Vol. 109, 2009, 1266–82.

11 Jonathan Safran Foer, *Eating Animals* (New York: Back Bay Books, 2009), pp. 129–31, 186–7, 229–30.

For more resources:

www.bloomsbury.com/holmes-introduction-to-applied-ethics

Part IV

Autonomy and the Individual

11

Privacy

The power of every state over its citizens has grown steadily during the last few hundred years, no less in countries where the power of the state has been exercised wisely, than in those where it has been used for brutal tyranny.

—Albert Einstein[1]

Introduction

There are philosophical, legal, and ethical dimensions to privacy. We shall in this chapter begin with the philosophical foundations of a conception of privacy as found in Plato and much later in John Stuart Mill. We shall, against that background, provide a definition of privacy, show the importance of privacy to individual autonomy, and then consider the various threats to privacy.

11.1 Why is privacy important?

For all of its progress, the twentieth century saw some of history's worst tyrannies. Through them the achievements of science and technology—particularly in the service of militarism—were turned into instruments of oppression and destruction. The twenty-first century has the potential for even greater tyrannies than the regimes of Hitler or Stalin, made possible by the technologies of the computer age.

In the past, governments couldn't monitor the lives of all their citizens. They could spy on some and apprehend others. If people didn't voluntarily tell them what they wanted to know, they could use threats, imprisonment, and torture to pry it out of them. Today governments have the capacity to get much of the information they want painlessly, without people even being aware that it's happening. In addition, there is growing commercial and fraudulent exploitation of personal information, all at the cost of the privacy of citizens.

Each step in the erosion of personal privacy has a plausible-sounding justification, whether it be providing better services or enhancing national security. But each increases the possibilities for control and manipulation of people. As the cruder forms of coercion and torture give way to unseen electronic devices, democracies can be transformed almost imperceptibly into tyrannies. The right to privacy—if sustained and nurtured—is a safeguard against the growing power of governments over individuals.

The many dimensions of the problem are highlighted in the following discussion.

Assaults on Privacy in America

[Jon] Penney's work is the sort of evidence for negative social effects that scholars (and courts of law) demand. If democratic self-governance relies on an informed citizenry, Penny wrote [in "Chilling Effects: Online Surveillance and Wikipedia Use," the *Berkeley Technology Law Review*, June 2016], then "surveillance-related chilling effects," by "deterring people from exercising their rights," including "... the freedom to read, think, and communicate privately," are "corrosive to political discourse." . . .

As a growing share of human interactions—social, political, and economic—are committed to the digital realm, privacy and security as values and as rights have risen in importance. When someone says, "My life is on my phone," it's meant almost literally: photos, passwords, texts, emails, music, address books, documents. It is not hard to imagine that the Declaration of Independence, redrafted for an information society, might well include "security and privacy," in addition to the familiar "life, liberty, and the pursuit of happiness," among its examples of "unalienable rights."

Although [Edward] Snowden highlighted government surveillance, it may not be the worst problem. Corporations holds vast and growing troves of personal information that is often inadequately protected, its use largely unregulated. Since 2005, hacks have stolen hundreds of millions of credit-card numbers from major retailers such as Target, Home Depot, TJX, and eBay. In 2014, someone stole the keys to half a *billion* Yahoo accounts without being detected. And everyday threats to privacy are so commonplace that most people are numb to them. In exchange for free email, consumers allow companies such as Google to scan the content of their digital messages in order to deliver targeted ads. Users of social media, eager to keep in touch with a circle of friends, rarely read the standard agreement that governs the rights and use of what they post online. Smartphones know their owners' habits better than they themselves do: where and with whom they sleep, what time they wake up, whom they meet, and where they have been. People accept such tradeoffs in exchange for convenience. They don't really have a choice . . .

In the past 15 years, entire corporations, even nations, have found their data and systems vulnerable to attack. The intrusion at the U.S. Office of Personnel and Management, disclosed in April 2015, was reportedly the most significant breach of federal networks to date: hackers, thought to be state-sponsored, took personal data for four million employees and political appointees, leading to the recall of American intelligence agents posted abroad. The 2016 digital break-in at the Democratic National Committee's headquarters was like a modern iteration of Watergate, but initiated by a foreign power seeking to interfere in the presidential election . . .

[The] Cyber Command is charged with protecting the Defense Department's weapons systems, millions of computing devices, and more than 15,000 data networks (say, in support of network operations for a battalion in Afghanistan fighting the Taliban). It also provides offense cyber capabilities to commanders around the world in the event that hostilities break out (analogous to the access they have to air and sea power capabilities). And it is responsible for defending the nation—including aviation, financial, and power-transmission systems—against a significant cyberattack.

The structure of the Internet itself makes that defensive mission difficult. Eviatar Matania, the head of Israel's National Cyber Bureau, discussed that challenge . . . at the Kennedy School. He noted that unlike the agricultural and industrial revolutions, the cyber revolution has both restructured society and created a space, "a new artificial domain" . . . But defending cyberspace is extremely difficult because it lacks both borders and distance. There are no clear boundaries between countries, and no clear divisions between corporate and government networks . . .

But secrecy is just "a very small slice" of what privacy is about, says Marc Rotenberg of the EPIC [Electronic Privacy and Information

Center] ... "Privacy is about accountability," he says. "It's about the fairness of decision making. It's about holding large government acts and private companies accountable for their decisionmaking. It turns out to be an extraordinarily powerful and comprehensive human-rights claim, particularly in the digital age, because so much about us is based on our data ... The Europeans were very upset, obviously, about the U.S. surveillance activities that Snowden had documented, but then you had the terrible tragedy of *Charlie Hebdo*, and suddenly the French government created new surveillance authorities that go beyond what the U.S. does . . ."

"When governments make these decisions," he reflects, "it is almost as if they're saying, 'We can't afford as much democracy, we can't afford as much openness, we can't afford to trust our citizens as much, we need to engage in more surveillance, we need less judicial review and less accountability.' ... A sacrifice of privacy is also a sac-rifice of democracy."

In the mid 1990s, *The New York Times* quoted Rotenberg saying that the protection of privacy in the Information Age would be like the protection of the environment in the Industrial Age—"which is to say it's so much a part of the nature of economic production today, you don't solve it, you have to manage it." Many people predicted the end of privacy. But Rotenberg believes people don't understand the full consequences: "Among other things, you would lose your democratic state if everyone said, 'Why do we care if the government knows everything about us? Who needs a private phone call? Who needs a building with walls? Why should data be accurate?' Everything col-lapses. And we know what that world looks like: that's what [Jeremy] Bentham described as the Panopticon"—designed so an observer can watch everything, but without being seen. "When you're under con-stant surveillance," says Rotenberg, "you're in a prison."[2]

As the above makes clear, privacy in the modern world has personal, social, and legal dimensions. But it also has a moral dimension underlying all of these, which is our primary concern. This moral dimension has evolved over the course of human social development. It presupposes certain ways of thinking about persons and their interrelationships. Let us consider some of the thinking in the philosophical, religious, and political realms that has shaped the conception of privacy that emerged in the eighteenth and nine-teenth centuries.[3]

11.2 The philosophical and legal foundations of privacy

Plato provided a metaphysical basis for a conception of privacy. He argued for an irreducible dualism between body and soul, the body being material, observable, and perishable, the soul being immaterial, unobservable, and immortal. Many hold this view today.

Theory Box 11A

Metaphysics
Etymologically, metaphysics means a going beyond physics. Thus, metaphysics stands for theories about the nature of ultimate reality that transcend what can be established scientifically.

Reason, Plato thought, resides within the soul. This implies that what a person thinks is hidden from others—unless the person discloses his or her thoughts (or they are somehow revealed by his conduct). The very idea of a person as a composite of soul and body implies the existence of a private realm.

Plato didn't make much of this fact. But Christianity did centuries later. For St. Augustine (354–430), the inner state of one's soul is more important than outward conduct. The state of one's soul—as measured by motives, intentions, thoughts, fantasies, desires, fears—determines whether one is virtuous in the eyes of God. Since one's soul is hidden from view, human law cannot regulate it. Human law can prohibit adultery, but it can't prohibit adulterous thoughts. And according to traditional Christianity, adultery in the heart is just as bad as adultery in fact. If persons wouldn't voluntarily reveal their innermost thoughts—as many did in the confessional booth—the temptation (if their thoughts were suspected of being heretical or blasphemous) was to try to pry them out of them by the rack or the thumbscrew, the techniques of the Inquisition. For these reasons, St. Thomas Aquinas (1224–74) stressed the importance of divine law as well as human law. Human law could regulate people's outward conduct. Divine law was needed to regulate their inner lives. Without divine law, many sins—those committed in the privacy of one's own thoughts—would go unregulated and unpunished.

With the development of the secular nation-state, the state as well as the church took increasing interest in people's inner lives insofar as they related to political stability and order. If a government knew in advance of subversive designs, it could counteract them before they were acted upon. Beyond the cruder forms of torture, there was spying, surveillance and data gathering—methods enhanced by the twentieth century's advanced technology.

There eventually came to be recognized an inner private realm. Descartes (1596–1650) had explored the metaphysical implications of such a realm in the seventeenth century. In the nineteenth century John Stuart Mill (1806–73) called this a "domain of consciousness" and made it the locus of human liberty. As he writes in a well-known passage:

Key Quote 11A

This, then, is the appropriate region of human liberty. It comprises, first, the inward domain of consciousness; demanding liberty of conscience, in the most comprehensive sense; liberty of thought and feeling; absolute freedom of opinion and sentiment on all subjects, practical or speculative, scientific, moral, or theological ... Secondly, the principle requires liberty of tastes and pursuits; of framing the plan of our life to suit our own character; of doing as we like, subject to such consequences as may follow: without impediment from our fellow creatures, so long as what we do does not harm them, even though they should think our conduct foolish, perverse, or wrong. Thirdly, from this liberty of each individual, follows the liberty, within the same limits, of combination among individuals; freedom to unite, for any purpose not involving harm to others: the persons combining being supposed to be of full age, and not forced or deceived.

No society in which these liberties are not, on the whole, respected, is free, whatever may be its form of government.[4]

Recognition of such a domain—and the associated liberties Mill enumerates—provides the foundation for philosophical liberalism (see Chapter 8, Section 8.4). Philosophical liberalism locates the ultimate worth of social, political, and economic schemes in their consequences for individual persons. This lays the groundwork for a tension between personal privacy, on the one hand, and stability and social order, on the other. Today governments want to know what is in the minds of potential terrorists before they put their thoughts into action.[5]

Although the US Constitution doesn't mention privacy, the law recognizes an implicit legal right to privacy in it. Such a right was central to the Supreme Court's reasoning in *Roe v. Wade* (1973) on the abortion issue, as we shall see in Chapter 12. As far back as 1890, Warren and Brandeis wrote on the legal foundation of a right of privacy.

Warren and Brandeis on Privacy

It is our purpose to consider whether the existing law affords a principle which can properly be invoked to protect the privacy of the individual; and, if it does, what the nature and extent of such protection is . . .

The common law secures to each individual the right of determining, ordinarily, to what extent his thoughts, sentiments, and emotions shall be communicated to others. Under our system of government, he can never be compelled to express them (except when upon the witness stand); and even if he has chosen to give them expression, he generally retains the power to fix the limits of the publicity which shall be given them. The existence of this right does not depend upon the particular method of expression adopted. It is immaterial whether it be by word or by signs, in painting, by sculpture, or in music. Neither does the existence of the right depend upon the nature or value of the thought or emotions, nor upon the excellence of the means of expression . . . In every such case the individual is entitled to decide whether that which is his shall be given to the public. No other has the right to publish his productions in any form, without his consent . . .

These considerations lead to the conclusion that the protection afforded to thoughts, sentiments, and emotions, expressed through the medium of writing or of the arts, so far as it consists in preventing publication, is merely an instance of the enforcement of the more general right of the individual to be let alone. It is like the right not to be assaulted or beaten, the right not to be imprisoned, the right not to be maliciously prosecuted, the right not to be defamed. In each of these rights, as indeed in all other rights recognized by the law, there inheres the quality of being owned or possessed—and (as that is the distinguishing attribute or property) there may be some propriety in speaking of those rights as property. But, obviously, they bear little resemblance to what is ordinarily comprehended under that term. The principle which protects personal writing and all other personal productions, not against theft and physical appropriation, but against publication in any form, is in reality not the principle of private property, but that of an inviolate personality.

If we are correct in this conclusion, the existing law affords a principle which may be invoked to protect the privacy of the individual from invasion either by the too enterprising press, the photographer, or the possessor of any other modern device for reworking or reproducing scenes or sounds. For the protection afforded is not confined by the authorities to those cases where any particular medium or form of expression has been adopted, not to products of the intellect. The same protection is afforded to emotions and sensations expressed in a musical composition or other work of art as to a literary composition; ... If, then, the decisions indicate a general right to privacy for thoughts, emotions, and sensations, these should receive the same protection, whether expressed in writing, or in conduct, in conversation, in attitudes, or in facial expression.

It may be urged that a distinction should be taken between the deliberate expression of thoughts and emotions in literary or artistic compositions and the casual and often involuntary expression given to them in the ordinary conduct of life. In other words, it may be contended that the protection afforded is granted to the conscious products of labor, perhaps as an encouragement to effort. This contention, however plausible, has, in fact, little to recommend it. If the amount of labor involved be adopted as the test, we might well find that the effort to conduct one's self properly in business and in domestic relations had been far greater than that involved in painting a picture or writing a book; one would find that it was far easier to express lofty sentiments in a diary than in the conduct of a noble life. If the test of deliberateness of the act be adopted, much casual correspondence which is now accorded full protection would be excluded from the beneficent operation of existing rules. After the decisions denying the distinction attempted to be made between those literary productions which it was intended to publish and those which it was not, all considerations of the amount of labor involved, the degree of deliberation, the value of the product, and the intention of publishing must be abandoned, and no basis is discerned upon which the right to restrain publication and reproduction of such so-called literary and artistic works can be rested, except the right to privacy, as part of the more general right to the immunity of the person—the right to one's personality.[6]

As the legal right to privacy evolved, it extended to such areas as marriage, contraception, and abortion as well as to privacy of the person and the home. The legal conception of privacy, as interesting and important as it is, however, isn't our primary concern. Our concern is with the moral issues that may be thought to underlie the legal issues. So let us proceed to try to understand better the very idea of privacy.

11.3   A definition of privacy

Central to the development of the concept of privacy is the notion of a domain of consciousness, as Mill calls it, that isn't accessible to others unless we open it to them. If we expand the notion of a domain of consciousness to the idea of "areas of one's life," we can define privacy as follows:

Definition Box 11A

Privacy: Freedom from intrusion into areas of one's life that one hasn't explicitly or implicitly opened to others.

Implied here is that there are areas of our lives that aren't normally open to others unless we choose to make them so. These represent the domain of privacy. I can observe you walking down a public street. But I don't know what you're thinking unless you tell me (or unless I can infer it from your behavior or things I know about you).[7] It normally requires consent on your part—either expressly or tacitly—to make those areas of your life accessible to others.

This definition lets in many acts that we don't normally think of as violations of privacy, such as burglary or rape. But they are. As a victim of a 2015 sexual assault said in a statement addressing her assailant in court:

Key Quote 11B

My damage was internal, unseen, I carry it with me. You took away my worth, my privacy, my energy, my time, my safety, my intimacy, my confidence, my own voice, until today.[8]

It's just that violations of privacy aren't all that burglary and rape are. And the rest of what they are—thievery and violence—is usually so much more serious than would be the mere intrusion by itself that we usually focus upon that rather than on the violation of privacy.

11.4 Personal autonomy

Closely related to the idea of a domain of privacy is the individual's capacity to control access to that domain. This brings to light the importance of autonomy, which in simplest terms can be defined as follows:

Definition Box 11B

Autonomy: The capacity to live one's life as one chooses.

This conception of autonomy is very close to what Warren and Brandeis characterize as the "right to the immunity of the person" or the "right to personality" at the end of the above passage. No one enjoys perfect autonomy. We can't choose to fly like a bird or leap tall buildings in a single bound. We're all constrained by personal limitations and the laws of nature. Within these constraints, to be autonomous is to be able to set goals for ourselves and, to the extent of our abilities, to strive to achieve them. To do this, we must be free of unwarranted interference by others.

Although they're intimately related, privacy and autonomy aren't identical. Privacy is a freedom. Autonomy a power or capacity.[9] This can be shown by means of an example.

Imagine a prisoner in solitary confinement for life. Suppose another person's life is monitored twenty-four hours a day on a television screen in the prisoner's cell. Suppose that person is you, and you're aware of it. With no books, newspapers, or magazines to read, the prisoner's sole contact with the outside world—and sole pastime—is to watch you in every detail of your life, from the most public to the most intimate. Because the prisoner has and never will have any control over you, your capacity to live your life as you choose (as measured by the absence of physical constraints) is unaffected. Your autonomy is intact. But you have absolutely no privacy (beyond your innermost thoughts, and those only insofar as they're never revealed).

Some people might shrug this off and say that so long as they never met the prisoner and he or she had no control over them they wouldn't be bothered by the situation. But most would probably be deeply disturbed by this invasion of their privacy. They would feel that it violated them as persons. Whether you'd be bothered or not, you have no privacy. But you do have autonomy. Privacy and autonomy are distinguishable.

If privacy is freedom from unauthorized intrusion into areas of our lives not normally open to others, then—except in rare circumstances, such as those of a hermit or a person stranded on a desert island—privacy depends upon our ability to control access to those areas. And that ability is a part of autonomy.

This means that although privacy and autonomy aren't identical, privacy *as a rule* presupposes some measure of autonomy (and vice versa). If others—whether individuals, groups, or governments—intrude into our personal lives against our will, then we have no privacy. Privacy presupposes some measure of control over what happens to us. But at the same time, when privacy is once achieved, it contributes to autonomy. Most people need and want some measure of privacy to be able to live their chosen lives. What that measure is varies from person to person, but it's an important underlying component in any conception of quality of life.

11.5 The paradox of privacy

Privacy, by this definition, is partly relative to individuals; specifically to the acts by which they open or close certain areas of their lives to others. The acts may be verbal or nonverbal. But they give or withhold permission to others to enter those areas. Those who enter without such consent violate the individual's privacy.

How extensive are the areas? There is no precise answer to this. Sometimes the notion of an "area" can be understood literally, in spatial terms. If I build a high fence around my house, you have intruded on my privacy if you climb a ladder and peer over the fence. At other times, "area" can be understood metaphorically. If through sophisticated data collection technologies I can monitor your travels, credit card purchases, iPhone calls, grocery purchases, bank transactions, book purchases, DVD rentals and restaurant charges, then by extrapolating from this data I can piece together a detailed picture of your life. In so doing, I can know things about you that wouldn't be open to me in the normal course of events and to which you may not have consented to my knowing. This area of your life isn't circumscribed spatially, as in the case of a house with a fence around it. Many (or even most) of the activities monitored may take place in full view of others. Yet when all of the information—bits and pieces of which are possessed by others—is pulled together, it may reveal a whole pattern of your life unknown by any one of the others.

The paradox of privacy is that knowledge of a collection of acts, each of which has been witnessed by some other people without any violation of privacy, may constitute such a violation if it reveals larger aspects of one's life one may not want to have cobbled together.[10]

11.6 Setting boundaries

To speak of "opening" areas of one's life implies also that those areas aren't open to begin with; that there are boundaries that one can lift or not as one chooses and for whom one chooses (as one does with a spouse or intimate friend). Some of these boundaries we set ourselves; others are set culturally or legally. But we can usually lift them if we choose.

The notion of boundaries can perhaps best be understood by examples. If you see me posting a letter at a public mailbox, even without my knowledge or consent, there's no violation of privacy. The act is a public one, open to others. But if you conceal a video camera in my bedroom you've invaded my privacy. Here the demarcation of the area of my life that is not open to you is partly physical—the walls of my house and the door to my bedroom—but also partly cultural and, in most countries, partly legal or constitutional as well. The boundaries defining areas of one's life not normally open to others may be set:

1. Expressly, by verbal announcement (e.g., a sign saying "Keep Out");
2. Tacitly, by physical boundaries (e.g., a fence enclosing one's property);
3. Culturally, by custom or tradition (e.g., the practice of segregating restrooms for males and females);
4 Legally, by statute (e.g., laws prohibiting stalking or voyeurism).

Some boundaries are set by individuals themselves. Some are set by others, past or present. Individuals normally have the right to lift boundaries they themselves have set, either for certain individuals or for people generally, and what the boundaries are will vary from person to person and culture to culture.

In some cultures, for example, a woman's privacy calls for wearing a veil in public and being clothed from head to foot. In others, it allows for bare breasts and only a minimum of other covering. And the boundaries vary to a considerable extent from individual to individual. Some people consider their lives an open book. Others are "private persons," disclosing facts about their personal lives only to a few. But whether intrusion into those areas constitutes a violation of privacy depends in large part upon the individual and whether he or she has consented to the intrusion.

11.7 The prima facie right to privacy

We don't have an unqualified right to privacy. No one would say that the privacy of terrorists plotting to bomb a crowded restaurant should be respected. We may say, rather, that we have a prima facie right to privacy; that is, a right, all other things being equal. (On prima facie rightness, see Chapter 4, Theory Box 4A, Section 4.7.) When all other things aren't equal—as in the case of terrorist plotters—it may not be wrong for others to intrude on privacy.

Thus, there is a range of possible cases, from the consensual sexual activities of married couples in the privacy of their bedrooms to the murderous conspiracy of terrorists in their hideaways. Clearly, privacy should be respected in the one case but not in the other. Where, in the vast range of cases lying between these two should the line be drawn between permissible intrusions and impermissible intrusions? Disagreement over the answer to that question gives rise to some of the moral dilemmas regarding privacy.

To understand these dilemmas we need to consider some of the values with which privacy may conflict. This requires considering some of the ends those who violate privacy seek to promote. Except for those motivated by curiosity, most who invade the privacy of others don't do so for its own sake; they do so because they believe the violation serves other ends. We shall consider three categories of such ends: political, social, and personal.

11.8 Violations of privacy for political, social, or personal ends

Political Ends: It's said that national leaders can recognize no higher value than the preservation of the state. If one accepts this view, the door is open to any and all methods of surveillance and information-gathering that a government may deem necessary for the preservation of the state. Most governments—perhaps all of them—will violate the privacy of their citizens if they believe it essential to maintaining order, stability, and security.[11]

Social Ends: Closely related to political ends are those which might broadly be considered social. Some of them are ends of governments (such as improving compliance with tax laws[12]); others are ends of businesses or corporations (such as efficiency, productivity, or profitability). Some employers deem it useful to require urinalyses or blood tests to identify employees who use drugs or alcohol or are HIV positive. Job efficiency of the workforce is one determinant of the profitability of a business. The health of employees is one factor in efficiency. The veracity of employees is also important to business, and it might be deemed valuable to require lie-detector tests.[13] In the case of another social end, freedom of speech, it might be argued that the right of individuals or newspapers to publicize information regarding the private lives of others—such as public figures—must be protected. In that case, the privacy of some persons might conflict with the freedom of speech of others.[14]

Personal Ends: Individuals may sometimes decide it's in their personal interest to disclose personal information to employers or governmental agencies in the belief that it will enhance their opportunities for recognition and advancement. Employers, for example, arguably are able to make more accurate comparative evaluations of employees the more information they have about them. For that reason some individuals may (wisely or not) gladly provide extensive information in the hope it will improve their prospects in competition with others or at least help ensure that they are accurately evaluated.[15] So it's not merely that invasions of privacy may seem to employers to advance their ends of profitability or efficiency. It may seem to employees as well that their best interests are also secured thereby.

11.9 Privacy and conflicting values

The problem of privacy isn't simply a matter of coping with sinister, totalitarian governments. If it were, there would be the practical problem of how to safeguard against such evil designs, but there would be no major moral problem. The issue would simply be one of right versus wrong. What we see in the contemporary world is more complex. It's often a problem *within morality* between conflicting values. In the first case above, privacy may conflict with the political goal of national security. In the second, it may conflict with social or economic goals, such as efficiency or productivity. In the third, it may conflict with the personal goal of wishing to see one's work evaluated fairly.

Privacy may also involve a conflict of rights within morality as well as a conflict of values. The following passage views privacy in that light and proposes a clear principle by which to resolve such conflicts.

The Right to Privacy

All conflicts of rights involving privacy can be resolved by an appeal to maximal autonomy. In other words, privacy conflicts with no rights where the conflict could not be resolved by asking which right best fosters autonomy in general. That is because privacy and all other rights with which it may conflict are necessary conditions for the very possibility of autonomy . . .

Privacy sets out the boundary within which the holder of the right is free to act. Other active rights also set out boundaries within which the holder is free to act. The boundaries of these different rights can overlap as, for example, when the press reports on the private lives of public officials. Consequently, the right to privacy can conflict with the active rights of others, as in the example, which is interpersonal . . .

By way of illustration, consider two examples in which the test for resolving conflict of rights might be applied. In the first situation the press publishes very personal information about a private citizen. In this situation, there is a conflict between freedom of the press and the citizen's right to privacy. The conflict is resolved by asking which right under these circumstances best promotes maximal autonomy. That is, which right better promotes the greatest amount of freedom for individuals to discover their interests? Clearly, a general practice of the press publishing personal information about individual citizens will hamper the actions of many citizens who might fear they will become the subject of an unwanted news story. Moreover, personal facts will not be a source of valuable information to readers. Consequently, here the consideration of promoting autonomy clearly favors the right to privacy over freedom of the press.

In contrast, for the press to report on a public official could serve the public interest since the official's actions can affect the interests of members of the public. Consequently, the information may be very important to voters' interests if it allows voters to determine whether the character or politics of the official will tend to advance their interests ... Thus, in this instance, the promotion of autonomy would favor freedom of the press over privacy.[16]

This passage focuses on the promotion of autonomy as the criterion by which to resolve conflicts of rights involving privacy. The most difficult problems arise over the question of where to draw the line between permissible and impermissible violations of privacy. Let us consider some of the principles and values that are most relevant to assessing these problems.

The issue can be seen as one of deciding between two different ways of thinking about morality. We have characterized these as macro ethics and micro ethics, depending upon whether they attach prime importance respectively to the well-being of collectivities or individuals. (See Chapter 4, Theory Box 4B, Section 4.9.)

In its starkest form, the issue between micro and macro ethics is posed in conflicts between the individual and the state. One may have to choose, in those cases, between sacrificing the rights of individuals and running risks to the security of the state. Macro ethics often resorts to utilitarian calculations in dealing with such conflicts. In the version of macro ethics that takes the state to be the highest value, this view says we must evaluate policies and legislation with a view to promoting the state's interests. If that requires sacrificing the interests of individuals (or in some cases, such as war, sacrificing the very lives of individuals), then that's the price that must be paid. That price includes violating the privacy of individuals to whatever extent is necessary.

There's a rationale to this way of thinking. To work efficiently craftsmen must understand their tools and materials. They must know how they function under different conditions. The more they know about them (up to a point, of course), the better they're able to use them to serve their purposes. Similarly, by this reasoning, those in charge of collectivities like the state can rule more efficiently and effectively the more they know about the citizens under them. Citizens are, in a sense, the instruments by which the state functions. If citizens don't voluntarily yield the necessary information about themselves, then it must be gotten by other means. Hence the macro-ethics based case for surveillance, monitoring, data-gathering, and, in the extreme cases, threats and torture.

On the other side, the state (and the same with corporations, races, religions, and other collectivities) is not itself a person. It doesn't live and breathe and has no value apart from the individual persons who make it up. Those individuals aren't machine parts, tools, or instruments to be manipulated according to some grand design that takes priority over their own individual life plans. The danger isn't that democratic societies will openly embrace totalitarianism in one fell swoop. It's that they will unwittingly drift so far in that direction that the final step into totalitarianism will be but a small one, taken almost imperceptibly. According to this way of thinking, we must risk some loss in efficiency and even security to safeguard the rights and privacy of individuals. Mill, again, captured the spirit of this way of thinking:

Key Quote 11C

The worth of a State, in the long run, is the worth of the individuals composing it; … a State which dwarfs its men, in order that they may be more docile instruments in its hands even for beneficial purposes, will find that with small men no great thing can really be accomplished; and that the perfection of machinery to which it has sacrificed everything, will in the end avail it nothing, for want of the vital power which, in order that the machine might work more smoothly, it has preferred to banish.[17]

Democratic peoples are, of course, aware of the threat of tyranny from dictatorship resulting from the overthrow of a government. They are less aware of the risks of sliding inadvertently into totalitarianism through the actions and policies of well-intentioned people.

11.10 Privacy and technology

The message isn't that we should be anti-technology. The development of security technology is no doubt worthwhile. But the problem, in the last analysis, is ethical, not technological. And there are no purely technical solutions to ethical problems. Indeed, an undue commitment to technical solutions may be part of the problem.

An ethical concern with the problem of privacy must include a concern for those who stand to be disadvantaged, not only by threats to privacy but also by proposed measures to counteract those threats. These will include those who—whether on principle or for economic reasons—do not or cannot avail themselves of the potential, privacy-threatening technologies (with their undeniable advantages) or the privacy technologies meant to counteract those threats. (You need to be able to afford a computer in the first place, e.g., before you can take advantage of advanced technologies meant to safeguard internet privacy.)

If you try to insulate yourself from surveillance and monitoring by the government or other groups, the day may come when there's virtually no market where you can buy your food, no store to purchase your clothing, no phone from which to call your friends, no restaurant where you can eat, nor any dealer from whom to buy a car. By no choice of your own, you may gradually be shut-off from services and opportunities that make for a normal life in advanced society. The poor and the homeless would be even more severely disadvantaged. Lacking computers, smart phones, or credit cards to begin with, they'd likely slip further and further behind the more affluent members of society. On the global level, the effect would almost certainly be an ever-widening gap between wealthy nations and lesser-developed nations.

11.11 Conclusion

Some will say these risks aren't the fault of technology, and we must not impede progress. That we mustn't impede progress can be granted so long as progress isn't defined to include increasing injustice in the comparative prospects of the rich and the poor. And that these risks are not the fault of technology can be granted as well. But not much follows from that. No one would argue that we shouldn't fear AIDS on the grounds that AIDS doesn't kill us. That AIDS doesn't kill us is, in a sense, true. What it does is to so weaken our immune systems that something else kills us—such as pneumonia or infection. The boundaries of our privacy are like an immune system. They're a defense against intrusions into our lives that can, at one end of the scale, merely annoy us, or at the other end seriously threaten our liberties.

In any event, those intrusions diminish the quality of our lives. Break down those defenses and we become vulnerable. Technology misused helps break down those defenses. The threat isn't to our lives, as it is with AIDS, but to our privacy, and beyond privacy to our autonomy. And autonomy is essential to our flourishing as social and moral beings.

Study questions

1. Why might the *right to privacy* be thought to be a *human right* (see shaded passage in Section 11.1)?
2. What are the three points *Mill* makes in a famous passage (Key Quote 11A)?
3. What is the *definition of privacy* (Definition Box 11A)?
4. What is the *definition of autonomy* (Definition Box 11B)? How do privacy and autonomy differ?
5. What is the *paradox of privacy* (Section 11.5)?
6. What are the ways in which privacy can be violated for *political, social, and personal ends* (Section 11.8)?
7. The text suggests that some of the problems with regard to privacy involve conflicts within morality. What does the shaded passage in Section 11.9 take to be a conflict of rights involving privacy?
8. How does the distinction between *macro ethics* and *micro ethics* (see Theory Box 4B in Chapter 4, Section 4.9) enter into the privacy issues in the relation between the *individual* and *the state* (Section 11.9)?
9. What are some of the obvious ways in which advances in technology pose a threat to privacy (Section 11.10)?
10. What does *Mill* (Key Quote 11C) take to be test of the worth of the state?

Notes

1 Albert Einstein, *Ideas and Opinions* (New York: Crown Publishers, Inc., 1962), p. 149.
2 Jonathan Shaw, "The Watchers: Assaults on Privacy in America," *Harvard Magazine*, January-February, 2017, pp. 56–61, 82–3. http://harvardmagazine.com/2017/01/the-watchers.

3 For an account of some of this history, see Morris L. Ernst and Alan U. Schwartz, *Privacy: The Right to be Let Alone* (New York: the Macmillan Company, 1962).

4 John Stuart Mill, *On Liberty* in *John Stuart Mill: A Selection of His Works*, John M. Robson (ed.) (Indianapolis: The Odyssey Press, 1966), pp. 16f.

5 Some even define individuality in terms of a right to privacy. Edward J. Boustein, for example, says that "our Western culture defines individuality as including the right to be free from certain types of intrusions." See "Privacy as an Aspect of Human Dignity: An Answer to Dean Prosser," in Ferdinand D. Schoeman (ed.), *Philosophical Dimensions of Privacy: An Anthology* (Cambridge: Cambridge University Press, 1984), p. 165.

6 From Samuel Warren and Louis D. Brandeis, "The Right to Privacy," *Harvard Law Review*, Vol. IV, No. 5, December 15, 1890.

7 Many philosophers have challenged the idea that thinking is a hidden, inner process. What I say isn't meant to resolve that issue one way or the other.

8 https://www.buzzfeed.com/katiejmbaker/heres-the-powerful-letter-the-stanford-victim-read-to-her-ra?utm_term=.vc4wd4Nx9#.umveN27w3.

9 As we shall see in Chapter 12, the landmark Supreme Court case *Roe v. Wade* in 1973 bases its decision upholding abortion on a supposed right to privacy implicit in the US Constitution. In fact, the court seems to have autonomy in mind rather than privacy.

10 Although he doesn't remark on anything paradoxical here, Kent Greenawalt notes court cases in which privacy can be protected even in public places. See Kent Greenawalt, "The Right of Privacy," in Norman Dorsen (ed.), *The Rights of Americans: What They Are—What They Should Be* (New York: Random House, 1970), pp. 300–301.

11 In the United States, for example, the Federal Government has for years conducted warrantless searches of the homes and offices of American citizens suspected of assisting foreign governments; this, despite Fourth Amendment guarantees against unwarranted searches and seizures.

12 Regarding the internal Revenue Service and privacy, see David F. Linowes, *Privacy in America: Is Your Private Life in the Public Eye?* (Urbana and Chicago: University of Illinois Press, 1989), pp. 87–90.

13 The use of lie detectors in employment was prohibited in the United States by the Employee Polygraph Protection Act of 1988.

14 The landmark article by Samuel D. Warren and Louis D. Brandeis, "The Right to Privacy" (*Harvard Law Review*, Vol. IV, No. 5, December 1890) expressly focuses on the issue of the privacy of individuals versus the rights of the press.

15 This point is made by the Privacy Protection Study Commission, *Personal Privacy in an Information Society* (Washington, DC: U.S. Government

Printing Office, 1977), p. 16. Cited in James Rule, et al., *The Politics of Privacy* (New York: Elsevier North Holland, Inc., 1980), p. 172.

16 From Vincent J. Samar, *The Right to Privacy: Gays, Lesbians and the Constitution* (Philadelphia: Temple University Press, 1991), pp. 104f., 109.

17 Mill, *On Liberty*.

For more resources:

www.bloomsbury.com/holmes-introduction-to-applied-ethics

12

Abortion

I will not give to a woman an abortive remedy.

—The Hippocratic Oath

Bring children into the world only if they are wanted.

—Peter Singer[1]

Introduction

In this chapter, we shall clarify the issues dividing the two sides in the abortion debate. In so doing we'll seek a neutral language in which to discuss the problem, then examine the medical, legal, and moral perspectives on abortion, including whether the unborn is a person and has rights along with the pregnant woman. Finally, as a way of finding common ground between the two sides, we shall propose shifting the issue away from abortion to that of unwanted pregnancy.

12.1 Is there neutral language with which to discuss the abortion issue?

Abortion is one of today's most emotional and confrontational issues. Even the language used to discuss it is contested. Let us begin with that.

With regard to any moral issue, we can distinguish the moral problem itself from the language used to discuss it. Where there are options within the language, it becomes necessary to choose among them.

We may take the central moral issue with regard to abortion to be whether abortion is morally permissible. What words should be used to discuss that question? This is important, because the choice of language can bias the discussion on one side or the other.

Each side chooses language that puts its position in the most favorable light and its opponent's in the least favorable light. Pro-life advocates often characterize pro-choice advocates as pro-abortion, as though they were advocating that more women should have abortions. Pro-choice advocates are sometimes referred to as "baby killers," transferring to them the negative emotive force of the word "killers." Pro-choice advocates, for their part, often refer to pro-life advocates as "anti-choice" or "anti-reproductive rights," as though they were saying that women should have no choice in whether they have children. As the preferred labels to describe their own positions are generally (though not invariably) "pro-choice" and "pro-life," we shall use those labels, bearing in mind that even they aren't without the taint of bias.

12.2 What is it that is aborted?

Consider the various options by which to refer to that entity, let us call it X, that is aborted in an abortion. The following are among the possibilities:

1. Zygote.	6. Unborn child.
2 Clump of tissue.	7. Potential human being.
3. Embryo.	8. Human being.
4. Fetus.	9. Potential person.
5. Unborn baby.	10. Person.

Which of these one chooses in discussing the morality of abortion makes a difference to the assessment of that issue. Persons (including children and babies) are presumed to have rights. (Recall Chapter 8, Section 8.3, Theory Box 8A.) So if one characterizes X as a person, he by implication imputes rights to X. As a right to life is one of the most basic rights, it would follow that X has a right to life. If so, then it would seem to be wrong to abort X. By choosing the word "person" to refer to X, one already tips the scales in the moral argument.

Theory Box 12A

Recall that in Theory Box 8A, Chapter 8, Section 8.3, we defined a right as a **human right** if and only if:

1. **It's possessed by all persons simply by virtue of their being human.**
2. **It's possessed by all persons equally and at all times.**
3. **It's (a) independent of one's position, social status, or role in the state or society, and (b) independent of whether it's honored or respected by others, individually or collectively.**

Recall also that the **UN's Universal Declaration of Human Rights** *(Chapter 1, Section 1.9) asserts:*

Article 3: Everyone has the right to life, liberty, and security of person.

However, the UN Declaration also says:

Article 1: All human beings are born free and equal in dignity and rights.

While Article 3 makes clear that everyone has a right to life, Article 1 may mean that such a right comes into existence only when one is born, which would leave the status of the unborn indeterminate with regard to rights.

On the other hand, if one characterizes X merely as a clump of tissue, then one tips the scales in the other direction. No one contends that clumps of tissue have rights. If you have a tumor removed, you destroy a clump of tissue. If the tumor is malignant, its removal may save your life. In terms of our earlier distinction between descriptive and emotive meaning (see Chapter 1, Section 1.3, Theory Box 1A), terms such as *zygote* or *clump of tissue* have a clear descriptive meaning but virtually no emotive meaning. Others such as *unborn child* or *person* have both descriptive and emotive meaning. If a physician said at the end of a day that he or she had destroyed so many clumps of tissue that day, no particular feelings on the part of a hearer would be aroused one way or the other. But if he or she announced the killing of a certain number of human beings that day, people would be shocked. The referent (X, the unborn as we have characterized it) would be the same in each case. But emotive meaning of the terms used in each case would vary dramatically, and would naturally tend to lead to different moral judgments.

In light of these considerations, consider the following passages:

> The greatest destroyer of peace today is the crime against the innocent unborn child [i.e., abortion].[2]
>
> We've been forced to endure unborn babies being mercilessly slaughtered and their bodies disposed of like so much garbage. We've been forced to pay our taxes and see those tax dollars used to pay for killing unborn innocent children. We've been arrested, convicted and jailed while abortion killers remain free. We've been ignored, scoffed at and vilified. We've been discredited in every way possible, not only by abortionists and their camp followers but by government agents and agencies as well.[3]
>
> My last patient today, a brave woman with a number of children who was fighting mental illness, as well as her estranged, abusive husband, decided she didn't have the strength for another child. Because of the inaccurate language of the anti-abortion movement, she thought her six-week pregnancy would be several inches long and crying, rather than a clump of placental tissue.[4]

If one labels X a person, it places the burden on pro-choice advocates to justify the violation of rights that abortion would then entail. If, on the other hand, one labels X a clump of tissue, then the burden is on pro-life advocates to explain why its destruction is wrong. The very choice of words to label X makes a difference to the moral coloration of the problem. That is why language itself has become pivotal in the battleground over abortion.

Notice that the choice of language to refer to X has implications for the terms that are appropriate for other entities whose interests are often thought to be at stake in the abortion issue. If X isn't a child, then it's inaccurate to refer to the pregnant woman as a mother (unless she has previously given birth), since a woman is a mother only if she has a child. And if it isn't a child, then it's inaccurate to refer to the man by whom she is pregnant as the father. Although we shall use the terms "woman" and "man," strictly speaking even they will sometimes be inappropriate, since the relevant parties are sometimes adolescents, more accurately characterized as "girls" and "boys."

12.3 A medical perspective

Let's consider briefly what medical science has to say. Both sides in the abortion issue can agree that X comes into existence at the moment of conception.

Theory Box 12B

Conception occurs in humans when a sperm and an ovum (egg) are united. The cell created by that union is a **zygote**. As the zygote divides, the resultant mass of cells is a **morula** (though "zygote" is sometimes used loosely to refer to the morula as well as to the original cell created by the union of egg and sperm). From the fourth day after fertilization until the end of the eighth week, X is an **embryo**. Following the eighth week it's a **fetus**.

To fill out this picture, we may note that medical science has a general term, "conceptus," to cover *everything* that results directly from fertilization, including all of the preceding but also including the umbilical cord and other membranes as well. So, in scientific terms the situation looks like this

One might refer to X by any of these terms at the appropriate stages. But while doing so is suitable for medical purposes, it has limitations for discussing the moral issues. "Embryo" and "fetus" are too narrow for this purpose. Strictly speaking, "fetus" is appropriate only after the eighth week, whereas "embryo" is appropriate only from the fourth day until the end of the eighth week. Countless spontaneous abortions occur naturally prior to either of these stages. The term "conceptus," however, is too broad, since it includes more than just X (e.g., the placenta and umbilical cord).

It'll be useful to have a single general term by which to refer to X alone, the developing organism, at any time from the moment of conception until birth (or abortion). I propose for this purpose to call X the unborn human offspring, or the unborn for short:

Definition Box 12A

The Unborn: The product of human fertilization from conception until spontaneous expulsion, miscarriage, abortion, or birth.

This makes clear that what's being talked about is a product of human reproductive processes. Sometimes unbeknownst to the woman that product is spontaneously expelled prior to pregnancy. (Pregnancy occurs when the embryo becomes implanted in the uterus wall and begins to develop.) If it's not expelled, miscarried, or aborted it will eventuate in birth.

This definition minimizes the risk of biasing the discussion of the moral problem. It allows that while the unborn is a clump of tissue (at least after the zygote begins the process of division), it's more than that. How much more is left open. Specifically left open is whether the unborn has rights or is a human being, a child, or a person, controversial issues we'll explore shortly. None of the options open to both sides in the abortion debate is foreclosed. This provides a common basis from which they can proceed without being disadvantaged at the outset by the choice of language.

12.4 Whose interests warrant moral consideration in the abortion issue?

We may indicate those whose interests are possibly at stake in the abortion issue as follows:

1. The unborn
2. The pregnant female
3. The impregnating male (husband, boyfriend, acquaintance, donor, rapist, et al.)
4. Medical personnel, friends, family
5. The state (and perhaps society)

The distinction between basic moral consideration (BMC) and derivative moral consideration (DMC) is relevant once again. (See Theory Box 9A in Chapter 9, Section 9.2 and Chapter 10, Section 10.1.) Unquestionably the pregnant woman warrants BMC. Her well-being, including her health and possibly even her life, are at risk when it comes to pregnancy. The unborn unquestionably warrants DMC, since its fate is a determinant of the well-being of the woman, whether she gives birth or ends the pregnancy. The difficult question is whether the unborn also warrants BMC, a topic we'll take up in Section 12.8. Whether the man in question deserves moral consideration of either sort we'll take up in Section 12.7. Whether the wishes of family and friends warrant any moral consideration we don't have space to go into, but they undoubtedly sometimes come into play as support for (or pressure upon) the pregnant woman. The state, as we shall see, according to *Roe v. Wade*, has a legal interest that comes into play in the later stages of pregnancy.

A word about medical personnel. There are moral issues surrounding their participation in abortions. Physicians who perform abortions risk harassment and sometimes violence. Some have been killed. Living under that kind of threat can undermine the quality of their professional and personal lives. But what of doctors and nurses who oppose abortion? Should they be expected to perform abortions when asked? And what about certain types of abortion, particularly at later stages of pregnancy? Medical personnel are sometimes disturbed by the procedures even if they don't disapprove of abortion. There is much that deserves discussion in this area, but it raises questions (e.g., about professional ethics and responsibilities) that we don't have space to explore here.

Before turning to the moral issue, let us consider briefly where abortion stands legally. Here we need to consider the landmark Supreme Court decision, *Roe v. Wade* (1973), wherein the court focused primarily upon the interests (and responsibility) of the pregnant female and the state. Possible interests of the unborn come in primarily by way of recognizing that the state has a legitimate interest in the unborn after a certain stage of pregnancy.

12.5 *Roe v. Wade* (1973)

A woman named Norma McCorvey challenged a Texas law prohibiting abortion. In *Roe v. Wade* the Supreme Court overturned the Texas law in a judgment that governed the abortion decision throughout the country. (McCorvey later became a pro-life advocate, but that didn't affect the legal ruling.)

The ruling focused on privacy. In its essentials, the court held that a woman's right to privacy is paramount during the first trimester of a pregnancy.

Although the Constitution doesn't mention privacy, courts have held that it contains an implied right of privacy. Recall our definition of privacy from Chapter 11, Section 11.3:

Definition Box 11A

Privacy: Freedom from intrusion into areas of one's life that one hasn't explicitly or implicitly opened to others.

The decision whether to continue a pregnancy during the first trimester is considered by *Roe v. Wade* to fall within that domain of a woman's personal life in which the state may not interfere. During the first trimester, the risks to the woman from abortion are less than the risks from childbirth. She minimizes the risk to herself by having an abortion during that phase. Additionally, the unborn during that phase is sufficiently undeveloped that it normally cannot survive outside of the womb.

During the second trimester, however, as the fetus develops and the risks associated with abortion increase, the state is deemed to have a legitimate interest in "maternal health." It can then regulate the procedure (e.g., facilities) under which abortion takes place. During the third trimester, which approximates the point at which the fetus becomes *viable*, that is capable of surviving outside the womb, the state acquires a compelling interest in the potential human life represented by the fetus. The state may (though need not) then prohibit abortion, except to save the life or protect the health of the woman.

Thus, the court balances the rights of the pregnant woman (the "mother," as it misleadingly calls her) against the rights of the state. The fetus isn't itself deemed to be legally a person, and hence to have legal rights.[5]

12.6 A woman's "right to choose"

Privacy, as we have seen, is freedom from interference in areas of one's life that one hasn't, implicitly or explicitly, opened to others. A right to privacy implies the prima facie wrongness of such interference. This, in turn, may be taken to imply a right to choose what will happen in and to your body (a "right to choose"). In the oft-quoted words of Benjamin Cardoza (who was later to become a Supreme Court Justice):

Key Quote 12A

Every human being of adult years and sound mind has a right to determine what shall be done with his own body.[6]

The case dealt with a woman under anesthesia who had experienced surgery to which she hadn't consented. It may be that Cardoza is speaking here of a legal right and not necessarily a moral right. In any event, a right to determine what happens in and to your body may be taken to imply a right to choose whether or not to have an abortion (a "right to choose"). Thus, the reasoning from a right to privacy to a right to abortion may be represented as proceeding from

1. A right to privacy (to be free from intrusion into areas of one's life that one hasn't implicitly or explicitly opened to others)

to

2. A right to choose (to decide what shall be done in and to one's own body)

to

3. A right to choose (whether or not to have an abortion)

The right to choose whether to have an abortion is said to be the woman's alone, as a result of the "biological reality" that the unborn is developing within her body and no one else's.

This is unquestionably correct. If we're talking about a free choice whether to have an abortion, no one but the woman can make that choice. Short of an abortion forcibly being performed against a woman's will, or her being forcibly prevented from having an abortion, the choice is hers. And if the choice is hers alone, only she can have the right to choose. That's in the nature of the case. It doesn't follow from this, however, that any choice she makes is morally permissible, which is still an open question.

Consider another example. If I'm strolling along a riverbank and see a child struggling in the water, I have the choice whether to rescue it or let it drown. If no one else is around, the choice is mine alone. Circumstances (though not biology, as in the case of the pregnant woman) dictate that. But it doesn't follow that it makes no difference morally which I do. I have an obligation to try to save the child. Failing to do so would be morally wrong.

The point is that being in a situation in which one has to make a choice (and in which not making a choice is effectively to choose one way or the other) doesn't necessarily mean that it doesn't matter what one chooses. By implication, it also implies that one may not have a right to choose in those situations. Having a right to do X (as opposed to having an obligation to do X) normally means that one may do X or not, as one pleases. All things being equal, either choice is morally acceptable. But in some situations in which one has, so to speak, no choice but to choose, it does matter which choice one makes. Whether in those situations we say that one doesn't have a right to choose or that one's right to choose is overridden by other moral considerations is immaterial. The fact that a choice is one's own and no one else's doesn't necessarily mean that any choice will do.

Likewise, from the fact that whether to have an abortion is ultimately a woman's decision—and biologically cannot be otherwise—it doesn't follow that she should make one choice rather than another. All things being equal, it's a matter of indifference legally which she does. It's perfectly permissible for a woman to have an abortion (subject to the constraints of *Roe v. Wade*) or to give birth. That issue has been resolved by the Supreme Court. But are there moral grounds for questioning that legal situation? Here is where controversy emerges.

Some don't think there really are two sides to the issue. They see the issue as clear-cut; that a woman has a moral right to an abortion. Consider the following reasoning:

Is Abortion Really a "Moral Dilemma"?

Quite apart from blowing up clinics and terrorizing patients, the anti-abortion movement can take credit for a more subtle and lasting kind of damage: It has succeeded in getting even pro-choice people to think of abortion as a "moral dilemma," an "agonizing decision" and related code phrases for something murky and compromising, like the traffic in infant formula mix. In liberal circles, it has become unstylish to discuss abortion without using words like "complex," "painful" and the rest of the mealy-mouthed vocabulary of evasion ... Many women, like myself, have felt free to choose the safest methods because legal abortion is available as a backup to contraception. Anyone who finds that a thoughtless, immoral choice should speak to the orphans of women whose wombs were perforated [*sic*] by Dalkon shields or whose strokes were brought on by high-estrogen birth-control pills.

I refer you to the orphans only because it no longer seems to be good form to mention women themselves in discussions of abortion. In most of the antiabortion literature I have seen, women are so invisible that an uninformed reader might conclude that fetuses reside in artificially warm tissue culture flasks or similar containers. It must be enormously difficult for the antiabortionist to face up to the fact that real fetuses can only survive inside women, who, unlike any kind of laboratory apparatus, have thoughts, feelings, aspirations, responsibilities and, very often, checkbooks . . .

From the point of view of a fetus, pregnancy is no doubt a good deal. But consider it for a moment from the point of view of the pregnant person (if "woman" is too incendiary and feminist a term) and without reference to its potential issue. We are talking about a nine-month bout of symptoms of varying severity, often including nausea, skin discolorations, extreme bloating and swelling, insomnia, narcolepsy, hair loss, varicose veins, hemorrhoids, indigestion and irreversible weight gain, and culminating in a physiological crisis which is occasionally fatal and almost always excruciatingly painful. If men were equally at risk for this condition—if they knew that their bellies might swell as if they were suffering from end-stage cirrhosis, that they would have to go for nearly a year without a stiff drink, a cigarette or even an aspirin, that they would be subject to fainting spells and unable to fight their way onto commuter trains—then I am sure that pregnancy would be classified as a sexually transmitted disease and abortions would be no more controversial than emergency appendectomies . . .

So I will admit that I might not have been so calm and determined about my abortions if I had had to cross a picket line of earnest people yelling "baby killer," or if I felt that I might be blown to bits in the middle of a vacuum aspiration . . . The question that worries me is: How is, say, a 16-year-old girl going to feel after an abortion? Like a convicted sex offender, a murderess on parole? Or like a young woman who is capable, as the guidance counselors say, of taking charge of her life?

This is our choice, for biology will never have an answer to that strange and cabalistic question of when a fetus becomes a person. Potential persons are lost every day as a result of miscarriage, contraception or someone's simple failure to respond to a friendly wink. What we can answer, with a minimum of throat-clearing and moral agonizing, is the question of when women themselves will finally achieve full personhood: And that is when we have the right, unquestioned and unabrogated, to *choose* not to be pregnant when we decide not to be pregnant.[7]

Many side with the above analysis. A woman's right to an abortion, they believe, should be unquestioned.

Even if one accepts that a woman's right to an abortion should be unquestioned, and that the decision should be hers and hers alone (as the above passage reasons), that doesn't answer the question whether the woman should take into account anyone else's interests or rights in making that decision. This brings us to a generally neglected issue in the discussion of abortion. It's whether the male by whom a female has become pregnant (the "responsible male," as we may call him) has or should have any rights with regard to the outcome of the pregnancy.

12.7 Do men have rights in the abortion issue?

It's usually assumed that the responsible male has no rights in this regard. When people speak of a "woman's right to choose," they usually mean that while she may discuss it with her husband or boyfriend (as well as with family, friends, and her physician), the decision is hers to make. Coupled with this is usually the assumption (which we questioned above) that whatever decision she makes is permissible. But there have been legal challenges to this position. Consider the following:

Ex-Boyfriend Loses Bid to Halt an Abortion
A Pennsylvania judge allowed a woman yesterday to end her pregnancy after a week's delay during which he had considered her ex-boyfriend's objections . . .
    "My preborn child at this moment is a living being who can feel and respond to pain, whose heart beats, who moves in Tanya's [the

ex-girlfriend] womb, who has brain activity and fully functioning organ systems," John Stachokus, 27, said in legal papers. "He or she is a living human being."

In an interview, Ms. Meyers said that having to explain herself to the court and then wait to hear what she would be allowed to do was hard. "It's not something the court system should entertain," she said. "I felt extremely violated. I still feel violated that my life was made so public. It's just been emotional torture."

Mr. Stachokus ... had told the court that he would take responsibility for the child's welfare once born ...

In his ruling, Judge Conahan said that both Ms. Meyers and Mr. Stachokus were "credible and sincere." But he held that Ms. Meyers had a constitutional right to have an abortion.

"This right is not subject to being vetoed by a woman's husband or partner," Judge Conahan wrote. "Neither an ex-boyfriend nor a fetus has standing to interfere with a woman's choice to terminate her pregnancy."[8]

This ruling takes a firm stand on the legal issue. The responsible male has no right to interfere with a woman's choice to have an abortion. Even where a couple is married, courts have ruled that a woman doesn't even have to notify her husband before having an abortion. But even a clear statement of the legal issue still leaves the moral issue open.

Whether or not the man has rights in the matter, he sometimes has interests. If the woman gives birth, he's legally responsible for child-support. This could run into tens and possibly even hundreds of thousands of dollars over a period of 18 years. Some men, for that reason, may want the woman to have an abortion. Moreover, assuming that the sexual intercourse that resulted in the pregnancy was consensual, the man is equally responsible for the pregnancy. In some cases (like the above, unusual though they are) the man may want a child, hence have an interest in seeing the woman give birth. In these two sorts of cases, it's obvious that the wishes of the woman and the man differ. If she wants a child, then she has an interest in giving birth; if he doesn't, he has an interest in seeing her have an abortion. If he wants a child, he has an interest in seeing her give birth; but if she doesn't, she has a strong interest in not undergoing the inconvenience or disruption to her life, not to mention the medical risks, associated with childbirth.

Although it's clear that both the woman and the man have *interests* in this regard, it doesn't follow from that fact alone that either necessarily has *rights*. Legally, as we have seen, the woman has a right—that of privacy. *Roe v. Wade* is silent on whether the man has any legal rights in the matter. This issue is explored in the following passage:

A Man's Right to Choose

I'm in favor of life, in favor of choice. Life is not easy. Neither is choice. My daughter and sons are biologically equipped for reproduction ... Each can choose what, if any precaution to take against an unplanned pregnancy. But should such precautions fail, the available choices take different directions along gender lines.

My daughter may choose to have the baby with or without the consent, cooperation, or co-parenting of the fellow (shall we call him the father now?) who impregnated her. Or she may choose, in light of her life's circumstances, that a child would be terribly inconvenient and she may avail herself of what the courts have declared as her constitutionally guaranteed right to a safe and legal medical procedure that terminates her pregnancy. Whatever discomfort—moral or personal or maternal—she might feel, a pregnancy that resulted from bilateral consent is legally undone by unilateral choice.

But if the choice as to when one is ready, willing and able to parent is a good thing, wouldn't it be good for my sons as well? And if that choice may be exercised by women after conception, then shouldn't men have the same option: to proclaim, legally and unilaterally, the end of their interest in the tissue or fetus or baby or what it is that sex between a man and a woman sometimes produces?

As it stands now, paternity, once determined, means fiscal responsibility for 18 years—not by choice, but by law. If they impregnate and the woman chooses to have the child, she has a legal claim against the father's earnings. They may, of course, refuse to pay, refuse their paternity, in which case they are "deadbeat dads" or some other media-made word for no good. Why oughtn't my sons have an equivalent choice—say, within the first two trimesters—to declare their decision not to parent, to void their paternity? Isn't this precisely the same choice given to women by *Roe v. Wade* and laws elsewhere that uphold this "right"? ...

The politics of reproduction involves not only our public interests, but our private ones. And in the longstanding debates, the terrible din of public rhetoric between politicos and archbishops has obscured the talk between fathers and daughters, mothers and sons, brothers and sisters, husbands and wives.

Women are right to abhor decisions about their bodies that leave them out. So are men. The reproductive life of the species is not a woman's issue. It is a human one. It requires the voices of human beings. And the language it deserves is intimate.[9]

However one answers the questions raised in this passage, they suggest that, morally, other interests and rights besides the woman's may be at stake in the abortion issue. Some point out that the woman is carrying the unborn; it's part of her body. She has the unqualified right to determine what shall be done in and to her own body. Others point out that the unborn is the product equally of the man and the woman. Although biology dictates that the unborn is contained within the woman's body, that doesn't give sole ownership to the woman (if, indeed, the unborn can be considered property). Its fate, on this view, should be decided by the two of them together, even if she of necessity has the final say.

12.8 Do the unborn have rights?

But what about the unborn itself? Does it (so to speak) have any say in the matter? Or is abortion solely a matter of the rights (and/or interests) of the woman, or of the man and the woman together? (Few, at least in American or British society, say it should be solely a matter of the rights of the man.) If the unborn has rights, then they must be weighed against the rights and/or interests of the woman and possibly the man as well.

On the legal issue, the judge in the above Pennsylvania case was clear: "Neither an ex-boyfriend nor a fetus has standing to interfere with a woman's choice to terminate her pregnancy."

Here language is critical again. If the unborn is considered a person or a human being, then (given the relatively uncontroversial assumption that human beings or persons have rights), it would appear that the unborn has rights. If the unborn has rights, then they must be weighed against the rights of the woman who may want the pregnancy terminated. If the unborn has no rights, then one may feel there is no problem with proceeding, as the Supreme Court did in *Roe v. Wade*, discussing the issue in terms of the rights of the woman. (Although the state has legal rights, we shall assume that it has no moral rights, and hence will not consider it in this connection.)

12.9 Human beings and persons

Some say the unborn is human but not yet a human *being*. By this they mean that it's not yet an independent entity. It's still part of the woman. This seems correct (though whether it's necessarily a part of the woman might be questioned once it reaches the stage of viability). At the same time the unborn, at least after the very earliest stages, is biologically a human organism. As such it may loosely be called a human being (though that would be challenged by some pro-choice advocates). The more problematic question is whether it's a person in a morally significant sense.

Sometimes "human being" and "person" are used interchangeably. When they are, let us call that sense of "person" *person$_1$*. In that sense, whether the unborn is a person is readily answerable. It is (assuming that it can be characterized as a human being in the loose sense above). But often people draw a distinction between human beings and persons. By this they have something like the following in mind. Whether a being is human can be answered in biological terms. As a living organism, a human being is an animal (as opposed, say, to a plant or fungus). More specifically it's a mammal. As such, it can be distinguished from a dog or a cat or a chimpanzee. But whether a human being is a person in a fuller sense depends upon whether it's conscious, self-aware, rational, capable of communicating and has purposes, values, and life plans. These are the characteristics of *personhood*. And there may be degrees of personhood, since someone might have some of these characteristics but not others. (An infant may be conscious and capable of minimal communication but not yet be self-aware or have life plans.) Someone might be a human being, biologically speaking (hence a *person$_1$*) but not be a person in this fuller sense (call it *person$_2$*). The characteristics that make one a human being are, so to speak, the foundation upon which are built the characteristics that make one a person$_2$. Although this is a matter of some philosophical controversy, we might represent the properties over and above that of being a human being that render one a person$_2$ by means of the following:

Theory Box 12C

Person$_1$: Human being.
Person$_2$: Human being with consciousness, self-awareness, use of language, rationality, purposes, values, and life plans.

Strip away enough of these characteristics (as happens when a person slips into an irreversible coma, a permanent vegetative state, or the advanced stages of Alzheimer's), and the being in question remains a human being but is no longer a person$_2$. There's no consensus as to precisely how many of the characteristics of personhood one must have to be a person$_2$ They're acquired gradually from the time of conception until adulthood and sometimes lost gradually if people slip into dementia. *Unless otherwise indicated, by "person" we shall henceforth mean person$_2$.*

The question then is whether the unborn, even if it's conceded to be a human being, can properly be said to be a person. Unlike someone in an irreversible coma, the unborn hasn't had the capacities associated with personhood and then lost them. It never had them in the first place. No one claims that an embryo or zygote is rational and capable of communicating. There is disagreement about how to characterize the unborn at the fetal stage. But even there it seems clear that it doesn't have the *full complement* of characteristics possessed by a normal, adult person. Indeed, it's not until the unborn comes into the world and begins to develop through infancy and childhood that it progresses toward full personhood. Where along that continuum it becomes appropriate to characterize the being in question as a person is probably undecidable with certainty in the present state of medical and psychological understanding.

What is at stake here is an issue for ethical theory. In order to have rights (such as a right to life), is it enough to be a human being or must one also be a person? Some would argue that being human isn't even necessary to having rights, since they believe, as we saw in Chapter 10, that animals have rights.

12.10 Abortion and the killing of the innocent

Suppose the unborn is a human being (person$_1$). And suppose that as such it has a right to life. Does that settle the abortion issue? Some have thought so on religious grounds. Pope John Paul II, for example, says:

> The acceptance of abortion in the popular mind, in behaviour and even in law itself, is a telling sign of an extremely dangerous crisis of the moral sense, which is becoming more and more incapable of

distinguishing between good and evil, even when the fundamental right to life is at stake. Given such a grave situation, we need now more than ever to have the courage to look the truth in the eye and to *call things by their proper name*, without yielding to convenient compromises or to the temptation of self-deception ... Especially in the case of abortion there is a widespread use of ambiguous terminology, such as "interruption of pregnancy," which tends to hide abortion's true nature and to attenuate its seriousness in public opinion ... But no word has the power to change the reality of things: procured abortion is *the deliberate and direct killing, by whatever means it is carried out, of a human being in the initial phase of his or her existence, extending from conception to birth.*

The moral gravity of procured abortion is apparent in all its truth if we recognize that we are dealing with murder ... It is true that the decision to have an abortion is often tragic and painful for the mother ... Nevertheless, these reasons and others like them ... *can never justify the deliberate killing of an innocent human being.*[10]

The pope stressed the importance of language here. He believed that the proper name for the unborn is human being (*person₁*). And he clearly believed that a human being has a right to life, and in the case of an innocent human being, an inviolable right to life.

What is it to "directly" kill someone? Direct killing means killing in which the intention is to kill as an end or as a means. If A has a grudge against B and kills B just to have B dead, A is directly killing B. Similarly, if A is a bounty hunter and kills B for the reward, A kills B as a means and again the killing is direct. If, on the other hand, A accidentally runs over B with his SUV, A's killing of B is indirect (it was neither intended as an end nor as a means).

If one is content to resolve the issue by an appeal to faith, and in particular, the Roman Catholic faith, the pope's declaration is definitive. But, religion aside, if one is concerned to determine whether there's a resolution to the issue that can in principle be universally accepted, this won't suffice.

Even if one doesn't subscribe to it on religious grounds, one might still think that the following *principle of innocence* (PI) is correct;

PI: One ought not to directly kill an innocent person.

Some have thought that even if the unborn is a person and innocent as well, that doesn't settle the problem. If it could be shown that abortion is permissible *even if* the unborn is a person, then it would seem to be even more incontrovertible that abortion is permissible if the unborn isn't a person or even a human being.

An influential argument to try to establish that abortion is permissible even on the assumption that the unborn is a person and has rights (specifically, a right to life) is by philosopher Judith Jarvis Thomson.

Abortion and Personhood

A newly fertilized ovum, a newly implanted clump of cells, is no more a person than an acorn is an oak tree. But I shall not discuss any of this. For it seems to me to be of great interest to ask what happens if, for the sake of argument, we allow the premise. How, precisely, are we supposed to get from there to the conclusion that abortion is morally impermissible? Opponents of abortion commonly spend most of their time establishing that the fetus is a person, and hardly any time explaining the step from there to the impermissibility of abortion. Perhaps they think the step too simple and obvious to require much comment. Or perhaps instead they are simply being economical in argument. Many of those who defend abortion rely on the premise that the fetus is not a person, but only a bit of tissue that will become a person at birth; and why pay out more arguments than you have to? Whatever the explanation, I suggest that the step they take is neither easy nor obvious, that it calls for closer examination than it is commonly given, and that when we do give it this closer examination we shall feel inclined to reject it.

I propose, then, that we grant that the fetus is a person from the moment of conception. How does the argument go from here? Something like this, I take it. Every person has a right to life. So the fetus has a right to life. No doubt the mother has a right to decide what shall happen in and to her body; everyone would grant that. But surely a person's right to life is stronger and more stringent than the mother's right to decide what happens in and to her body, and so outweighs it. So the fetus may not be killed; an abortion may not be performed.

It sounds plausible. But now let me ask you to imagine this. You wake up in the morning and find yourself back to back in bed with an unconscious violinist. A famous unconscious violinist. He has been found to have a fatal kidney ailment, and the Society of Music Lovers has canvassed all the available medical records and found that you alone have the right blood type to help. They have therefore kidnapped you, and last night the violinist's circulatory system was plugged into yours, so that your kidneys can be used to extract poisons from his blood as well as your own. The director of the hospital now tells you, "Look, we're sorry the Society of Music Lovers did this to you—we would never have permitted it if we had known. But still, they did it, and the violinist now is plugged into you. To unplug you would be to kill him. But never mind, it's only for nine months. By then he will have recovered from his ailment, and can safely be unplugged from you." Is it morally incumbent on you to accede to this situation? No doubt it would be very nice of you if you did, a great kindness. But do you *have* to accede to it? What if it were not nine months, but nine years? Or longer still? What if the director of the hospital says, "Tough luck, I agree, but you've now got to stay in bed, with the violinist plugged into you, for the rest of your life. Because remember this. All persons have a right to life, and violinists are persons. Granted you have a right to decide what happens in and to your body, but a person's right to life outweighs your right to decide what happens in and to your body. So you cannot ever be unplugged from him." I imagine you would regard this as outrageous, which suggests that something really is wrong with that plausible-sounding argument I mentioned a moment ago.

In this case, of course, you were kidnapped; you didn't volunteer for the operation that plugged the violinist into your kidneys. Can those who oppose abortion on the ground I mentioned make an exception for a pregnancy due to rape? Certainly. They can say that persons have a right to life only if they didn't come into existence because of rape; or they can say that all persons have a right to life, but that some have less of a right to life than others, in particular, that those who came into existence because of rape have less. But these statements have a rather unpleasant sound. Surely the question of whether you have a right to life at all, or how much of it you have, shouldn't turn on the question of whether or not you are the product of a rape. And in fact the people who oppose abortion on the ground I mentioned do not make this distinction, and hence do not make an exception in case of rape.[11]

Thomson's point is that the right to life, which persons may be presumed to have, isn't absolute. Even the killing of an innocent person is justified. An innocent person doesn't have a right to make use of your body even for nine months if you haven't consented to such use.

This raises a host of questions. Among them is whether the unborn is in fact a person. Thomson assumes for the sake of argument that it is but doesn't otherwise justify the assumption. Nor does she explore the broader implications of the taking of innocent human life. Both of these are addressed by philosopher Richard Werner.

Abortion and Human Life

There are two major issues to be decided concerning the topic of abortion: first, whether an embryo or fetus is a human being; and, second, if so, whether being human is sufficient to render abortion morally wrong in some or all cases. Most pro-abortionists ... deny that being human is sufficient to render abortion, at least in most cases, morally wrong. They contend either, with J.J. Thomson, that the moral prohibition against the taking of innocent human life is not strong enough to rule out most abortions, or that persons, rather than humans, have a full right to life, and that embryos, fetuses and infants do not qualify as bona fide persons ...

When I claim that a fetus or embryo is a human being, I am not merely stipulating what I shall take the sign 'human being' to mean, nor am I giving the results of a random sample poll conducted among ordinary language users. Instead, I am claiming that any fully informed, conceptually clear, fair-minded and rational individual would agree, upon reflection and deliberation, that the arguments I present show that one is a human being from the point of conception onward ...

Here, then, is my argument:

1. An adult human being is the end result of the continuous growth of the organism from conception.
2. From conception to adulthood, there is no break in this development which is relevant to the ontological status of the organism.
3. Therefore, one is a human being from the point of conception onward.

... Having argued that one is a human being from the point of conception onward, I shall now turn my attention to the moral aspect of the abortion issue. It is my contention that there is a basic prima facie moral obligation against the taking of innocent human life. This obligation can only be overridden by an equally basic moral obligation or an extreme situation such that the value of bringing about some set of consequences *greatly* outweighs the value of abiding by our basic prima facie obligation. In more familiar terms, I am claiming that an innocent human life is intrinsically valuable and can only be taken in the direst of circumstances ... Here then is my argument:

> M1. One has a basic prima facie moral obligation to refrain from the killing of innocent human beings.
>
> M2. Embryos and fetuses are innocent human beings.
>
> M3. Therefore, one has a basic prima facie moral obligation to refrain from the killing or aborting of embryos and fetuses.
>
> Conception is the only clear cutoff point in human development which is relevant to the abortion issue. As we have seen, if one is ever a human being one has been human since conception and, further, being human is the morally relevant criterion for a right to life. So, if one is willing to grant that the wanton killing of innocent humans is morally wrong, then one must be prepared to accept that abortion, at least in the majority of cases, is also wrong. In the interest of consistency, one can neither draw an arbitrary line at some point in human development prior to which one has no right to life nor weaken the prohibition against the killing of innocent humans without stopping short of all out homicide. To legitimize abortion or infanticide is to take one more step toward the total breakdown of the prohibition against the killing of innocents.[12]

For Werner, one needn't assume that the unborn is a person, as Thomson does. It's a human being, and undeniably innocent, and as such has a right to life. Moreover, Werner believes legitimizing the practice of abortion risks breaking down the prohibition against killing the innocent.

Abortion is understood by some as the intentional killing (murder) of the unborn. Others regard the death of the unborn as a result of a procedure performed for other compelling reasons. We can't resolve this deeply emotional aspect of the debate here, but we can seek a clearer understanding of the issue of what abortion is. We've been assuming thus far that it's clear what abortion is. And for most purposes it is. But greater precision than is provided by ordinary language is needed in discussing certain issues. This is the case with abortion.

12.11 What precisely is abortion?

Consider the following definitions of abortion, one medical, one legal:

Key quotes 12B

Abortion: the premature expulsion from the uterus of the products of conception—of the embryo or of a nonviable fetus. (*Dorland's Medical Dictionary*)

Abortion: The spontaneous or artificially induced expulsion of an embryo or fetus. (*Black's Law Dictionary (abridged)*)

Both definitions have shortcomings. The first identifies the "products" of conception with an embryo or nonviable fetus. But there are spontaneous abortions prior to the stage at which the unborn becomes an embryo. It's estimated that two out of three fertilized eggs are expelled before becoming an embryo. And at the stage at which the unborn becomes a fetus, abortions are conducted in the case of both nonviable and viable fetuses (though the latter are less common). Also, the second definition doesn't take into account that spontaneous expulsions of fetuses prior to viability are considered miscarriages rather than abortions.

It will be useful here to distinguish between spontaneous abortions and those which are the result of deliberate human action ("procured abortions," as the pope calls them in the earlier passage). It's the latter that's controversial, so let's define abortion in this sense as follows:

Definition Box 12B

Abortion: The intentional premature termination of pregnancy by the removal or induced expulsion of the unborn.

A caesarian section, of course, is the removal of the unborn by surgical means, but it's not usually a premature removal. And although it in fact terminates a pregnancy, that's not its purpose, which is to produce a live birth.

Notice that this definition and the preceding two say nothing about killing. Although it almost always results in the death of the unborn, abortion isn't by its nature the killing of the unborn. In abortion prior to viability, the unborn, of course, dies. At that stage it hasn't developed sufficiently to survive outside of the womb. And even at later stages it nearly always dies, if not in the process of abortion, then shortly thereafter. But the *idea* of abortion is different from that of the killing of the fetus. Abortion doesn't by definition require the intention to kill the unborn. For that we have another term.

Definition Box 12C

Feticide: The act of killing a fetus. (*Webster's Third International Dictionary*)

That there is a distinction between abortion and feticide is clear from the fact that sometimes an abortion can be successfully performed and yet the fetus emerges as a premature baby. Although the baby in those cases doesn't usually live long, the outcome of abortion is a live birth. But this is rare. It happens only with later pregnancies and depends upon the abortion procedure that is used. (Prior to twenty weeks, or if the unborn weighs less than seventeen ounces, the product of abortion is called an *abortus*.)

Often, however, abortion involves killing the fetus. When a saline solution is injected into the amniotic sac to induce expulsion, it poisons the unborn, thereby killing it. Arguably, sometimes there is even an intentional killing of the unborn, as, for example, when its skull is crushed or it's dismembered inside the womb to facilitate removal. If that is deemed intentional killing, then abortion sometimes involves direct killing as a means. But even then the end that is sought is the termination of the pregnancy, not the killing of the unborn. So, sometimes the unborn is killed as a means in abortion; but most often the unborn dies from the trauma of removal or induced expulsion. Sometimes it's allowed to die (by withholding medical care) after its removal. In any event, abortion is conceptually distinguished from feticide.

This means that sometimes abortion does indeed involve killing the innocent unborn. And it almost always results in the death of the unborn. But it's not by its nature the killing—much less the direct killing—of the unborn.

Even if abortion isn't, per se, a direct killing of the unborn, still it's sometimes direct killing. In any event, it involves knowingly performing an act that is expected to result in the death of the unborn and almost always does so.

12.12 Hare's golden rule argument

Some, on the other hand, believe it's possible to show that abortion is impermissible (at least usually) without assuming that the unborn is a person. The late British philosopher R. M. Hare (1919–2002) argues this. In so doing, he adapts a version of the Golden Rule, yielding what he calls a Golden Rule Argument.

Abortion and the Golden Rule

The single, or at least the main, thing about the fetus that raises the moral question is that, if not terminated, the pregnancy is highly likely to result in the birth and growth to maturity of a person just like the rest of us. The word "person" here re-enters the argument, but in a context and with a meaning that does not give rise to the old troubles; for it is clear at least that we ordinary adults are persons . . .

We can explain why the potentiality of the fetus for becoming a person raises a moral problem if we appeal to a type of argument which, in one guise or another, has been the formal basis of almost all theories of moral reasoning that have contributed much that is worthwhile to our understanding of it. I am alluding to the (and indeed pre-Christian) "Golden Rule," the Kantian Categorical Imperative, the ideal observer theory, the rational contractor theory, various kinds of utilitarianism, and my own universal prescriptivism . . . I shall use that form of the argument which rests on the Golden Rule that we should do to others as we wish them to do to us. It is a logical extension of this form of argument to say that we should do to others what *we are glad was* done to us. Two (surely readily admissible) changes are involved here. The first is a mere difference in the two tenses which cannot be morally relevant. Instead of saying that we should do to others as we wish them (in the future) to do to us, we say that we should do to others as we wish that they had done to us (in the past). The second is a change from the hypothetical to the actual: instead of saying that we should do to others as we wish that they had done to us, we say that we should do to others as we are glad that they did do to us. I cannot see that this could make any difference to the spirit of the injunction, and logical grounds could in any case be given, based on the universal prescriptivist thesis, for extending the Golden Rule in this way.

The application of this injunction to the problem of abortion is obvious. If we are glad that nobody terminated the pregnancy that resulted in *our* birth, then we are enjoined not, *ceteris paribus*, to terminate any pregnancy which will result in the birth of a person having a life like ours. Close attention obviously needs to be paid to the *"ceteris paribus"* clause, and also to the expression "like ours." The "universalizability" of moral judgments, which is one of the logical bases of the Golden Rule, requires us to make the same moral judgment about qualitatively identical cases, and about cases which are *relevantly* similar. Since no cases in this area are going to be qualitatively *identical*, we shall have to rely on relevant similarity. Without raising a very large topic in moral philosophy, we can perhaps address the difficulty by pointing out that the relevant respects here are going to be those things about our life which make us glad that we were born. These can be stated in a general enough way to cover all those persons who are, or who are going to be or would be, glad that they were born ... So, although I have, for the sake of simplicity, put the injunction in a way that makes it apply only to the abortion of people who will have a life just like that of the aborter, it is generalizable to cover the abortion of any fetus which will, if aborted, turn into someone who will be glad to be alive.[13]

In Hare's analysis, all that is required is that the fetus be a *potential* person. It need not be a person, as Thomson assumes in her argument, nor an actual human being, as Werner argues. That presumably can be agreed by pro-choice advocates. But then rather than appealing to religion, Hare presents an argument based on a moral principle, the Golden Rule, that can be accepted by anyone, pro-life or pro-choice. And if his modification of the argument is sound, then his reasoning constitutes a secular argument opposing abortion (at least in many cases), in addition to the religious pronouncement of the pope.

Perhaps the conclusion to be drawn from the preceding discussion is that there is no objective, decisive way in which to determine whether the unborn is a person$_2$; that is, whether it has enough of the characteristics that make for personhood to entail that it has a right to life. Perhaps it's neither a person nor a nonperson. Perhaps, that is, the term "person," which derives its meaning principally in the context of discourse about human beings that have been born and are in the world interacting with other persons, simply is too vague to cover the status of the unborn (meaning that there are gray boundaries where it's unclear whether it applies). In that case the question—in objective terms—may be undecidable. If so, how do we deal with the issue?

A statement from the National Academy of Sciences may prove instructive here. The academy was responding to a Congressional bill to specify that human life begins at conception.

The Onset of Human Life

The introduction by anti-abortion Senators of a bill that would define the legal commencement of human life as the moment of conception has given new urgency to a debate among scientists that began in July 1978, after the birth of Louise Brown, the first person born after being conceived in a glass dish.

The discussion has focused on defining the extent to which a newly conceived embryo enjoys "human rights."

According to the Senate bill, proposed by Senator Jesse Helms, Republican of North Carolina, and Representative Henry J. Hyde, Republican of Illinois: "The Congress finds that present day scientific evidence indicates a significant likelihood that actual human life exists from conception." Last week, at the annual meeting of the National Academy of Sciences, some 150 academy members, representing the nation's scientific elite, debated how to respond. They then passed a resolution, almost unanimously, that said such a statement "cannot stand up to the scrutiny of science."

It deals with a question, the resolution added, "to which science can provide no answer." The definition of when a developing embryo becomes "a person," the resolution said, "must remain a matter of moral and religious values."[14]

The idea we may derive from this statement is that if the abortion issue is thought to turn on the notion of rights, and if the notion of rights involves the question of whether the unborn has a right to life, then the abortion issue may be unresolvable in moral terms that are acceptable to both pro-choice and pro-life sides. It may be undecidable in any way satisfactory to both sides whether the unborn is a person$_2$ or even (at least in the embryonic and morula stages) a human being.

12.13 Toward a new perspective on abortion

Perhaps there is some possible common ground between pro-choice and pro-life advocates. Perhaps there is another perspective from which they can view the problem without giving up the basic convictions that animate them in the current debate.

Let's note that the abortion issue has medical, social and personal dimensions. It's a divisive issue in society, one that has led to violence and even murder. Although studies suggest that having an abortion doesn't have long term traumatic emotional consequences for most women, it's a difficult personal issue for some. All things being equal, it would benefit society, not to mention millions of women, and a much smaller number of men, if the problem could successfully be resolved.

As the abortion issue is being framed today, both sides are at loggerheads. Two changes in the approach to the problem can provide a new perspective in which common ground may be achievable.

First, the ethical language of the debate could be changed. The abortion issue is framed in terms of rights. The alleged *rights* of the unborn are pitted against the *rights* of the pregnant woman. Sometimes the rights of the responsible man and of the State are thrown into the mix. But, as others have pointed out, the language of rights tends to be divisive. Rights are commonly understood as claims against others; claims not to be interfered with or to be provided with certain benefits. By the very nature of rights, some people are set against others.

Theory Box 12D

The language of rights is dispensable in ethics from a theoretical standpoint. Everything we want to say by means of rights can be said by means of other ethical language (right, wrong, good, bad, etc.), without any loss in our capacity to assess problems morally.

This doesn't mean that there aren't rights; only that they aren't fundamental, and to frame an issue exclusively in terms of rights introduces a division among people at the outset.

An alternative is to frame the issue in terms of what is good, specifically in terms of what would be *best* overall, taking into account the well-being of all who are affected. This isn't to embrace utilitarianism, however. Utilitarianism (see Theory Box 1E, Chapter 1, Section 1.8) bases rightness solely on the value of consequences. An axiological ethics, on the other hand, factors in the value of the act itself, and perhaps the motives and intentions, as well as the consequences.

> **Theory Box 12E**
>
> **Axiological Ethics:** An act is right if, and only if, it actualizes at least as great a balance of good over bad (in the act itself, or its consequences, or a combination of the two) as any other alternative available to the agent.

The pursuit of what is best overall doesn't set people at odds with one another at the outset. Instead, it involves a shift in emphasis regarding what is taken to be morally most important.

The second helpful change in the approach to the problem would be to recognize that abortion isn't the central issue. The central issue is that of *unwanted pregnancy*. In virtually every case of abortion there is an unwanted pregnancy. Even in cases in which pregnancy was initially wanted but is terminated for the health of the woman, at the time of the abortion the pregnancy is unwanted. Most of the most vexing moral problems surrounding abortion wouldn't occur but for an unwanted pregnancy.

12.14 The basic problem of unwanted pregnancy

If we shift from the issue of abortion to the problem of unwanted pregnancy, we may ask two questions.

A. How may one deal with an unwanted pregnancy?
B. How may one avoid unwanted pregnancy?

Let us take these in turn. Regarding (A), there are two options:

1. Terminate the pregnancy (abortion).
2. Give birth to an unwanted child.

If one gives birth to an unwanted child, the options are basically four:

a. parenting
b. adoption
c. infanticide
d. abandonment

Strictly, these aren't the only options. In some societies, children are sold into prostitution or virtual slavery. In purely economic terms, children are often treated as commodities. However, this tends not to happen when they are infants, and in any event it is not an ethical option and not one that is considered seriously in the majority of contemporary societies.

Giving birth to an unwanted child raises serious issues. To the woman, there are risks in giving birth that are greater than if she has an abortion at an early stage. There are financial burdens in raising a child that typically run into tens of thousands of dollars. Additionally there are the unquantifiable but equally serious problems of the psychological effects upon a child who is unwanted and upon the mother and possibly the father. Raising a child imposes long-term demands on a parent that many don't want to bear. And there are the effects on society at large of children who are raised by a parent (or parents) who don't want them. Some parents come to love a child that was initially unwanted; but many don't. Much of the neglect of children—often by poor and overburdened single mothers but often by the affluent as well—may owe at least in part to the fact that the children are unwanted. Giving a newborn up for adoption may help minimize these problems, but there are far more orphans in the world than there are adoptive parents, and the health risks of childbirth are the same for a woman whether she keeps the child or gives it up for adoption.

Putting a child up for adoption is sometimes psychologically difficult for a mother. If a woman sees her newborn, she sometimes wants to keep it, even if it has been promised to a couple for adoption. And adoptive children and adults sometimes long to know who their birth parents are. On the positive side, adoption may be considered a moral alternative to reproducing. To adopt an unwanted child provides a family for a child that wouldn't otherwise have one. It also helps to curb overpopulation. If one reproduces, one adds to the world's population. If one adopts an already existing child, the world's population remains unchanged.

Infanticide is, of course, illegal. A newborn is considered a person from a legal standpoint, even though it doesn't acquire many of the characteristics necessary to its being a *person*$_2$ (ability to reason, use language, form life plans, etc.) until later. Abandonment is often tantamount to infanticide. Leaving a newborn untended in a remote area seals its fate. But sometimes, as in Russia and China, newborns are abandoned in locations where it is virtually certain they'll be found and looked after.

These considerations aside, the main problem is how to avoid being confronted with any of these options in the first place. This brings us to question (B) earlier. Here the options are clear.

B. How may one avoid unwanted pregnancy?
    1. Abstinence.
    2. Safe-sex:
        a. rhythm method
        b. contraception
        c. selective sexual practices

Both abortion and childbirth involve risks to the woman. But there are no known health risks to not getting pregnant. Nor are there any social problems generated by nonexistent offspring who were never conceived. They don't do drugs, aren't disruptive at school, and don't commit crimes—and they don't have to pay college tuition. So there are clear advantages to avoiding unwanted pregnancy rather than dealing with it once it has occurred.

Abstinence avoids pregnancy. But it's not for everyone. Even if it were clear that abstinence should be preached to young people (just say no, not me, not now, etc.), what about unmarried adults who don't want children? Should they be celibate throughout their lives (or at least those years when they are capable of reproducing)?

Safe-sex seems to be a more realistic alternative. Contraceptives, properly used, are highly effective at preventing pregnancy (as well as preventing sexually transmitted diseases). For those who have religious objections to contraception, there is both a rhythm method which, though less effective than contraceptives, is still highly effective when carefully practiced. It involves abstaining from sexual intercourse, though not necessarily from other sexual practices, on those days of a month when a woman's menstrual cycle makes her most likely to become pregnant. And for those who aren't comfortable with either of these, there are selective sexual practices (e.g., oral or anal sex) that are 100 percent effective in avoiding pregnancy.

Both sides in the abortion debate can agree that unwanted pregnancies are bad. And they can both agree that it's legally and morally permissible to avoid getting pregnant. Moreover, both can agree (as scientific data establishes) that there are effective ways to avoid unwanted pregnancies. Even if pro-choice and pro-life advocates can find little common ground on how to deal with an unwanted pregnancy once it has occurred, it seems they can find common ground in agreeing that it is best to avoid unwanted pregnancy in the first place. This shifts the emphasis away from abortion onto the question of how best to avoid unwanted pregnancy. If virtually all unwanted pregnancies ceased (excepting the small percentage resulting from rape and failure of contraception and safe-sex methods), then the wrenching personal decisions that some women confront would end. And most of the divisive social problems the issue raises, and the broader social effects of countless unwanted children in the world, could be avoided. Are there moral grounds for shifting the focus from abortion to avoidance of unwanted pregnancies?

The following makes some suggestions in this regard.

Reinterpreting a Woman's "Choice"

I am pro-choice—reluctantly. For the sole reason that if made illegal, abortions would continue to occur under unsafe circumstances . . .

I believe, and can admit, that abortion is a life being discarded. And I'd ask any woman having an abortion to admit the same, to at least accept this much responsibility now, which she didn't earlier, when egg and sperm were still separate, and not an embryo.

Most of my fellow wanderers in the pro-choice camp won't ask even this much . . . Instead, my co-ideologists demand rights without responsibilities. The loudest message when it comes to abortion remains a *fait accompli*: Just accept sex is going to happen; forget about prevention and go straight to the reckless cure.

But sex—especially unprotected sex—doesn't *have* to happen. Why should the assumption be that human beings can't control themselves? If everyone understands that sex can lead to conception, self-control isn't an unlikely message to promote . . .

While promoting and providing contraception, why can't we also just as strongly promote an ethic of self-control and the selflessness that comes with thinking of the "possible life" first and ourselves second? . . .

According to 1998 data from the Alan Guttmacher Institute for Reproductive Health, close to half—47 percent—of unintended pregnancies occur in women who do not use contraception at all. The majority of the remaining 53 percent of unintended pregnancies are due to inconsistent or incorrect use of contraceptive methods . . .

A 1998 study by James Trussell, of Princeton University's Office of Population Research, found that while "perfect use" of the pill resulted in a 0.5 percent pregnancy rate, "typical use" resulted in 5 percent. Similarly, the 3 percent failure rate resulting from "perfect use" of the male condom became 14 percent when used typically.

Somewhere, pretense must end and an honest argument begin. As the numbers suggest, "choice" was made when a couple chose to have unprotected sex . . .

> The right shoots itself in the foot by seeking unilaterally to mandate on a moral issue, but the left does the same with its abortion-on-demand zeal and its zero tolerance for dissent.
>
> Each side forces the other to its extreme, and so the extremists emerge to commandeer the dialogue, thereby alienating the movements from each other. The essence of the debate subsists on each side shutting the other out, when what they need to do is work together to encourage a woman's choice *not* to get pregnant. This way, maybe accountability will kick in first, before the dialogue has to turn to rights.[15]

Both sides, again, can agree that unwanted pregnancies are bad, and that it's permissible to avoid unwanted pregnancies. Is there, beyond this, a moral obligation to avoid unwanted pregnancies? On this many will likely disagree.

Absolutists on the pro-choice side will argue that a woman's right to decide what happens in and to her body includes a right to have sex without regard to pregnancy if she chooses. A right to privacy prohibits anyone from intervening or even intruding moralistically into that dimension of her life. Many on the pro-life side will argue that with rights go responsibilities, and that a right to do what you want with your body includes a responsibility not to use it in ways that have consequences (like unwanted pregnancy) that affect many others (medical personnel who have to perform the abortion if that is elected, insurance companies who pay the cost, the responsible male if he should want the child, society as a whole if an unwanted child is brought into the world, etc.). But as difficult as this issue is, it's one that both sides should be able to discuss without entrenched opinions that currently characterize the debate. The problem of abortion would, for all practical purposes, nearly disappear in nine months if unwanted pregnancies ceased.

12.15 Conclusion

Highly effective and widely available birth control could go a long way toward reducing the rate of abortion. But it wouldn't entirely eliminate the problem. There would still be pregnancies resulting from rape and from the failure of safe-sex practices and contraceptives. And there would still be wanted pregnancies that endangered women's lives. But these are relatively few. Broadening one's perspective away from rights and emphasizing reducing unwanted pregnancies is an approach to which both pro-choice and pro-life might profitably devote their time and energies. Though not perfect, it isn't beset with the probably undecidable questions of whether the unborn is a person (in a meaningful sense or to a significant degree) and whether it has a right to life that supersedes all other considerations.

Study questions

1. Why is it important to try to find a *neutral language* with which to discuss the moral issue of abortion (Section 12.1)?
2. What is it that is aborted when an abortion takes place (Section 12.2)? Why is the way in which this question is answered important to understanding the debate between *pro-life* and *pro-choice* advocates?
3. What did the Supreme Court decide in *Roe v. Wade (1973)* (Section 12.5)?
4. What is Cardoza's point in Key Quote 12A (Section 12.6)? How does it support a woman's *"right to choose"*?
5. For what reasons might some argue that *men* have rights in the abortion issue (Section 12.7)?
6. Do the *unborn have rights* (Section 12.8)?
7. How does the text *define "abortion"* (Definition Box 12B, Section 12.11)? How does abortion differ from feticide (Definition Box 12C)?
8. How does the text distinguish between *human beings* and *persons* (Theory Box 12C, Section 12.9)?
9. What positions do *Thomson, Werner* (Section 12.10), and *Hare* (Section 12.12) take on abortion?
10. How does the text argue that shifting from abortion to the problem of *unwanted pregnancy* may provide some common ground between pro-choice and pro-life advocates?

Notes

1   Peter Singer, *Rethinking Life and Death* (New York: St. Martin's Griffin, 1994), p. 200.
2   Mother Teresa, Nobel Prize Winner, *The New York Times*, December 11, 1979.

3 Ladd Alexander, National Right to Life News, Vol. 7, No. 16, November 10, 1980. Official Publication of the National Right to Life Association.

4 Elizabeth Karlin, Letter to the Editors, *The New York Times*, January 11, 1995.

5 Interestingly, although *Roe v. Wade* is taken to uphold a woman's right to choose, the court actually represents the choice as a medical decision that is the responsibility of the woman's physician.

6 Justice Benjamin Cardoza, *Schloendorff v. Society*, New York (1914).

7 From Barbara Ehrenreich, *Hers* Column, *The New York Times*, February 7, 1985; emphasis in the original.

8 *The New York Times*, August 6, 2002.

9 From Thomas Lynch, "A Man's Right to Choose," Op-Ed, *The New York Times*, July 5, 2000.

10 Pope John Paul II, From *Evangelium Vitae*, Encyclical letter of John Paul II, March 25, 1995; emphases in the original.

11 From Judith Jarvis Thomson, "A Defense of Abortion," *Philosophy & Public Affairs*, Vol. I, No. 1, Fall 1971, 48f.; emphasis in the original.

12 Richard Werner, "Abortion: The Moral Status of the Unborn," *Social Theory and Practice*, Vol. 3, No. 2, Fall 1974, 201–202, 209–11, 216, 218–19.

13 R. M. Hare, "Abortion and the Golden Rule," *Philosophy & Public Affairs*, Vol. 4, No. 3, Spring 1975, 207f.; emphases in the original.

14 *The New York Times*, May 4, 1981.

15 From Julia Gorin, Opinion, *The Christian Science Monitor*, August 14, 2000; emphases in the original.

For more resources:

www.bloomsbury.com/holmes-introduction-to-applied-ethics

13

Medical Aid in Dying, Physician-Assisted Suicide, and Euthanasia

I will neither give a deadly drug to anybody if asked for it, nor will I make a suggestion to this effect.

—The Hippocratic Oath.

For truly, the man who does not know when to die, does not know how to live.

—John Ruskin[1]

Introduction

In this chapter we'll explore the moral issues involved in the question of whether a person has a right to die. In particular, we'll consider suicide, physician-assisted suicide (PAS; or aid in dying, as it's sometimes called), and euthanasia. In so doing, we shall examine the distinctions between killing and letting die and between active and passive euthanasia. We'll consider legal rulings in controversial cases (Quinlan, Cruzan, and Schiavo) as well as the moral issues. Finally, we will consider whether there is a slippery slope from suicide to assisted suicide to euthanasia, such that if one accepts suicide, one is led to accept assisted suicide and euthanasia as well.

13.1 Suicide

More than 44,000 Americans commit suicide each year, 5,000 of them teens and young adults. That's more than die by homicide and more than are killed by drunk drivers.

Although people often feel sad that someone (e.g., a troubled teenager) has committed suicide, they don't usually speak of what they did as a moral wrong. Killing yourself isn't condemned the way killing another person is. To that extent, suicide isn't a compelling moral issue for most people. They think of it as *bad*—or often tragic—but not as wrong.

The issue becomes more complex, however, if we ask whether we have a *right* to commit suicide or to assist others in doing so. Here the lines are sharply drawn. Some believe we should prevent others from taking their own lives if we can, whatever the circumstances. Others feel that sometimes we should actually assist others in committing suicide. It's the second of these views that shall primarily concern us.

While the broader moral issue concerns whether *anyone* (spouse, partner, friend) has a right to assist another in suicide, the more specific issue—and the one that shall primarily concern us—is whether physicians should be allowed to assist suicide in carefully defined circumstances. The circumstances are crucial. No one argues that we should help troubled teens or otherwise healthy adults suffering from depression commit suicide. But many feel it's merciful to help someone end his or her own life if the alternative is a drawn-out, painful death from a terminal illness.

13.2 Self-administering lethal medication versus committing suicide

Choice of language becomes important here, as in discussing abortion. It's illegal in most states in the United States to assist someone in committing suicide. One can usually be charged with manslaughter for the offense. In Illinois one can be charged with inducement to commit suicide if he or she, among other things, exercises substantial control over a person through use of "actual or ostensible religious, political, social, philosophical or other principles" and the person then commits or attempts to commit suicide. But six states (California, Colorado, Montana, Oregon, Vermont, and Washington) allow medical assistance in dying to competent terminally ill adults with six months or fewer to live. The question is how to describe the giving of that aid, which typically consists of providing lethal medication which the patient then self-administers. Is it assisting a person to commit suicide or is it merely assisting a person with dying? Some of the laws specifically state that the provision of the medical aid in question (which is meant to hasten an end to life) shall not for any purpose constitute assisting suicide, which would be illegal. We shall return to this topic in Section 13.7. Quite apart from what various state laws say, we can consider what suicide consists of in ordinary language.

Definition Box 13A

Suicide: Intentionally or knowingly taking your own life.

If a physician sets a lethal medication by your bedside for you to take if pain from a terminal illness becomes too severe, have you committed suicide when you take the medication and die? If so, then the physician has assisted you in committing suicide, which is called PAS. If you haven't committed suicide, then the physician has done something else; he or she has helped you take control of the process of dying by providing you with what might be called medical aid in dying (MAD). You've had the benefit of physician-assisted dying (PAD).

In plain English, if you perform an act (taking a lethal medication) intended to end your life, and it does end your life, then you've killed yourself. And if you've killed yourself intentionally or knowingly, that's suicide. Even if you were suffering from a terminal illness which would have killed you within six months, it's not the illness that killed you but the act you performed. In fact, the point of taking the medication is so that you wouldn't have to die from the illness with all of the suffering that process would entail. If officials of the state give a lethal injection to a person under a death sentence, and he dies from the injection, that's an execution. They've killed him. If you self-administer a comparable substance and die as a result, you've killed yourself. The main difference conceptually (there are many differences ethically and legally, of course) is that the act causing death in the one case is performed by others; in the other case, by you yourself.

Although we speak of dying as something that people do, that can be misleading. Dying is not something you do in the way in which you do something when you perform an action or engage in an activity. It's something that happens to you. Everyone dies, and unless they die instantaneously, they go through a process of dying. That process can be shortened or prolonged, but it can't be stopped. It's like aging, which also is something that people do but isn't an act or activity; it, too, is something that happens to you. It can possibly be slowed (say, by healthy living) and can definitely be hastened (say, by alcoholism and heavy drug use), but it can't be stopped. If a physician gives you pain killers when you're dying from a terminal illness, he or she may be able to minimize the suffering you undergo until the illness kills you. But if he or she gives you a lethal medication that ends your life before the illness does, then the physician has killed you, and that's euthanasia. If, on the other hand, the physician provides you with a lethal medication, and you take it yourself, then you've killed yourself, and that's suicide. Because the physician has assisted you, it's PAS.

Legislators in some states want competent adults suffering from terminal illness to be able to hasten the end of their lives, but they don't want to call it suicide. And they want physicians to be able to assist such people in that undertaking, but they don't want to call it assisted suicide. So, they characterize the patient as having died (which is true) and the physician as having assisted the patient in dying (which also is true). That way, in the eyes of the law the patient hasn't taken his or her own life; hence there's no suicide. And if there's no suicide, there's no PAS.

> ## Key Quote 13A
>
> Factually, legally and medically speaking, it is inaccurate to equate aid in dying with assisted suicide … The Oregon, Washington, Vermont and California laws emphasize that:
>
> *"Actions taken in accordance with [the Act] shall not, for any purpose, constitute suicide, assisted suicide, mercy killing or homicide."*
>
> This is because a person who is choosing medical aid in dying already has a terminal prognosis of six months or less to live. They are not choosing to die; the disease is taking their life.
>
> *Compassion & Choices: Medical Aid in Dying Fact Sheet.*
> *CompassionAndChoices.org*
> *info@compassionandchoices.org*

Left unspecified by this reasoning is what the precise cause of death is. It's not the underlying medical condition (since the whole point of taking the lethal medication is to prevent the medical condition from running its course) and not the termination of his own life by the patient (which would be suicide). The disease is in the process of taking the person's life, as the above statement indicates; but it doesn't do so. It's the cause of the person's dying (a process that may go on for weeks or months) but not of his death (an event that brings that process to an end). The lethal medication is the cause of death.

Because MAD and PAD leave unspecified what causes death when one takes the lethal medication provided by a physician, we shall follow plain English in saying that the patient has committed suicide and the physician has assisted the patient in that act. Bearing in mind that this choice of language is controversial and departs from much of the language recent law uses, we shall define PAS as follows:

Definition Box 13B

Physician-Assisted Suicide
Physician-Assisted Suicide: The provision of assistance, by a physician, to a competent terminally ill person in ending his or her own life.

This definition leaves it open whether either suicide or PAS is morally justified, and if they are, under what conditions. Some of the laws authorizing PAD (but not PAS), for example, require that two physicians confirm that the illness is terminal and two confirm that the patient is competent to make end-of-life decisions. A practical problem that has emerged is that of prescribing the right medication to bring about a swift and painless death, as the following report indicates:

Preventing Prolonged Death in Aid-In-Dying
Two years after an abrupt price increase for a lethal drug used by terminally ill patients to end their lives, doctors in the Northwest are again rethinking aid-in-dying medications—this time because they're taking too long to work.

The concerned physicians say they've come up with yet another alternative to Seconal, the powerful sedative that was the drug of choice under Death with Dignity laws until prices charged by a Canadian company doubled to more than $3,000 per dose. It's the third drug mixture recommended by the doctors whose medication protocols help guide decisions for prescribers in the six states where aid-in-dying is allowed.

The first Seconal alternative turned out to be too harsh, burning patients' mouths and throats, causing some to scream in pain. The second mix, used 67 times, has led to deaths that stretched out hours in some patients—and up to 31 hours in one case . . .

Patients and families are told to expect sleep within 10 minutes and death within four hours. When it takes far longer, family members get worried, even distressed . . . The doctors say this can be addressed with larger doses of the three drugs they have been using . . . plus another heart medication . . . in a four-drug cocktail aimed at quickly inducing death.[2]

The problem of finding the right medication for PAS (or aid-in-dying as the article calls it) is not unlike that of finding the right chemicals to use in death penalty executions, with undesired results being common enough to cause concern. That problem, however, is a practical one.

A moral problem is highlighted by the objection that if practiced, PAS would lead eventually to the acceptance of euthanasia. Euthanasia, as we shall consider in Section 13.4 is performed by someone other than the patient. PAS involves an act by the physician and an act by the patient, the patient's act (say, of self-administering the lethal medication) being the final act leading to death. So, in addition to the question of whether PAS is wrong, there's the question of whether euthanasia is wrong. If PAS (considered in itself) should be permissible but euthanasia wrong, then if the former would lead to the latter, that could be one reason for opposing PAS as a social practice.

13.3 Is there a right to die?

Although, as indicated earlier, the problem of PAS can be framed independently of the question of rights, most of the discussions turn on the notion of rights, and we shall therefore use the language of rights for convenience.

Both abortion and PAS raise questions of privacy rights. We've defined "privacy" as freedom from intrusion into areas of one's life that one hasn't, implicitly or explicitly, opened to others. (See Definition Box 11A, Chapter 11, Section 11.3.) In abortion, the question is whether a pregnant woman has the right to do what she wants with her own body. In PAS, the question is whether people have a right to do what they want with their own lives. More specifically, do people have a right to die—that is, a right to decide when and how their lives shall end? And if so, do they have a right to enlist the help of others in ending their lives? On the face of it, it would seem that prohibiting people from doing what they want with their own lives violates their right to privacy.

Many who are pro-life on the abortion issue (supporting the unborn's right to life) deny there's a right to die. Many who are pro-choice (denying that the unborn has a right to life) affirm a right to die. Although the right to die presumably encompasses a right to commit suicide, and suicide has long been considered a moral issue, many of the problems raised by the question of a right to die are of recent origin, because of advances in medical technology. We can now keep people alive under conditions that would have been impossible in the past, which gives rise to moral and legal problems that didn't arise for earlier generations.

Do you have a right to take your own life? Some feel that your life is yours to do with what you want, at least as long as you don't hurt others. For them, suicide is permissible. Others, often for religious reasons, think that because you didn't give yourself life, it's wrong for you to take it away. For them, suicide is impermissible.

The notion of a right to die might be taken to encompass some or all of three distinguishable rights:

1. The right to kill yourself.
2. The right to be provided with assistance in killing yourself.
3. The right to authorize your killing by another person (euthanasia).

Numbers (2) and (3) might be taken as general rights, in which you're entitled to seek assistance from others in taking your own life or in authorizing others to do it for you. Some people enlist the help of friends or partners, but we'll focus upon the problems for bioethics, where it's the participation of physicians that's at issue; hence we'll take (2) to relate specifically to PAS. With regard to (3), we'll discuss such authorizations only in the context of terminal illness, in which the question is whether "mercy killing" (as euthanasia is sometimes called) is justified.

As with many contemporary issues, the discussion of PAS tends to be framed in terms of rights. As we have seen with the abortion issue, one can also speak simply of what is morally right or wrong, permissible or impermissible. The following passage does so, and provides a useful illustration of the case for PAS:

Legal, Moral and Social Implications of Physician-Assisted Suicide

If one accepts the premise that it is morally permissible for a person to terminate or refuse medical treatment with the intent that it shall cause his death then, I propose, it must be morally permissible for another person to provide assistance to help in the accomplishment of that same end. By way of illustration, consider the following scenarios.

Background: John was a male fashion model and fiercely independent. He has no close friends or family. Before he became ill he took great pride and pleasure in his outward appearance. John is now bedridden with an incurable illness. He remains competent and rational and understands his prognosis and medical options. He has open sores on his face which ooze and produce a foul odor. He cannot bear the sight of himself. He is incontinent and must rely upon others to perform his most intimate personal hygiene. He experiences severe abdominal pain due to the cancerous tumor on his liver. He *can* be medicated sufficiently to dull the pain, but it will leave him in a "medically-induced coma." He is not on life-sustaining machines, so none can be turned off. He has been advised by his long-time physician that he may live another six months in a condition of continual deterioration. He has repeatedly expressed his desire to terminate his life. His requests have been persistent and voluntary. His physician (Sam) intends to honor, as the law permits, John's medical treatment decisions.

Scenario 1: John has consulted with Sam and is informed that if he wishes to terminate his life his only recourse is to starve himself to death. This will take several days and, in order that he not feel pain, he would need to be sedated into a condition of unconsciousness. John does not want to die in pain nor does he wish to linger for days in an unconscious condition. However, he finds his existence intolerable. He refuses food and water, intending that it should cause his death. After suffering the predicted pain, he dies several days later.

Scenario 2: John has consulted with Sam and is informed that Sam can provide a medicine which if taken in the prescribed dose will cause him to die a peaceful death in a matter of minutes. John obtains the medicine and, when he feels the time is right, and intending his death, he takes the medication and dies a few minutes later.

In order to succeed in showing that PAS is *not* morally permissible, one would have to demonstrate a morally relevant difference between these two situations. Let us look first at the morality of John's actions.

The morality of John's actions: In both situations John's intent (to bring about his death), his motive (to end his suffering), and his end (death) are the same. Also, in both scenarios it is John's action (for I would argue that an action is involved in his directive that he not be given nourishment or hydration) that is the *direct cause* of his death. In neither case was John's death directly caused by his underlying medical condition. The sole difference is that in the second scenario, John has obtained the means to achieve his desired end from his physician . . .

The morality of the physician's (Sam) actions: In both situations Sam's intent is not to cause John's death, but to honor the reasonable directives of his patient. In the first scenario, Sam acted by failing to forcefully feed John when it was clear that he would die if he were not fed. In the second, he acted by providing the means for John to kill himself. The end, of course, was the same in both instances. On this analysis, I see no reason to distinguish morally between the acts of Sam in the two scenarios. If anything, one could make the argument that the differences which do exist should lead one to prefer the acts of Sam in scenario #2, for in scenario #2, although Sam did perform an act (the provision of medication) his is not the act that directly causes John's death. There is an intervening action by John that is the direct cause of his death. The last NECESSARY act leading to John's death in scenario #2 is performed by John himself. This constitutes one difference between the two scenarios. Another difference is the fact that in scenario #1, John suffers, whereas in scenario #2, he does not. True, he dies in both instances, but hasn't Sam performed a beneficent act in scenario #2, by decreasing the amount of suffering that John will experience? **In any event, there is no morally relevant difference between these two scenarios such that we should prefer scenario #1 over scenario #2.**[3]

The above reasoning, again, frames the issue in terms of what is permissible (or morally right) rather than in terms of rights—entitlements. And though it doesn't expressly mention the principle of universalizability (see Theory Box 1F, Chapter 1, Section 1.10), it makes use of the same reasoning involved in the principle by asking whether there are morally relevant dissimilarities between the two scenarios and concluding that there are not. Hence, so the argument goes, if the first scenario is permissible, then the second must be also.

Whether they are framed in terms of rights or not, the issues that arise in connection with terminal illness turn on a distinction between killing and "letting die." If you're suffering from a terminal illness, then you're presumed to be going to die (usually within six months), no matter what anyone does. The only options, so far as life and death are concerned, are whether to shorten your life (by suicide or euthanasia) or allow yourself to die from the illness or injury. The only choices are between killing yourself (or having someone else kill you), and letting yourself die; or between killing and letting die, as it is termed by ethicists.

The problem of killing versus letting die arises in a small percentage of abortion cases as well. Sometimes if a woman gives birth she'll die in the process, whereas if she has an abortion she'll live but the unborn will die in the process. The option is whether to kill the unborn through abortion (ignoring for the moment the complications with the definition of abortion discussed in Chapter 12, Section 12.11) or to let the woman die. There, however, the issue is whether to let one person die (the pregnant woman) or to kill another being (the unborn). In the cases at hand, as in the above example of the physician and his patient, the question is whether to kill or let die one and the same person: the patient who is suffering from the terminal illness.

13.4 Active and passive euthanasia

Euthanasia is often thought of as "mercy killing"—the killing of terminally ill persons to end their suffering. It's not suicide, because the act bringing about their death isn't performed by the persons themselves; it's performed by someone else, presumably (we shall assume) a physician. When it involves an *act* of killing (e.g., giving a person a lethal injection) it's called *active euthanasia*. But letting a person die, on the other hand (e.g., by withholding medication or not resuscitating him if he suffers cardio or respiratory failure), has sometimes been called *passive euthanasia*, as in the following passage from philosopher James Rachels (1941–2003):

> The distinction between active and passive euthanasia is thought to be crucial for medical ethics. The idea is that it is permissible, at least in some cases, to withhold treatment and allow a patient to die, but it is never permissible to take any direct action designed to kill the

patient ... However, a strong case can be made against this doctrine ... To begin with a familiar type of situation, a patient who is dying of incurable cancer of the throat is in terrible pain, which can no longer be satisfactorily alleviated. He is certain to die within a few days, even if present treatment is continued, but he does not want to go on living for those days since the pain is unbearable. So he asks the doctor for an end to it, and his family joins in the request.

Suppose the doctor agrees to withhold treatment, as the conventional doctrine says he may. The justification for his doing so is that the patient is in terrible agony, and since he is going to die anyway, it would be wrong to prolong his suffering needlessly. But now notice this. If one simply withholds treatment, it may take the patient longer to die, and so he may suffer more than he would if more direct action were taken and a lethal injection given. This fact provides strong reason for thinking that, once the initial decision not to prolong his agony has been made, active euthanasia is actually preferable to passive euthanasia, rather than the reverse ... Part of my point is that the process of being "allowed to die" can be relatively slow and painful, whereas being given a lethal injection is relatively quick and painless.[4]

It should be noted that so-called passive euthanasia—that is, withholding medical treatment from the terminally ill—is now widely practiced with advance consent from the patient. It just isn't called euthanasia. Euthanasia is killing, and killing is illegal even if done to end a person's suffering. Passive euthanasia is considered "letting die," which supposedly is distinguished from killing. Three landmark cases dealt with the issue.

13.5 The Quinlan, Cruzan, and Schiavo cases

The widely publicized Quinlan case was pivotal in the development of the "right to die" movement. In 1975, 21-year-old Karen Ann Quinlan, who had been taking tranquilizers, collapsed after having a few drinks. The combination of drugs and alcohol caused her to slip into a coma. She was put on a respirator from which her parents wanted her removed when they became convinced the coma was irreversible. In 1976 the New

Jersey Supreme Court authorized the removal. It was thought that removing her from the respirator would allow her to die. But against all expectations, she survived in a coma before dying from pneumonia more than 9 years later.

In a second case, 25-year-old Nancy Beth Cruzan was first in a coma, then in a persistent vegetative state (PVS) following an auto accident in 1983. Her parents wanted nutrition and hydration tubes removed so that she might be allowed to die. In 1988, a Missouri court ruled that the tubes could be removed. But the Missouri Supreme Court overruled the lower court and said that such removal was impermissible unless there was "clear and convincing evidence" that such would have been her wish. That ruling was upheld by the US Supreme Court. When subsequent evidence proved "clear and convincing" to the Missouri court, the tubes were removed and she died soon afterward in 1990.

In the Quinlan case, the authorization was to remove a ventilator, that is, an instrument of medical technology designed to keep people alive who are unable to breathe on their own. In the Cruzan case, authorization was extended to removing the means of providing food and water. The administering of food and water under such circumstances came to be viewed as forms of medical treatment. Since a person has a right to refuse medical treatment, a person has a right to refuse nutrition and hydration. Because Cruzan was unable to communicate her wishes, the court relied upon prior evidence regarding what would have been her wish had she been able to express herself.

Many people now have living wills, in which they put in writing what they would or would not want done if they're ever terminally ill and incapable of communicating their wishes. They also often authorize "do not resuscitate" (DNR) orders, instructing medical personnel not to resort to emergency measures to revive them if, say, their heart should stop or they should stop breathing.

Also of interest here is that Quinlan was in a *coma*; Cruzan was in a *PVS*. It's sometimes difficult to be certain whether a coma is irreversible or whether a PVS is permanent.

Such issues were at stake in a much-publicized Florida case. Twenty-six-year-old Terri Schiavo's heart stopped temporarily in 1990, causing severe brain damage and leaving her in a PVS. As reported in the *New York Times*, September 24, 2004, this meant "that her eyes are open and might widen, stare or follow objects, but that her brain is incapable of emotion, memory or thought. She breathes on her own, often moaning, but depends on a gastric tube for sustenance." After she had been in that condition for years, her husband—who was her legal guardian—wanted feeding and hydration tubes removed. He said that was what she would want, and that she had once made him promise that he wouldn't let her be kept alive artificially in that way. Her parents and siblings, however, wanted her kept alive, believing she would improve with therapy. They said *that* was what she would want. The husband's wishes eventually prevailed legally, and she died after the tubes were removed.

13.6 Consciousness, coma, and persistent vegetative states

It's important to distinguish between a coma and a PVS, and between both of these and more recently recognized conditions. All are understood by reference to the notion of consciousness, as the following passage emphasizes:

> Consciousness has two dimensions: wakefulness and awareness … Unconsciousness implies global or total unawareness and is characteristic of both coma and the vegetative state. Patients in a coma are unconscious because they lack both wakefulness and awareness. Patients in a vegetative state are unconscious because, though they are wakeful, they lack awareness …
>
> A wakeful unconscious state that lasts longer than a few weeks is referred to as a persistent vegetative state … A permanent vegetative state, on the other hand, means an irreversible state, which like all clinical diagnoses in medicine, is based on probabilities, not absolutes.[5]

For our purposes, we may define these as follows[6]:

Definition Box 13C

Coma and Vegetative States
Coma: A sleep-like state of unconsciousness from which one cannot be roused.

> **Persistent Vegetative State: An unconscious state, with sleep-wake cycles, lasting roughly more than one month (PVS).**
> **Permanent Vegetative State (PmVS): A persistent vegetative state judged to be irreversible.**

Each of the above should be distinguished from so-called locked-in states (LIS) and minimally conscious states:

Definition Box 13D

Locked-in State (LIS): A state in which consciousness and cognition are retained but movement and communication are impossible because of paralysis of the voluntary motor system.

Unlike those who are comatose or in a PVS, a person in an LIS may be fully conscious and rational, often able to communicate with others through blinking the eyes. In one such case in France, a man succeeded in writing a novel through these means.

Since 2002, a new category has been recognized, marking a state between coma and PVS, on the one hand, and consciousness on the other. Sometimes it's represented as an area between a PVS and a PmVS. In this area, there is some evidence of limited and fluctuating awareness of self and environment. This can be defined as follows:

Definition Box 13E

Minimally Conscious State (MCS): Limited and intermittent awareness of self and environment.

Various of these conditions are sometimes confused with one another, even by some in the medical profession. People often come out of comas, but sometimes—often to the amazement of doctors—people in these other states surprisingly regain consciousness (or in the case of an LIS, the ability to move and speak). The following are some examples:

Injured in '88, Officer Awakes in '96

Mr. Dockery, a member of the four-person police force in Walden, Tenn ... was shot when responding to a call on Sept. 17, 1988.

Most of the years since he has been in a nursing home, but last weekend ... he was moved to Columbia Parkridge Medical Center here, where he spoke for the first time since he had been shot.

Mr. Dockery's relatives said that in his first 18 hours after awakening he talked almost nonstop, recalling names and middle names of a host of people, the names of his horses and the color of his jeep, and fending off suggestions that he rest. . .

Doctors at the hospital call Mr. Dockery's improvement a miracle as well. They have stopped short of calling the state from which he emerged a coma.

Instead, they have used the phrase "persistent vegetative state" or "locked-in state" because Mr. Dockery remained conscious, was able to breathe on his own and could respond with eye motions to some questions at times.[7]

* * *

After 16 Years, Woman Awakens to Life

For 16 years, Patricia White Bull was unresponsive to the world: unable to speak, swallow or move much. On Dec. 24 she snapped back to consciousness ... Doctors cannot explain why Ms. White Bull, 42, awakened from the catatonic state she slipped into while delivering her fourth child ... Since then, Ms. White Bull has been speaking her children's names and catching up on family history.[8]

* * *

Mute 19 Years, He Helps Reveal Brain's Mysteries

Terry Wallis showed no improvement in the first year [after a 1984 auto accident], and doctors soon pronounced him to be in a persistent vegetative state, and gave him virtually no chance of recovery, his parents said . . .

But at some point after his accident, probably within months, Mr. Wallis ... entered what is called a minimally conscious state ... The diagnosis, established formally in 2002 is given to people who are severely brain damaged but occasionally responsive. In their good

> moments, they can track objects with their eyes, respond to com-
> mands by blinking, grunting or making small movements . . .
>   None of which made the day he said "Mom" any less thrilling . . .
> He was suddenly speaking; it was a transformation. He was still disa-
> bled, barely able to move or speak, but he was recognizable as Terry.[9]

Cases of these sorts are rare. But they show that it's sometimes difficult to
be certain that a coma is irreversible or that a PVS has become a PmVS.
They also indicate the uncertainty about how most accurately to label
those in various states of mental incapacitation. In the first example
above, the doctors appear to be using PVS and LIS synonymously and
to be distinguishing both from coma. In the third example, Terry Wallis
is represented as having evolved from a PVS to a MCS, yet in 2003 when
he first began speaking, he was represented as having been in a coma for
19 years.

13.7 Killing and letting die

Most people think there's a strong moral presumption against killing people.
If the presumption can be overridden at all, it can be overridden only for
compelling reasons, such as self-defense. There's also a presumption against
letting people die, but in commonsense thinking it's probably not nearly as
strong a presumption. If you could easily save someone from dying (say,
by picking up a phone and calling 911), most would agree that you should
do so. But if you had to leave school or quit your job, sell your car to raise
the money, and then travel ten thousand miles to save the life of someone
unknown to you, many people would think twice. Even if they decided to
do it, they might think they were going beyond what's morally required of
them. But if you could prolong your dying grandmother's life for only a few
days—and at great cost in suffering to her—many would say it's far better to
withhold life-preserving treatment and allow her to die. These issues, however, are complex, both philosophically and morally. Let us separate and
consider in turn two questions:

1. Is there a distinction between killing and letting die?
2. If so, is there a moral difference between killing and letting die?

Specifically:

a. Is killing worse than letting die?
b. Is the obligation not to kill more stringent than the obligation not to let die (i.e., to save)?

In answer to (1), it's clear that there's a distinction between the two (meaning, a distinction conceptually or by definition). But it's more complex than is sometimes assumed.

It's often assumed that to kill is actively to *do* something (like shooting or stabbing), whereas letting die is merely *not* doing something (like not giving a life-saving medicine). That is, it's assumed that killing is an *act of commission*, whereas letting die is merely an *act of omission*. Thus, if—in anticipation of inheriting his fortune—you deliberately give your sick uncle a poison instead of his medication, you've killed him. On the other hand, if you simply withhold life-saving medication and he dies as a result, you've let him die. In the one case, you have performed an act of commission. In the other, you have performed an act of omission. But there's more complexity to this than meets the eye.

This distinction between acts of commission and acts of omission figures in many difficult moral problems. Let us try to understand it more clearly.

Theory Box 13A

Acts of Commission and Acts of Omission
Act of Commission: Intentionally or knowingly bringing about a certain state of affairs.
Act of Omission: intentionally or knowingly refraining from bringing about a certain state of affairs.

Putting the cat out is an act of commission. You have to get up, open the door, and let the cat through. Not letting the cat out is an act of omission. You simply decide not to get up and open the door, which you can do without physically doing anything other than what you're already doing, for example, sitting and watching TV. An observer can see you perform the first act, because you have to move to perform it. An observer can't see you perform the second act, because it's a mental act and doesn't require doing anything readily observable.

Though it might seem from this that killing is an act of commission and letting die an act of omission, sometimes letting die is an act of commission.

For example, in the Quinlan case earlier (Section 13.5), somebody had to perform an act of commission (turning off the respirator) in order (so they thought) to let Karen Quinlan die. In the second and third cases, someone had to remove the tubes providing nutrition and hydration to Nancy Ann Cruzan and Terri Schiavo in order to let them die. Those are both acts of commission. So sometimes letting die is an act of omission, but other times it can be an act of commission.

Further, when letting die is an act of commission, it involves *withdrawing* continuous medical support that's keeping a person alive (as was true in both the Quinlan and Cruzan cases), but it might also sometimes involve *discontinuing* medical treatment which isn't continuous but is no less essential to keeping a person alive. Those who need dialysis (to compensate for kidney malfunction) don't need to remain hooked up to the dialysis machine twenty-four hours a day in the way in which someone on a respirator does. Rather, they go in for treatment periodically. Similarly, someone undergoing chemotherapy doesn't receive the chemicals constantly but only intermittently. This suggests that we need to recognize three different kinds of letting die, which requires more precise definitions. Let us begin by giving plain English definitions of some key terms:

Definition Box 13F

Death: The cessation of life.
Dying: A pathological process which, if uninterrupted, will result in death.
Being Dead: The state of one who was once alive but is no longer.

The definition of "dead" leaves open whether or not death is permanent. With advances in medical technology and the science of resuscitation, people now sometimes speak of people coming back from the dead—if, for example, their hearts have stopped and they're not breathing for extended periods but can then be revived. Regarding dying, it's important to specify that the process is pathological, otherwise life itself would constitute dying, since living is a process which eventuates in death.

Death is an event that everyone will experience. Being dead is a state everyone will eventually be in. Dying is a process everyone will go through who hasn't died instantaneously. In other words, death, dying, and being dead *happen* to people; they're not things people do in the sense of acting.

But death and dying relate to actions people perform, because people sometimes have some control over the process of dying, hence over the timing and circumstances of their death. So let us define two notions referring to actions that figure prominently in some of the more vexing medical cases.

Definition Box 13G

Killing: Causing death.
Letting Die: Refraining from intervening in pathological processes (e.g., terminal illness) which, if uninterrupted, will cause death.

There are three main ways of intervening in the process of dying:

1. Stopping the process, for example, by providing cardio-pulmonary resuscitation (CPR), placing a person on life support (e.g., a respirator), or administering a life-preserving medication. Each of these interventions can be said to save the person's life.
2. Prolonging the process, for example, by placing a person on life support, artificially providing nutrition and hydration or administering life-extending medication. These measures don't save the person's life but they extend that life.
3. Hastening the process, for example, by removing life-support (such as by taking a person off a respirator) or discontinuing life-sustaining treatment (such as by withholding nutrition and hydration).

But suppose the process can't be stopped by the above means, and there's no way to hasten it further (the patient isn't on life support or being fed intravenously, so there's no technological support to withhold or withdraw); and yet the patient doesn't want to endure the pain that a continuation of the process would entail? The only option is to stop the process, but by other means than those enumerated in (1). The main options that need to be added to those in (1) are:

1. Administering a lethal injection (euthanasia).
2. Providing the patient with the means to self-administer a lethal medication.

If a physician gives the patient a lethal injection, he or she kills the patient, and that's euthanasia. That seems clear. But if the patient self-administers the same (or comparable) chemicals, now called medication, orally, is that suicide, and has the physician assisted in suicide by providing the medication?

Whether we call the patient's death suicide depends upon what we consider the cause of death to be. If the lethal medication is the cause, then it's suicide; if the underlying medical condition is the cause (the disease, the pathological process), then it's not suicide. If a physician kills a patient by giving a lethal injection with the intention of ending the patient's suffering by terminating his life, it's hard to see why a patient's self-administering a lethal medication with the intention of ending his suffering by terminating his life isn't killing himself. In other words, the same reasoning by which the physician's act is said to be a killing would seem to apply to the patient's act. If that's so, then the patient's act is one of suicide. Yet the laws permitting the self-administration of lethal medication in these circumstances don't call it suicide; they hold that death is the result of the disease.

Recall Key Quote 13A in Section 13.2, which says: "People who consider aid in dying find the suggestion that they are committing suicide deeply offensive, stigmatizing and inaccurate." This suggests that the reason legislators and some supporters of the right to die don't want to call the deaths in question suicides is because of the emotive meaning of the term. Remember the distinction between descriptive and emotive meaning in Theory Box 1A, in Chapter 1, Section 1.3:

> **Descriptive Meaning**: The beliefs a word or sentence tends to express (on the part of the speaker) or to produce in others.
>
> **Emotive Meaning**: The feelings or attitudes a word or sentence tends to express (on the part of the speaker) or evoke in others.

The fact that the word "suicide" has negative associations that make it "deeply offensive" and "stigmatizing" helps explain the reluctance to use the term in this connection. That is, it may be the term's emotive meaning that is objectionable. But part of the reluctance may be because the term's descriptive meaning (intentionally or knowingly taking your own life) triggers legal problems, because providing assistance in these circumstances would seem to be assisting suicide, and assisting suicide is illegal. So there are psychological and legal reasons for the reluctance to characterize the patient's act as suicide and the physician's as assisting suicide. For those reasons, there's strong motivation to choose other terms to describe the process, such as medically assisted dying or physician-assisted dying, even though they're arguably imprecise and euphemistic. It's interesting to note that we think of Socrates as having been put to death after his conviction in Athens, not as having committed suicide, even though he self-administered the hemlock that killed him; but we think of Seneca, the Stoic philosopher (4 BCE–65 CE) as having committed suicide when he took his own life under orders to do so by the emperor Nero.

We can now distinguish three ways the term "letting die" may be understood:

Definition Box 13H

Letting Die

Letting Die₁: Refraining from intervening in pathological processes (e.g., the progression of terminal illness) which, if uninterrupted, will cause death. There are three kinds of circumstances:

1. Intervening would *save* life, in which case the issue is between **letting die** and **saving**. (Thus, if A withholds medication B needs to recover from an otherwise fatal illness, A lets B die.)

2. Intervening would *prolong* but not save life, in which case the issue is between **letting die** and **prolonging life**. (Thus, if A withholds medication needed to extend B's life, though the illness will eventually prove fatal, A lets B die.)

3. Intervening would *terminate* life, in which case the issue is between **letting die** and **killing**. Two kinds of cases:
   a. A refrains from giving B a *lethal injection* that would spare B the final stages of a terminal disease. (Thus, if life can neither be saved nor prolonged, A lets B die from the disease if A refrains from killing B by giving the lethal injection.)
   b. A refrains from providing B with a *lethal medication* that would spare B the final stages of a terminal disease. (Thus,

A lets B die from the disease rather than assisting B in killing himself by taking the lethal medication.)

Letting Die$_2$: Removing conditions that are impeding patho-logical processes which would otherwise cause death. (Thus, if A unplugs a respirator that's keeping B alive, A lets B die in this sense by allowing the disease to cause B's death.)

Letting Die$_3$: Discontinuing intermittent interventions in patho-logical processes which would otherwise cause death. (Thus, terminating treatment like dialysis that has been begun but isn't con-tinuous is letting die in this sense.)

It may be helpful to have a visual representation of these relationships. In the following, we may take "intentional action" to be deliberate behavior undertaken for specific purposes, as opposed to inadvertent acts or reflexive bodily movements.

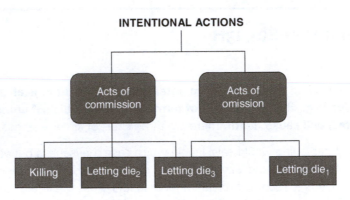

Letting die$_1$ and letting die$_3$ are acts of omission; letting die$_2$ an act of commission.[10] In the standard medical situation, letting die$_1$ would be wrong; the responsibility of physicians is to restore health and preserve life where they can. Letting die$_2$ would normally be the patient's choice; if he or she wanted life prolonged as long as possible, it would be wrong to stop medical treatment that would make that possible; if he or she didn't, it would be permissible to discontinue treatment. Letting die$_2$ and letting die$_3$ would presumably be permissible if the patient was competent and expressed a wish to be allowed to die, or was incompetent but had left a directive (e.g., a Living Will) indicating that such would be his or her preference.

What is most problematic is letting die$_1$ in situations like (3) in Definition Box 13H above. Options like the intervention specified in (3a) (giving a lethal injection) are illegal, because they would constitute euthanasia, but many people think they're a moral option. So letting die in that sense is legally required unless the physician opts for the intervention specified in (3b). Interventions such as that specified in (3b) (providing lethal medication for the patient to take) is legal in six states, as we've said, and is held to be moral by many people (though the procedure is described by many of its advocates as receiving medical aid in dying rather than as suicide).

There is one more complexity we need to take account of. It's that killing and letting die aren't always mutually exclusive. Sometimes letting die (in any of the three senses) is part of killing. If A shoots B and then refrains from getting help while B bleeds to death, A has killed B, even though a component of what he does in the process is to let B die. In a case more directly relevant to the bioethical issues, consider the following from philosopher Shelly Kagan:

> Consider this case: my rival is sure to win the coveted Wise Prize for Living Philosophers, unless he dies before a given date—in which case the lucrative award will go to me. Fortunately for me, he lies comatose in the hospital, and his condition is deteriorating. Unfortunately for me, he is being sustained by a variety of life-support equipment, and he will not die in time for me to win in his stead. Seizing my chance, I sneak into his room late at night, and turn the machinery off. He breathes a last breath—and dies. I have killed him.
>
> Contrast this with the following case: after months of seeing their comatose son kept alive through the use of exotic and resource-consuming medical equipment, the parents decide it would be better to let their son die than to meaninglessly prolong his deteriorating life. The proper legal/medical boards add their consent, the duly authorized doctor disconnects the life-support machines—and the boy dies. After months of prolonging life, the doctor has allowed him to die.
>
> Not everyone, perhaps, will agree with the intuitive judgments I have offered about these two cases. But many, I think will be inclined to accept them. When I maliciously unplug my rival's life-support machines, I kill him; when the doctor—acting out of due concern for all those involved—disconnects the machines preserving the comatose boy, she merely allows him to die.[11]

Interestingly, most people would say that if they were locked in a room without food and water until they died, the person who did this had killed them.

But when food and water are withheld from a terminally ill person (or one in a PmVS), the resultant death isn't called killing (which would be illegal) but merely letting die.

Simplifying the above, we may say that, in the medical contexts, *withholding*, *withdrawing*, and *discontinuing* medical treatment may all be considered instances of letting die. All three are practiced. They simply aren't called passive euthanasia, since passive euthanasia is still euthanasia, and euthanasia is illegal.

13.8 Is there a moral difference between killing and letting die?

Whether there is a moral difference between killing and letting die is posed in this well-known example, again from philosopher James Rachels, in which he describes two hypothetical cases.

> In the first, Smith stands to gain a large inheritance if anything should happen to his six-year- old cousin. One evening while the child is taking his bath, Smith sneaks into the bathroom and drowns the child, and then arranges things so that it will look like an accident.
>
> In the second, Jones also stands to gain if anything should happen to his six-year-old cousin. Like Smith, Jones sneaks in planning to drown the child in his bath. However, just as he enters the bathroom Jones sees the child slip and hit his head, and fall face down in the water. Jones is delighted; he stands by, ready to push the child's head back under if it is necessary, but it is not necessary. With only a little thrashing about the child drowns all by himself, "accidentally," as Jones watches and does nothing.
>
> Now Smith killed the child, whereas Jones "merely" let the child die. That is the only difference between them. Did either man behave better, from a moral point of view? If the difference between killing and letting die were in itself a morally important matter, one should say that Jones's behavior was less reprehensible than Smith's. But does one really want to say that? I think not.[12]

Rachels's contention is that killing isn't in itself any worse morally than letting die, hence active euthanasia (which involves killing) isn't any worse than passive euthanasia (which involves letting die). If one accepts this conclusion, one might argue that, since passive euthanasia is now practiced, there is no good reason not to legalize active euthanasia as well.

We've seen that there is a clear—if complex—distinction between killing and letting die. But is there a moral difference between the two? And if so, is killing worse than letting die, or is the reverse sometimes true?

Killing and letting die are doings, actions people perform. As such they may be considered events. And as events, they may be considered abstractively or contextually.

Theory Box 13B

Perspectives on Killing and Letting Die

Abstractively Considered: Considered in detailed, morally neutral terms in isolation from motives, intentions, and the broader social context of practices, purposes, and values.
Contextually Considered: Considered from a moral point of view in light of motives, intentions, and the broader social setting of practices, purposes, and values.

Considered abstractively, there's no moral difference between killing and letting die. But in that sense, there's no moral difference between any two acts. Separate acts from their context and describe them in sufficient detail—as but movements of bodies, or more microscopically still, as movements of molecules and atoms—and they're stripped of everything that could give them moral significance. The same with their consequences. Take them pragmatically, however, in the living contexts in which we encounter them, and they come laden with moral significance.

The issue over killing and letting die admits of this solution: considered abstractively, there is and can be no moral distinction between the two. Considered contextually, there's sometimes a moral difference between them and sometimes not. When there is a moral difference, sometimes (probably most of the time, though this is debatable) killing is worse than letting die and sometimes letting die is worse than killing.

In the Rachels case of Smith and Jones, the examples are set up contextually—replete with motives and intentions and assumptions of a social context that contains a system of inheritance. As framed contextually, there's no discernible moral difference between Smith and Jones. Both are rotten to the core. But Rachels concludes from this that there's no intrinsic difference between killing and letting die. If that's thought to follow from the judgment that there's no moral difference between the two men, it's a non-sequitur. What is at issue is whether there's a moral difference between the two acts, not between the two men.

Theory Box 13C

Persons, Acts, and Consequences
In commonsense terms, we can distinguish among **persons**, the **acts** they perform, and the **consequences** of the acts they perform. The moral judgments we make of persons and acts differ. Persons we judge as **good or bad**, virtuous or vicious, honorable or dishonorable, kind or unkind, and so on, usually with reference to their motives and intentions. Actions we judge not only as good or bad, but also as **right or wrong, permissible or impermissible, prohibited or obligatory**, typically with regard to rules or principles or the consequences of the acts. Although all acts (in a morally relevant sense) have motives and intentions, they're primarily relevant to the evaluation of persons, not acts. Consequences can only be good or bad. It's with actions that morality is primarily concerned (though so-called **virtue ethics** shifts the emphasis to persons). Judgments of right and wrong often depend upon our evaluation of consequences (consequentialists say they always depend on consequences) and sometimes on the evaluation of persons.

As we've said, there's no moral difference between the two men, Smith and Jones. If we focus upon the particular acts in the example (one of killing, the other of letting die) there is, of course, no moral difference between them either. As the example is designed, the particular acts are both wrong. But it doesn't follow from this that there's no moral difference between killing and letting die as *kinds* of acts. Indeed, Rachels acknowledges this when he says:

> [I]t is very easy to conflate the question of whether killing is, in itself, worse than letting die, with the very different question of whether most actual cases of killing and more reprehensible than most actual

cases of letting die. Most actual cases of killing are clearly terrible . . . and one hears of such cases every day. On the other hand, one hardly ever hears of a case of letting die, except for the actions of doctors who are motivated by humanitarian reasons. So one learns to think of killing in a much worse light than of letting die. But this does not mean that there is something about killing that makes it in itself worse than letting die. Rather, the other factors—the murderer's motive of personal gain, for example, contrasted with the doctor's humanitarian motivation—account for different reactions to the different cases.

I have argued that killing is not in itself any worse than letting die; if my contention is right, it follows that active euthanasia is not any worse than passive euthanasia.[13]

13.9 Is there a slippery slope from suicide to assisted suicide to euthanasia?

We've said that many people fear that if suicide were generally accepted, then PAS would come to be practiced, and if it were practiced, euthanasia would eventually be accepted.

For those who oppose euthanasia that would be bad. For those who support it that would be good. (We'll confine ourselves to consensual euthanasia for medical reasons.) Whether or not both sides can be brought into agreement on the issue, they should in principle be able to agree on whether there is a slippery slope here.

The notion of a slippery slope is a useful metaphor, but it can be understood in different ways:

Theory Box 13D

Contingent and Logical Slippery Slopes
A Contingently Slippery Slope (CSS): Any situation in which the acceptance of one position will *in fact* (or with high probability) lead to the acceptance of a second position.

> **A Logically Slippery Slope (LSS): Any situation in which accept-ance of one position *logically or morally* requires the acceptance of a second position (whether the second is in fact eventually accepted or not).**

Whether there is a CSS from suicide to PAS to euthanasia is a factual ques-tion. It depends on religious, psychological, sociological, and perhaps pol-itical considerations that can vary from culture to culture. From a purely practical standpoint, it's one of the most important questions. But it doesn't raise the central philosophical issues.[14]

The interesting philosophical question is whether there is an LSS from sui-cide to PAS to euthanasia. Does *consistency* require that if one accepts suicide, one should accept PAS and euthanasia as well? Or are there dissimilarities among the three such that one can quite consistently regard suicide as mor-ally permissible but deny—or at least seriously question—the permissibility of the other two? And remember, we're talking about moral permissibility, not legal. Suicide isn't illegal, though attempting suicide is illegal in some states. Assisted suicide is illegal, though the provision of medical aid in dying (what we've been calling PAS) is legal in six states. Euthanasia is illegal.

Notice that there might be a CSS without there being an LSS, and vice versa. People might come to accept PAS and euthanasia if suicide were com-monly accepted without there being compelling logical or moral reasons to do so. By the same token, there might be logical and/or moral reasons why people *should* accept PAS and euthanasia (if they accept suicide), even if they don't.

13.10 The case for a logically slippery slope

Consider a line of reasoning that might be thought to lead down the LSS.

A. 1. One may permissibly take one's own life.[15]
    2. Whatever one may permissibly do, one may permissibly request another's assistance in doing.
    3. Therefore: One may permissibly request a physician's assistance in taking one's own life (PAS).

4. Whatever one may permissibly request a physician's assistance in doing, one may permissibly request a physician to do on one's behalf.
5. Therefore: One may permissibly request a physician to end one's life.
6. Therefore a physician may permissibly end one's life on request (euthanasia).

The question of a slippery slope arises only if one assumes that suicide is morally permissible, so we'll make that assumption for purposes of argument. And we'll assume in (2) through (6) that we're talking about situations of terminal illness that involve considerable suffering. If we assume that suicide is morally permissible, then we may take premise (1) to be true. The question, then, so far as a possible LSS is concerned, is whether steps (2) through (6) follow from (1).

There are two problems with the argument as it stands, however. The first is that premises (2) and (4) are suspect; (2) can be taken to be an extrapolation from (1).There are some things that one may permissibly do but may not permissibly request another's help in doing. If I'm writing a book to be published under my own name, it's wrong to ask someone's help in writing it (I'm mindful that celebrities and politicians regularly to this) if there's not to be attribution. It's permissible to play in a chess tournament, but it isn't permissible to ask for help in playing. The second problem is that even when requesting help from someone is permissible, it doesn't follow that the other person may permissibly comply with the request. In order for PAS to be morally justified, physicians must be morally justified in actually assisting suicide; it's not enough that the patient be justified in making the request. And in order for euthanasia to be justified, physicians must be justified in actually performing euthanasia. It's not enough that those asking for assistance in committing suicide or asking to be euthanized be justified in requesting that those particular acts be performed. Requesting something is a different act from that of complying with the request. Both must be justified.

To take account of this, let us modify the argument in the following way. In the following argument, unlike the first, it's assumed (in premise 3) that PAS is justified.

B. 1. One may permissibly take one's own life.
   2. Whatever one may permissibly do to oneself one may permissibly enlist another's assistance in doing.
   3. One may permissibly enlist a physician's assistance in taking one's own life (PAS).

4. Whatever one may permissibly enlist a physician's assistance in doing to oneself, one may authorize a physician to do on one's behalf.

5. Therefore: One may permissibly authorize a physician to take one's own life (euthanasia).

Even if we assume that the argument is good through steps (1), (2), and (3) (hence that it justifies PAS), there's still a problem with (4). The act of authorizing someone to kill you is different from the act of killing that is authorized. Asking is different from performing the act requested. By the same token, killing another person (performing euthanasia) is a different act—and arguably a different *kind* of act—from killing yourself (suicide) or enlisting help in killing yourself (PAS) or authorizing someone to kill you on your behalf. Every act must be susceptible of moral assessment. Not only must the primary agent (the person intending to commit suicide or to be euthanized) be justified in what he or she does, the secondary agent (the physician whose assistance is enlisted or who is authorized to kill the primary agent) must also be justified in what he or she does. That justification doesn't follow logically or morally from the primary agent's justification in making the request or granting permission.

It's part of the very idea of morality that every act (meaning every free, uncoerced, voluntary act) is susceptible of moral assessment. Every act, in other words, is either right or wrong; and if right, is either merely permissible or obligatory.

The mere fact that I may be morally justified in consenting to your killing me (as 5 establishes), or in authorizing your so doing if I'm entitled to, doesn't in and of itself suffice to establish that it's right for you to kill me. My authorizing you is one act; your killing me is another. The fact that I've consented to your doing something to me, or authorized you to do it, or even ordered you to do it doesn't in and of itself entail that it is morally permissible for you *to do* it.

Once it's recognized that these are two acts, the possibility must be acknowledged that they may have radically different consequences. If I ask you to assist me in suicide, or to kill me on my behalf, one consequence of your complying with my request or authorization is my death. It's not a consequence of the request alone or the authorization alone. Another consequence might be your arrest and conviction for homicide (if PAS or euthanasia isn't legal). That's not a consequence of what I do, considered in itself. A third consequence might be that, justifiably or not, you come to feel guilty for having dispatched me, take to strong drink, and your life falls hopelessly into ruin. With a little imagination, one could likewise hypothesize equally felicitous consequences that would ensue from the one act and not from the other. This suggests that the moral evaluation of the two acts might differ radically on any view of morality that weighs consequences of individual acts (even without giving them decisive weight) in the determination of right and wrong.

13.11 Conclusion

If the preceding is correct, there is no LSS from suicide to PAS to euthanasia. It doesn't follow from this, however, that euthanasia cannot be morally justified. Nothing in the preceding argument answers that question one way or the other. All that follows is that it cannot be shown to be permissible by reasoning from the assumed permissibility of suicide, or even of PAS, alone. To make their case, supporters of euthanasia must do more than just argue for the permissibility of suicide or PAS. And opponents of euthanasia, to make their case, must do more than just argue for the impermissibility of suicide or PAS.

Both PAS and euthanasia normally involve the consensual taking of life, one's own or that of someone who requests that you do it for him or her. But many people support the nonconsensual taking of human life as well. In one case, it takes the form of the death penalty. In another, it takes the form of terrorism and war. We shall take up both in the next section.

Study questions

1. What is *suicide* (Definition Box 13A)? What difference does it make whether assisting a terminally ill person in ending his or her life is called *assisted-suicide* or *aid in dying*?
2. What does it mean to have a *right to die* (Section 13.3)?
3. What is the distinction between *active* and *passive euthanasia* (Section 13.4)?
4. What were the main issues in the *Quinlan, Cruzan*, and *Schiavo* cases, and how were those issues resolved legally (Section 13.5)?
5. What are differences among a *coma*, a *vegetative state*, a *locked-in state*, and a *minimally conscious state* (Section 13.6)?

6. What is the distinction between *acts of commission* and *acts of omission* (Theory Box 13A)?
7. What is the distinction between *killing* and *letting die* (Definition Box 13G)?
8. Given that there's a conceptual (or definitional) distinction between killing and letting die, what issues are there in deciding whether there's a *moral difference* between the two (Section 13.8)?
9. What is the distinction between a *contingent* and a *logically slippery slope* (Theory Box 13D)?
10. What argument does the text consider for a logical slippery slope from *suicide* to *physician-assisted suicide* to *euthanasia* (Section 13.10)?

Notes

1   "Unto This Last," *Ruskin's Works*, Vol. 6 (Boston: Aldine Book Publishing Company, n.d.), p. 162.
2   *USA TODAY—Rochester Democrat and Chronicle*, Sunday, February 19, 2017.
3   From Rebecca Holmes-Farley, "The Legal, Moral and Social Implications of Physician-Assisted Suicide," unpublished manuscript.
4   From James Rachels, "Active and Passive Euthanasia," *The New England Journal of Medicine*, Vol. 292, No. 2, January 9, 1975, 78–80.
5   From "Medical Aspects of the Persistent Vegetative State," Part One, Multi-Society Task Force on PVS, American Academy of Neurology, *The New England Journal of Medicine*, Vol. 330, No. 21, May 26, 1994.
6   The definition of a "locked-in state" is taken from ibid., p. 1501. The other definitions are mine.
7   *The New York Times*, February 16, 1996.
8   *The New York Times*, January 5, 2000.
9   *The New York Times*, July 4, 2006.
10 That letting die$_3$ is an act of omission is arguable, since normally the decision to discontinue intermittent treatment would involve acts of commission (e.g., discussion between physician and patient). The flow chart allows that it may be regarded as omission or commission.
11 Shelly Kagan, *The Limits of Morality* (Oxford: Clarendon Press, 1991), p. 101.
12 From Rachels, "Active and Passive Euthanasia."
13 Ibid.

14 This isn't quite true. There is at least one important philosophical issue it raises. Some forms of consequentialist reasoning in ethics would say that were euthanasia to follow from the acceptance of suicide and PAS, then euthanasia would be among their consequences for purposes of moral assessment. That would raise the question of what should be counted among the consequences of an action or practice, and that is an important issue. But as it is far more complex than we can take up here, we shall not deal with it.

15 Premise (1) isn't meant to imply that suicide is *absolutely* permissible, that is, permissible, under all conceivable circumstances. Those who believe that suicide is permissible typically think that there is some set of conditions under which killing yourself is permissible—such as that continued life would bring only unrelieved suffering—not that you're justified in ending your own life for any reason whatever.

For more resources:

www.bloomsbury.com/holmes-introduction-to-applied-ethics

Part V

The Nonconsensual Taking of Human Life

14

The Death Penalty

I believe we have no right to risk additional future victims of murder for the sake of sparing convicted murderers.

—Ernest van den Haag[1]

But precisely because ... [man] is not absolutely good, no one among us can pose as an absolute judge and pronounce the definitive elimination of the worst among the guilty, because no one of us can lay claim to absolute innocence.

—Albert Camus[2]

Introduction

We shall in this chapter explore the moral issues bound up in the death penalty. Since the death penalty is a form of punishment, we'll explain what punishment is and examine the two main rationales for punishment, deterrence and retribution. Morally speaking, the former is a consequentialist theory, the second nonconsequentialist. Both deterrence and retribution face serious objections as moral justifications of the death penalty, and we'll examine those objections in detail.

14.1 The death penalty in America

Early colonists brought the death penalty with them from England, where it was widely practiced for more than 300 offenses—including shoplifting, forging a birth certificate, or stealing a handkerchief. Its victims included children. A 7-year-old girl was hanged in 1808, a 9-year-old boy in 1831.

In addition to more usual offenses like murder, arson, and rape, the early colonists prescribed death for striking one's parents (New York), witchcraft (Massachusetts), and stealing slaves (North Carolina). A Virginia man was put to death in 1622 for stealing a pig and a cow and a Massachusetts woman in 1660 for defying the colony's ban on Quakers. Hanging was the preferred method, but shooting was used. Some slaves were burned at the stake. At least one man in Salem was reportedly crushed by a heavy weight.

The colonists believed that if the death penalty was to deter, executions must be public. People must not only know that an execution has taken place, they must see for themselves its horror. And the colonists' executions were public, often drawing huge crowds.

If public executions were meant to encourage sober reflection on the virtues of rectitude, however, they seemed to have the opposite effect. In England, the crowds they drew reportedly provided excellent opportunities for pickpockets—even though picking pockets was one of the offenses for which people were executed. Drunkenness and rowdiness came to characterize the crowds in the United States—prompting authorities to begin to move executions behind closed doors in the 1830s, where they are in the United States today.

Opposition to the death penalty began most notably with an abolitionist speech in 1787 by Benjamin Rush, a physician, peace advocate, and signer of the Declaration of Independence. The abolitionist movement gained momentum, with Michigan abolishing the death penalty except for treason in 1847, and Rhode Island abolishing the penalty for all crimes in 1852. But the momentum wasn't sustained, and abolitionist sentiment has waxed and waned to the present day.

Even many who weren't opposed to the death penalty were concerned about the method of killing. People were squeamish about hanging. Too short a rope and the person strangled slowly; too long a rope and his head might be torn off. New York State appointed a commission in 1886 to find the most humane way to kill people known to modern science. Physics pointed the way, and electrocution won out.

New York secured its place in history when it strapped convicted murderer William Kemmler to a crude electric chair at Auburn State Prison on August 6, 1890. It thereby became the first government ever to kill a person with electricity. Kemmler had protested that this would be a cruel and unusual punishment. If so, it would violate the Eighth Amendment.

Key Quote 14A

Amendment VIII
Excessive bail shall not be required, nor excessive fines imposed, nor cruel and unusual punishments inflicted. (US Constitution)

He was right, of course, that it would be unusual. After all, it hadn't been done before. But the Supreme Court ruled that it wouldn't be cruel because death would be instantaneous and painless.

The court was dead wrong. Kemmler's death was far from instantaneous, and his groans cast doubt on whether it was painless. Some witnesses fainted at the gruesome spectacle.

Nonetheless, other states followed New York's lead in harnessing the laws of physics to judicial purposes. Electrocution eventually became the country's method of choice for legal homicide. Modern chemistry made its bid in 1923, however, and gassing ran a strong second for a time. Eventually, both gassing and electrocution gave way to medical technology. Since 1982, more and more states use lethal injection, combining deadliness with a bizarre hint of humanity: they swab the victim's arm before inserting the needle, as though to protect against infection. "The people that are involved in this are very concerned that what they do is proper, done professionally and with decorum," according to an Arkansas Correction Department spokesman following the execution of three men in less than three hours by lethal injection.[3]

Although it was widely believed that death by legal injection was painless, it has been reported, nonetheless, that several men "have had bad reactions to the drugs, moaning and heaving as they died."[4] Some critics fear that execution by lethal injection places the prisoner in what, in medical terms, is a locked-in state—one in which the person is fully conscious and experiencing pain but is incapable of speaking or moving (see Chapter 13, Section 13.6).

Amid diminishing public support for the death penalty, its use waned during the mid-twentieth century, with no executions taking place between June 2, 1967, and January 17, 1977. Juries, with considerable discretionary power to choose between the death penalty and life imprisonment, were voting against the death penalty. But they were inflicting it at a disproportionately high rate on minorities. In 1972 the Supreme Court

(*Furman v. Georgia*) struck down existing death penalty laws which gave juries such discretion. Death-penalty states quickly redrafted their laws to take account of the court's objections, and in 1976 (*Gregg v. Georgia*) the court effectively opened the way to resumption of the death penalty. By 2016, the imposition of the penalty had dropped to a 40-year low, with only thirty new executions. As of 2016, thirty-three states and the Federal Government had the death penalty, with nearly 3,000 persons on death row. More than 18,000 executions have taken place overall in America. As the death penalty is a form of punishment, let us begin by asking what punishment is.

14.2 What is punishment?

Morality has two dimensions: the first, governing ordinary conduct toward others; the second, governing responses to wrongdoing by others. Depending upon circumstances, when others do wrong (at least to us) we can, among other things, either forgive them or retaliate. Often people respond in kind, repaying harm or injury with harm or injury. That is, they think in terms of retribution. Retribution can take many forms. But it will either be limited or unlimited in terms of the kind or quantity of harm it inflicts upon wrongdoers. The best example of unlimited retribution is *revenge*: retaliation for hurt or harm received by you or those you identify with. Revenge as an action is often disproportionate and done in anger or with malice. As a motive, revenge is the desire to inflict hurt or harm for hurt or harm received. *Vengeance* is closely related. Although often used interchangeably with revenge, it may stand for justified retaliation without necessarily any anger or malice. (An avenger might, for pay, harm someone on behalf of someone else, without knowing or harboring any anger toward the person he harms.) An example of limited retaliation is *Lex Talionis*, the Law of Hammurabai and the Bible.

Key Quote 14B

Lex Talionis
And if *any* mischief follow, then thou shalt give life for life, eye for eye, tooth for tooth, hand for hand, foot for foot, burning for burning, wound for wound, stripe for stripe. (Exod. 21:23)

In *Lex Talionis* we find an important element in punishment as an institutionalized practice in society: it typically involves a measured, rule-governed response to wrongdoing that has some sort of societal sanction. With that in mind, we can now define punishment as a societal response to wrongdoing as follows:

Definition Box 14A

Punishment: The deliberate infliction of (usually predetermined) pain, suffering, deprivation, or death in response to alleged offenses.

So understood, punishment is a retributing of something bad for wrongdoing. It's like retaliation, except that it isn't necessarily repayment for harm to the particular individuals who inflict the punishment. It's society's response to perceived offenses regardless of who is victimized by them. It's necessary to specify "alleged" offenses, because sometimes innocent people are mistakenly (and occasionally intentionally) punished. Punishment sometimes extends to those associated with the offenders, such as family, friends, or community, in which case it constitutes *collective punishment*. There are, it should be noted, nonviolent as well as violent forms of punishment, such as exile, economic sanctions, ostracism, or shunning.

14.3 Deterrence and retribution

Much of the discussion of the death penalty centers about deterrence and retribution. Those who support the death penalty (retentionists) argue from either or both of these viewpoints. Those who appeal to deterrence claim that the death penalty is justified because it deters others from committing similar crimes. In that way it safeguards society and promotes a social good. Those who appeal to retribution maintain that, whether or not the death penalty promotes a social good through deterrence, it's justified because those guilty of the most serious crimes simply *deserve* to die.

Underlying these two appeals are two different moral theories of punishment: *consequentialist* and *retributivist*. These center around three considerations:

1. The nature of the offense
2. The nature of the offender
3. The consequences of punishment

The first two considerations are central to retributivism; the third is central to consequentialism. Consequentialist theories of punishment typically appeal to a good to be promoted by punishment. The commonest of consequentialist theories is utilitarian, appealing to the good of society or the community or the state, that is, to some collectivity. (See Theory Box 1E in Chapter 1, Section 1.8, and Theory Box 6A in Chapter 6, Section 6.5.) The good is usually thought to be grounded in the deterrent value of the death penalty, or (as in the *Gregg v. Georgia* case mentioned in 14.1) to the promotion and maintenance of stability in society. But it's also possible to argue that punishment is justified because of its consequences for the victims of crimes (or in the case of murder, also for the families of victims). It's possible, still further, to argue (as Plato did) for the promotion of the good of the offender. Thus we have the following principal theories:

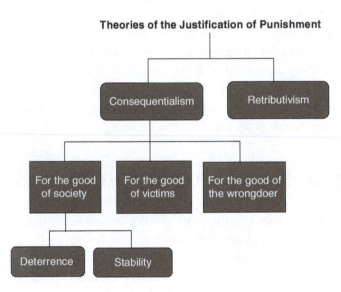

Theories of the Justification of Punishment

Consequentialism

Retributivism

For the good of society

For the good of victims

For the good of the wrongdoer

Deterrence

Stability

14.4 What is retributivism?

The underlying idea of retributivism is simple. It's captured in a statement by a waitress concerning Timothy McVeigh, the 1995 Oklahoma City bomber who was at the time under a death sentence. (He was executed in 2001.)

Key Quote 14C

He took another person's life. He deserves to die. (*The New York Times*, April 19, 2001)

This is the simplest and probably commonest of the ideas underlying the death penalty. It says, first of all, what McVeigh *did*: he took another person's life (actually 168 persons' lives). Second, it concludes from this what should be done to him. The one is intended to follow from the other. This simple idea receives elaboration in the philosophy of Hegel, one of the chief historical proponents of a retributivist justification of the death penalty. Consider the following passage from Hegel:

> The injury [the penalty] which falls on the criminal is not merely *implicitly* just—as just, it is *eo ipso* his implicit will, an embodiment of his freedom, his right; on the contrary, it is also a right *established* within the criminal himself, i.e., in his objectively embodied will, in his action. The reason for this is that his action is the action of a rational being and this implies that it is something universal and that by doing it the criminal has laid down a law which he has explicitly recognized in his action and under which in consequence he should be brought as under his right ... Since that is so, punishment is regarded as containing the criminal's right and hence by being punished he is honoured as a rational being. He does not receive this due of honour unless the concept and measure of his punishment are derived from his own act.[5]

The main point, in Hegel's view, is that even the murderer is a rational being; and respect for rational beings demands that they be accountable for wrongdoing and punished accordingly. When the offense warrants it, the death penalty is demanded by respect for the offender as a rational being.

We cannot consider Hegel's reasoning fully here, but he believes it's possible to derive the moral necessity of punishment from consideration of the offender's own nature and his offense. The aim isn't deterrence. Or to promote a social good. It's to nullify the wrong that was done. The wrong is a negation. Punishing the wrong negates that negation. (Recall from Chapter 8, Section 8.6, that the negation of the negation is one of the laws of dialectic which Marx adapted from Hegel.)[6]

So, in its simplest terms, the retributivist theory of the death penalty asserts:

Theory Box 14A

Retributivism
The death penalty is justified if, and only if, it puts to death those, and only those, who *deserve* to die.

Whether one deserves to die is determined principally by one's offense and one's character. The consequences of the death penalty may or may not also be relevant, but in any event they are not the paramount consideration and are not in and of themselves decisive. A retributivist view is the following by contemporary philosopher Igor Primoratz:

> This view that the value of human life is not commensurable with other values, and that consequently there is only one truly equivalent punishment for murder, namely death, does not necessarily presuppose a theistic outlook. It can be claimed that, simply because we have to be alive if we are to experience and realize any other value at all, there is nothing equivalent to the murderous destruction of a human life except the destruction of the life of the murderer. Any other retribution, no matter how severe, would still be less than what is proportionate, deserved, and just ... Accordingly, capital punishment ought to be retained where it obtains, and reintroduced in those jurisdictions that have abolished it, although we have no reason to believe that, as a means of deterrence, it is any better than a very long prison term. It ought to be retained, or reintroduced, for one simple reason: that justice be done in cases of murder, that murderers be punished according to their deserts.[7]

The Supreme Court justice in Stewart in *Furman v. Georgia* highlights such a consideration when he says:

Key Quote 14D

The instinct of retribution is part of the nature of man, and channeling that instinct in the administration of criminal justice serves an important purpose in promoting the stability of a society governed by law. When people begin to believe that organized society is unwilling or unable to impose upon criminal offenders the punishment they "deserve," then there are sown the seeds of anarchy—of self-help, vigilante justice, and lynch law. (*Furman v. Georgia*, 1972, Justice Stewart)

Sometimes retributivists emphasize the aspect of the offender that Hegel plays down, the fact that he or she may be evil or malicious. In fact, when juries consider a death penalty they weigh such considerations among the so-called *aggravating circumstances*. At other times, retributivists appeal to the fact that, by his offense, the criminal has violated the law. This is a non-consequentialist consideration. One needn't look to the consequences of punishing a person to know that he has broken the law. At other times it is the viciousness of the crime that is appealed to. At other times, the act is seen more broadly as upsetting the moral order. Punishment is thought to restore that order (what Hegel apparently means above by negating the negation). Thus, retributivists typically appeal to one or more of the following characteristics of the act or person:

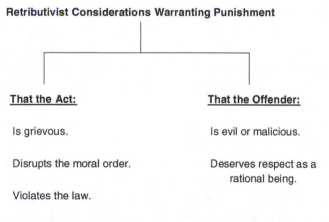

Retributivist Considerations Warranting Punishment

That the Act:

Is grievous.

Disrupts the moral order.

Violates the law.

Unfairly benefits the offender.

That the Offender:

Is evil or malicious.

Deserves respect as a rational being.

Sometimes the necessity of punishment is presumed to follow immediately from these considerations. At other times, it's thought demonstrable by argument from one or more of these considerations.

14.5 Objections to the retributivist justification of the death penalty

We shall consider the consequentialist objection to the retributivist rationale for the death penalty in a moment. First, let's consider another objection. It pertains to the nature of morality and the scope of our responsibility as moral agents.

It's arguable that everything we do (leaving aside reflexive, unintentional, and involuntary acts) is susceptible of moral evaluation. It's always relevant to ask whether what we do is morally right or wrong. Not that there is always a need to do so. Many of our acts raise no moral questions in the contexts in which they occur (whether you put your right shoe on before your left raises no moral issues, though it conceivably could in some contexts). But this just means that we can justifiably assume that they are permissible, not that they aren't susceptible of moral evaluation.

If every act is susceptible of moral evaluation, the same is true of responses to wrongdoing. It's one thing to establish that an act is wrong. It's another to say that any particular response to that wrongdoing is permissible. The wrong is one act, the response to it another. The wrong act doesn't itself tell us which of many possible responses to it is morally permissible. Whatever *we* do in response to a wrongful act itself needs to be justified.

Some responses to wrongful acts are themselves wrong. It would be wrong, for example, to impose the death penalty for parking violations or for fishing without a license. Retributivists often speak as though there's one and only one proper response to offenses, and that it follows immediately from the nature of the offense what that is. But if the principle we just cited is correct (that every act must be susceptible of moral evaluation), this is a non sequitur. There are always options in responding to wrongdoing (e.g., imprisonment, forgiveness). Which is the correct one is an open question morally. This doesn't mean that the retributivist is necessarily wrong in saying that the death penalty is the right option, say, for the offense of murder. It just means that it must be shown to be the correct option; it cannot simply be assumed to follow immediately from the character of the offense.

There are some who argue that the retributivist idea of responding in kind to severe offenses is itself wrong. Socrates said as much when he was himself awaiting execution after a death sentence in ancient Athens. In an exchange with a friend, Crito, depicted in Plato's dialogue, *Crito*, Socrates says:

Socrates:	Then in no circumstances must one do wrong.
Crito:	No.
Socrates:	In that case one must not even do wrong when one is wronged, which most people regard as the natural course.
Crito:	Apparently not.
Socrates:	Tell me another thing, Crito. Ought one to do injuries or not?
Crito:	Surely not, Socrates.
Socrates:	And tell me, is it right to do an injury in retaliation, as most people believe, or not?
Crito:	No, never.
Socrates:	Because, I suppose, there is no difference between injuring people and wronging them.
Crito:	Exactly.
Socrates:	So one ought not to return a wrong or an injury to any person, whatever the provocation is.[8]

Centuries later a similar thought is attributed to Jesus in the *New Testament*:

You have heard it said, "An eye for an eye and a tooth for a tooth." But I say to you, do not resist one who is evil. But if anyone strike you on the right check, turn to him the other also and if anyone would sue you and take your coat, let him have your cloak as well; and if anyone force you to go one mile, go with him two miles … You have heard that it was said, "You shall love your neighbor and hate your enemy." But, I say to you, love your enemies and pray for those who persecute you. (Matt. 5:38–41; 43–44)

The reference to "an eye for an eye," you recall, is a reference *Lex Talionis* (see Section 14.2). This leaves it open, of course, what constitutes returning "evil for evil" or "injustice for injustice." Hegel would deny that imposing the death penalty is returning evil for evil. He would say it's returning right for wrong, justice for injustice. The issue between Socrates and Jesus, on the one hand, and Hegel, on the other, would then be over the proper moral evaluation of the death penalty. The point is that it's possible to maintain, in the spirit of Socrates and Jesus, that putting people to death isn't honoring them as rational beings. It's treating them inhumanely when they're defenseless before the power of the state.

A second and related objection is that the death penalty is excessive. It goes beyond the proper function of the state. The state's function, on this view, is to protect society. (It has other functions, of course, but this is the one that pertains specifically to the issue of wrongdoing.) To presume to judge individuals morally is not the state's business. It can protect society by imprisoning people for life. It doesn't need to kill them. In so doing it exceeds its legitimate role.

Supreme Court Justice Thurgood Marshall in effect makes this argument in his dissent from the majority decision in *Gregg v. Georgia*. His point is that the death penalty violates the Eighth Amendment prohibition of "cruel and unusual" punishment because it's excessive.

There remains for consideration, however, what might be termed the purely retributive justification for the death penalty—that the death penalty is appropriate, not because of its beneficial effect on society, but because the taking of the murderer's life is itself morally good. Some of the language of the opinion of my Brothers Stewart, Powell, and Stevens ... appears positively to embrace this notion of retribution for its own sake as a justification for capital punishment.

[T]he decision that capital punishment may be the appropriate sanction in extreme cases is an expression of the community's belief that certain crimes are themselves so grievous an affront to humanity that the only adequate response may be the penalty of death.

Then they quote with approval from Lord Justice Denning's remarks before the British Royal Commission on Capital Punishment:

The truth is that some crimes are so outrageous that society insists on adequate punishment, because the wrong-doer deserves it, irrespective of whether it is a deterrent or not.

Of course, it may be that these statements are intended as no more than observations as to the popular demands that it is thought must be responded to in order to prevent anarchy. But the implication of the statements appears to me to be quite different—namely, that society's judgment that the murderer "deserves" death must be respected not simply because the preservation of order requires it, but because it is appropriate that society make the judgment and carry it out. It is this latter notion, in particular, that I consider to be fundamentally at odds with the Eighth Amendment. The mere fact that the community demands the murderer's life in return for the evil he has done cannot sustain the death penalty, for as Justice Stewart, Powell, and Stevens remind us, "the Eight Amendment demands more than that a challenged punishment be acceptable to contemporary society." To be sustained under the Eighth Amendment, the death penalty must "comport with the basic concept of human dignity at the core of the Amendment;" the objective in imposing it must be "[consistent] with our respect for the dignity of [other] men." Under these standards, the taking of life "because the wrongdoer deserves it" surely must fail, for such a punishment has as its very basis the total denial of the wrongdoer's dignity and worth.[9]

While Marshall's concern as a Supreme Court justice is with the constitutionality of the death penalty, one can raise the moral issue independently of that concern. To do so opens up the broader range of issues concerning the legitimacy of the state and its proper functions.

This concern brings us to the other principal line of justification for the death penalty, namely, that it promotes a social good by deterring other potential criminals.

14.6 The consequentialist justification of the death penalty as a deterrent

Remember that we have distinguished *persons*, *acts*, and *consequences* (Chapter 13, Theory Box 13C, Section 13.8). In these terms, retributivism appeals to the nature of persons (e.g., the fact that they are rational beings) and/or the nature of their acts (e.g., committing murder) in justification of the death penalty. Some people, in the retributivist view, deserve to die quite independently of the consequences of putting them to death. Consequentialists (or utilitarians in particular) who defend the death penalty justify their position by appeal to the consequences of putting people to death for certain offenses. In their view, it serves to deter others from committing similar crimes in the future, hence promotes a social good.

In assessing this rationale, there are two questions: (1) is the death penalty a deterrent? And (2) if it is, is it a better deterrent than life imprisonment (or some other response)? It wouldn't be enough to establish that a death penalty is a deterrent if life imprisonment (or some other punishment or mode of treatment) were at least as good or even better as a deterrent.

The prior question is: what is deterrence? Notice that deterrence differs from prevention. I can prevent you from crossing my lawn by building a fence around it. That way you *can't* cross it. But I've deterred you only if I've led you to refrain from crossing it when you otherwise would have—which I might do by putting up a sign that says "No trespassing" or "Beware of dog." Deterrence presupposes a mental act that is part of the explanation of why a person didn't perform the act in question. In the cases of greatest interest legally and morally, one is deterred only if one chooses not to do something because of the threatened consequences if one does. To put this a little more formally, where A and B can be individual persons, or nation states:

Theory Box 14B

What Is It to Deter?
A has deterred B from doing x if and only if:

1. A has threatened to do y if B does x,
2. B has not done x,
3. B has refrained from doing x because of the threat of y if B does x.

In other words, deterrence says more than simply that someone hasn't done something in the face of threatened consequences; it says they've chosen not to do it because of those consequences. It provides an explanation for their failure to do the act. Nuclear deterrence, for example, purports to lead an adversary to refrain from a nuclear attack because of threatened nuclear retaliation. Deterrence can occur in legal and nonlegal contexts. In light of this, let us define deterrence, in a sense specifically relevant to the death penalty, as follows:

Definition Box 14B

Deterrence: Causing people to refrain from committing certain crimes for fear of execution if they do.

Notice, further, that refraining implies that but for the threatened consequences, the person would have performed the act in question. You haven't refrained from doing something unless you otherwise would have done it.

To know that someone has been deterred requires *counterfactual knowledge*. It requires knowing what *would have* happened (but didn't) but for something that did happen (the threat of consequences). It requires knowing something contrary to the actual course of events.

Thus, to know that the death penalty functions as a deterrent, one would have to know that but for it as a threatened punishment for murder, some people would have committed murder but chose not to in order to avoid execution.

Now most people never commit murder. But most of them don't do so because they were deterred. Most of them don't do so because they've never had any inclination to or because they think it's wrong. It's not that they would commit murder if the death penalty were removed. If that were so, one would expect the murder rate to skyrocket when a state abolishes the death penalty, which doesn't happen. And one would expect soaring murder rates in states (or countries) which don't have a death penalty, which isn't borne out. In other words, the explanation why most people don't commit murder isn't because there is a death penalty for it.

If doesn't follow from this that some people aren't deterred by the death penalty. They might be. But it means it would be difficult to know that. To know that certain persons have been deterred by the death penalty would require knowing that, but for the death penalty, those persons would have committed murder. And this would require knowledge of the motives and intentions of those particular individuals, and counterfactual knowledge of what their behavior would have been but for the death penalty. More than this, it would require our knowing that:

1. They knew or believed there was a death penalty in the jurisdiction in which they contemplated committing murder.
2. They believed they would likely be caught if they committed murder.
3. They believed they would likely be convicted, sentenced to death, and the sentence would be carried out if they committed murder.

Absent any one of these beliefs, the death penalty would fail to deter potential murderers even if it *would have* deterred them if they had possessed this knowledge. And absent knowledge that potential murderers had all of these beliefs and refrained from murder because of them, one couldn't know that the death penalty functioned as a deterrent. It seems clear that over a population of millions of people, we simply don't have that kind of knowledge.

Simply compiling statistics on the number of homicides with and without a death penalty isn't enough. Any homicide rate is compatible both with the death penalty's being a deterrent (meaning that it would deter if potential murderers had the requisite beliefs or knowledge) and with it's not being a deterrent (meaning that some potential murderers commit murder even if they possess all of the requisite knowledge or beliefs in (1) through (3)). The same should be said for life imprisonment. Precisely the same kind of evidence would be required to know whether life imprisonment is a deterrent and whether, if it is, it's as good, less good, or better a deterrent than the death penalty.

We know the extent to which the death penalty fails as a deterrent. Every time there's a crime for which there's a death penalty there's a failure of deterrence, whether it's because the perpetrators lack the requisite beliefs to be deterred or because they have the beliefs but commit the crimes anyway. That we know for certain. In fact, some states that have the death penalty have higher murder rates than those that don't. This means that some of the statistics cited as reasons for retaining the death penalty (e.g., high murder rates) actually show the extent of its failure as a deterrent.

If people aren't deterred from speeding, smoking, or having unsafe sex by the threat of death from auto accident, lung cancer, or AIDS, it's not surprising that those who are inclined to kill aren't deterred by a death penalty. Indeed, some psychologists believe that self-destructive people sometimes kill in order to receive the death penalty—raising the possibility that capital punishment may actually help produce some homicides (just as some persons commit "suicide by cop," as it is sometimes called, by provoking the police into shooting them).

14.7 The role of fear in deterrence

Deterrence and retribution are the only remotely plausible nonreligious justifications for a death penalty. Deterrence requires instilling fear; retribution requires doing to offenders as they have done to others. Holding executions behind closed doors defeats the first purpose. Potential murderers are unlikely to read newspaper accounts of executions or to be much troubled if they do. No punishment deters if you don't expect to be caught, and few murderers expect to be caught. Many people don't even know which states have a death penalty. Making executions "humane," on the other hand, defeats the second purpose. Diminish the pain and terror traditionally associated with the death penalty, and you widen the gap between criminal homicide and judicial homicide. After Pedro Medina's death mask burst into flame during his electrocution on March 25, 1997, Florida Attorney General Bob Butterworth said that Medina's death, which many considered horrifying, would be a deterrent to crime. Those who wish to commit murder, he said, "better not do it in the state of Florida because we may have a problem with our electric chair." Commenting on lethal injection as an alternative to electrocution, the state's Senate Majority Leader said the next day, "A painless death is not punishment."[10]

There's a dilemma here that society must confront. If one hoped to deter crime by the death penalty, that would seem to argue for spreading the fear of the penalty as widely as possible through public executions, perhaps requiring children—among whom are tomorrow's criminals—to witness them. But then one risks the very brutalization of people that led American states to move executions behind closed doors in the 1830s. A special committee of the New York State Assembly spoke to this issue nearly 150 years ago in recommending abolition of the death penalty. It wrote:

Key Quote 14E

If the child never sees the sanctity of human life invaded, his early reverence for it will remain in his maturer years; but if he sees society frequently cutting off its members ... [his reverence for life] will pass away like the early dew, and the morning cloud; and he, perhaps in a moment of passion or excitement will follow the example which has been set him by the State.

On the other hand, if one defends the death penalty on retributivist grounds, one runs the risk that the message to people—and in particular to children—will be that it's permissible to kill people if you have the power to do so and are convinced you have the wisdom to judge who is and who isn't deserving of life. Such a message isn't lost on those who attack abortion clinics or assassinate world leaders or who engage in terrorism, much less those who initiate wars.

Finally, even if there were a compelling moral justification for the death penalty in theory, the practice of judicial execution is flawed, and numerous innocent people—as many as one in twenty-five in a 2014 study by the National Academy of Sciences—have erroneously been sentenced to death.

Part of the problem is the nature of the judicial system. At its best, it seeks to provide an impartial and fair process for determination of guilt or innocence. But the system is imperfect and errors can and do result. Moreover, eyewitness reports, which often are key elements in a finding of guilt for homicides, have come to be seen as highly unreliable, thus contributing to erroneous convictions.

14.8 Conclusion

The only safe conclusion, then, is that we simply don't know whether the death penalty is a deterrent, or if it is, how effective a deterrent it is, and whether it's better or worse as a deterrent than life imprisonment. But both sides on the death penalty question can agree on some things. In America today, thousands of children begin their lives poisoned by drugs or alcohol; hundreds of thousands of troubled teenagers flee their homes; millions grow up in poverty. At a time when violent crime is decreasing overall, it's increasing by young people. Privileged or disadvantaged, all children begin life innocent. Yet among them are tomorrow's criminals. We can, if we choose, regard them all as our children, and the adults they will become, as our brothers and sisters. We can, if we choose, help them to a better life now, in which respect for others becomes easy and natural for them. Or we can pour millions into concrete, barbed-wire, and execution chambers to contain or kill them later. The challenge to abolitionists and retentionists alike is to reflect on what kind of society we aspire to be.

Study questions

1. What does the *Eighth Amendment* to the US Constitution assert (Key Quote 14A)?
2. What is *Lex Talionis* (Key Quote 14B)?
3. How does the text define *punishment* (Definition Box 14A)?
4. What is *retributivism* (Theory Box 14A)?
5. What kinds of considerations do retributivists believe justify the death penalty (take note of characteristics of the *act* and of the *offender*) (Section 14.4)?
6. How do the views attributed to *Socrates* and later to the historical *Jesus* go against the retributivist argument for the death penalty (Section 14.5)?

7. What is *deterrence* (Definition Box 14B)?
8. In what sense is deterrence a *consequentialist justification* of the death penalty and retribution a *nonconsequentialist justification* (Sections 14.4–14.6)?
9. What is the role of *fear* in deterrence (Section 14.7)?
10. What possible *effect on children* of the death penalty is pointed out in Key Quote 14E?

Notes

1 "On Deterrence and the Death Penalty," in Robert M. Baird and Stuart E. Rosenbaum, *Punishment and the Death Penalty: The Current Debate* (Amherst, NY: Prometheus Books, 1995), p. 134.
2 "Reflections on the Guillotine," in *Resistance, Rebellion, and Death* (New York: Modern Library, 1960), p. 170.
3 The spokesman was defending multiple executions by lethal injection on the grounds of efficiency and diminished strain on prison workers. *New York Times*, August 5, 1995.
4 *New York Times*, February 17, 1995.
5 *Hegel's Philosophy of Right*, trans. with notes by T. M. Knox (Oxford: Clarendon Press, 1967), pp. 71f.
6 Interestingly, this aspect of Hegel makes it sound as though the death penalty is for the good of the offender. In his view, in a sense it is. But this doesn't make his theory consequentialist. It is a moral good that Hegel is concerned with here, one that is entailed by the infliction of the penalty. It is not a nonmoral good brought about by the causal consequences of the penalty (as consequentialists believe).
7 From Igor Primoratz, *Justifying Legal Punishment* (Atlantic Highlands, NJ: Humanities Press, 1989), p. 158f.
8 Plato, *Crito*, Stephanus 49.
9 Justice Thurgood Marshall, *Gregg v. Georgia* (1976), Dissenting Opinion.
10 *The New York Times*, March 26 and 27, 1997.

For more resources:

www.bloomsbury.com/holmes-introduction-to-applied-ethics

15

Terrorism and War

We stand, therefore, at the parting of the ways. Whether we find the way of peace or continue along the old road of brute force, so unworthy of our civilization, depends on ourselves.

—Albert Einstein[1]

Introduction

Most people understand terrorism and war well enough for ordinary discourse, but both concepts need clarification to understand fully the moral issues they raise. We'll define them, and then explore the just war theory, which is the main theory people appeal to in trying to justify war. Terrorism often involves intentionally killing innocent people, and war inevitably kills innocent people, if only unintentionally. We'll ask whether such killing can be justified, as well as whether the intentional killing of soldiers in warfare can be justified. Warists (those who hold that war can be morally justified) believe that the intentional killing of soldiers is justified and that the killing of innocents can be excused if it's unintentional. Pacifists (those who believe that war, at least in the modern world, cannot be justified) deny both claims. We'll clarify the pacifist position and conclude by considering possible common ground between pacifists and warists.

15.1 The problem

The September 11, 2001, attack on the World Trade Center and the Pentagon stunned the world and left Americans feeling threatened as never before. The United States responded by launching an open-ended "war" against terrorism, attacking Afghanistan and Iraq. A full assessment of these events isn't possible here, but a starting point is to try to understand better the two notions they center about: *terrorism* and *war*.

The common association of terror with cunning, deceit, and violence highlights the fact that violence is at the heart of terrorism. Violence that maintains the status quo (whether in the way of police action or war) tends to be approved by those who are its beneficiaries; that which threatens the status quo tends to be condemned. But the mode of violence that is almost universally condemned is terrorism. Although it's at the other end of the scale of destructiveness from nuclear war, terrorism rivals nuclear war in the dread it inspires.

15.2 What is terrorism?

The term "terrorism" is often used emotively, to stand for virtually any use of political violence of which we disapprove. (See Theory Box 1A, Chapter 1, Section 1.3, on emotive and descriptive meaning.) One and the same person is a terrorist or a freedom fighter, depending upon whether we approve or disapprove of his cause.

It's tempting to define terrorism in such a way that it's wrong by definition. When many people speak of terrorism, they mean by it something approximating the following:

Definition Box 15A

A Persuasive Definition of Terrorism
Terrorism₁: The merciless killing of innocent people for evil ends.

Definitions of this sort have been called evaluative or persuasive. In this case, the definition is evaluative because the moral assessment of terrorism has already been included in the definition, and it's persuasive because such a definition would normally be intended to convince others to share that assessment. You can't acknowledge that something is an act of terrorism without already condemning it as morally wrong. Thus from

1. X is an instance of terrorism,

it would follow:

2. Therefore X is morally wrong.

But terrorism has an underlying descriptive meaning, one that may point to a moral evaluation but which doesn't entail it in the way in which the above definition does. To terrorize is to instill extreme fear. Although this can be done for its own sake, terrorism becomes of moral and political interest when it causes and manipulates fear for a purpose. So understood, it can be defined as:

Definition Box 15B

A Descriptive Definition of Terrorism
Terrorism$_2$: Pursuit of one's ends by causing fear, usually by the use or threat of violence, often against innocent persons.

According to this second definition, one can acknowledge that something is an instance of terrorism but still consider it an open question whether it's morally justified. Thus from

1. X is an instance of terrorism,

one can still intelligibly ask (in a way in which one cannot with the first definition):

2. Is X morally permissible?

We'll proceed on the assumption that the moral evaluation of terrorism is best not decided by definition. This doesn't preclude any moral issues from consideration in connection with terrorism; it just moves them outside of the definition. So, by "terrorism" we shall henceforth mean *terrorism$_2$*.

According to this definition, who does the terrorizing doesn't matter. What counts is what is done and why. Individuals acting alone can terrorize. But so can groups, governments, or armies. And what the ends are doesn't matter. They may be social, political, religious, or moral. What makes one a terrorist are the means by which ends are pursued, not the ends themselves. One can terrorize in the service of just causes as well as unjust causes.

15.3 Rationalizations of terrorism

Terrorism is most important to understand when undertaken for a cause. For terrorism isn't necessarily a less rational choice—purely in the sense of being a perceived means to an end—than many conventionally accepted modes of violence.[2] The revolutionary Leon Trotsky (1879–1940) saw this when writing of the Russian revolution.

Key Quote 15A

A victorious war, Trotsky observed, usually destroys "only an insignificant part of the conquered army, intimidating the remainder and breaking their will. The revolution works in the same way: it kills individuals, and intimidates thousands."[3]

Although Trotsky was describing the terror used by a revolutionary class, what he said applies to terrorism of any sort. Terrorism typically kills few people by comparison with warfare. That may change if terrorists acquire weapons of mass destruction, including nuclear and chemical/biological weapons. Philanthropist Bill Gates warns of the dangers of bioterrorism in particular at a 2017 Munich Security Conference:

Bioterrorism and Pandemics
The point is, we ignore the link between health security and international security at our peril. Whether it occurs by a quirk of nature or at the hand of a terrorist, epidemiologists say a fast-moving airborne pathogen could kill more than 30 million people in less than a year. And they say there is a reasonable probability the world will experience such an outbreak in the next 10–15 years ... The good news is that with advances in biotechnology, new vaccines and drugs can help prevent epidemics from spreading out of control. And, most of the things we need to do to protect against a naturally occurring pandemic are the same things we must prepare for an intentional biological attack ... I view the threat of deadly pandemics right up there with nuclear war and climate change ... When the next pandemic strikes, it could be another catastrophe in the annals of the human race. Or it could be something else altogether. An extraordinary triumph of human will. A moment when we prove yet again that, together, we

are capable of taking on the world's biggest challenges to create a safer, healthier, more stable world.[4]

Whatever the scale of violence represented by terrorism, it instills fear, and typically tries to manipulate that fear to achieve the ends of those who use it.

Often it's not known what the justification for terrorism is alleged to be, but sometimes a rationale is set forth, as in a 1998 document by Osama bin Laden and other leaders of militant Islamist groups, entitled "Declaration of the World Islamic Front for Jihad against the Jews and the Crusaders." Writing in *Foreign Affairs*, Bernard Lewis says: "The statement—a magnificent piece of eloquent, at times even poetic Arabic prose—reveals a version of history that most Westerners will find unfamiliar. Bin Ladin's grievances are not quite what many would expect." The document says, in part:

Osama Bin Laden on Jihad

First—For more than seven years the United States is occupying the lands of Islam in the holiest of its territories, Arabia, plundering its riches, overwhelming its rulers, humiliating its people, threatening its neighbors, and using its bases in the peninsula as a spearhead to fight against the neighboring Islamic peoples . . .

Second—Despite the immense destruction inflicted on the Iraqi people at the hands of the Crusader-Jewish alliance . . . the Americans nevertheless . . . are trying once more to repeat this dreadful slaughter . . . So they come again today to destroy what remains of this people and to humiliate their Muslim neighbors.

Third—While the purposes of the Americans in these wars are religious and economic, they also serve . . . to divert attention from [Jewish] occupation of Jerusalem and their killing of Muslims in it.[5]

In a similar vein, one of the suicide bombers in the 2005 London subway bombings provided his rationale for that action. As reported by ABC News:

The video also contained a long testimonial from one of the London bombers, Tanweer, in which he gave his motives for taking part in the attacks and warned of more to come. Some of it appeared in the edited version broadcast by al-Jazeera.

"For the non-Muslims in Britain, you may wonder what you have done to deserve this," Tanweer said in a thick north English accent. Britons oppress "our mothers and children, brothers and sisters from the east to the west in Palestine, Afghanistan, Iraq and Chechnya," he said.

"Your government has openly supported the genocide of more than 150,000 innocent Muslims in Fallujah," he added, referring to the west Iraqi town where U.S. troops fought Islamic militants for several weeks.

"You have openly declared war on Islam ... I tell every British citizen to stop your support to your lying British government and to the so-called war on terror. And ask yourselves: Why would thousands of men be ready to give their lives for the cause of Muslims?"

"What you have witnessed now is only the beginning of a series of attacks that will continue and increase in strength until you withdraw your soldiers from Afghanistan and Iraq," he warned.[6]

Whatever one thinks of the ends terrorists pursue, one cannot understand terrorism without considering what those ends are and the motives of those who pursue them in this way.

Terrorism seeks to achieve its ends by breaking the will of the thousands who learn of it. That's why publicity is important to its success. Whereas war intimidates by inflicting losses, terrorism—at least until, or unless, terrorists acquire weapons of mass destruction—intimidates by instilling fear.

Conventional war, however, *may* also be terroristic. Its rationale then is usually military necessity. This was put bluntly by Germany's Kaiser during the First World War. He said:

Terroristic Warfare

My soul is torn, but everything must be put to fire and sword; men, women, and children and old men must be slaughtered and not a tree or house be left standing. With these methods of terrorism, which are alone capable of affecting a people as degenerate as the French, the war will be over in two months, whereas if I admit considerations of humanity it will be prolonged for years.[7]

Much the same rationale, though never stated as directly, underlay the US fire-bombings of Tokyo and Dresden and the atomic bombings of Hiroshima and Nagasaki during the Second World War. They employed massive, indiscriminate violence against mostly innocent people. The aim, in each case, was to destroy the morale of the country.

Because of the resources at a government's command, *state terror* is often the most systematic kind. When governments terrorize openly, they have a propaganda apparatus to justify what they do. When they terrorize surreptitiously, they can recruit, train, and finance operatives beyond the reach of public view. And they can direct terror against their own people. Stalin did this in the 1930s, as did South Africa and many Latin American governments in the past. But whereas many governments operate through torture and death squads, some enlist the country's legal system in the service of terrorism. Stalin worked though the Soviet Union's legal institutions. There was no gunfire in the night, no bodies on Moscow's outskirts in the morning. Yet through trial, conviction, and execution, perceived enemies were eliminated as effectively as though they had been gunned down. In the process, countless others were terrified into submission.

15.4 Who are terrorists?

Terrorism is commonly represented as primarily Arab and Muslim. When a toy manufacturer produced a doll representing a terrorist, the doll was named Nomad, dressed in Arab garb and, according to the company's description, engaged in "terrorist assaults on innocent villages."[8] Political cartoonists often depict terrorists as grizzled and wearing keffiyehs. US President Trump's 2017 executive order designed to keep terrorists from entering the country was directed against six Muslim countries, and all of them except Iran were also Arab countries.

It's true that some of the most dramatic acts of terrorism, from the Munich Olympics in 1972 to the 9/11 attacks in the United States, were by Arabs. But it's wrong to represent even Middle East terrorism as exclusively Arab. The Jewish underground used terrorism against the British in Palestine. Both Yitzhak Shamir and Menachem Begin who later became Israeli prime ministers led such groups.[9] Iran, which is high on the US list of terrorist governments, isn't even an Arab country (it's Persian). Nor is Arab terrorism all the work of Muslims. The Phalangists who massacred Palestinians in the Sabra and Shatila refugee camps of Lebanon in 1982 were Christians. Also Christian were the founders of the two principal PLO factions after Fatah: George Habash[10] of the Popular Front for the Liberation of

Palestine and Nawef Hawatmeh of the Democratic Front for the Liberation of Palestine. Nor is terrorism by any means confined to the Middle East. The Pol Pot regime undertook a campaign of genocidal terror in Cambodia exceeded in recent history only by the Nazis' extermination of Jews. Terror was used by the IRA in Northern Ireland, the Basques in Spain, the Tamil Tigers in Sri Lanka, and the African National Congress in South Africa.[11] The 1995 Oklahoma City terror bombing—second in casualties only to 9/11 in American history—was by Timothy McVeigh, a white middle-class veteran who had earned a Bronze Star in the Gulf War.

15.5 How some terrorists view themselves

Is the terrorist as a person necessarily any worse than the soldier in uniform? Both are prepared to kill other human beings. If the one uses unconventional means, that's likely because they're all he has. It would be odd to say that if terrorists had an army, navy, and air force at their disposal, it would be all right to use them, but since they don't, they may not use homemade bombs (as the Boston marathon bombers did) or box-cutters (as the 9/11 hijackers did). Rank and file soldiers do what they do because they're told to. Often they've been drafted or recruited and have little understanding of the issues for which they're required to kill. No doubt the same is true of many terrorists, who are recruited by propaganda. But terrorists often do what they do knowledgeably and with belief in the rightness of their cause. Nigerian Umar Farouk Abdulmutallab, a shy, serious son of a wealthy banker, reportedly thought that "God was guiding him to jihad" in his failed attempt in 2009 to blow up a US airliner on route to Detroit with explosives hidden in his underwear.[12] They also often think of themselves as engaged in a legitimate military struggle. When Palestinian Georges Abdalla was convicted of terrorist activities in France, he claimed that he was a "Palestinian fighter," not a terrorist.[13] Former Jewish terrorists gathered to reminisce about their 1946 bombing of the King David Hotel in Jerusalem that left ninety-one dead. One reportedly said, "I am very proud of the operation militarily. I felt myself like a soldier of these Jewish forces."[14] As Algerian-born suspected terrorist Kamel Daoudi awaited trial in Paris, he said: "I accept the name of terrorist if it is used to mean that I terrorize a one-sided system of iniquitous power and a perversity that comes in many forms. I have never terrorized innocent individuals and I will never do so. But I will fight any form of injustice and those who support it."[15] Aimal Khan Kasi, in a death row interview before his execution for killing two CIA employees, said, "What I did was in retaliation against the US government" for its Middle Eastern policy and support of Israel. "It had nothing to do with terrorism," he said, adding that he opposed the killing of American citizens in the September 11, 2001, attack.[16] To all appearances, these are people who commit themselves to a cause and pursue it with conviction. It's precisely because their conviction—at least as measured by their willingness to sacrifice and kill—is stronger than that of the average person that they're willing to do things most people consider abhorrent.

The point is that it's a mistake to represent terrorism as the work of one people or one religion or one government. Any people desperate enough are capable of engaging in it, any government unscrupulous enough is capable of using it.

15.6 Terrorism and the killing of innocents

Terrorism is intentionally directed against civilians more often than is standard warfare, and it's widely assumed that doing so is its primary objective. That assumption apparently underlay the 2011 killing of an American, Anwar al-Awlaki, a supporter of jihad, by a US drone strike in Yemen.

Key Quote 15B

Mr. Awlaki became the first American citizen deliberately killed on the order of a president, without criminal charges or trial, since the Civil War ... Mr. Obama argued that killing Mr. Awlaki was the equivalent of a justified police shooting of a gunman who was threatening civilians.[17]

But, as the preceding quotation from the Kaiser (Section 15.3) attests, warfare can and does target civilians. The terror bombings of Dresden, Hiroshima, and Nagasaki probably killed more civilians than have been killed by ter-rorists throughout the world in all the years since.[18] The majority of the fifty million or so killed in the Second World War were civilians, as most likely would be the majority of persons killed in any sizable war in the future. While most of them were not targeted as civilians, many of their deaths were foreseeable from the military actions that caused them.

During the Vietnam War, both sides terrorized the civilians whose sup-port they needed. The Vietcong, for example, would steal into villages that collaborated with the South Vietnamese and US troops and disembowel the village leader in front the rest of the villagers. On the American side, a US officer who had commented upon the gloomy prospects of success in opera-tions in the delta area was asked what the answer was:

> "Terror," he said pleasantly. "The Vietcong have terrorized the peas-ants to get their cooperation ... We must terrorize the villagers even more, so they see that their real self-interest lies with us. We've got to start bombing and strafing the villages that aren't friendly to the Government." He then added, "Of course we won't do it. That's not our way of doing things ... But terror is what it takes."[19]

It was reported soon after: "U.S. and allied forces are adopting a program of destroying homes and crops in areas which feed and shield the communist forces. For years, Americans have refused to participate in 'scorched earth' efforts, leaving them to the Vietnamese. Now Americans are directly involved."[20]

Washington Post correspondent John T. Wheeler reported on one such operation on March 30, 1967:

> The Vietnamese woman ignored the crying baby in her arms. She stared in hatred as the American infantrymen with shotguns blasted away at chickens and ducks. Others shot a water buffalo and the family dog. While her husband, father and young son were led away, the torch was put to the hut that still contained the family belongings. The flames consumed everything—including the shrine to the family ancestors. The GIs didn't have much stomach for the job, but orders were orders ... "God, my wife would faint if she could see what I'm doing now," an infantryman said. "Killing ... [Vietcong] is one thing, but killing puppies and baby ducks and stuff like that—it's something else, man."

More recently, US fighter pilots reportedly were prepared to shoot down United Airlines Flight 93 if necessary to prevent it from reaching Washington on 9/11. They were prepared to kill the innocent passengers to achieve their objective (to prevent the plane from reaching its target). The hijackers, for their part, were prepared to kill those same people in the course of trying to achieve *their* objective (perhaps to destroy the White House[21]). Would the killing of innocents have been permissible in the one case but not in the other?

It might be argued that the US pilots wouldn't have intended to kill the passengers, even though they knew that they would do so if they shot the plane down. But such reasoning is available to terrorists as well. The hijackers of Flight 93 might not have intended to kill those particular persons either. But it was foreseeable that they would do so, and they were willing to do so in pursuit of their objective (believed to be to strike a target in Washington). In fact, the hijackers of the four planes on 9/11 probably would have preferred to fly empty planes that day; it would have simplified their task. (Rebellious passengers, after all, are believed to have caused the premature crash of Flight 93.) It's hard to believe, though, that they didn't intend to kill the persons in the World Trade Center and Pentagon. But even there, with a little philosophical ingenuity they might have argued that their objective wasn't to kill civilians at all, though it was foreseeable that they would do so; it was, rather, to destroy symbols of US military and economic power. Had the nearly 3,000 persons who were killed on 9/11 been assembled in an open field and the hijackers been confronted with the choice of killing them or striking an empty World Trade Center, Pentagon, and White House, they might well have chosen to do the latter. If their aim had been simply to kill Americans, they could more easily have done that by attacking crowded football stadiums, and they could have done so (and spared their own lives) simply by planting explosives rather than by crashing airliners into buildings.

In the case of the hijackers, most people would be quick to say that such reasoning isn't good enough; that if the hijackers could foresee that they would kill innocents, they are culpable. But if we say that, then we must be prepared to point out a moral difference between that and the cases in which military power is used in ways that will foreseeably though not intentionally kill innocents. For example, on July 23, 2002, Israel dropped a 2,000-pound bomb in a Gaza neighborhood that killed not only the targeted Hamas leader but 15 others as well, including 9 children.[22] They weren't targeting the children. But it was foreseeable that they would kill them. Estimates of the number of Iraqi civilian casualties by the London-based Iraq Body Count range from 170,635 to 190,240. These, too, no doubt weren't targeted as civilians. Yet such deaths are foreseeable in urban warfare. If we cannot point to a moral difference between the killing of innocents by terrorists and the killing of innocents by soldiers in warfare, then it might be argued that they should be judged similarly. This would represent an application of the principle of universalizability discussed in Theory Box 1F in Chapter 1, Section 1.10, slightly modified to deal with actions rather than treatment of persons:

Theory Box 15A

As formulated in Theory Box 1F, the **principle of universalizability (U)** asserts:

U: Persons ought to be treated similarly unless there are morally relevant dissimilarities among them.

We may take this to imply also:

U$_1$: Acts should be judged similarly unless there are morally relevant dissimilarities among them.

The point is that the deliberate killing of innocents doesn't in itself suffice to distinguish terrorism from much of conventionally accepted military violence. For that reason, it's unclear why the same logic thought to justify the killing of civilians in wartime—namely, that so doing is believed unavoidable, useful, or necessary in the pursuit of one's ends—doesn't equally justify killing them in terroristic violence. Or, to turn the matter around, it's unclear why the killing of civilians by soldiers in wartime isn't as bad as the killing of them by terrorists.

15.7 What is war?

In any event, while terrorism is almost universally condemned, war is almost universally accepted. By that is meant that nearly everyone thinks that war is sometimes morally justified. The so-called *just war tradition* attempts to provide a moral justification for war.

As with terrorism, there's no consensus as to precisely what war is. Over the centuries it has been given many definitions. One of the most famous is by the nineteenth-century German writer Karl von Clausewitz (1792–1831).

1. "War is ... an act of force to compel our enemy to do our will."[23]

This is overly broad, of course. Unless one thinks of an "act" as possibly extending over 5, 10, or 20 years—as wars sometimes do—war cannot plausibly be identified with a single act. Sticking a gun in someone's ribs and saying "Your money or your life" is an act of violence intended to compel another person (whether an opponent or not) to fulfill one's will, but it surely doesn't represent war.

Another definition is offered by political scientist Quincy Wright (1890–1970):

2. War is "the *legal condition* which *equally* permits two or more hostile groups to carry on a *conflict* by *armed* force."[24]

Unlike definition (1), this definition introduces the notion of law; war is understood as a legal condition. It also represents the condition as one that permits groups to use armed force. The notion of "groups" is, however, vague and sets no limits to what may count as groups for purposes of understanding war (states, societies, militias?). And obviously, "hostile groups" can go to war illegally if their conflict is in violation of international law.

Still another definition, offered by Francis Lieber (1798–1872), the nineteenth-century writer on the laws of war, identifies the groups in question:

3. War is "a state of armed hostility between sovereign nations or governments."[25]

Unlike definitions (1) and (2), definition (3) identifies sovereign states as the actors in war. Whether or not armed hostility rises to the level of warfare, however, might be questioned. There often are border skirmishes between states (as, e.g., between India and Pakistan over Kashmir) that arguably represent armed hostilities but which do not amount to war.

There are important elements in these conceptions of war, however—particularly those of violence and states. So let us propose the following as a definition of war in what we may call a standard sense:

Definition Box 15C

War: The pursuit of ends by two or more states through the use of organized, systematic violence against one another.

The term "war" is, of course, used in many ways—such as "civil war" and "guerilla war"—that depart from this standard sense. The further removed one gets from the standard sense, the more attenuated the sense of war that is utilized, to the point where when we speak of "war on poverty" or "war on drugs" we are using "war" in a metaphorical sense, not a literal sense. An interesting question is whether the so-called war on terrorism represents a literal sense of war or is merely metaphorical. It would appear to stand somewhere between the literal and metaphorical senses.

15.8 Can war be morally justified?

No one thinks that war is *always* justified. People usually believe that wars are bad because of the death and destruction they cause but can nonetheless sometimes be justified. Those who believe that some wars are justified we shall call *warists*. Following philosopher Duane Cady, in his book *From Warism to Pacifism: A Moral Continuum*, we shall define "warism" as follows:

Definition Box 15D

Warism: The view that war is sometimes morally justified in practice as well as in theory.

On the other hand, those who say that war cannot be morally justified usually hold that war in the world we live in and as we know it is wrong, not that every conceivable war in hypothetical situations is wrong. That is, they believe that even if some wars could be justified in theory, war in practice is wrong. Those who hold this view are *conditional pacifists* as opposed to *absolute pacifists*—or pacifists for short. We'll define pacifism in Definition Box 15E.

In these terms, most people are warists. They support the armament of their country and the willingness of their governments to go to war if deemed necessary.

Why is there a moral problem with war? The obvious answer is because it causes death and destruction. More specifically, the problem for modern war can be posed in the following way:

1. Modern war makes large-scale, systematic use of lethal weapons for the purpose of killing human beings.

2. Whatever is done for that purpose is done with the intention to kill human beings.
3. The large-scale, systematic use of such weapons with that intention inevitably kills innocent human beings as well.
4. That it does so can be known.
5. What can be known (of the future) is foreseeable.
6. Therefore: Modern war intentionally kills human beings and foreseeably kills innocent human beings.

Intentionally killing tens of thousands or even millions of human beings is presumptively wrong. Even more so is foreseeably killing tens of thousands or even millions of innocent persons. If an act is presumptively wrong, the burden is on those who would perform it to show that the presumption can be defeated in the circumstances in which they propose to perform it. So there is a moral problem with war. Can war be justified?

15.9 The just war theory

War might be morally assessed from any of the basic positions in ethical theory regarding moral justification. Two main types of ethical theory are utilitarianism (already considered briefly in Chapter 1, Theory Box 1E, Section 1.8) and deontologism:

Theory Box 15B

Utilitarianism: An act is right if and only if it produces at least as great a balance of good over bad in its consequences as any other act available to the agent.
Deontologism: Value and consequences are either irrelevant or relevant but not decisive to the determination of right and wrong.

For example, war might be morally assessed purely in terms of its consequences, and more specifically, in terms of the value of its consequences. (See Chapter 6, Theory Box 6B, Section 6.5.) Such a consequentialist (or more specifically, utilitarian) justification would require that one consider nothing other than the consequences of war and the balance of good and evil in those consequences. In its simplest form, a consequentialist justification would say that if a particular war produced at least as great a balance of good over evil in its consequences as any other alternative, then it was justified; otherwise it wasn't. If it brought about a greater balance of good over evil, then it was not only justified, it was morally obligatory.

Deontological ethical theories, on the other hand, would say that either the consequences of a war are irrelevant to its justification; or if they are relevant, they aren't decisive in assessing whether the war was justified. A deontologist might say, for example, that if a war violates trust as embodied in international treaties, or if it kills innocent people, then it may fail to be justified even if it brings about a greater good. Some things, the deontologist says, are equally, or even more, important than the value of consequences.

The just war theory (JWT) has roots in Cicero (106–43 BCE), the Roman lawyer and philosopher, and St. Augustine (354–430), an early church bishop who is often thought of as the father of the JWT. Over the centuries there evolved both religious and secular versions, and today it's widely considered the main ethical approach to the justification of war. The JWT has a deontological moral foundation. It attaches weight to consequences but holds that other types of considerations are relevant as well. The JWT has received many formulations. but it typically consists of two parts, referred to by Latin terms.

Theory Box 15C

Jus ad bellum (justice in the resort to war) sets forth the conditions that must be met in order for a state to be justified in resorting to war in the first place.

Jus in bello (justice in the conduct of war) sets forth the conditions that must be met in the conduct of war once it's begun, whether or not one was justified in going to war in the first place.

A standard representation of these conditions is the following:

Theory Box 15D

Just War Theory

Jus ad bellum (JAB)	Jus in bello (JIB)
Just cause	**Proportionality**

Competent authority   **Discrimination**
Right intention
Probability of success
Comparative justice
Proportionality
Last resort

According to JWT, all of the conditions in the first column must be met in order to be justified in going to war in the first place. The two conditions in the second column must be met in order for the war to be conducted justly once begun. For a war as conducted by a state to be fully just, the conditions of both *jus ad bellum* (JAB) and *jus in bello* (JIB) must be met. One might be justified in going to war (assuming that some wars are justified) but conduct the war abominably—for example, by committing atrocities and wantonly killing civilians. By the same token, one might have wrongfully gone to war in the first place (hence have violated the conditions of JAB) but conduct the war scrupulously according to the provisions of JIB. Although JWT tends to say that a war cannot be just if it fails to meet the conditions of JAB, it has no clear answer to the question whether a war is just that meets the conditions of JAB but fails (sometimes, often, or much of the time) to meet the conditions of JIB.

As indicated, the JWT has both religious and secular forms. They emphasize more or less the same conditions, though sometimes with different interpretations of those conditions. The JWT plays a prominent role in the Catholic Church, and in a 1983 Pastoral Letter the American Catholic bishops explained the conditions of a just war. These constitute a representative example of modern thinking about JWT:

Jus Ad Bellum

Just Cause: War is permissible only to confront "a real and certain danger," i.e., to protect innocent life, to preserve conditions necessary for decent human existence, and to secure basic human rights . . .

Competent Authority: In the Catholic tradition the right to use force has always been joined to the common good; war must be declared by those with responsibility for public order, not by private groups or individuals . . .

Comparative Justice: Every party to a conflict should acknowledge the limits of its "just cause" and the consequent requirement to use *only* limited means in pursuit of its objectives. Far from legitimizing a crusade mentality, comparative justice is designed to relativize absolute claims and to restrain the use of force in a "justified" conflict . . .

Right Intention: Right intention is related to just cause—war can be legitimately intended only for the reasons set forth above as a just cause. During the conflict, right intention means pursuit of peace and reconciliation, including avoiding unnecessarily destructive acts or imposing unreasonable conditions (e.g., unconditional surrender).

Last Resort: For resort to war to be justified, all peaceful alternatives must have been exhausted . . .

Probability of Success: This is a difficult criterion to apply, but its purpose is to prevent irrational resort to force or hopeless resistance when the outcome of either will clearly be disproportionate or futile. The determination includes a recognition that at times defense of key values, even against great odds, may be a "proportionate" witness.

Proportionality: In terms of the *jus ad bellum* criteria, proportionality means that the damage to be inflicted and the costs incurred by war must be proportionate to the good expected by taking up arms . . . This principle of proportionality applies throughout the conduct of the war as well as to the decision to begin warfare.

Jus in Bello: Even when the stringent conditions which justify resort to war are met, the conduct of war (i.e., strategy, tactics, and individual actions) remains subject to continuous scrutiny in light of two principles . . . These principle are proportionality and discrimination . . . Just response to aggression must be discriminate; it must be directed against unjust aggressors, not against innocent people caught up in a war not of their making . . . The principle prohibits directly intended attacks on non-combatants and non-military targets . . .

When confronting choices among specific military options, the question asked by proportionality is: once we take into account not only the military advantages that will be achieved by using this means but also all the harms reasonably expected to follow from using it, can its use still be justified?[26]

These conditions each admit of substantial elaboration. We cannot go into all of them here, but particularly noteworthy is the understanding of **just cause**, which according to the bishops' account consists of any or all of the following:

1. Avenging the violation of a right
2. Self-defense
3. Protecting the innocent

Self-defense normally implies that one has been aggressed against. Hence the notion of aggression figures prominently in discussions of war and international relations. But both (1) and (2) leave open the possibility that the side with a just cause may initiate a war (in that sense, aggressing against another state). In the case of avenging the violation of a right, one might hold that a state needn't wait until it's aggressed against to initiate a war against another state; it may initiate a war itself if it has a just cause. In the case of (3), for example, if a state is committing atrocities against its own citizens, another state may (assuming that other conditions are met) wage war against the first state on behalf of the rights of the oppressed (the rationale for so-called humanitarian military intervention). Even the notion of self-defense in (2) is sometimes expanded to mean "pre-emptive" or even "preventive" self-defense, in which case one may claim to be acting in self-defense if one initiates the actual fighting, either to anticipate an imminent attack by an adversary or to forestall an attack that may not be imminent. The result in the first case is *preemptive war*, in the second case it is *preventive war*. This option was made explicit by President George W. Bush:

Key Quote 15C

The greater the threat, the greater is the risk of inaction—and the more compelling the case for taking anticipatory action to defend ourselves, even if uncertainty remains as to the time and place of the enemy's attack. There are few greater threats than a terrorist attack with WMD [weapons of mass destruction]. To forestall or prevent such hostile acts by our adversaries, the United States will, if necessary, act preemptively in exercising our inherent right of self-defense [Contained in Article 51 of the UN Charter].[27]

15.10 War and the killing of innocents

Even the most ardent warists are troubled by the killing of innocent persons in wartime. The JWT, in the principle of discrimination under JIB, addresses this issue. That principle requires that in the conduct of war (whether the war was justly entered into or not) one must discriminate between those one may permissibly kill (combatants on the other side) and those one may not permissibly kill (civilians or innocent persons).

When warfare was hand-to-hand, one could easily abide by this principle. If you were fighting with clubs, swords, spears, and even bows and arrows you could clearly choose whether or not to kill persons who weren't directly engaged in combat with you. In modern warfare it's more difficult and sometimes impossible. With bombs, artillery, drones, and missiles it's impossible to be certain that you won't sometimes kill noncombatants or innocent persons.

Just warists (as we may call advocates of the JWT) tend to appeal to a principle we encountered in connection with terrorism. The principle distinguishes between the *intentional* killing of innocents/noncombatants, either as a means or as an end, and the foreseeable killing of innocents/noncombatants incidental to the pursuit of other, legitimate ends. The central element of this principle—*right intention*—is one of the conditions of JAB. There, the requirement is that if one is to go to war justly, one must intend only to bring about a good. Even though it's foreseeable that if you wage war you will cause death, destruction, pain, and suffering, these cannot be what you aim at; bringing them about cannot be your intention. You have a *right* intention only if you intend to promote a good (such as any of the ends encompassed by a just cause).

The notion of right intention also figures prominently in the understanding of discrimination in JIB. For in the conduct of war, you may not intend to kill innocents/noncombatants either as an end (killing them for the sake of killing them) or as a means (to achieving some good). But you may kill them if their deaths are incidental and even foreseeable in the pursuit of legitimate ends. In the former case (killing them as an end or as a means) their killing is said to be *direct*, and that's prohibited. In the latter case, their killing is said to be *indirect*, and that's permissible (provided certain other conditions are met, such as that a greater good is expected to be achieved by the action that results in their deaths). An incident early in the Iraq War is illustrative:

Either Take a Shot or Take a Chance

At the base camp of the Fifth marine Regiment here, two sharpshooters ... sat on a sand berm and swapped combat tales while their column stood at a halt on the road toward Baghdad ... They said Iraqi fighters had often mixed in with civilians from nearby villages, jumping out of houses and cars to shoot at them, and then often running away. The marines said they had little trouble dispatching their foes, most of whom they characterized as ill trained and cowardly.

"We had a great day," [one marine said]. "We killed a lot of people."

Both marines said they were most frustrated by the practice of some Iraqi soldiers to use unarmed women and children as shields against American bullets. They called the tactic cowardly but agreed that it had been effective … [T]hey said they had declined several times to shoot at Iraqi soldiers out of fear they might hit civilians.

"It's a judgment call," [one marine said]. "If the risks outweigh the losses, then you don't take the shot."

But in the heat of a firefight, both men conceded, when the calculus often warps, a shot not taken in one set of circumstances may suddenly present itself as a life-or-death necessity.

"We dropped a few civilians," [one said], "but what do you do?"

To illustrate, the sergeant offered a pair of examples from earlier in the week.

"There was one Iraqi soldier, and 25 women and children," he said. "I didn't take the shot."

But more than once … he faced a different choice: one Iraqi soldier standing among two or three civilians. He recalled one such incident, in which he and other men in his unit opened fire. He recalled watching one of the women standing near the Iraqi soldier go down.

"I'm sorry," the sergeant said. "But the chick was in the way."[28]

There is a second and even more complex problem with the killing of innocents/noncombatants in war. We've been speaking as though the categories of innocents and noncombatants were the same. They aren't. Noncombatant is a morally neutral category. It simply designates someone who's not a certifiable participant in combat—someone who's not in the military, not wearing a uniform, and not engaged in fighting. Innocence implies that one is free of guilt or wrongdoing. That implies a moral judgment. It signifies that one is free of guilt or wrongdoing with regard to the particular war in question. Many noncombatants (e.g., members of government) may not be innocent in this sense; and many combatants may be innocent. It's more difficult to be confident that one isn't killing innocent persons in warfare than it is to be confident that one isn't killing noncombatants.

We can illustrate these points by means of a mythical example. Suppose King Mighty the Great launches an unjust aggressive war against King Great the Mighty. All of those fighting for King Great will be fighting a just war (assuming that the other conditions of JAB and JIB are met). They'll be free of any wrongdoing relative to that particular war. Although they're combatants, they'll be innocent. The killing of them by King Mighty's soldiers will be the killing of innocent persons. In principle—and almost certainly always in fact—the killing of innocent persons will be unavoidable in any war in which one side is acting justly and the other is acting unjustly. Not only that, but many—and perhaps most—of the soldiers who are fighting for King Mighty may be innocent as well. They'll include farmers, cobblers, and blacksmiths who have been pressed into service by the king. They may have little or no knowledge of why King Mighty attacked King Great and have no responsibility for any wrongdoing. They may be innocent as well, by which the killing of them by King Great's soldiers will also be the killing of innocent persons.[29]

The upshot is that while in principle it's possible to avoid killing noncombatants in warfare (if, e.g., all combat were hand-to-hand), it's virtually impossible to avoid killing innocent persons. It's not the point of war to kill innocent persons, but modern war inevitably does so.

15.11 War and the killing of soldiers

It is in the nature of war, however, to kill soldiers. While one could hypothesize wars fought with water pistols or paintballs, one cannot have a war in any standard sense without the killing of soldiers. That's what the conduct of war is about. If the killing of soldiers by one another in warfare is impermissible, then war is impermissible.

It's often assumed without question that it's permissible for soldiers on all sides to kill one another, whether they're fighting in a just war or not. Once one has entered the military, it's thought that one becomes licensed, so to speak, to kill other human beings without limit in warfare. It's just that those one kills must be combatants, which means that they're similarly licensed to kill you. In these circumstances, according to this thinking, in the process of becoming licensed to kill you also forfeit a right to life at the hands of others who, like you, have been given identical licensure by their government. The essentials of this outlook are expressed by political scientist Michael Walzer.

In our judgments of the fighting, we abstract from all consideration of the justice of the cause. We do this because the moral status of individual soldiers on both sides is very much the same: they are led to fight by their loyalty to their own states and by their lawful obedience. They are most likely to believe that their wars are just, and while the basis of that belief is not necessarily rational inquiry but, more often, a kind of unquestioning acceptance of official propaganda, nevertheless they are not criminals; they face one another as moral equals . . .

Now, aggression is ... a criminal activity, but our view of its participants is very different; ... In the course of an aggressive war, a soldier shoots another soldier, a member of the enemy army defending his homeland. Assuming a conventional firefight, this is not called murder; nor is the soldier regarded after the war as a murderer, even by his former enemies. The case is in fact no different from what it would be if the second soldier shot the first. Neither man is a criminal, and so both can be said to act in self-defense ... [S]o long as they fight in accordance with the rules of war, no condemnation is possible.[30]

This condition, in which soldiers may permissibly kill one another in wartime, has sometimes been called the moral equality of soldiers. I shall refer to it as the *moral expendability of soldiers* (MES). The permissibility of war depends upon MES.

15.12 Are soldiers morally expendable?

One line of reasoning to try to establish MES contends that the guilt or innocence of soldiers is irrelevant to judgments we make of the conduct of war. Soldiers, in this view, are dangerous people. Through their training they've allowed themselves to become dangerous people. Hence when they meet on the battlefield, they're all fighting in self-defense, which they have a right to do. As Walzer puts it in another passage:

Key Quote 15D

Simply by fighting, whatever their private hopes and intentions, they [soldiers] have lost their title to life and liberty, and they have lost it even though, unlike aggressor states, they have committed no crime.[31]

Hence soldiers may permissibly kill one another, regardless of the justice of the cause for which they do so.

We might formulate this reasoning a little more precisely:

1. If soldiers forfeit their right to life, then the killing of soldiers by one another is morally permissible.
   a. Persons forfeit their right to life when they allow themselves to become dangerous persons.
   b. Persons allow themselves to become dangerous persons when they enter the military.
   c. The soldiers (by definition) have entered the military.
   d. Therefore: The soldiers are dangerous persons.
2. Therefore: Soldiers forfeit their right to life.
3. Therefore: The killing of soldiers by one another is morally permissible (MES).

The claim in 1(d) doesn't mean, of course, that every soldier at every moment is dangerous. All soldiers sleep and many repair equipment, cook meals, or do paperwork as their main duties. The point is, rather, that in wartime they're all part of a war effort, hence are dangerous to the soldiers on the other side. In the military everyone trains to kill. But not everyone's main duty is to kill. Those who don't kill (which is often true of most soldiers in a war) support those who do in various ways. It's in that sense that they may be considered dangerous.

Does it follow, however, that soldiers forfeit their right to life, as (2) asserts? One line of reasoning to try to support that conclusion is that when soldiers, as dangerous people, meet on the battlefield, they're all fighting in self-defense. Since everyone (according to this reasoning) has a right to self-defense, soldiers have a right to kill one another.

15.13 Is there an absolute right to kill in self-defense?

Many people believe that war is justified in self-defense. They believe that individuals are justified in killing in self-defense, hence that states are justified in killing in national defense. Thus at least defensive wars are morally justified.

The argument we considered in the previous section doesn't purport to show that states are justified in waging war (and killing) in self-defense, though it's consistent with that view. It purports to show that since soldiers on both sides in a war are justified in killing in self-defense, soldiers are morally expendable. They may kill one another with moral impunity, because they're all acting in self-defense.

But is the right to kill in self-defense an absolute right? Are you justified in killing other persons in any circumstances in which you believe yourself threatened by them?

The problem of self-defense arises only when one is in a dangerous situation and there is some imminent threat to life or limb. Whether one is justified in killing in such situations may depend upon whether one has *knowingly* and *voluntarily* entered into the situation. And it may depend upon whether one bears some responsibility for the situation's being dangerous in the first place.

If you deliberately enter the den of a hungry lion, are you then justified in killing the lion if it attacks you? You had the option not to enter the den in the first place. Let's suppose that you have the option to retreat and close a gate behind you if the lion approaches. You could have chosen not to enter the den; and you could choose to leave the den unharmed (at least until the lions' jaws clamp down on you). Only if you choose to stay is your life in jeopardy. Do you have the right to kill the lion with the gun you carry?

Take another case. Suppose you favor stern action to wipe out drug addiction and crime, as do some governments. You'd like nothing better than to kill some of those responsible for the drug problem. So you venture out in the middle of the night and walk alone in a high-crime area where there's a likelihood of being mugged. Sure enough, someone tries to mug you, and you draw your gun and kill him. You were under assault. You were acting in self-defense. Were you justified in so doing? You chose to enter the dangerous situation. You did so in the hope of being assaulted. Your intention was to kill someone in the course of defending yourself.

Cases of this sort raise serious questions about whether there's an absolute right of self-defense. At the least, avoiding dangerous situations—or removing oneself from them when that is possible—are moral options that must be weighed into the scales.

Soldiers know that if they enter the military they're agreeing to being sent into dangerous situations on the orders of others. They also know that if they were to remove themselves from dangerous situations once they are in them, which might not be possible, there would no longer be an issue of self-defense. (There might be severe penalties, though, at the hands of their superiors if they were to do this.) They also know, if they've reflected on the argument for MES, that their adversaries have a moral right to kill them only if they—the adversaries—are in imminent danger from them. Adversaries are entitled to kill you, on the view we're considering, only on grounds of self-defense. If you cease to be a threat to them, they no longer have a moral right to kill you (unless they have some other reason than self-defense). You've defused the dangerous situation. If soldiers on both sides cease their threat to one another, none of them has a license to kill. And none of them has forfeited his right to life.

15.14 The paradox of the moral expendability of soldiers

Things aren't this simple in practice. In the stress and confusion of war (or the threat of war) it'll often be difficult to know precisely whether others pose a threat to you and you to them. In practice, it would no doubt be virtually impossible for soldiers to cease being the threats they are to one another when fighting is under way. They might be court-martialed or shot on the spot by their commanding officers. However, the principle is clear: by the above argument, soldiers can render it morally impermissible for other soldiers to kill them by ceasing to be a threat to those other soldiers. Soldiers on all sides can render it morally wrong to kill them by renouncing their license to kill. If they can in principle do that, then it's an open question whether the right to self-defense is justifiably exercised in these circumstances. If the MES doesn't obtain, then it's difficult to see how war can be morally justified, whatever one says of the rights of collectivities to self-defense.

Even if this were not correct, there is something paradoxical about MES. If it's morally permissible for soldiers on all sides to kill one another, then (assuming that they are abiding by the laws of war and the constraints of *jus in bello*), nothing they do is wrong. Virtually everything that happens once a war begins is morally permissible, irrespective of the justice or injustice of the reasons for the war. It's difficult, in that case, to make any sense of saying that any such a war is unjust. For this reason, one of the main tenets of JWT—the MES—seems to conflict with the whole point of the JWT, which is to enable one to distinguish just from unjust wars. It's paradoxical to say that a country acts unjustly in going to war but that everything it does once the fighting commences is morally permissible.

15.15 Pacifism

Pacifism is opposition to war. As such, it's distinguished from nonviolence, since you might oppose war but think violence in some situations is permissible. Nonetheless, early pacifism usually derived from an explicit or implicit commitment to *nonviolence*. This is true of early Christianity, Buddhism, Jainism, Taoism, and the Hinduism espoused by Gandhi in his interpretation of the *Bhagavad Gita*. An exception is Moism in ancient China, which is expressly pacifistic but doesn't espouse nonviolence.

Pacifism may be personal, principled, or pragmatic, depending upon how it's grounded. We may distinguish the following forms of pacifism:

Definition Box 15E

Personal Pacifism: Opposition to war as a personal commitment not considered binding on others.
Principled Pacifism: Opposition to war on grounds considered valid for all. For example:

   a. **Religious Pacifism: Pacifism based on religious or spiritual grounds.**
   b. **Moral Pacifism: Pacifism based on moral grounds.**
   c. **Pragmatic Pacifism: Pacifism based on purely rational and practical grounds, such as the belief that war is an irrational, costly, and ineffective way to pursue one's ends.**

Personal pacifists might agree with pragmatic pacifists that war is impractical. And like principled pacifists, they might take their renunciation of war to have a moral or religious character. They just don't insist that others make that same commitment they do. Personal commitment, rather than general principles about religion, morality, or practicality are central to their pacifism.

Principled pacifists, for their part, can also agree that war is ineffective. That is, they can secondarily be pragmatic pacifists as well. But that isn't their main reason for being pacifists. Their main reason is their belief that war is wrong for everyone (moral pacifism) and/or contrary to certain religious or spiritual commitments everyone should espouse (religious pacifism).

Pragmatic pacifists can agree that war is morally wrong or contrary to various religious or spiritual outlooks. That is, they can secondarily be principled pacifists. But their main reason for being pacifists is their conviction that war is impractical. Whereas principled pacifists are likely to think of war as wrong, pragmatic pacifists are likely to think of it first of all as wasteful or irrational.

15.16 Conclusion: a common ground between warists and pacifists

There's a little-noticed aspect of war: that it's a cooperative activity on the part of those engaged in it. (This is implied in the definition of war by Quincy Wright in Section 15.7, though the emphasis there is on a legal condition.) It's as though both sides tacitly agree to try to settle their differences by means of large-scale, systematic military violence. In times past, there were often formal declarations of war, in which these intentions were made explicit. Today that rarely happens. But the cooperative nature of war remains. If either side refuses to try to resolve the differences between it and the other side by fighting, war cannot take place. The other side could still attack the side that refuses to wage war. That would be aggression, but it wouldn't be war. War wouldn't begin until the side aggressed against chose to fight back. War requires that both sides agree, expressly or implicitly, to fight.

This is one of the points of difference between war and terrorism. Terrorism requires only the unilateral decision by one side (individual, group, state) to use violence. It doesn't require a cooperative response by the other side.

A simple example illustrates the point. High-speed chases involving police and suspects are common. They frequently result in death or injury. But they occur only because the police and the suspects tacitly agree to them. It's not as though the police say, "Okay, we'll give you a head start and then try to catch you." Rather, when they see a traffic violation or suspect a crime, they attempt to pull the person over. The driver of the car then makes the decision to try to evade arrest and speeds off. The police then turn on their sirens and give chase. If either the police didn't give chase or the suspect pulled over at the sign of the flashing lights there would be no high-speed chase. The chase depends upon the willingness of both to try to achieve their ends (the police to apprehend the suspect, the suspect to evade apprehension) by outracing each other.

So with war. Wars can take place only if two (or more) sides tacitly agree to try to resolve their differences by fighting. War *cannot* take place otherwise. Moreover, just as neither the police nor the suspects can engage in a high-speed chase unless their cars have gasoline and the engines are working, so states cannot wage war unless they have armies and weapons and unless some persons in those armies are willing to command others to kill and those others are prepared to obey those commands. That is the structure of every army in the world.

This suggests, therefore, an argument that can provide a starting point for discussing the justifiability of war:

1. War is a cooperative undertaking between warring parties. If either side refuses to fight, war cannot take place.
2. For both sides to cooperate in fighting:
   a. Some persons on each side must command others to kill;
   b. Some persons on each side must obey commands to kill.
3. Therefore: If enough people on either side refuse to kill on command or to command others to kill, war cannot take place.

Both warists and pacifists should be able to agree on all of these points. Where they will disagree will be on such issues as what the consequences would be if one side refuses to fight when the other is bent on aggression, or whether persons have a moral right to command others to kill (and to enforce those commands) or a moral right to kill on the command of others. These are all legitimate questions and can provide a focus for the discussion of the morality of war. But it should be understood that the common view that there's no way to end war is mistaken. War ends if human beings cease to fight wars.

Study questions

1. What are the definitions of terrorism in Definition Boxes 15A and 15B? Why is the first called a *persuasive definition* and the second a *descriptive definition*? What difference does it make which definition one uses?
2. What are some of the *rationalizations for terrorism* considered in Section 15.3?

3. What is *war* (Definition Box 15C)?

4. What is *warism* (Definition Box 15D)?

5. What is the *Just War Theory* (Section 15.9)? What are the components of the theory *jus ad bellum* and *jus in bello* (Theory Box 15C)?

6. What is the *moral expendability of soldiers* (Section 15.12)?

7. What is *Walzer's position* on the moral expendability of soldiers (Key Quote 15D)?

8. Is there an absolute right to kill in self-defense (Section 15.13)?

9. What is the *paradox of the moral expendability of soldiers* (Section 15.14)?

10. What is *pacifism* (Definition Box 15E)? How does considering war a cooperative undertaking between warring parties provide a possible common ground between *warists* and *pacifists* (Section 15.16)?

Notes

1   Albert Einstein, *Ideas and Opinions* (New York: Crown Publishers, Inc., 1962), p. 103.

2   Not that terrorism has a good track record at achieving its ends. As Walter Laqueur writes, "The decision to use terrorist violence is not always a rational one; if it were, there would be much less terrorism, since terrorist activity seldom achieves its aims." "Post Modern Terrorism," *Foreign Affairs*, Vol. 75, No. 5, September/October 1996, 31.

3   Leon Trotsky, *Terrorism and Communism* (Ann Arbor: The University of Michigan Press, 1963), p. 58.

4   http://www.businessinsider.com/bill-gates-op-ed-bio-terrorism-epidemic-world-threat-2017-2.

5   Quoted from Bernard Lewis, "License to Kill: Usama [*sic*] bin Ladin's Declaration of Jihad," *Foreign Affairs*, Vol. 77, No. 6, November/December 1998, 14–19.

6   Copyright 2006 The Associated Press. Copyright 2006 ABC News Internet Ventures.

7   Quoted in Richard A. Falk, Gabriel Kolka, and Robert Jay Lifton (eds), *Crimes of War* (New York: Vintage Books, 1971), p. 135.

8   *The Christian Science Monitor*, December 10, 1986.

9   Begin's group, Irgun, was responsible for the 1946 bombing of the King David Hotel in Jerusalem. Shamir was one of the leaders of the Lehi (Fighters for the Freedom of Israel) responsible for the assassination in 1944 of Lord Moyne, Britain's minister of state for the Middle East, and

in 1948 of Sweden's Count Folke Benadotte, the UN representative to the Middle East. Although Shamir claims to have had no direct knowledge of the Bernadotte assassination, Israeli scholars disagree. Interestingly, Geula Cohen, former Knesset member who worked with Lehi at the time, reportedly says the assassination "was no less moral than other wartime actions." *Jerusalem Post International Edition*, Week Ending October 10, 1998. James Bennet says that after ignoring a British plea to him and other prisoners to renounce their terrorist activities, Yitzhak Shamir "later escaped and returned to the underground, to a campaign of assassination, bombing and arms smuggling, with bank robbery thrown in to finance the effort." "How Ben-Gurion Did It: Is Everyone Listening?," *The New York Times*, August 13, 2003.

10　George Habash, trained as a pediatrician, retired as head of the PFLP in 2000. He had been living in Syria. His successor, Ali Mustafa, who was living in the West Bank city of Ramallah, was assassinated soon after by the Israelis.

11　"Necklacing," burning to death by a gasoline-filled tire around the neck, was a particularly ghastly form of terrorism used by black South Africans against other black South Africans.

12　*The New York Times*, February 23, 2017.

13　*The New York Times*, September 26, 1981.

14　Ibid.

15　*The New York Times*, September 22, 2002. Notice that, unlike the Palestinian and Jewish terrorists quoted, Daoudi accepts the label "terrorist" if (and presumably only if) it represents a struggle against iniquity. By implication— at least as it applies to himself—it precludes attacks upon innocents. Most who discuss terrorism accept the emotively pejorative force the term has, and then apply the term only to those of whom they strongly disapprove. Daoudi, on the other hand, tacitly redefines the term in such a way that it acquires a descriptive meaning that most people would find unobjectionable, provided they do not object in principle to the use of violence.

16　*The New York Times*, November 8, 2002. Abu Abbas, alleged mastermind of the 1985 hijacking of the Achille Lauro, an Italian cruise ship, in which a wheelchair-bound passenger, Leon Klinghoffer, was thrown overboard, has reportedly condemned the 9/11 attack and denounced both Osama bin Laden and Al Qaeda. He died in US custody after being apprehended in Iraq. *The New York Times*, November 3, 2003.

17　*The New York Times*, February 23, 2017.

18　This excludes the genocidal slaughters of the Pol Pot regime in Cambodia and of Tutsi's in Rwanda. Genocide is meant to eradicate a people, not to terrorize them into submission. The case of Cambodia was complex, of course. It arguably was the elimination of a particular class (the educated and well-to-do) that was intended to terrorize others into submission. Thus it combined terrorism and genocide.

19 Jack Langguth, *The New York Times Magazine*, September 19, 1965.

20 *Rochester Times-Union*, January 6, 1966.

21 It is also reported that two mid-level generals are authorized to order the destruction of US and other passenger planes in the future if it is believed that they constitute a comparable threat to the United States.

22 When US forces bombed Afghan villages in July of 2002, killing 48 civilians and wounding 117, mostly women and children (according to Afghan government figures; the Pentagon claims they killed only 34 and wounded 50), they denied targeting them, and blamed the Taliban for "placing women and children near valid military targets." *The New York Times*, September 7, 2002.

23 Carl Von Clausewitz, *On War*, ed. and trans. Michael Howard and Bernard Brodie (Princeton: Princeton University Press, 1989), p. 75.

24 Quincy Wright, *A Study of War*, 2nd ed. (Chicago: University of Chicago Press, 1965), p. 8; emphases in the original.

25 Lieber's Code (US War Department, Gen. Ord. 100 [1863], art. 20). Citation taken from ibid., p. 9, n. 2.

26 Excerpted from *The Challenge of Peace: God's Promise and Our Response*, A Pastoral Letter on War and Peace, May 3, 1983, National Conference of Catholic Bishops.

27 President George W. Bush, *National Security Strategy of the United States*, September 20, 2002.

28 *The New York Times*.com/2003/03/29international/worldspecial/29HALT. html (April 1, 2003).

29 I have adapted this example from one used by Liane Norman.

30 Michael Walzer, *Just and Unjust Wars*, 3rd ed. (New York: Basic Books, 2000), pp. 127f.

31 *Just and Unjust Wars*, p. 136.

For more resources:

www.bloomsbury.com/holmes-introduction-to-applied-ethics

Glossary

DB = Definition Box.
TB = Theory Box.
KQ = Key Quote.
Section: The first numeral denotes the chapter and the second the actual section number. For example, 5.1 indicates Chapter 5, section 1.

Abortion: The intentional premature termination of pregnancy by the removal or induced expulsion of the unborn. (DB 12B, Section 12.11)

Absolute Freedom: Absence of all constraints to action; possible only for a supreme being. (Section 8.2)

Absolute Rights (not to be confused with absolute rightness): A right is absolute if, and only if, it should be honored irrespective of any other considerations, moral or nonmoral. (TB 10B, Section 10.10)

Accidental Property: A property that a person or object can have at one time and not at another without any change in what the person or object is (e.g., being a student is an accidental property of some people; being painted a certain color is an accidental property of some houses). (TB 1C, Section 1.6)

Act of Commission: Intentionally or knowingly bringing about a certain state of affairs. (TB 13A, Section 13.7)

Act of Omission: Intentionally or knowingly refraining from bringing about a certain state of affairs. (TB 13A, Section 13.7)

Active Euthanasia: The act of killing a terminally ill person to end his or her suffering (e.g., by lethal injection, normally with consent). (Section 13.4)

Affirmative Action: Voluntary or mandated measures to end discrimination, compensate for past discrimination, or promote diversity (or all three). (DB 4A, Section 4.5)

Anarchism: The view that government is morally illegitimate. (Section 8.4)

Antecedent: The proposition following the "if" in a conditional proposition (e.g., the sentence "you want your car to run" in the conditional "If you want your car to run, then put gas in it." (TB 5B)

Anthropocentrism: The view that humans are the most important entities in the universe and for that reason are the only ones warranting basic moral consideration. (DB 9A, Section 9.4)

Autonomy: The capacity to live one's life as one chooses. (DB 11B, Section 11.4)

Axiological Ethics: The theory that an act is morally right if, and only if, it actualizes at least as great a balance of good over bad (in the act itself, or its consequences, or a combination of the two) as any other alternative available to the agent. (TB 12E, Section 12.13)

Basic Moral Consideration (BMC): Concern for something (living or nonliving) for its own sake, usually because it is thought to have interests, rights, or value. (TB 9A, Section 9.2)

Beneficence: Doing good. The principle of beneficence is that one ought to do good. (TB 7A, Section 7.4)

Bigot: A person obstinately, often fanatically, devoted to his or her own religion, party, or opinions in ways that are intolerant of others. (KQ 1A, Section 1.3)

Biocentrism: The view that all living things warrant some measure of basic moral consideration. (DB 9C, Section 9.6)

Bourgeoisie: Marx's term for the class of capitalists who own the means of production in capitalist society. (Section 8.7)

Capital: Wealth that can be owned, traded, transferred, or sold through the market on a permanent basis. (KQ 8A, Section 8.1)

Capitalism: A competitive economic system in which the means of production are privately owned and used for profit. (DB 8A, Section 8.1)

Capitalist Principle of Distributive Justice: As formulated by Milton Friedman—To each according to what he, and the instruments he owns, produces. (DB 8D, Section 8.9)

Chauvinism: An unreasoning, intolerant, and often fanatical devotion to one's own country, race, or sex (e.g., male sexists are sometimes called male chauvinists). (DB 2E, Section 2.3)

Civil Liberty: Freedom to do whatever isn't prohibited by law and not to do whatever isn't required by law. (Section 8.2)

Civil Rights: Specific legal entitlements to be free of interference in certain areas of one's life or to receive certain benefits. (Section 8.2)

Collective Morality: Morality understood to guide the conduct of collectivities (e.g., states, societies, groups) in their relation to other collectivities. (TB 6A, Section 6.5)

Coma: A sleep-like state of unconsciousness from which one cannot be roused. (DB 13C, Section 13.6)

Complete Freedom: Conditional freedom accompanied by lack of constraints by others (e.g., as would be true if one lived on an otherwise deserted island). (Section 8.2)

Conceptus: Everything that results directly from fertilization (up to the termination of pregnancy), including zygote, morula, embryo, fetus, umbilical cord, and other membranes. (Section 12.3)

Conditional Freedom: Freedom restricted by one's own mental and physical limitations, the actions of others, and the constraints of the natural environment. (Section 8.2)

Conditional Proposition: An if-then compound of two propositions (e.g., "If you want to be healthy, then eat your spinach"). (TB 5B, Section 5.4)

Connotation (logical): The properties common to all the things to which a general term refers. (TB 3B, Section 3.5)

Consequent: The proposition following the "then" in a conditional proposition (e.g., "he is mortal" in the conditional "If Socrates is a man, then he is mortal"). (TB 5B, Section 5.4)

Consequentialism: The theory that moral right and wrong are determined solely by the consequences of actions. (TB 6B, Section 6.5)

Conservatism: In capitalist societies, a political outlook that favors democracy, capitalism, and little or no governmental interference in the economy. (Section 8.4)

Contingently Slippery Slope: Any situation in which the acceptance of one position will *in fact* (or with high probability) lead to the acceptance of a second position, whether it ought to or not. (TB 13D, Section 13.9)

De Facto Meaning: The literal or commonsense meaning of a term that ordinary speakers of a language typically have in mind when using it. (TB 3A, Section 3.2)

Democratic Socialism: An economic system in which the means of production are publicly owned and used for the benefit of all under a democratic political system. (Section 8.1)

Denotation: The particular things to which a general term refers (e.g., the term "philosophers" denotes Plato, Aristotle, Epicurus, etc.). (TB 3B, Section 3.5)

Deontologism: The theory that value and consequences are either irrelevant or relevant but not decisive, to the determination of moral right and wrong. Contrasts notably with utilitarianism. (TB 15B, Section 15.9)

Derivative Moral Consideration (DMC): Concern for something (living or nonliving) for the sake of something else (e.g., because it is useful to humans). (TB 9A, Section 9.2)

Descriptive Meaning: The beliefs a word or sentence tends to express (on the part of the speaker) or to produce in others (the hearers). (TB 1A, Section 1.3)

Descriptive (Factual) Statement: A sentence that reports a fact (or facts) about persons, objects, or states of affairs. (TB 1D, Section 1.7)

Destitution: The state of being deprived of what is necessary for a minimally decent human life. (DB 7C, Section 7.2)

Deterrence (with regard to the death penalty): Causing people to refrain from committing certain crimes for fear of execution if they do. (DB 14B, Section 14.6)

Dialectic: As discussed in this text, a philosophical methodology based on the interplay among three elements (thesis, antithesis, synthesis); used by Hegel and adapted by Marx to a materialistic philosophy. (Section 8.6)

Distributive Justice: Fairness in the distribution of benefits and/or burdens to individuals or groups. (TB 3D, Section 3.9)

Divine Will Theory: The theory that moral rightness and obligation are determined by God's will. When expressed in terms of God's commands, this is called the Divine Command Theory. (TB 1E, Section 1.8)

Dying: A process (other than aging) which, if uninterrupted, will result in death. (DB 13F, Section 13.7)

Elitism: The view that some individuals are superior (e.g., mentally, physically, or morally) overall to others. (Section 1.9)

Embryo: The unborn from the fourth day after fertilization until the end of the eighth week. (TB 12B, Section 12.3)

Emotive Meaning: The feelings or attitudes a word or sentence tends to express (on the part of the speaker) or to evoke in others (the hearers). (TB 1A, Section 1.3)

Essential Property: An unchangeable property that is part of what makes a person or object what it is (e.g., having three sides is an essential property of a triangle). (TB 1C, Section 1.6)

Ethical Relativism: The theory that what is morally right or wrong (as opposed to what is merely thought to be right or wrong) may vary fundamentally from person to person or culture to culture. (TB 2A, Section 2.6)

Ethnicity: Characteristics (other than racial) such as language, traditions, religion, music, and art that are common to a group of people and tend to create a sense of identity among them. (Section 3.2)

Ethnorace: A term proposed for a people (as some think is true of Hispanic/ Latinos) who have a common identity but can't accurately be characterized as either a race or an ethnic group. (DB 3A, Section 3.2)

Euthanasia ("mercy killing"): the act of killing (or allowing to die) a terminally ill person to end his or her suffering. (Section 13.4)

Evil: Intentionally causing or taking pleasure in the undeserved and unjustified suffering of others for its own sake. (DB 10C, Section 10.9)

Extrinsic Value: Value that depends at least in part upon the relationship of what has value to other things (e.g., a hammer has extrinsic value because it can be used to drive nails). (TB 9B, Section 9.8)

Famine: Severe food shortage in an area or suffered by a people. (DB 7B, Section 7.2)

Fertilization: The union of an egg and sperm, often leading to a replication of cells eventuating in pregnancy. (TB 12B, Section 12.3)

Feticide: The killing of a fetus. (DB 12C, Section 12.11)

Fetus: The unborn following the eighth week after fertilization. (TB 12C, Section 12.3)

Gender: Chromosomal, anatomical, hormonal, psychological, and cultural determinants (varying in importance according to different accounts) of whether a person is male or female or a blend of the two. (Section 2.4)

Gender Harassment: Repeated unwanted behavior toward people because of their sex or gender. (DB 5B, Section 5.1)

Golden Rule Argument: An argument advanced by R. M. Hare that purports to show that the golden rule, properly adapted, shows some abortions to be wrong. (Section 12.12)

Heightism: The fictitious theory that tall people are superior overall to short people. (Section 1.10)

Historical Materialism: Marx's term for the operation of dialectical laws to explain the evolution and operation of socioeconomic systems. (Section 8.7)

Hostile Environment Harassment: An uncomfortable work or study environment owing to sexual harassment directed against oneself or others. Sometimes used to stand for an uncomfortable work or study environment owing to sexual language or depictions that one finds offensive even in the absence of sexual harassment. (Section 5.3)

Humanitarian Military Intervention: The use of military force in other countries, usually without the consent of their governments, on behalf of the rights of oppressed or threatened innocents within those countries. (Section 15.9)

Human Rights: Moral (as opposed to merely legal) rights that are possessed by all persons equally and at all times simply by virtue of their being human. They are possessed independently of law, status, or social position and independently of whether they are acknowledged or respected by others. (TB 8A, Section 8.3)

Incomplete Freedom: Freedom limited by others (individually or collectively) by custom, practice, or law. (Section 8.2)

Individual Morality: Morality understood basically to guide the conduct of individuals in relation to other individuals. (TB 6A, Section 6.5)

Intrinsic Value: Value dependent solely upon the nature of what has value, apart from its relations to other things. Pleasure is often thought to have intrinsic value, because its value (goodness) depends only on the experience of pleasure. But the experience might be caused by eating wholesome food or by smoking cigarettes. In each case the pleasure is intrinsically good. But in the first case it's extrinsically good as well (because it contributes to good health); in the other case it's extrinsically bad (because it contributes to ill health). (TB 9B, Section 9.8)

Is/Ought: Shorthand for a distinction between descriptive statements and prescriptive ought judgments. (TB 1D, Section 1.7)

Jains: A religious/philosophical people found primarily in India who are committed to nonviolence, vegetarianism, and respect for all living things. See the Jain Declaration on Nature. (Section 9.6)

***Jus ad Bellum*:** A dimension of the Just War Theory that sets forth conditions that must be met in order for a state to be justified in resorting to war. (TB 15C, Section 15.9)

***Jus in Bello*:** A dimension of the Just War Theory that sets forth conditions that must be met in the conduct of war once it's begun, whether or not one was justified in going to war in the first place. (TB 15C, Section 15.9)

Just War Theory: A theory having religious and secular forms that has evolved since the time of Cicero and St. Augustine for the moral assessment of war. (TB 15D, Section 15.9)

Killing: Causing death. (DB 13G, Section 13.7)

Labor Power: For Marx, one's mental and physical capacities that can be put to work for (i.e., sold to) capitalists in exchange for money. (Section 8.8)

Laws of Dialectic: As discussed by Marx and Engels, three laws (transformation from quantity to quality, negation of the negation, and interpenetration of opposites) that explain the operation of the natural order as well as the evolution of socioeconomic systems. (Section 8.6)

Letting Die: Refraining from intervening in pathological processes (e.g., a terminal illness) which, if uninterrupted, will cause death. (DB 13G and DB 13H, Section 13.7)

***Lex Talionis*:** Punishment according to the rule: An eye for an eye, a tooth for a tooth, and so on. (KQ 14B, Section 14.2)

Liberalism: In capitalist countries, a political outlook that favors capitalism and democracy combined with significant involvement of the government in the economy in order to provide health, education, welfare, and other benefits. (Section 8.4)

Libertarianism: The view that government is minimally justified only in securing life, liberty, and property. (Section 8.4)

Liberty: Freedom defined by reference to law. (Section 8.2)

Locked-In State: A medical state in which consciousness and cognition are retained but movement and communication are impossible (sometimes other than by blinking of the eyes) because of paralysis of the voluntary motor system. (DB 13D, Section 13.6)

Logically Slippery Slope: Any situation in which acceptance of one position *logically or morally* requires the acceptance of a second position (whether the second position is in fact eventually accepted or not). (TB 13D, Section 13.9)

Macro Ethics: A theory that takes the primary concern of ethics to be the survival, well-being, and rights of groups (states, societies, religions, races, etc.). (TB 4B, Section 4.9)

Marxian Principle of Justice: From each according to ability; to each according to need. (DB 8C, Section 8.8)

Metaphysics: Theories about the nature of ultimate reality that transcend what can be established scientifically. (TB 11A, Section 11.2)

Micro Ethics: A theory that takes the primary concern of ethics to be the survival, well-being, and rights of individuals. (TB 4B, Section 4.9)

Minimally Conscious State: A medical condition in which there is limited and intermittent awareness of self and environment. (DB 13E, Section 13.6)

Morula: The mass of cells that form from the zygote up to the fourth day after fertilization (union of egg and sperm). (TB 12B, Section 12.3)

Natural Freedom: Freedom limited by the presence of others in the absence of law. (Section 8.2)

Natural Law Ethics: The theory that moral rightness and obligation are grounded in nature (cosmic nature or human nature). (TB 1E, Section 1.8)

Naturalistic Fallacy: The allegedly illegitimate attempt to derive an "ought" from an "is." (e.g., "pleasure is desired," therefore "pleasure ought to be pursued.") (See Is/Ought, Section 1.7)

Negative Golden Rule: Do not do unto others what you would not have them do unto you. (KQ 7B, Section 7.4)

Negative (or Autonomy) Rights: Legal or moral rights not to be interfered with in certain areas of one's life (e.g., in expressing opinions, worshipping, etc.). (TB 8B, Section 8.3)

Nihilist (moral): one who denies that there is such a thing as morality. (TB 2A, Section 2.6)

Nonconsequentialism: Any theory of moral right and wrong that is not consequentialist; that is, that does not hold that right and wrong are determined solely by the consequences of actions. (TB 6B, Section 6.5)

Non-maleficence: Not doing harm. The principle of non-maleficence holds that one ought to do no harm. (TB 7A, Section 7.4)

Overt Primary Racism: A situation in which racist beliefs and attitudes are openly held; as opposed to covert primary racism, a situation in which racist beliefs and attitudes are consciously or subconsciously concealed.

Pacifism: Opposition to war, whether on personal, moral, religious, or practical grounds. (Section 15.15)

Paradox of Privacy: The fact that knowledge of a number of one's acts over time, each of which can be witnessed by others without a violation of privacy (e.g., whom one visits, what political rallies one attends, where one dines, shops, worships, travels, and seeks entertainment), may constitute such a violation if that knowledge is collected and reveals larger aspects of one's life one would rather not have known. (Section 11.5)

Passive Euthanasia: Withholding medical treatment from the terminally ill in the expectation of hastening their death. (Section 13.4)

Peer Harassment: Sexual harassment between individuals neither of whom has power or authority over the other. (Section 5.3)

Permanent Vegetative State: A persistent vegetative state judged to be irreversible. (DB 13C, Section 13.6)

Persistent Vegetative State: An unconscious state, with sleep-wake cycles, lasting roughly more than one month. (DB 13C, Section 13.6)

Personal Pacifism: Opposition to war as a personal commitment not considered binding on others. (DB 15E, Section 15.15)

Personhood: Characteristics, such as consciousness, rationality, and ability to communicate, that a human being (simply as a living organism) may or may not have (i.e., may come to acquire as it develops and may lose through accident or deterioration). (Section 12.9)

Persuasive Definition: A definition in which the moral assessment of an act or practice has been included for the purpose of inducing others to accept that assessment. (DB 15A, Section 15.2)

Philosophical Liberalism: A relatively recent development historically, supporting individualism, human rights, democracy, and capitalism; both liberalism and conservatism (as political positions) tend to be products of philosophical liberalism. (Section 8.4)

Phrenology: A pseudo-science which claims that mental properties can be inferred from the shape and protuberances of the skull. (Section 1.6)

Physician-Assisted Suicide: The provision of help by a physician to a competent terminally ill person in ending his or her own life. (DB 13B, Section 13.2)

Physiognomy: A pseudo-science which claims that mental properties can be inferred from general physical properties. (Section 1.6)

Positive Golden Rule: Do unto others as you would have them do unto you. (KQ 7C, Section 7.4)

Positive Rights: Legal or moral entitlements to certain benefits (e.g., health care, education). (TB 8B, Section 8.3)

Poverty: Possession of little or no money and material goods. (DB 7A, Section 7.1)

Pragmatic Pacifism: Pacifism based on purely rational and practical grounds, such as the belief that war is an irrational, costly, and ineffective way to pursue one's ends. (DB 15E, Section 15.15)

Preemptive War: The initiation of a war that one believes an adversary is about to start. (KQ 15C, Section 15.9)

Prescriptive Judgments: Those which purport to guide conduct, typically by the use of "ought," either on moral grounds (e.g., "You ought to keep that promise") or nonmoral grounds (e.g., "You ought to take your umbrella"). (Section 3.2)

Prescriptive Meaning: The meaning one thinks a term *should* have, even if it differs from its de facto meaning. (TB 3A, Section 3.2)

Preventive War: The initiation of a war thought necessary to forestall an attack by an adversary which may or not be imminent. (KQ 15C)

Prima Facie Obligatory: Obligatory in at least one respect. (TB 4A, Section 4.7)

Prima Facie Right: Right in at least one respect. (TB 4A, Section 4.7)

Prima Facie Rights (not to be confused with prima facie right): A right is prima facie if, and only if, it should be honored, all other things being equal (i.e., if the right is not overridden by other moral considerations). (TB 10B, Section 10.10)

Prima Facie Wrong: Wrong in at least one respect. (TB 4A, Section 4.7)

Primary Racism: The beliefs, attitudes, and practices of racists. (DB 1A, Section1.2)

Primary Sexism: The beliefs, attitudes, and practices of sexists. (DB 2A, Section 2.2)

Principle of Innocence: The principle that one ought not to directly kill an innocent person. (Section 12.10)

Principle of Organic Unities: The principle that the intrinsic value of a whole may be more or less than the sum of the intrinsic values of its parts. (TB 9D, Section 9.8)

Principled Pacifism: Opposition to war on grounds (e.g., moral) considered valid for all. (DB 15E, Section 15.15)

Privacy: Freedom from intrusion into areas of one's life that one hasn't explicitly or implicitly opened to others. (DB 11A, Section 11.3)

Proletariat: Marx's term for the workers (those wielding the instruments of production) in capitalist society. (Section 8.7)

Punishment: The deliberate infliction of pain, suffering, deprivation, or death in response to alleged offenses. (DB 14A, Section 14.2)

Pure Procedural Justice: A process of distributing benefits and burdens whose outcomes are fair (whatever they may be) if the process itself is fair. (Section 8.9)

Quid Pro Quo Harassment: Sexual harassment, typically where one person has power or authority over another, in which benefits (e.g., pay raises) are exchanged for sexual favors or detriments (e.g., firing) are threatened unless sexual favors are provided. (Section 5.3)

Race: A contested term for the categorization of groups of people according to supposedly invariable properties such as skin color, body structure, facial features, and hair texture, which are then often correlated with other properties such as intelligence, initiative, creativity, and moral character. (Section 1.6)

Racial Discrimination: The prejudicial treatment of persons on the basis of supposedly racial characteristics. (DB 1D, Section 1.3)

Racialist (as used in this text): One who believes that some races are innately superior to others. (DB 1F, Section 1.3)

Racist₁: One who practices racial discrimination. (DB 1C, Section 1.3)

Racist₂: A racial bigot. (DB 1E, Section 1.3) (See bigot)

Racist₃: One who knowingly practices or approves of racial discrimination in the belief (a) that some races are innately superior to others, and (b) that innately superior races ought to dominate inferior races. (DB 1G, Section 1.3)

Religious Pacifism: Pacifism based on religious or spiritual grounds. (DB 15E, Section 15.15)

Reparations: Restitution (often financial) for past wrongs. (Section 4.7)

Retributivism (regarding the death penalty): The theory that the death penalty is justified if, and only if, it puts to death those, and only those, who *deserve* to die. (TB 14A, Section 14.4)

Rights: Moral or legal entitlements to certain benefits or to be free of interference in certain areas of one's life. Moral rights are sometimes taken to be the foundation of morality; at other times (as in this text), they are considered dispensable because everything that can be said about rights can be said using moral words such as right and wrong. (Sections 1.9 and 2.2 See also Human rights)

***Roe v. Wade* (1973):** US Supreme Court Decision that legalized abortion under specific circumstances. (Section 12.5)

Secondary Racism: The perpetuation of racial inequality, sometimes unwittingly, through conduct motivated primarily by nonracial (e.g., economic) considerations. (DB 1B, Section 1.2)

Secondary Sexism: The perpetuation of sex-inequality by conduct that is motivated primarily by nonsexist (e.g., economic) considerations. (DB 2B, Section 2.2)

Sentientism: The view that all sentient beings (those capable of experiencing pain), and only sentient beings, warrant basic moral consideration. (DB 9B, Section 9.5)

Sex Discrimination: Prejudicial treatment of individuals or groups because of their sex (Section 5.4)

Sexist₁: One who practices sex discrimination. (DB 2C, Section 2.3)

Sexist₂: A chauvinist with regard to sex (DB 2D, Section 2.3) (See Chauvinist)

Sexist₃: One who knowingly practices or approves of sex discrimination in the belief (a) that one sex is innately superior to the other, and (b) that the innately superior sex ought to dominate the inferior sex. (DB 2G, Section 2.3)

Sextist (as defined specifically for this text): One who believes in the innate superiority of one sex over the other. (DB 2F, Section 2.3)

Sexual Harassment: Repeated unwanted sexual attention. (DB 5A, Section 5.1)

Skeptic (moral): One who questions whether any acts are right or wrong. (TB 2A, Section 2.6)

Socialism: A cooperative economic system with public ownership of the means of production, which are used for the benefit of all. (DB 8A, Section 8.1)

Socratic Definition: A definition which specifies properties common to, unique to, and essential to all instances of what is being defined. (TB 3C, Section 3.5)

Sound Argument: A valid argument whose premises are true (and whose conclusion must therefore also be true). (TB 5A, Section 5.4)

Speciesism: The beliefs, attitudes, and practices of speciesists (DB 10A, Section 10.2)

Speciesist: One who practices or approves of discrimination against animals in the belief (a) that humans are innately superior to animals, and (b) that humans ought to dominate animals. (DB 10B, Section 10.2)

State of Nature: State of affairs in which one is either unconstrained by others (as on an otherwise deserted island) or in which oneself and others are not governed by laws. (Section 8.2)

State Socialism: Ownership or control of the economy by the state. (Section 8.1)

Strong Affirmative Action: Preferential treatment of minorities and/or women in education or employment to compensate for present or past discrimination or to promote diversity (or both). (DB 4C, Section 4.5)

Suicide: Intentionally or knowingly taking one's own life. (DB 13A, Section 13.2)

Surplus Value: Marx's term for the value human labor produces over and above the cost of the labor embodied in it (i.e., the cost of food, clothing, shelter, etc., enabling the person to work for the contracted length of time). Even if the capitalist pays a fair price for a person's labor power when he hires the person, that labor power creates additional value when put to use. This surplus value constitutes profit for the capitalist, which constitutes capital and is the source of wealth. (Section 8.8)

Terrorism (proposed descriptive definition in the text): Pursuit of one's ends by causing fear, usually by the use or threat of violence, often against innocent persons. (DB 15B, Section 15.2)

The Moral Expendability of Soldiers (sometimes called the moral equality of soldiers): The view that soldiers on all sides may legally and/or morally kill one another, provided they abide by the rules of war. (Section 15.12)

The Unborn: The product of human fertilization from conception until expulsion, miscarriage, abortion, or birth. (DB 12A, Section 12.3)

Tragedy of the Commons: Allegedly disastrous effects of common ownership of land or property detailed by Garret Hardin. (Section 7.5)

Universalizability: The principle that persons ought to be treated similarly unless there are morally relevant dissimilarities among them. (TB 1F, Section 1.10)

University of California v. Bakke (1978): Landmark US Supreme Court Case ruling unconstitutional affirmative action based on a quota system. (Section 4.2)

Utilitarianism: The theory that moral rightness and obligation are determined by what maximizes value in the consequences of actions. (TB 1E, Section 1.8) (TB 15B)

Valid Argument: An argument in which it is impossible for the premises to be true and the conclusion false. (TB 5A, Section 5.4)

Value Judgment: An assessment of persons, objects or states of affairs as good, bad, better, or worse, whether on moral grounds (e.g., "She's a good person") or nonmoral grounds (e.g., "That's a good car"). (TB 1D, Section 1.7)

War (a standard sense): The pursuit of ends by two or more states through the use of organized, systematic violence against one another. (DB 15C, Section 15.7)

Warism: The view that war is sometimes morally justified in practice as well as in theory. (DB 15D, Section 15.8)

Weak Affirmative Action: Measures short of preferential treatment of behalf of minorities and/or women in employment or education. (DB 4B, Section 4.5)

Zygote: A cell created by the union of an egg and a sperm. (TB 12B, Section 12.3)

Selected Bibliography

Aiken, William and Hugh LaFollette, eds. *World Hunger and Morality*.
Englewood Cliffs, NJ: Prentice-Hall, 1996.

Alfino, Mark and G. Randolph Mayers. "Reconstructing the Right to Privacy."
Social Theory and Practice, 29.1 (January 2003), 1–19.

Beauchamp, Tom L. and Norman E. Bowie, eds. *Ethical Theory and Business*,
7th ed. Upper Saddle River, NJ: Pearson/Prentice-Hall, 2004.

Bedau, Hugo A., ed. *The Death Penalty in America: Current Controversies*.
New York: Oxford University Press, 1997.

Boxill, Bernard, ed. *Race and Racism*. New York: Oxford University
Press, 2001.

Cahn, Steven M., ed. *The Affirmative Action Debate*, 2nd ed.
New York: Routledge, 2002.

Cohen, G. A. *Why Not Socialism?* Princeton, NJ: Princeton University
Press, 2009.

DeBeavoir, Simone. *The Second Sex*. New York: Vintage Books, 1989.

Friedman, Milton. *Capitalism and Freedom*. Chicago: The University of
Chicago Press, 1970.

Gracia, Jorge J. E. and Pablo DeGreiff, eds. *Hispanic/Latinos in the United
States: Ethnicity, Race, and Rights*. New York: Routledge, 2000.

Jamieson, Dale. *Ethics and the Environment: An Introduction*.
New York: Cambridge University Press, 2008.

Kopelman, Loretta M. and Kenneth A. De Ville. *Physician-Assisted
Suicide: What Are the Issues?* Boston, MA: Kluwer Academic, 2001.

LeMoncheck, Linda and James P. Sterba, eds. *Sexual Harassment: Issues and
Answers*. New York: Oxford University Press, 2001.

Nathanson, Stephen. *Terrorism and the Ethics of War*. Cambridge: Cambridge
University Press, 2010.

Regan, Tom. *Defending Animal Rights*. Urbana: University of Illinois
Press, 2001.

Roleff, Tamara L., ed. *Abortion: Opposing Viewpoints*. San Diego,
CA: Greenhaven Press, 1997.

Index